THE

METALWORKER'S
BENCHTOP REFERENCE
MANUAL

THE

METALWORKER'S
BENCHTOP REFERENCE
MANUAL

JOSEPH W. SERAFIN

TAB BOOKS Inc.
Blue Ridge Summit, PA 17214

FIRST EDITION
FIRST PRINTING

Copyright © 1987 by TAB BOOKS Inc.
Printed in the United States of America

Library of Congress Cataloging in Publication Data

Serafin, Joseph W.
The metalworker's benchtop reference manual.

Includes index.
1. Metal-work. I. Title.
TT205.S35 1986 684′.09 86-14368

ISBN 0-8306-0805-2
ISBN 0-8306-1705-1

Front cover photograph by Deborah Teeuws.

Contents

Acknowledgments

Instead of permitting a lifetime of valuable experience in machine shop practice to just fade and die, I believed it to be genuinely worthwhile to put this knowhow into a book, whereby countless thousands of persons who might not be at all familiar with the art of precision metalworking can benefit from my experience.

I wish to express my sincere appreciation to the following for permissions granted to copy from some of their work:

American Machinist Handbook, McGraw-Hill Book Co.
American Society of Mechanical Engineers
Cincinnati Milling Machine Co.
Dercks Gage Dial
Industrial Press
Prentice-Hall, Inc.

ALIGNMENT

ALIGNMENT BY SWEEP INDICATING. Any machine having a swiveling head or table can best be set absolutely square with its spindle's axial center by sweep indicating as shown in Fig. A-1. The test indicator is mounted on the end of a bent rod. The rod's shank can be held either in a drill chuck or collet or clamped to the rotatable spindle of the machine.

First, touch the indicator spindle down on one side of the table or work, and note the indicator's reading. Then manually rotate the machine spindle one-half revolution to see how the second side compares with the first. Swivel the spindle head or table either way until the indicator's readings become exactly the same at both ends of the indicator's sweep.

In indicating wider surfaces, the indicator must read the same at four places, such as at twelve o'clock and six o'clock, as well as at nine o'clock and three o'clock.

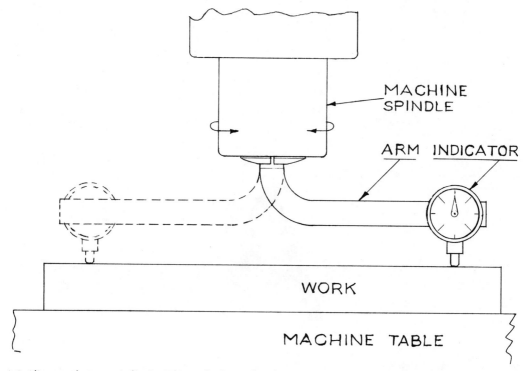

Fig. A-1. Alignment by sweep indicating. This method is used in determining whether, for example, the spindle of any machine is fixed at 90° to the table on which the work rests.

B

BORING

BORING BAR. Figure B-1 shows a most versatile boring bar and holder for use in an engine lathe. It is as sturdy as it is simple.

The bars are made double-ended; that is, having cutting tool slots at both ends. The squared tool hole at one end is made at right angles to the axis of the bar, while the hole at the other end is made at 60° to the bar's axial centerline. The 60° angular hole permits the cutting tool to face off the bottoms of blind bores, which might be only slightly larger than twice the bar's diameter. The 60° tool

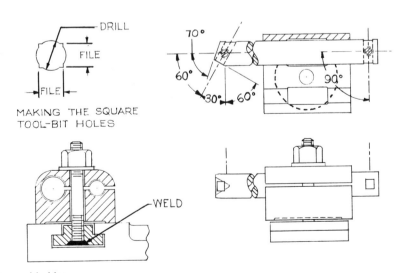

Fig. B-1. Boring bar and holder.

3

slot angle permits the tool to project ahead of the bar, for facing bore bottoms without having to project out to excess.

For cutting 60° internal threads, the 60° tool angle is ideal. One side of the tool bit is ground parallel with the bit, while the 60° angle is all ground-off from the other side of the bit. This design permits the boring bar to always be positioned very near parallel with the bore of the work.

The holder is generally made with two sizes of holes bored to receive bars, for example, 1 1/4 inch and 3/4-inch in diameter. Of course, adapter sleeves, split lengthwise on one side, can be easily made up to support any in-between bar diameters. For heavier cutting, strips of emery cloth placed between the holder and the lathe's compound rest will prevent the bar holder from swiveling away from the increased load.

BAR FOR INTERNAL SLOTTING. Figure B-2 shows how a bar for internal slotting in a shaper can easily be made. The bar (A) can be made to almost any convenient diameter and length. Its back end resembles the shaper's tool post and fits into the clapper (C), as does the tool post.

The bar is secured in position by the nut (N), which screws on over the bar against the washer (W). The bar can be used in any radial position by partially rotating the

bar, the shaper's head, or both. However, if the slotting is to be done in the upper side of the bore, the clapper holding the bar must be kept from opening by tightening the screw (S).

BORING BAR, SPADE DRILL. Figure B-3 shows a spade drill as used in an engine lathe. To prevent the drill and shank from turning, tighten a lathe dog around the shank, with the dog's tail rested against the boring bar's support block.

LINE BORING BAR. Figure B-4 shows a line boring bar. These can be made quite slender, with the cutting bits projecting only slightly above the bar's periphery. The square tool-bit holes can be easily drilled into the bar with a Watts Brothers square hole drill. These types of bars must be supported at both ends, and are also used in boring in and through work that holds fixtures.

STAR-WHEEL BORING HEAD. Figure B-5 shows a star wheel fed boring and facing head. As the head rotates with the machine's spindle, the star wheel (A) strikes the fixed pin (B). The holder (C) carrying the pin is bolted to any convenient part of the machine or the work. As the head rotates, the star wheel strikes the pin, rotating the feed screw (E) 1/5 revolution, which in turn causes the cutting tool

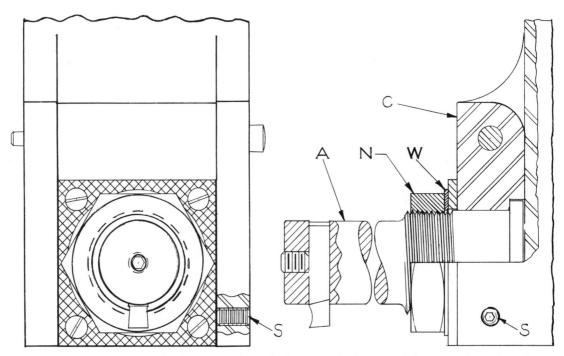

Fig. B-2. Bar for internal slotting. A bar for use in a shaper for key seat and other internal slotting can be made as shown.

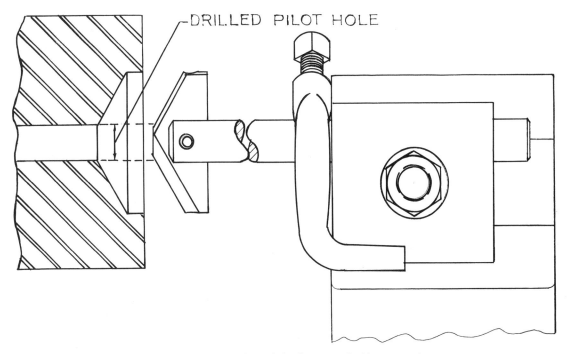

Fig. B-3. Boring bar spade drill. This bar can be used in a lathe for removal of heavy metal.

holder (F) to move away or toward the spindle's axial center. The direction of tool movement depends on whether the pin strikes the star wheel on its back or front sides. The body (D) is threaded as at G for easy adaptation to different types of shanks, as might exist in different machines.

HORIZONTAL BORING MILL BAR. Larger boring and milling work is done in horizontal bar-type milling machines, usually referred to as *bar mills*. The machine's spindle generally has a Morse taper into which various lengths and diameters of bars and cutting tools are inserted and driven.

The bar (Fig. B-6) is held in the tapered spindle by key K, which runs transversely through the bar's tapered shank, simultaneously engaging the machine's spindle. The outer end of the bar is supported by an outboard member—the tail stock—holding the bushing (B) in which the bar rotates. The tail stock's bushing housing (T) is raised or lowered by a translating screw through a set of bevel gears. The head elevating screw functions in conjunction with the tail-stock elevating screw. The head spindle (S) and the tail-stock bushing (B) are synchronized, traveling up or down the exact same amount, thus always keeping the bar parallel with the machine's base or table.

The machine's spindle telescopes into and out of the head, often up to several feet, depending on the size of the machine. Telescoping permits boring or machining of the more distant areas.

Boring is done with tool bits projecting out of the bar.

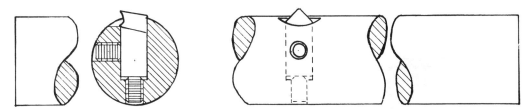

Fig. B-4. Line boring bar. The cutting bits are held in a longer boring bar.

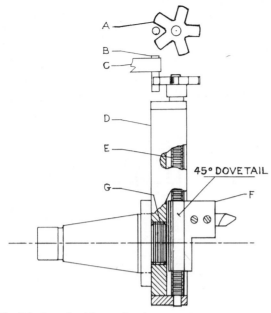

45° DOVETAIL

Fig. B-5. Star wheel boring head.

These bits are hammered either inward or outward to bore the required diameters. For boring comparatively large diameters, collars of a suitable diameter—as at C—are fastened over the bar. This collar, in turn, supports the cutting tools. Sometimes these collars are made in two 180° sections for easier mounting and moving, without needing to remove the bar in each case.

Tools that are ground with a long cutting edge parallel with the side of the tool are used for facing cuts. If the face surface is to be unusually wide, then it is better to employ a star wheel fed facing tool for the purpose.

Shell and regular end mills, as well as numerous other types of cutting tools, can be used in the horizontal bar mills, providing they have suitable adapters to fit the spindle.

For smaller machine work, such as might be done in a horizontal knee column type of milling machine or a smaller horizontal bar mill, the work is moved up, down, and sideways with the machine's table. In large work where the job is bolted to a stationary base of the machine, it cannot be moved over for each machining location. Instead, the machine's head, bar, and tail stock are moved around to suit the machining location.

LARGE CYLINDRICAL BORING. Figure B-7 shows a method of machining the interior of a large cylinder in an engine lathe. The work is first chucked on its open end while the closed end is supported by a pipe (bull) center in the tail stock spindle. Two sufficiently wide "spots," one at each end of the work, are turned for a steady rest. This procedure is followed by the installation of the large steady rest to support the work, then the withdrawal of the pipe center. The small bore is finished to size with the inside face cutting being done through the bore using a boring bar. Next, the work is turned around, end for end, and gripped by the closed end. The open end is now supported in the steady rest.

A shouldered, oil-impregnated bronze bushing is inserted into the small bore. C, the small end of the bar (D), fits into the bronze bushing (B). The outer end of the bar is supported in a secondary steady rest (E). The bar, with the keyway (F) running its full length, also fits the key (G), which is fixed in the bore of the steady rest. The boring tool head (T) is keyed and slides along the bar. Longitudinal boring head feeding is done by the push rod (I), which connects the boring head with the lathe's carriage (J), through the clamping block (K), bolted atop the compound rest. The push rod passes through a hole (not shown) in the secondary rest. The push rod can be made in sections, screwing together only those lengths required for the particular length of job.

The boring head is made to receive tool bits for the boring. For smoothing the bored surface, a special hone

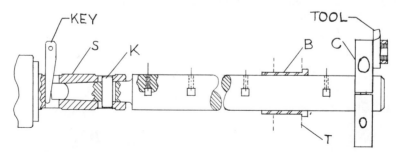

Fig. B-6. Horizontal boring mill bar. This bar can be adapted for boring and facing in a horizontal bar mill.

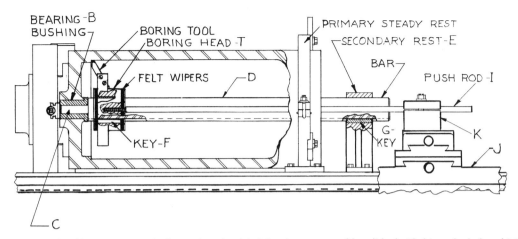

Fig. B-7. Large cylindrical boring. Larger cylinders are bored and their interiors are smoothly polished with this method of machining.

with holder is provided (Fig. B-8). It is held in the tool-bit slot of the boring head, and is spring loaded and propelled the full length of the bore. Before increasing the rate of rotation, it is customary to apply a generous amount of oil; sulphurized cutting oil is preferred. If the hone were motorized in a fashion that would cause it to oscillate in and out in short strokes, it would then approach the same principles as are involved in superfinishing of cylindrical surfaces.

ACCURATE MULTIHOLE BORING. When a job comes up calling for a large number of closely and accurately spaced bored holes in several heavy steel plates, set up and do the job as illustrated in Fig. B-9.

Because there are several plates to be drilled and bored exactly alike, first make the drill jig plate (J), with all the holes accurately spaced and bored in a jig-boring machine, as per print specifications.

The drill jig plate is then properly aligned and fastened

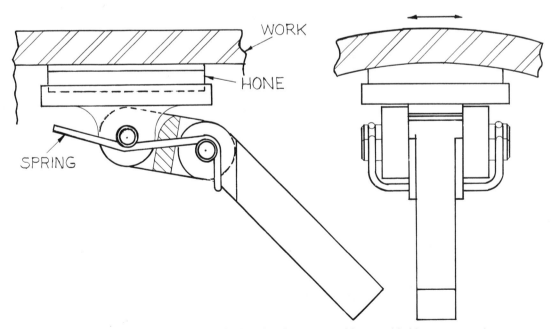

Fig. B-8. Large cylindrical boring. For smoothing the bored surface, a special hone and holder are provided.

7

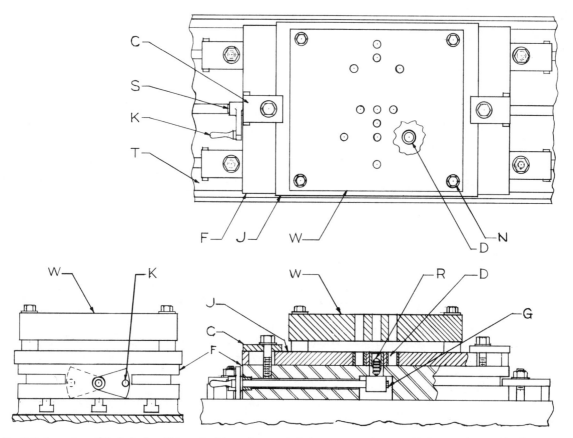

Fig. B-9. Accurate multihole boring. This method is used to precisely bore accurately spaced holes in a knee-and-column type of vertical milling machine.

atop the work (W). All holes are drilled through in a drill press. To relieve the work load in the jig borer, bore the many holes in a vertical milling machine.

To accurately locate each hole, a fixture (F) is made. This fixture is clamped atop the mill's table (T). Running longitudinally through one end of the fixture is a hand-operated pinion gear shaft (G). The pinion gear raises or lowers a cylindrically shaped rack (R), whose upper diameter engages any one of the holes in the jig plate, as in D.

Before the work fastened to the jig plate (J) is positioned on the fixture, the pin rack is moved upward by the handle (K) to project above the fixture. The projecting rack is test-indicated to be sure its axial center is true with the axial center of the machine's spindle. The top face of the fixture is also sweep-indicated (see Fig. A-1) to ensure its squareness both ways with the axial centerline of the spindle.

After indicating, the work is placed atop the fixture, locating each hole by elevating the rack pin to engage any

one of the holes in the jig plate. A boring bar with a cemented tantalum-carbide tip is used for boring the holes to size.

Since varying temperatures, in the room and in the machine, alter the pilot pin's alignment with the vertical spindle, you should indicate the pin before starting the finish boring each morning. Do so only after the machine has been run for at least two hours before the day shift's starting time.

After pin alignment, no part of the machine table is moved up, down, or sideways. For changing hole locations, only clamps (C) are used.

HEAVY BORING TO SIZE. It is possible to take comparatively heavy boring cuts close to the finished dimension and remain confident of not boring oversize. All heavier boring in the lathe is accomplished with less difficulty when the cutting tool is positioned upside down and the cutting is done on the back side of the bore.

Figure B-10 illustrates how the bar, under the cutting

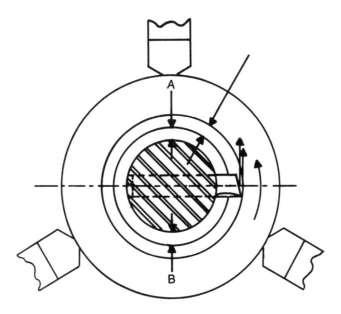

Fig. B-10. Heavy boring to size. In heavy boring, a boring bar flexes away from the cut.

pressure, is forced up and away from the finished diameter. For example, if you need to remove 3/8 inch from the side of a bore, you feed the tool inward slightly more than 3/8 inch. With the feed engaged, you cut into the work approximately 1/16 inch, then disengage the feed and rapidly withdraw the carriage.

Here the rough bore is measured for size. Any lesser adjustments to increase or decrease the bore diameter can be made without seriously affecting the bar's flexing.

Decide on the feed rate before you take the first trial bore cut. Do not change the feed rate without resetting the cutting depth. In doing so, the bore diameter changes also. If the short trial bore is oversize (it usually is), and does not clean up the finish cutting, it is not serious. The bore is almost always either rounded, chamfered, or faced off to depth.

BALL BEARINGS

CONE-TYPE BALL BEARING. Figure B-11 shows a cone-type ball bearing. The balls roll in a transverse, concave raceway. Each transverse raceway arc is not more than 90° wide.

The retainer (R) is made of brass or soft steel. The ball holes are not drilled completely through. After loading the balls into the retainer, the outer end of the holes are swaged inward slightly, using a hollow punch. This procedure prevents the balls from falling out during assembly and disassembly.

This type of bearing can carry as much end thrust as it does radial loads.

LINEAR-TYPE BALL BEARING. For rapid linear motions, bearings as shown in Fig. B-12 can be made up. This design permits little, if any, radial play. Like a caterpillar tractor, it lays down and picks up its own track (balls in this case). The raceways are generally spaced 120° apart, running longitudinally parallel with the axial centerline of the moving member.

RADIAL BALL BEARINGS. Figure B-13 shows a radial-type ball bearing, which can be made up in an emergency

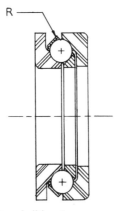

Fig. B-11. Cone-type ball bearing.

9

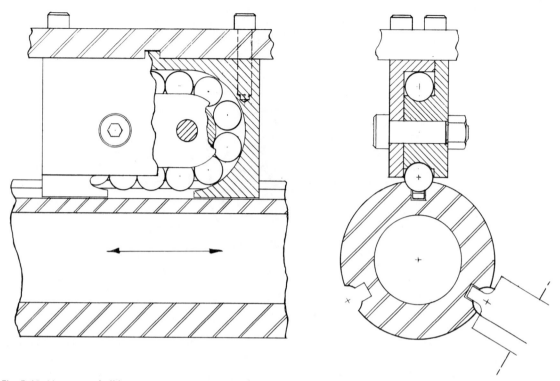

Fig. B-12. Linear-type ball bearing. This type of ball bearing is used to support a shaft's rapid linear back-and-forth movement.

for special and lower-speed applications.

The procedure involves the grooving of the outer periphery of the inner ring, and also the grooving of the inside of the outer ring. The standard depths of both grooves are each equal to 18 to 20 percent of the ball's diameter. Balls of any diameter can be readily purchased. They are made (graded) into many size variations. For example, each nominal ball size can be purchased with diameter variations in the tenths of one thousandths of an inch, or up to 20 diameter variations for any one nominal ball size.

The better ball bearings are selectively fitted. The balls themselves make only a line contact in the very bottom of

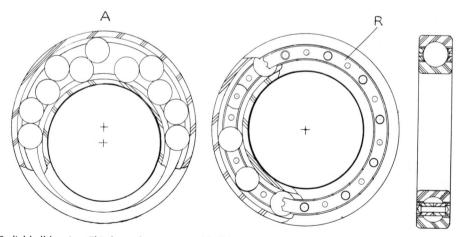

Fig. B-13. Radial ball bearing. This better-known type of ball bearing can be made as shown if and when the need arises.

the grooves because the raceways are purposely made .0003 to .0005 inch greater in their transverse diameter than is the ball's diameter. This difference in diameter is made for purposes of reducing side friction, which in turn reduces excessive heating.

The ball retainer (R) can be made of two pieces, as shown. The two half sections are riveted together, over the balls.

When the inner ring is eccentric with the inside of the outer ring, as shown in A, the bearing will usually accept only the number of balls for which it was designed.

THRUST BEARINGS. Figure B-14 shows a typical thrust ball bearing. These can vary widely in their design and applications. Perhaps the most common type of thrust ball bearing is one in which a single row of balls roll in a grooved raceway. the depth of the raceway should be no more than 18 to 20 percent of the ball's diameter.

A thrust bearing having grooved raceways has several advantages over the plain, flat-washer types. Because the balls ride on something slightly wider than a mere line contact, they afford considerably more radial, as well as end thrust, capacities.

The retaining ring (R) can be made of soft steel, brass, or fiber. To keep the balls from falling out of the ring, the ball holes are not drilled completely through. After the holes are filled with balls, the open or top side of the holes are swaged over, using a hollow punch. Any tight-fitting balls can be readily loosened by tapping it against the swaged

side. Use either brass or aluminum against the ball's surface.

THRUST BEARING, (PLAIN) SINGLE ROW. Figure B-15 shows a plain, or ungrooved, thrust ball bearing. These, of course, are more simple to make than the typical grooved bearing because they consist of two hardened washers and a retaining washer (R). Because the balls roll on a flat surface, resulting in a thin line contact, their load-carrying capacity is somewhat limited. This load capacity can be increased by employing more than one row of balls. The retainer's ball holes can be staggered, permitting more balls to be used with each annular row of balls running in its own path.

To be sure, in the case of the ungrooved thrust bearing, there is the tendency for the ball retainer assembly to run eccentric with the shaft's axial center. Therefore, the inside diameter of the retainer should be a free fit on the shaft of which it is to operate. These types of bearings offer no radial support.

BEARING, ROUGH-SURFACE APPLICATION. Occasionally it becomes necessary to install bearings on a rough surface when you cannot machine a suitable flat surface for its mounting. This situation can occur for any number of reasons.

Figure B-16 shows how a bearing support is mounted on the rough surface. In the illustration, bronze sleeve bushings (B) are used, although ball or roller type bearings can

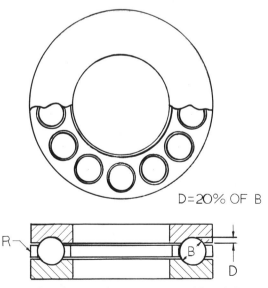

Fig. B-14. Thrust bearing. The common grooved thrust ball bearing can be made as shown.

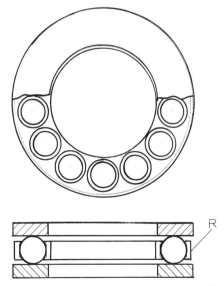

Fig. B-15. Thrust bearing, (plain) single row. This ball bearing can be made by the simple method shown if the need arises.

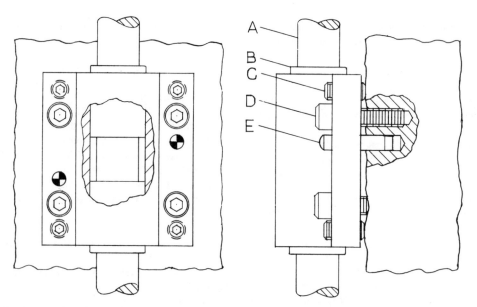

Fig. B-16. Bearing, rough-surface application. Occasionally a bearing must be added to a machine where no machined surface is present to accommodate it. In such cases a support as shown works very nicely.

also be used if space permits. The type of bearing used also depends on whether the shaft (A) is to rotate or operate in a linear motion.

The four set screws (C) are used for purposes of leveling only, and must have flat bottoms. The four bolts (D) hold the complete bearing assembly to the machine wall, or whatever. Dowel pins (E) fitting looser in the bearing housing and snug in the machine wall can be used for cases of disassembly. However, be sure the lineup is near to perfection before you ream out the dowel pin holes.

BENDING

G.M. BENDING EXHIBIT. Figure B-17 shows a very important exhibit put on by General Motors Corporation at one of its manufacturing shows. It demonstrates the amount of flexing in a heavy I-beam, when it is only under the pressure of the human hand.

The beam was about 3 feet in length, 1 foot in height, and 4 inches wide. Atop this beam was a fine dial indicator, mounted on its own, independent, stand. When the top of this beam was pressed downward, by hand, the dial indicator would register the amount of flexing in the beam.

The amount of flexing was very little, of course. However, the fact remains that it did bend. If a locomotive passed over this same beam, the bending would be multiplied many hundreds of thousands of times. The demonstration proves that few, if any, objects or materials,

regardless of their massiveness or hardness, are so rigid that they will not bend, even slightly.

It is well to always keep these facts in mind, especially when you are setting up a job for machining or designing any type of equipment. In setting up for machining, always consider how the work can be held, how much and where the holding pressure can be, how much and where any distortion can be tolerated. Even in assembling, the tightening down of small-diameter screws will often distort an accurately machined part beyond the allowed tolerance.

BENDING AND FORMING CYLINDERS. Figure B-18 shows a method of bending flat stock into cylindrical and other rounded shapes. This method involves the use of a bench vise (V), a mallet, and random spacing blocks (B and C). Plates (P) should be long enough to merely increase the throat depth of the vise for the length of the stock. For the mandrel (A), choose a somewhat smaller diameter, about 10 percent less than the cylinder's inside diameter. The amount depends on the springiness of the material being bent. The springier the material, the smaller the mandrel's diameter must be.

Most metals can be bent into a "round" cylinder, if some proper planning is done beforehand. Some metals might require heating before bending.

There are at least three ways to find the length of stock needed to form any diameter of cylinder:

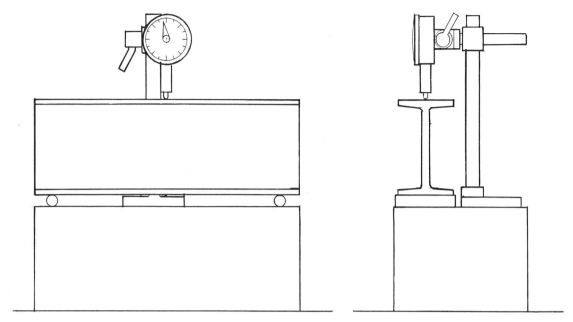

Fig. B-17. G.M. bending exhibit.

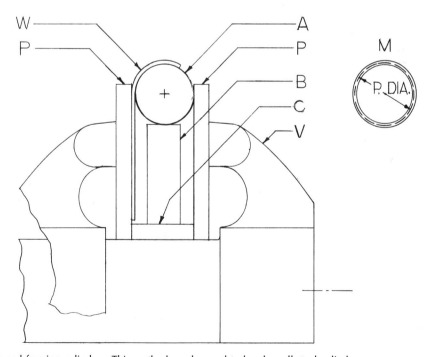

Fig. B-18. Bending and forming cylinders. This method can be used to bend small steel cylinders.

- By closely estimating the pitch diameter—by measuring from the center of one wall and across to the center of the opposite wall (as shown in M—then multiplying this diameter by the constant 3.1416.
- By adding one wall thickness to the inside diameter of the proposed cylinder, then multiplying by 3.1416.
- By subtracting one wall thickness from the outside diameter of the proposed cylinder, then multiplying by 3.1416.

ROLLING CYLINDERS. In employing the conventional three-roller method of rolling flat and other shapes of stock—such as square or round rods—into cylinders, rings, etc., both ends of the stock always must be bent to nearly the correct curve first, as illustrated at A in Fig. B-19.

The end-forming can be done by any available means. The general practice is to bend the ends, a little at a time, in a steel bending brake. The bending should be gaged with a radius template. If the ends are not prebent, the material will not negotiate between the three rolls, as shown at B.

Rolling rings, cylinders, and other cross-sectional shapes can be done in an engine lathe. The driver roller is positioned between centers, while the other two rollers are mounted as a unit, fastened to and moved in and out with the compound rest.

TUBE-BENDING FIXTURE. Tube bending, as such, can be interesting and a pleasure, if and when the process is properly carried out. There are numerous tube-bending

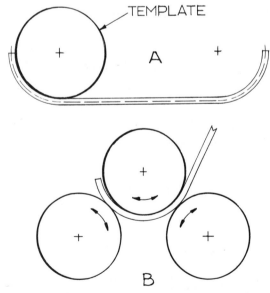

Fig. B-19. Rolling cylinders. Steel sheets are preformed before being rolled into cylinders using the three-roller method.

methods and equipment. The one to employ depends on the material, size, wall thickness, and function, and also on what equipment is readily available.

Figure B-20 shows a method of bending a thin-walled steel tubing to form a helical coil. Two bolts (B) anchor the fixture to some solid object such as a heavier mill table, planer, or whatever. The plate (C) represents the diameter around which the tube is formed. (D) represents the cross-sectional view of the forming roller (E).

The roller which does the bending has a somewhat elongated cross-sectional groove. Instead of a clean 180° transverse arc, the sides are straight, slanting inward from the open side. Each side slants at approximately 30°. The plate and roller are spaced closely together and are connected by steel straps (F), one on each side, held in place by two axial center pins (G and H). The handle (I), bolted between the inner sides of the straps, is rounded to receive a pipe, thus providing the necessary leverage.

(A) represents a locking (holding) block. For better gripping, this block has a fine internal thread, of any random pitch, and is hinged as shown. Instead of the internal thread, emery cloth with its grit facing the tube can also be used for better gripping.

In the case of thin-walled tubing, better bending can be had by filling the tube with Cerro-Bend, a brand of metal that melts at a low temperature. In every case, the tube should be heated to about 450° F then flushed through with oil to prevent droplets of Cerro-Bend from adhering to the inner wall of the tube. Place a sufficient amount of Cerro-Bend into a steel bucket then cover the metal with water. Heat the water over a flame, furnace, etc. to the boiling point. Then pour the molten metal and water into the tube, filling it completely. Plug one end of the tube with a cork to prevent fluid leakage. After coiling, the work is placed into a large enough steel vessel and again covered with water. The water is heated here also. The higher water temperature melts the Cerro-Bend, permitting it to run out as would mercury (quick silver).

The plate has no groove on its periphery for approximately 200° to permit advancing the helix. The cross-sectional shape of the bent tube's outer half does not permanently take on the shape as shown in D. Because of some stretching in the bending process, the work very nearly rounds out after the passage of the roller. In helical coiling, the tube is rolled (bent) in sections, each section consisting of arcs 60° to 70° wide.

BROACHES

FLAT BROACH. Figure B-21 shows a simple, flat type of broach that might be used to finish slots to correct size.

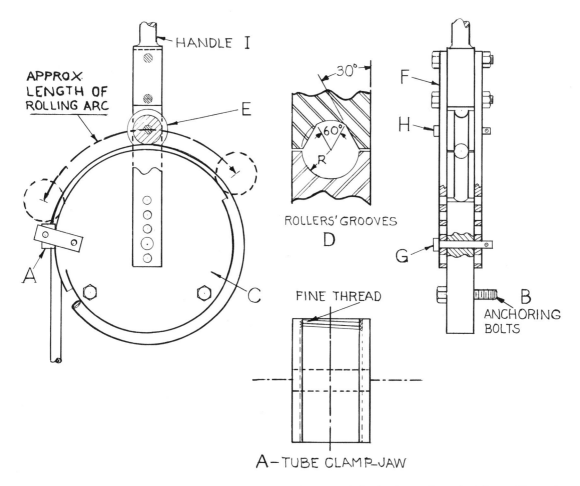

HANDLE I

APPROX LENGTH OF ROLLING ARC

E

30°

ROLLERS' GROOVES

D

A

C

F

H

G

FINE THREAD

A—TUBE CLAMP JAW

B ANCHORING BOLTS

Fig. B-20. Tube-bending fixture. A thin-walled steel tubing can be bent into a helical coil using the method shown. The particular cross section of the bending rolls and work is also shown.

This is a push-through type of broach and is usually backed up by hardened blocks of varied, desired thicknesses.

SQUARE-HOLE BROACH. Figure B-22 shows a type of push broach used for making square holes. It would be interesting to know how many internal, as well as external, surfaces are finished by broaching. Broaching applications are almost limitless. They are particularly adaptable to high-volume production. Broaches are made to be pushed or pulled through. They also vary in lengths and in their tooth spacings.

Their in-between teeth, throat depth diameters, as well as tooth spacing, must be designed to adequately accommodate the rolled-up chip. The diameter of the rolled chip depends on the depth of cut by each tooth, the length of the cut (thickness of the work), and the type of material.

For example: if the work is 2 inches thick (E), the chip in theory is also 2 inches long. If the tooth is made to cut a chip .004 inches thick, then you roll a piece of .004-inch thick paper into a tight roll and measure its diameter. The throat depth (D) and width is made about 30 percent greater than the rolled-chip diameter to avoid jamming up.

As the broaching progresses, the depth of the cut is decreased. The last tooth merely burnishes the surface.

It is a good idea to space the teeth unevenly, which generally results in a smoother finish. Where cutting is too much of a load for one broach, it can be divided up between two or more broaches.

A series of shorter sections coupled together to make up a long broach, up to 8 or 12 feet in length, can be set up in a planer to cut out intricate shapes on the periphery of a blank.

15

FLAT PUSH BROACH

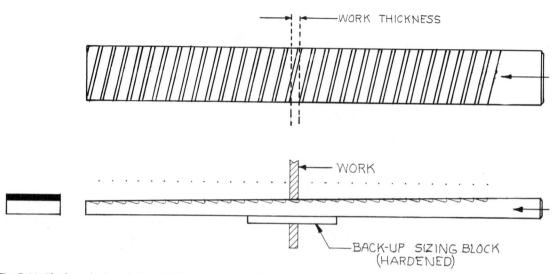

Fig. B-21. Flat broach. A push-through flat-surface sizing broach is shown, as well as the method for controlling its cut.

¾" SQUARE HOLE BROACH

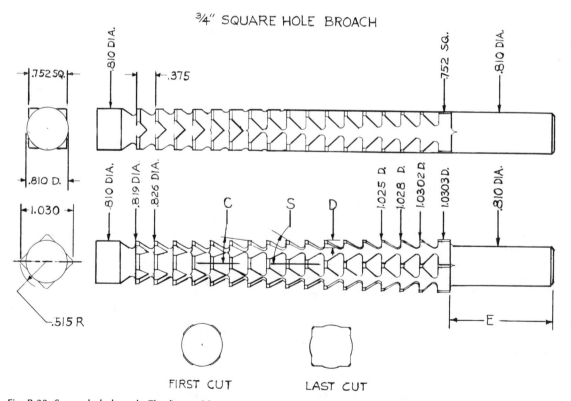

Fig. B-22. Square-hole broach. The first and last sizing cuts of a square-hole push-through broach are shown.

Note: In the illustration, C = the cutting clearance of teeth and S = the secondary tooth clearance.

KEY-SEATING BROACH. In Fig. B-23, A shows a type of internal, key-seating broach. These can be purchased in sizes that satisfy the key and bore dimensions. However, because bores can be of infinite diameters, it often becomes necessary to make up guide bushings to fit the particular diameters. The hole in the bushing is bored eccentric to the bushing's outside diameter. The amount of eccentricity depending on the bore's diameter in the work, as well as the depth of the key seat to be cut.

These broaches are pushed through the work in an arbor press. Since you must assume that your work does not set perfectly square in the press, it is advisable to release the pressure on the broach after the first initial short push. Doing so permits the broach to conform parallel with the axial center of the bore, thus preventing excessive bending and possible breakage of the broach.

In Fig. B-23, B shows a flat type of internal key-seating broach, which can be made up quite easily. This broach must be guided and backed up by a slotted bushing, as shown. Push this broach through the work as described in A.

KEY SEATING IN A LATHE. Figure B-24 shows a method of cutting smaller, internal key seats in a lathe by using a boring bar. Although this method involves considerable

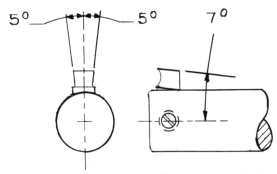

Fig. B-24. Key seating in a lathe. Although this method of cutting key seats involves considerable manual labor, it nonetheless is most convenient in a pinch.

manual labor, it nonetheless is very convenient in the pinches. The square-nosed cutting tool is ground nearly the same as for roughing a square thread, and is inserted into the right-angled tool slot of the boring bar.

Set the tool's radial position by partially rotating the bar until the two corners of the cutting tool touch the bore of the work at the same time. This tool-positioning method produces a key seat bottom that will be more nearly at right angles to the bore's centerline and the key seat's walls.

Of course, the lathe's carriage must be hand-cranked, in and out, the length of the key seat.

The cutting tool is cross-fed into the work .003 to .005 inch per cut.

A somewhat larger and/or truer key seat can be cut using this method by first cutting a narrower and deeper slot. Then finish with the correct width of tool, cutting both walls down to the correct depth.

KEY-SEAT SLOTTING IN THE SHAPER. Figure B-25 shows the general method of work setup in a shaper for key-seat slotting.

A indicates the width of the key slot, while B indicates the key slot's depth. Note that the depth of the key seat is always one half the key's width. The depth is measured from the corners of the bore, where they meet the key slot.

It is better to use a cutting tool about 20 percent narrower than the desired width of the key slot. You should also cut in a few thousandths of an inch deeper than the finish depth is to be. Follow by inserting a finishing tool as wide as you want the key slot to be, shaving both walls down to the required depth (B).

BUSHINGS, SPLIT

SPLIT BUSHING, TURNING AND BORING. The machining of bronze or other split bushings, such as used in heavy machine bearing journals, can be done quite easily if cer-

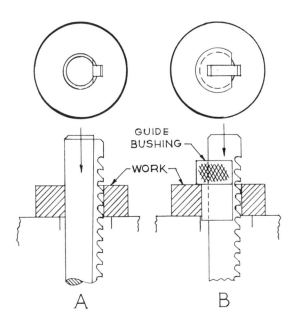

Fig. B-23. Key-seating broach. This broach is used for key seating in different bore sizes.

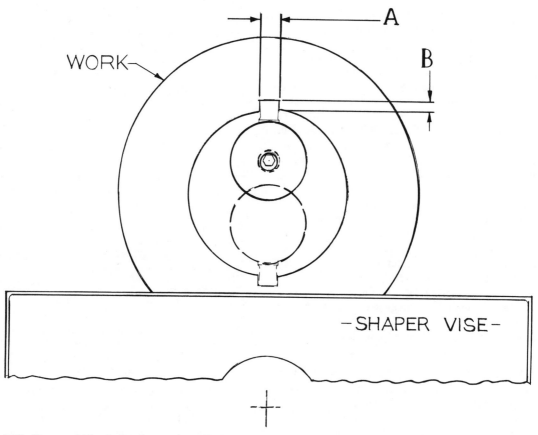

Fig. B-25. Key-seat slotting in the shaper. The general method of work setup in a shaper for internal key-slotting is shown.

tain steps are followed.

The rough-cast bushing should first be rough turned and bored (only a cleanup cut). Both ends must also be faced, but not to length.

The splitting can be done in a shaper using a regular lathe-type cutoff tool. The shaper method is probably more simple than setting up in a milling machine, using a slitting saw.

After splitting, take a light cleanup cut off the split surfaces to ensure some degree of flatness and parallelism.

Using the corner of a file, cut a **V** notch into one corner of each half's front end, as shown at A in Fig. B-26. Then set up the two halves in the four-jaw chuck of a lathe, as shown in Fig. B-26 or Fig. B-27, depending on the diameter of the bushing. For example, if the bushing O.D. is only 4 to 12 inches in diameter, the setup is fairly simple as shown. Roughly preadjust the chuck jaws to approximate the diameters of the bushing. To support the outer bushing end, lay wooden blocks or such across the ways of the

lathe, equal in height with the bottom chuck jaw. Place one of the halves into the chuck, allowing enough space for cutting off. Place narrow strips of paper, .004 to .006 inch thick and 1/8 inch wide, a short but equal distance from the back ends of the half bushing. Next, place the second half-bushing atop the first, being careful not to disturb the paper shims.

Before the jaws are tightened, place two narrow strips of coarse emery cloth, doubled by folding inwardly, between the jaws and the bushing on the two nonsplit sides, as shown at B. These strips are placed an equal distance inward from the jaw ends. Make sure they are positioned farther away from the chuck's face than are the shims in the split. They are used to keep the outer ends of the two bushing halves pressing against each other.

After you tighten the jaws, you can remove the supporting blocks. The bushing can now be trued up closer, as follows. Lay a smooth, flat piece of steel across the ways near to the chuck. This piece is used as a base for support-

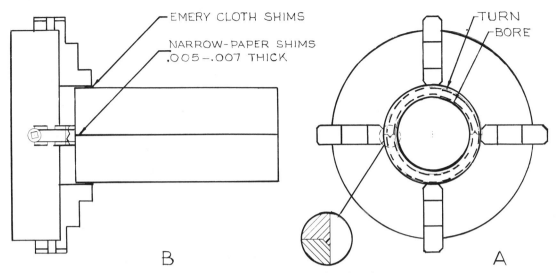

Fig. B-26. Split bushing, turning and boring. Split-type bushings are machined as shown.

ing a surface gage. Tentatively adjust the gage so that it points to the machine spindle's axial center height. Compare the gage pointer to the slit of the bushing next to the jaws, on the front side then the back side. Rotate the work

1/2 turn and repeat the comparison, simultaneously adjusting the surface gage pointer.

After you have centered the slit at the back end of the bushing, make the same comparison on the front end. By

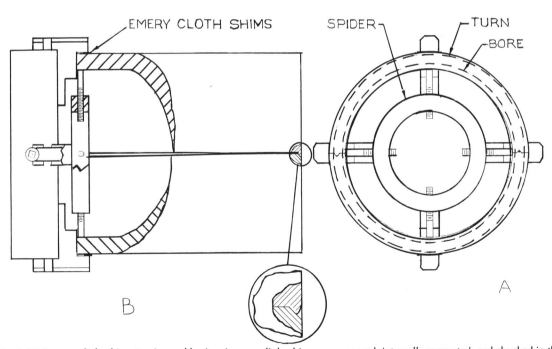

Fig. B-27. Larger split bushing, turning and boring. Larger split bushings are prepared, internally supported, and chucked in the method shown. The method of cutting off is also illustrated.

leaving the gage pointer closer to the front end, the non-split sides of the bushing are centralized.

At this point the bushing halves are tightened down a bit more securely in the chuck. Then use a blunt, narrow chisel and a light hammer to flare the unnotched end's corner into the filed **V** notch, as shown. This step prevents the ends of the two half sections from sliding away as a result of the cutting pressures. *Note:* the notching and flaring is done in two places only.

LARGER SPLIT BUSHING, TURNING AND BORING. In machining split bushings of a larger diameter, the chuck jaws must be reversed, as shown in Fig. B-27. In this position, their gripping lengths are much shorter. The preparation and setting up procedure is very nearly the same as for the smaller bushings described in Fig. B-26. Paper and emery shims are used similarly. So are the two **V** notches.

In setting up the two half sections, butt against the jaws for easier trueing and more gripping. To prevent excessive warping from jaw pressures, a four-legged spider (as shown in Fig. B-27) is positioned internally and next to the jaws. Its four studs are unscrewed to exert pressure outwardly against the jaws. The two emery cloth shims between the two jaws and the bushing are positioned slightly forward of the spider studs, causing the two front ends of the half sections to press toward each other. The trueing procedure is done as described in Fig. B-26, so is the notch flaring.

BRONZE TOOL

With everything lined up and secure, the rough-finishing cuts are done by using a somewhat unorthodox bronze cutting tool (it can be of high-speed steel), ground as illustrated in Fig. B-28. This type of tool has been used safely over an extended period of time without mishaps. It is used with the condition that its tip is slanted downward and positioned slightly below center. The big trick is in the starting of each heavier cut, and holds true for machining solid bronze bushings, as well.

To start each heavier cut, engage the lateral feed when the cutting tool is only a short distance from the work. Start the work rotation very gradually by nudging the switch or clutch of the machine until the tool begins to cut into the work. Continue this gradual increase in rotational speed until the tool has cut from one to two revolutions at the full depth of the cut, then allow the work to rotate fully at the predetermined rate.

This gradual starting of all heavier cuts permits the tool and cut to become adjusted to each other's pressures. Otherwise, this type of tool would pull itself into the bronze instantly and so severely it would tear the bushing out of the chuck.

A similar type of cutting tool, using the same gradual starting procedure, is used for the heavy internal boring. The purpose of this type of tool is that much freer, heavy cuts can be made without the chips flying across the shop.

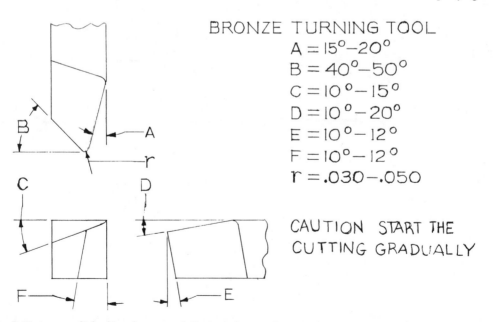

BRONZE TURNING TOOL
A = 15°–20°
B = 40°–50°
C = 10°–15°
D = 10°–20°
E = 10°–12°
F = 10°–12°
r = .030–.050

CAUTION START THE
CUTTING GRADUALLY

Fig. B-28. Larger split bushing, bronze tool. Begin each cut only as described to prevent disaster.

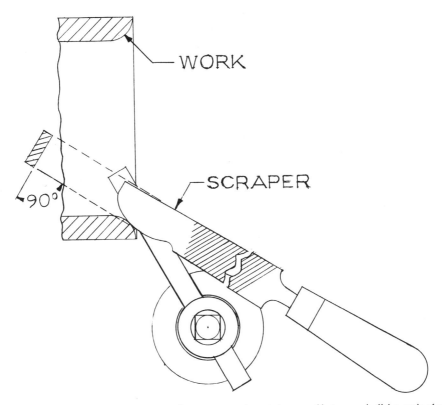

Fig. B-29. Larger split bushing, cutting sequence. Use a flat scraper made out of a worn file to round off the ends of split bushings after you have roughed with a sharp-pointed tool positioned above center.

CUTTING SEQUENCE

Rough cut the outside to within .030 to .040 inch over the finish dimension. Rough-bore the inside and finish to +.003 inch over the finish dimension. Come back and finish the outside to finish dimensions.

If the bushing end is to be rounded off to a given radius, no particular difficulties are encountered. *Caution:* Do not use a radius-form tool in these cases. Instead, rough out the bulk of the radius material with a sharp-pointed negative rake tool in the tool holder, manipulating the cross and lateral feeds manually. Then insert a suitable piece of steel into the tool post, projecting into the bore at approximately 45° and slightly above center, becoming a rest for a flat scraper.

A flat scraper can be made from a worn larger flat file. (See Fig. B-29.) The scraper, pressed down on the rest, is hand-manipulated over and around the roughed bushing end. A gage is used for checking the required size of radius. Any scraper marks can be smoothed out with a pad of emery cloth, held by hand and moving in and out over the scraped surface as the work revolves more rapidly.

The bushing halves can be cut off with a conventional cutoff tool, ground with a negative rake. However, when the tool has nearly cut through, the cross feed is engaged and the work is rotated quite slowly by nudging the machine's switch or clutch. Block up under the bushing with wooden boards or such to prevent damaging the bushing halves as they drop off. To prevent accidents and disappointments, a light blow with a soft mallet or piece of wood—striking from the inside out after the sections are practically cut off—will also sever the halves.

If a radius is required on the cutoff end, true up two assembled halves as you would a solid bushing. Insert the halves into the chuck as far as possible. A long bushing might require a steel band tightened around and close to the outboard end to help keep the two halves together. Use the same rounding and radiusing procedure as on the first end.

C

CAMS

A CAMS APPLICATION. Figure C-1 shows a drum-type cam specifically designed to perform with a semiautomatic lathe to do a specific job. The work performed was the rough straight and rough and finish spherical boring of cast-iron pillow block bearing housings.

The requirements were to first bore straight through the rough cored casting, as shown in G. This step was done in one pass since this bore diameter was not critical, being in the area of plus or minus .003 inch.

A parallel bar type of spherical generating mechanism was mounted on the main tool carriage block. The cam roller follower (R) was attached to the tail end of the horizontally oscillating parallel bar (P), carrying a two-tool boring bar attached to its front end.

The drum cam (C) was mounted—in such a way that it can be rotated—on a stub shaft attached to the back end of the mechanism. It was rotated at a 1 to 1 ratio by a roller chain and sprocket (S), which was driven from a sprocket sliding along an existing shaft and running through the length of the lathe's bed.

Upon starting, the machine tool (Y) in the boring bar rapidly approached the work to within 1/16 inch or so. Simultaneously, the cam drum had also rapidly but partially revolved, slowing down to the predetermined feeding rate. This speed decrease took place at about 275°, as

illustrated in D. Tool Y bored straight through, and was prevented from cutting any arcs by the cam follower negotiating in a straight nonactuating section of the cam's groove, as at G.

The straight-boring cut ended at around 320° on the cam. The forward advancement of the tool carriage block was then stopped. At this point the boring bar came into play. The oscillating parallel bar was actuated by the cam's roller follower coming in contract with the angular side of the cam's groove at 320°, causing tool Z to swing about its two common centers, and cut an arc, as shown in H. The first was an arced roughing cut. However, because the cut was too heavy and uneven, no accurate sizing was possible.

The tool's travel direction was then automatically reversed, starting at around 360°. The cam started to swing (pull) the tool back over the previous cut. The tool was not fed into the work for the finish cutting. Instead, it removed only the stock it left as it sprung away in its roughing cut (I).

The amount of metal remaining for the final finishing cut varied from .001 to .004 inch on the side. Without exploiting the system's full possibilities, it was possible to finish approximately 150 larger pillow block housings in less than 8 hours on one machine. The spherical bore di-

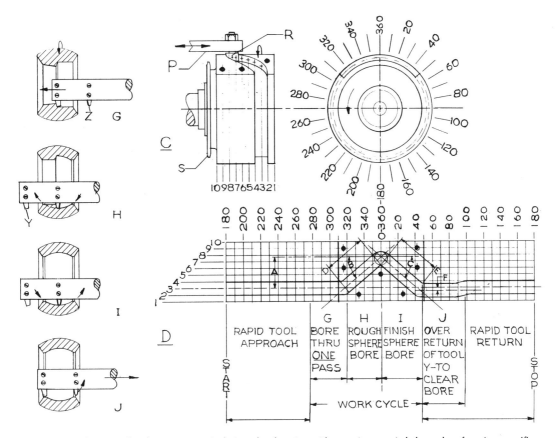

Fig. C-1. A cams application. This drum-type cam is designed to function with a semiautomatic lathe and perform in a specific way.

ameter was consistently held within .0002 inch, both radially and transversely, producing an almost perfect spherical surface and eliminating practically all selective assembly.

Shortly after the sperical boring was finished, the whole tool block and spherical cutting mechanism was automatically withdrawn. The machine's spindle rotation also stopped, awaiting unloading and reloading.

To prevent unsightly tool marks in the straight bore, caused by the return of tool Y, the cam was made to pull the bar, with tool, back and out slightly farther than when entering into the work. This amount is shown at F, illustration D.

The cam proper was constructed separately and screwed onto the drum. A method that offered more choices in best cam angles (B and C) and also lengths of cycling time, as differentiating between the chordal widths of the various sizes of castings. Cam angles (B and C) of 42° gave suitable cutting feed rates for the rough and finish boring of the sphere.

More than one size of boring bars was made available for machining the smallest to the largest castings. The tool slots in the bars were spaced to suit the various chordal widths of each size of casting, thereby shortening the cycle time. The work was supported on an angle plate, and bolted and balanced on the face of a pneumatic chuck.

Except for the carbide-tool sharpening and settings, the job could be run by almost anyone having no particular skills.

ENGINE CAM. Figure C-2 shows the end view of a general type of cam used in an internal combustion engine for opening and closing the intake and exhaust valves. The illustration shows a somewhat exaggerated high cam lobe. Nevertheless, this cam is also laid out much the same as a heart cam.

To avoid most side thrust to the follower, the cam's bottom diameter is made wide enough to span the widest extent of the lobe's sweep as at B. The cam's lobe on its following (back) side can be cut away from its apex, down to the shaft's diameter. The follower's bottom can also be

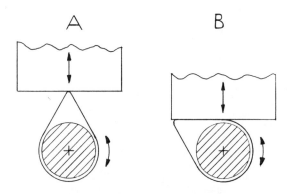

cut away on its falling side. Doing so results in a more rapid closing action.

This type of cam can also be readily milled between centers in a dividing head and milling machine.

INVOLUTE PLATE CAM, LAYOUT. Figure C-3 shows an involute plate cam. Cams of this type have a great many applications, designs, actions, and purposes. Regardless of their make, design, or name, the same cam can be made to vary its action by utilizing a pointed follower, either a roller type or a flat headed one. The size of the cam does not change its action. Whether the follower is positively returned, brought back by gravity, or returned by springs, would depend on its angular position or the type of actions required.

The illustration shows how these cams can be laid out

Fig. C-2. Engine cam. Although gasoline engine cams vary considerably, this illustration represents the general shape of the internal combustion engine cam. They can be milled between centers in a dividing head and milling machine.

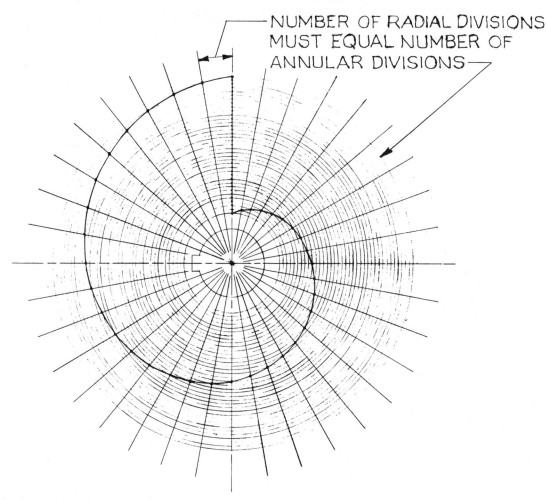

Fig. C-3. Involute plate cam, layout.

by drawing a circle somewhat larger than the hub of the cam. Add the amount of rise required in the cam to the first drawn circle. This amount of rise is divided equally into 36 spaces with a divider caliper.

Prick, punch, or mark each of the 36 divisions. Adjust the divider caliper from the cam blank's axial center to the first mark of the 36 divisions and draw a complete circle. Continue drawing circles, each with a radius equal to one of the 36 layouts marks.

The next step is to draw 36 straight lines, 10° apart, radiating outward from the blank's axial center, as shown. Starting at the top, and progressing to the left or right, punch or mark the intersecting point of the largest circle and one radiating line. Repeat the procedure by moving down one circle and over one radial spacing until 360° have been punched. Using a French curve, draw a line connecting the 36 intersection points.

You can now either saw out or shape the blank according to the layout line. Smooth the surface by hand or machine filing.

This type of cam also can be mounted on a mandrel and cut in a knee-column type of milling machine.

HEART CAM. Figure C-4 shows a heart-shaped cam, the

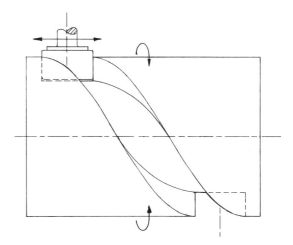

Fig. C-5. Helical cam, positive action.

purpose of which is to impart a uniform, harmonic back and forth motion to the cam follower. You can lay out and cut this type of cam much like the involute plate cam, except that in a heart cam you deal only with half of the cam's periphery at a time. Therefore, the annular lines must be spaced twice as far apart as would be those for an involute plate cam.

You can also mill the heart cam between the centers of a dividing head and tail stock. Starting at the highest or lowest points of the cam, after you make the first cut, partially rotate the cam a specific radial amount (in degrees). Then, raise or lower the table the amount of the annular spacing. Repeat this procedure for just half of the cam's revolution. Then do the table feeding in the opposite direction to cut the second half of the cam's periphery. In each case some file finishing will be required.

If the cam is planned for a roller follower, use a rounded (convex) circular cutter or an end mill for the milling.

HELICAL CAM, POSITIVE ACTION. Figure C-5 shows a positive-action, helical type of cam. The follower requires no springs or such to keep it constantly returning.

HELICAL CAM LAYOUT. Figure C-6 shows a method of laying out the harmonic rise and fall of the cam groove. It becomes more simplified to work out (lay out) the cam on paper first. When it is carefully laid out, it gives you an exact idea of where the follower will be at any particular degree in the cam's revolution.

Assuming you know the required extent of the follower's travel (stroke), as shown by A in Fig. C-6, at one end of the paper draw a half circle having a diameter equal to the planned cam stroke. Divide the half circle into as many

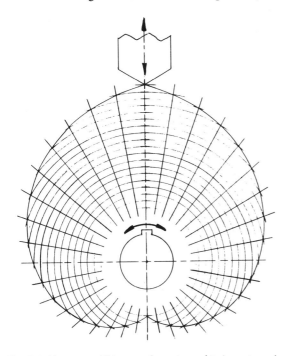

Fig. C-4. Heart cam. This type of cam is used to impart a uniform, harmonic back-and-forth motion to the cam follower. Its layout and cutting is much like the involute plate cam.

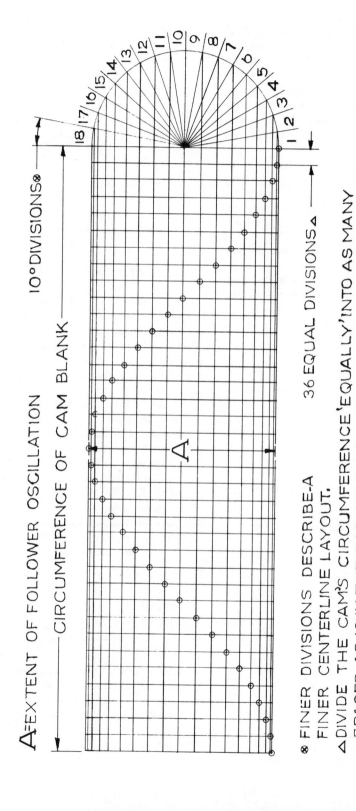

A = EXTENT OF FOLLOWER OSCILLATION

CIRCUMFERENCE OF CAM BLANK

10° DIVISIONS ⊗

36 EQUAL DIVISIONS △

⊗ FINER DIVISIONS DESCRIBE-A
FINER CENTERLINE LAYOUT.

△ DIVIDE THE CAM'S CIRCUMFERENCE 'EQUALLY' INTO AS MANY
SPACES AS IS IN THE RADIALLY DIVIDED HALF CIRCLE. MULTIPLY THE
NUMBER OF 'SPACES' BY 2, FOR A 360° LAYOUT, AS ABOVE.

Fig. C-6. Helical cam layout. A method of laying out the harmonic rise and fall of the cam follower groove is shown.

equal radial spaces (not lines) as is convenient, without excessive crowding. In the sample layout, I chose these spaces to be 10° apart.

From the center point of the half circle, draw a horizontal line equal in length to the circumference of the cam blank's outside diameter. Divide the horizontal line into twice as many equal spaces as there are radial spaces in the half circle. In the sample layout, there are 360 spaces. The width of these spaces is found by dividing 36 into the cam's circumference. Adjust a pair of dividers to this division measurement, then step off the 36 spaces.

Next draw the 36 vertical lines that will represent longitudinal lines running parallel with the cam blank's axial centerline.

The next step is to draw lines the length of the layout to represent the circumferential measurement. These lines start at the intersection of each radial division line and the half circle. Punch or otherwise mark the intersecting points of the vertical and horizontal lines, with each mark being one space apart both ways. These markings plot the harmonic centerline of the groove to be.

To make this type of cam, special machinery must be used that will cut exacting, smooth working surfaces on the cam walls. However, if cam milling equipment is not readily available, you can begin by mounting the blank between the dividing head and tail stock centers in a milling machine. (A vertical mill is preferred.) Use a two-lipped end mill, somewhat smaller in diameter than the finished groove width.

Plunge the end mill to the full depth of the groove, at both ends. After withdrawing the cutter, move the machine's table longitudinally for a distance of one space. Also, rotate the dividing head spindle 1/36 of a revolution. This position is now end milled, as was the preceding position. The indexing and table advancing are repeated until 18 places plus 1 are roughed out.

When you reach the halfway point, or 180° around the cam blank, continue with the indexing and table moving as before, but reverse the table's advancing direction. In this way, the groove of the cam will be brought around and back to the original starting point.

At this point, change to the finish-sized end mill, preferably one having more than two flutes. Perform the finish cutting of the groove by cutting in exactly the same path as in the roughing. In every such procedure the groove's side walls are left with a series of scallops from the cutter. To lessen the scalloped depth and width, multiply the original layout spacings by 2, 4, or whatever, to result in more finely spaced cuts and shallower scallops.

The final step is the hand-smoothing of the side walls by filing or sanding.

Of course, you also can cut a helical grooved cam in the milling machine by gearing the table and dividing head in the same way as for cutting helical gears. The difference is that an end mill instead of a circular cutter must be used. Also, the table's feeding direction must be reversed after you cut the groove halfway around the blank. See Table M-3.

INSTANT-RETURN CAM. Figure C-7 shows a very rapid

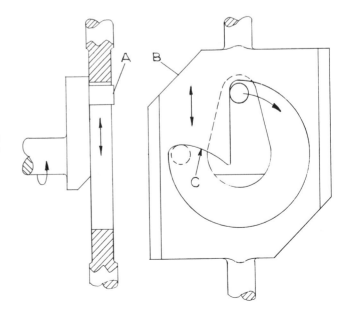

Fig. C-7. Instant-return cam. This rapid-acting cam can go in one direction only. Its follower returns either by springs or gravity.

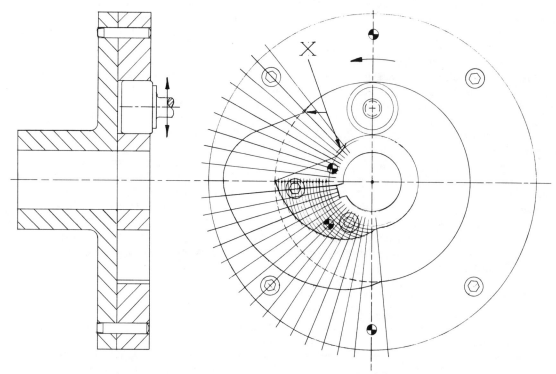

Fig. C-8. Positive-acting cam. This positive type of cam is made primarily of three pieces.

acting cam. In this particular system the activating crank can rotate in one direction only.

The follower is returned by springs or gravity. The crank's pin (A) lifts the plate follower (B) by bearing upward against the lip (C). The lip's bottom can be straight, or curved downward to compensate for the diminishing rate of rise of the rotating crank pin.

POSITIVE-ACTING CAM. Figure C-8 shows a positive-acting type of cam, and does not necessarily depend on springs or weights to bring the follower back to its starting point. The cam can be made of three parts, as illustrated. You can lay out, finish, bolt, and dowel the inner cam member to the face of the shank's plate.

Position and bolt the outer cam ring blank to the face of the same shank's plate. Then, using a round plug of the same diameter as the cam follower's diameter, you can readily scribe the ring's cam outline according to the contours of the inner cam member. Removing the ring from the plate, you can mill, saw out, shape, and file the cam to the laid-out line.

It is always best to lay out the complete cam on paper first. The indexing and cutting procedure is carried out much like that of the involute plate cam, guiding yourself by the intersecting points of the annular layout circles and the radial spacings.

Note the slight indentation in the inner cam and the slight protrusion in the outer cam ring, marked by X. This indentation is used to take up the slack in the linkage on the return stroke.

In assembling the cam sections, use short round plugs in the groove for proper spacing. Fix this spacing by doweling.

CRANK AND SLOT CAM. Figure C-9 shows a cam action where the pin (A) of the rotating crank shaft (B) operates in slot C. This action changes the crank's rotary into a linear motion to slot C.

This cam action is positive, requiring no springs or weights.

BACKING-OFF CAM. Figure C-10 shows the general principle of cam usage in the backing off of taps and other cutting tools. The cam is geared to make one complete revolution for each cutting edge on the tool. Lathes specially equipped for back-off work can be purchased.

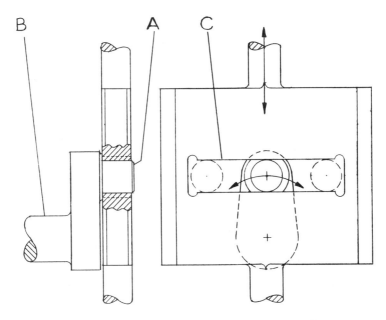

Fig. C-9. Crank and slot cam. A rotating shaft's action is turned into a linear motion without springs or weights.

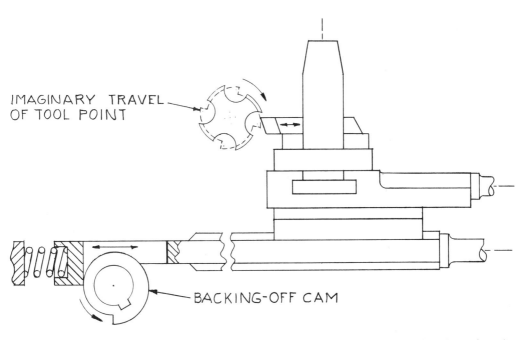

IMAGINARY TRAVEL OF TOOL POINT

BACKING-OFF CAM

Fig. C-10. Backing-off cam. Toolroom lathes can be purchased already equipped for doing back-off work on taps and cutters.

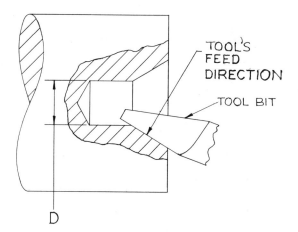

Fig. C-11. Centering shafts. Use a tool bit ground to a straight cutting edge, as shown.

CENTERING

CENTERING SHAFTS. Figures C-11 and 12 show a method of centering large or out-of-round shafts in a lathe when higher rotational speeds cannot be used. This method uses a drill and tool bit.

For example, if a job set up in a steady rest cannot be aligned properly with the machine spindle's axial center-line, all you need to do is drill into the full depth of the proposed center hole. Then, using a tool bit ground to a straight cutting edge, as shown in Fig. C-11, bore out the 60° center angle. To check the tool's angular setting use a thread tool centering gage, as shown in Fig. C-12.

The countersink angle need not always be exact because the pressure of the work, while cutting, will burnish the hole to match the 60° tail stock's center angle within a short time.

MOVING OVER CENTER HOLES. Figure C-13 shows a method of moving over a partially drilled center hole so that it registers more centrally with the layout.

After laying out and center-punching the center hole location, use a small divider caliper to scribe a circle approximating the diameter of the countersunk hole to be. Then prick-punch this circle in four places, or about 90° apart, as shown.

Use a drill with a smaller diameter to begin, then follow with a larger one, to full depth. Instead of the common center drill, use a pilotless 60° countersink. The countersunk hole's relationship to the prick-punched marks in the layout must be observed. Groove the inside of the hole, farthest from the punched marked circle, along its beveled surface, as shown.

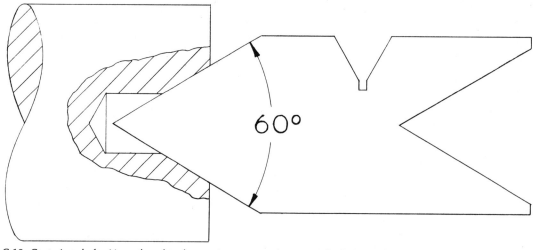

Fig. C-12. Centering shafts. Use a thread tool centering gate, as shown, to check the tool's angular setting.

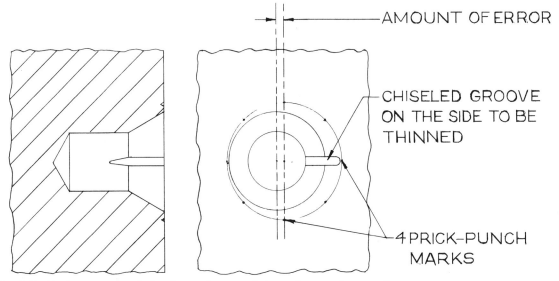

AMOUNT OF ERROR

CHISELED GROOVE
ON THE SIDE TO BE
THINNED

4 PRICK-PUNCH
MARKS

Fig. C-13. Moving over center holes. An angular center hole can be moved over easily.

Now use the countersink tool to cut more off the grooved side. Repeat the grooving and countersinking on the hole until the countersink tool cuts away half of each of the four punch marks.

DOUBLE CENTER-PUNCHING. Often in the development and building of special equipment, it becomes necessary to cut out some section of the machine. However, because of its shape or size, the machine cannot be readily moved for machining. In this situation, you must use a different method, that of drilling a series of overlapping holes through the section, then punching out the slug. As easy as it sounds, though, this method can be frustrating if the hole spacings were not laid out uniformly. You can lay out the hole locations (A) with a divider caliper, or with a double-pointed centering and spacing punch, as shown in Fig. C-14. Of course, using the double centering punch is easier and faster.

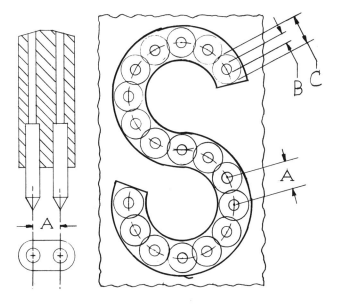

Fig. C-14. Double center-punching. The better method of removing the desired configuration without the use of large machines is shown.

After the hole locations are center-punched, use a comparatively small-diameter drill (1/8 to 3/16 inch), and drill completely through. These smaller-diameter holes (B) then serve as pilots for guiding the larger drill, which must be large enough to slightly overlap and break through into the previously drilled hole (C).

After the slug is hammered or otherwise pushed out, the sharp hole edges can be chiseled, filed or ground smooth and to size.

CENTERS

RELIEVED CENTERS. Figure C-15 shows a typical relieved tail-stock center, which is very useful when you are facing off shaft ends between centers. However, this type of center is not at all recommended for heavier turning.

PIPE (BULL) CENTER. Figure C-16 shows a very handy pipe center, also known as a bull center. For rigid-walled types of work, three blades (preferably hardened) are equally spaced and soldered to the 60° cone. The blades imbed themselves into the corner of the work, preventing the center from partially rotating in an out-of-round hole. Various sizes of these centers can be made up, as shown, without any particular difficulty.

CHUCKS

POT CHUCK NO. 1. A very convenient chuck for accurately holding partially machined pieces in a secondary operation is shown in Fig. C-17. It is generally known as a pot chuck. This type of chuck often is made just for the job at hand, but, it also can be taken out and rechucked for similar-sized jobs. A smaller pot chuck can be run in

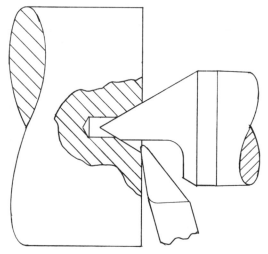

Fig. C-15. Relieved centers. A typical relieved center often is used to permit facing off of shaft ends between centers.

a collet. Otherwise, it requires some trueing by indicating and slight reboring. However, it can be rebored only a limited number of times for any one diameter of work.

The body of this chuck is taper-threaded and uses a threaded nut for closing and opening the chuck. The chuck body is sawed through at its front end and divided into four or eight equal sections, as shown.

Before you start boring the body to size and depth, screw on the nut just snug enough to compress the sawed end. When you unscrew the nut, the chuck springs open to admit the workpiece.

POT CHUCK NO. 2. Another type of pot chuck that can

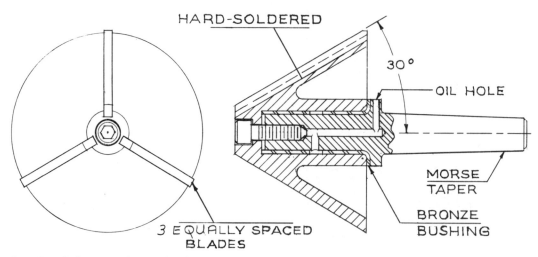

Fig. C-16. Pipe (bull) center. This very handy pipe center is used for supporting hollow work.

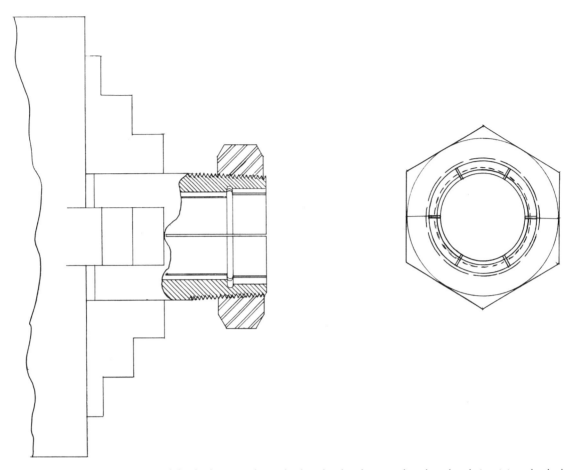

Fig. C-17. Pot chuck no. 1. This type of chuck often is made just for the job at hand. It must be rebored each time it is rechucked to ensure trueness.

be made in a hurry, out of a piece of pipe and a bolt, is shown in Fig. C-18. After you have sawed across the end of the pipe, drill and tap a cross hole at right angles to the saw out.

Tighten the pipe in the lathe's chuck. Screw in the bolt and tighten it just snugly while you finish the bore to the desired diameter and depth.

Upon loosening the bolt, the pot chuck springs open enough to insert and to extract the work.

DIAPHRAGM CHUCK. Figure C-19 shows a type of chuck used for holding work extremely accurately, and repeatedly so. It is called a diaphragm chuck and is primarily designed to function with a grinding machine for doing both external and internal work. Because of its design principles, it will not hold work tight enough except for very light turning, boring, or grinding.

Work held in a diaphragm chuck will repeatedly run within .0001 inch, full indicator reading. This type of chuck does not open or shut much more than .005 inch across the diameter (or just enough to freely slip the work on and off).

Depending on whether it is made for inside or outside work, the fingers (A) are opened by either pulling or pushing the rod (B), which screws into and deflects the diaphragm (C). The fingers, being an integral part of the diaphragm, close or spread with the pull or push of the rod. During the working process, the rod neither pulls nor pushes. It rotates freely under no end pressures.

The outer part of the diaphragm, being thicker and in the form of a flange, is bolted to the nose of the machine's spindle (D). The chuck proper is of one piece, and made to hold work of one specific diameter only. To increase or decrease the chuck's capacity, screws with lock nuts are

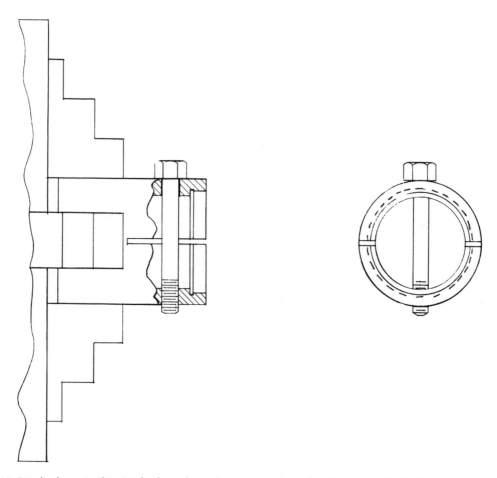

Fig. C-18. Pot chuck no. 2. This pot chuck can be made in a hurry. It needs only a pipe and a bolt.

screwed radially into the fingers. Then the bolt heads are cylindrically ground in the machine to the required chuck's diameter.

FOUR-JAW CHUCK, SCREW MARKINGS. Figure C-20 shows a speedy method of trueing-up work in a four-jaw chuck. To begin with, true-up a random-sized, smooth-surfaced piece of steel (C), exerting an even pressure on all four jaws. Then center-punch, file, or grind small matching marks (A and B) at each of the four screw locations. By observing the jaw locations in relation to the annular grooves on the chuck's face, together with the uniform alignment of the marks on the screws, work can be easily and more quickly trued-up.

COILING

COILING HEAVIER ROD AND WIRE. Figure C-21 shows a method of helical coiling a tube or rod. The process is much like coiling a wire spring, except that the tube or rod is clamped to the mandrel, as shown. In the case of a tube, you should not drill holes through the mandrel and then sharply bend over the tube's end.

If it is required that the rod or tube be uncoiled or straight for some length before winding, the end can be very loosely wound around the mandrel only tight enough to clear the swing capacity of the lathe. That generous bend in this end can easily be later straightened or bent into any shape necessary.

It becomes more difficult to negotiate the heavier material through holes and bends. To retard its flow, use a clamping method, as illustrated. You can use various materials for the split block, including iron, brass, fiber, or wood, depending on the work material's hardness. You can vary the clamping tension to suit by turning the tool

34

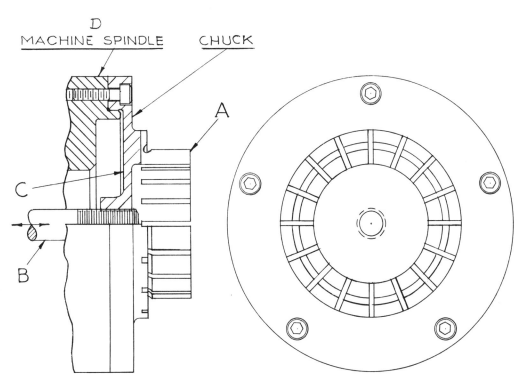

Fig. C-19. Diaphragm chuck. This chuck is used for lightly holding work with extreme accuracy, repeatedly. It is usually used in grinding ball-bearing raceways.

post screw. Heavy springs are wound in their soft state, then heat-treated afterward.

In every case, you must exercise extreme caution when you are removing a heavy spring from the mandrel. Perhaps the safest method is to shut off the machine's motor. Then, while it is still in gear, you can manually reverse the machine spindle for a couple of revolutions. Then carefully loosen the tool post screw.

Be very careful when you are coiling heavy rod or wire. It can be dangerous.

CRANKSHAFTS

LAYING OUT AND TURNING CRANKSHAFTS. Figure C-22 shows a method of laying out and turning heavier crankshafts. This method varies with the number of throws (cranks), as well as with the size. Also, there are different methods of supporting the shafts in their turning or grinding.

In Fig. C-22A, the stock comes as a rough forging. The first step is to weld on extensions at both ends of the forging to accommodate the eccentric centers. These extensions can be of hot-rolled 1020 steel. Avoid carbon steel for this purpose.

At B, the forging is laid on a flat surface plate or planer table. Adjusting a surface gage to one-half of the forging's thickness, scribe a horizontal line across both ends, as shown.

At C, the forging is rolled 90° according to a square. Use old files for shimming, if need be. Adjust the surface gage to one-half of the main journal's diameter, and scribe horizontal lines across both ends, as shown in C. Prick-punch the intersecting lines on both journals' ends. Adjust a pair of divider calipers to the amount of eccentric offset, and scribe an arc intersecting the vertical line. Prick-punch this intersection.

At D, the center of the crank cheeks is located by making a flat layout on paper. To the amount of offset, add one-half of the main bearing's diameter, plus one fillet radius. To this subtotal, add one-half the crankpin diameter, plus one fillet radius. This sum gives you the overall diameter of the cheeks. To find the center of the cheeks, divide the calculated cheek diameter by two. Set the divider calipers to this finding, and scribe an arc across the vertical line. Then prick-punch this intersection. The only time the cheek's center point is exactly halfway between

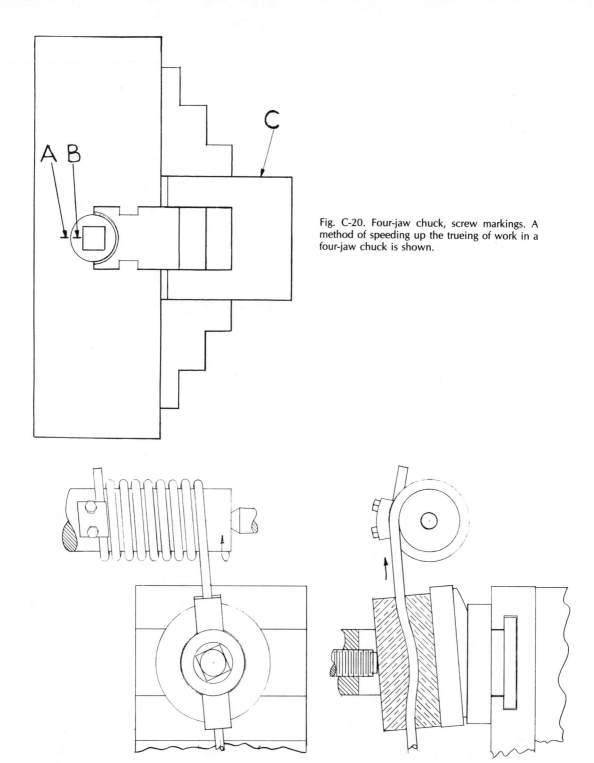

Fig. C-20. Four-jaw chuck, screw markings. A method of speeding up the trueing of work in a four-jaw chuck is shown.

Fig. C-21. Coiling heavier rod and wire. Shown is a method of helically coiling a tube or rod.

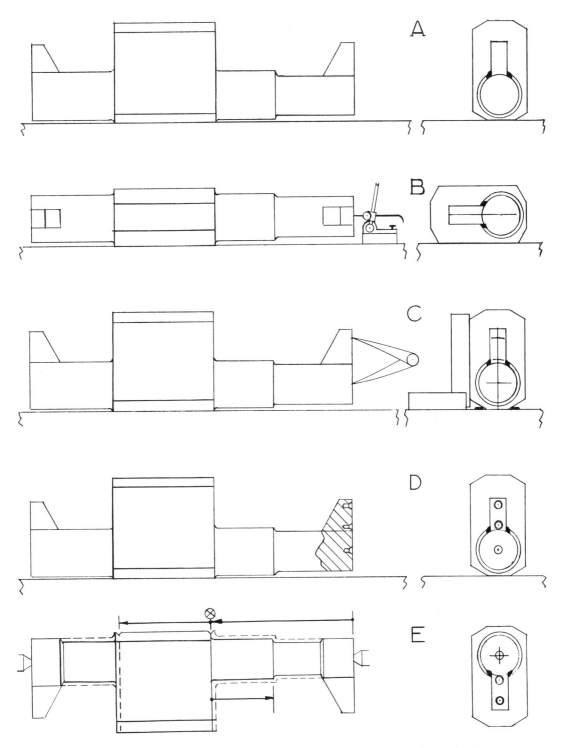

Fig. C-22. Laying out and turning crankshafts. This method is used to lay out and turn heavier crankshafts.

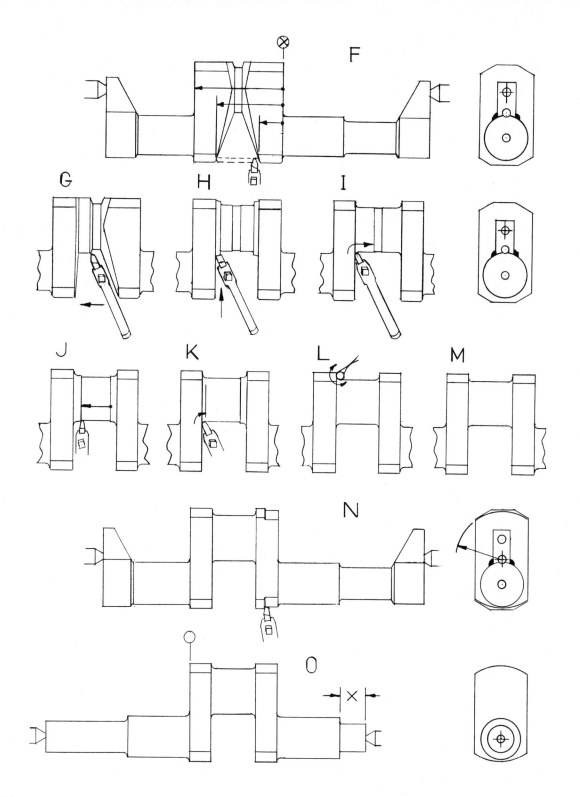

the cranks and the main bearing centers is when both of their diameters are the same.

For D, the center-drilling operation, you can clamp the forging onto a flat plate then drill the center holes of one end in a horizontal bar mill. Next, the whole combination is turned end for end to drill the second end, or by enlarging the center punch marks, you can drill the shaft very satisfactorily by using a hand electric drill motor. A pilot hole of about 3/16 inch is drilled to full depth. It is followed by a 5/16-inch-diameter drill, then finished with a 60° countersink. The center drilling procedure, as described in Fig. C-13, should be followed.

On some crankshafts, the ends can be turned to receive clamped-on center extensions. See Fig. C-23.

After you have done the center drilling, suspend the forging between centers in a large enough engine lathe (Fig. C-22E). It is usually best to use a very heavy dog for driving the work. Counter-balancing is not really required for the roughing operation.

Measure off the distance from the shaft's end to the point on the eccentric's cheek, as shown at x on Fig. C-22E.

Mark this distance by filing a notch on the peripheral corner of the cheek. The notched mark now serves as a datum line from which other longitudinal measurements will be made. Do not use chalk or paint for the marking; these are too easily rubbed off by chip abrasion.

The driving dog's tail should be located on the same side of the shaft as the eccentric section, or on the heavier side. Begin roughing by facing-off both ends of the eccentric section, going down as far as possible and close to the datum notches. Turn the main journals, taking as heavy a cut as the work and equipment will stand. Caliper the turned diameter frequently to guard against any sudden dimension change, possibly resulting from the swiveling of the tool holder. Continue the roughing by digging into the smaller diameter of the shaft, measuring the shoulder's distance from the datum notch. Also rough-out the main journal to the left side of the eccentric section. Leave 1/8 inch on all roughed diameters for warpage and finishing. It is better to rough all fillets to approximately 60 percent of their finished sizes to eliminate much extra cutting in the finishing of the fillets.

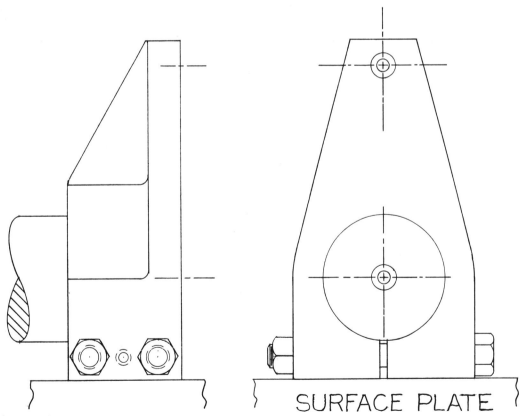

SURFACE PLATE

Fig. C-23. Laying out and turning crankshafts. On some crankshafts, the ends can be turned to receive clamped-on center extensions.

At Fig. C-22F, the shaft is suspended by its eccentric pin's center as shown in Fig. C-24, so the crank pin can be roughed out. Instead of a driving dog, drive the shaft by a heavy angle plate, which is bolted very securely to the face plate and butting up against the shaft. To prevent any intermittent shaft flip-flopping, bolt a second angle plate to the face plate opposite the first, as shown in Fig. C-24.

The idea here is to reach the bottom of the crank's throat (Fig. C-22F). Measure off and notch the cheeks' rough thickness. These notches should be 1/8 inch wider than the print's finish size. The rough throat width will now measure 1/8 inch narrower than the print's dimension.

Using an elongated, rounded nose tool with considerably more side rake, begin by digging in to the left and adjacent to the throat notch. Dig in a little, then hand-feed laterally to the left for a few revolutions. Come back and dig in a little more, then hand-feed to the left some more. Repeat this procedure until the cut becomes 1/2 to 1 inch deep.

Continue the lateral hand-feeding until the tool is far enough away from its starting point to allow the passage of the cut chip. Do not engage the feed until at least 1/2 inch of space appears in back of the tool. Since the chips coming off are individual, unattached, short pieces, there is no need to curl them. Therefore, a cutting tool with a much steeper top rake is used. To take advantage of the machine's power, increase the depth of the cuts.

After the bottom has been reached, change to a side-cutting tool, widening the throat first on the inner right side, then changing over to widen the left side. Swivel the tool and holder to the most advantageous angles as illustrated at Fig. C-22.

After you have worked out both sides of the throat, change to an end-cutting tool as shown at Fig. C-22H, face-cutting inwardly and closer to the notched datum mark. Stop the inward feeding a little less (about 30°) than one fillet radius above the finished crankpin's diameter.

At this stage, the job must be balanced by attaching weights to the face plate, as shown in Fig. C-24 View A-A. Without counterbalancing it becomes impossible to produce round work. With a shorter round nose tool, complete the roughing of both fillets and even up the varied rough crank pin diameters, shown at Fig. C-22I.

With a narrower and a slightly more elongated round nose tool, begin rough-finishing the crank pin's diameter. First, measure the pin's diameter with a micrometer, then feed the tool into the revolving work, leaving 1/5 to 1/4 inch for the final finishing cut. After you have run this cut across as far as possible, remeasure the starting diameter.

On the final finish cut, purposely avoid shaving the shoulders of the previous cut. Feed the tool into the work the remaining required amount, minus .003 inch for filing and polishing, as shown at Fig. C-22J.

Note: Always set the tool for the depth of the finish cutting by touching it against the rotating chalked surface.

Using a round nose tool, set slightly below center, finish the two fillets. This procedure is easily done by manipulating the lateral- and cross-feed handles simultaneously.

To gage the size of the fillets, use any smooth, round rod or pipe of the required diameter (Fig. C-25). First, smear the rod with a light, thin coat of Prussian blue paste or blackened oil off the machine's ways. With the work stationary, lightly press and partially rotate the rod down

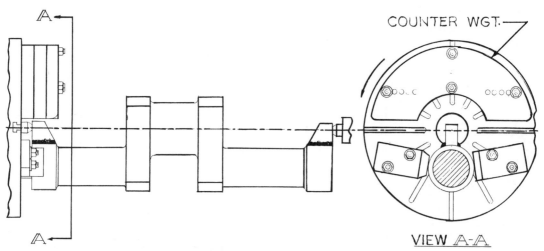

Fig. C-24. Laying out and turning crankshafts. Suspend the shaft by its eccentric pin's center. Also bolt a second angle plate to the face plate.

and against the vertical side of the fillet. The marks left on the fillet are then elongated somewhat with a soft lead pencil or chalk to make the high points easier to see when the work rotation is resumed. Also, use a sharp-cornered blade or block, pressing down and sliding it along the finished pin's diameter toward the fillet being worked. The blade or block should stop sliding at a distance equal to the radius of the fillet before rising, measuring from the vertical side.

Caution! Before any fillet finish-turning is done, touch the tool against the stationary diameter of the work to establish the inward feeding limit. Then mark the cross-feed dial with chalk, as shown in Fig. C-26. Occasionally glance down at the chalk mark to prevent overfeeding inwardly.

The fillets are then smoothed by stroking dry emery cloth, wrapped or folded around a rod or pipe of a suitable size, over the fillets, as in Fig. C-27. Start with a coarser, then finish with a finer emery.

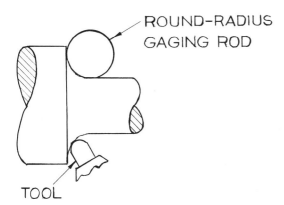

Fig. C-25. Laying out and turning crankshafts. Use any smooth, round rod or pipe of the required diameter to gage the size of the fillets.

Fig. C-26. Laying out and turning crankshafts. Mark the cross-feed dial with chalk, as shown.

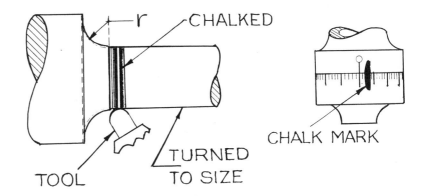

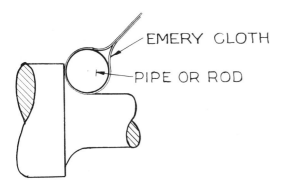

Fig. C-27. Laying out and turning crankshafts. Stroke dry emery cloth wrapped or folded around a rod or pipe of a suitable size over the fillets to smooth them.

To cut fillets on large work that, for its size, cannot be speeded up enough, or on a machine that is just too large to easily manipulate in the previously mentioned manner, then you must use a radius form-cutting tool, as shown in Fig. T-49. Here you also touch the form tool against the stationary finished diameter to establish the inward feeding limit. After marking the cross-feed dial, begin by cutting down along the vertical side of the fillet, at a relatively low rotational speed. As the limit mark approaches, the shaft's rpm should be at its lowest. Use sulphurized cutting oil for the last few revolutions.

Pull the form tool away as soon as the bottom is reached. Operate with the cutting tool set below center. After the fillets are finished, file the crankpin to size. In every case, be extra careful so that the file does not strike the finished fillets. You must develop the ability to file left, as well as right, handed.

Polish the crank pin and fillets to a smooth finish using a cutout wooden block (Fig. C-28), emery cloth, and oil. The block should be narrow enough to permit lateral movement. At this point the fillet and the straight shaft should blend together, showing no junction marks of any kind.

Note: Always use several thicknesses of emery cloth in the polishing block. Doing so results in a softer pad.

Next, you have the diameters of the cheeks to turn down to size, as at Fig. C-22N.

You can now remove the center's extension blocks. If they are welded on, you can turn them off. If longer, they can be burned off with an acetylene torch. Another method is to remove the shaft from the lathe and break off the extensions with a sledgehammer. The welds, on the shaft ends, pose no particular problems. You can cut away the hardened areas with a high-speed tool bit at a slightly lower rotational speed.

For the remaining finish turning, you must rebalance the shaft. Also, you should finish-turn the two main journals in the one setting.

Generally, the end of the shaft at X in Fig. C-22O is finished to print length only if specifically required to save considerable extra work.

Although crankshaft turning involves many operations and much metal removal, the whole procedure is quite rapid when it is done correctly by an experienced machinist. You must have a large enough lathe with enough horsepower to permit heavy cuts. You also need an assortment of cutting tools and tool holders.

When crankshafts having much greater strokes are to be turned, it is often advantageous to drill a series of overlapping holes close to the crank pin. Then, saw through inside of each cheek to remove the unwanted metal slug. In these situations, it is also advantageous to employ an adjustable tool holder jack, as shown in Fig. C-29, for the

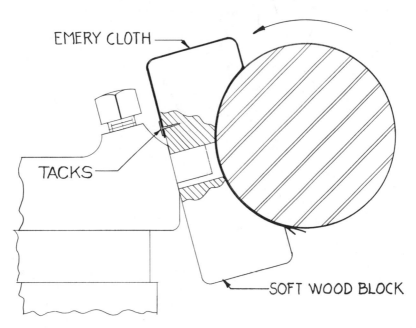

Fig. C-28. Laying out and turning crankshafts. Polish the crank pin and fillets to a smooth finish using a cutout wooden block, emery cloth, and oil.

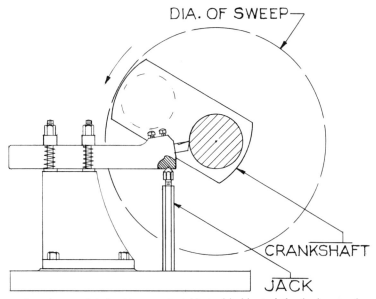

Fig. C-29. Laying out and turning crankshafts. Use an adjustable tool holder jack for the heavier, long-stroke crank-turning.

heavier, long-stroke crank-turning.

CUTOFF TOOL HOLDER

COMMON TYPE. Figure C-30 shows one of the more common types of cutoff tools, primarily designed for use in a lathe. The cutting blade (B) is supported in the for-ward end of the holder. The blade is held in place by the tapered head of a bolt (C).

This type of holder differs from a standard and nearly similar type of holder by the slit (D), which allows the blade to spring away from the cut slightly. This springing away prevents the usual and undesirable jamming, which invariably causes the blade to break off.

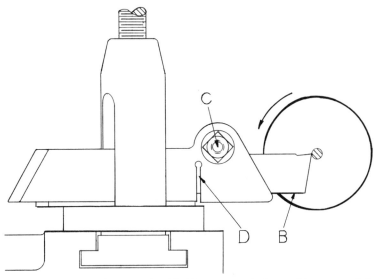

Fig. C-30. Cutoff tool holder, common type. This type of tool holder is primarily designed for use in a lathe. The vertical split prevents jamming while it is cutting by springing away.

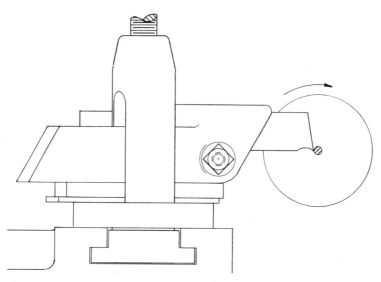

Fig. C-31. Cutoff tool holder, variation. The work is run in reverse for this tool, which is at least 400 percent better than the conventional cutoff tool, and does not jam.

This type of tool holder works on the same principle as when you are boring in the lathe, with the tool positioned upside down, and cutting on the back side of the bore.

VARIATION. Figure C-31 illustrates a somewhat different type of cutoff tool holder, in that the holder is solid but is designed to hold the cutoff blade upside down. The work is run in reverse for this tool.

The pressure of the cut—instead of lifting the work, and consequently the lathe spindle—presses it down into the spindle's journals. Although no slits are provided or necessary, this type of cutoff holder still functions better than the best of the conventional types of cutoff tools.

The very slight amount of flexing and play in the tool holder, tool post, compound, and cross-slide gib provide all of the springing away that the cut might require and so prevent jamming.

A straight, instead of a left- or right-hand holder using this upside down principle, will operate quite satisfactorily, even if the blade must be projected outward for several inches, as for cutting larger work diameters. Of course, the blade must be thick enough for this type of work.

CUTTING TOOLS

FLY CUTTERS. Figure C-32 shows a typical flycutter, which is as versatile a cutting tool as any made. A fly cutter is employed in much the same fashion as end and shell mills. Although it cuts off only one chip per revolution, it nonetheless exerts only a fraction of the pressure on the

work than an end or shell mill does, and thereby produces a truer surface.

The arm (A) can be adjusted to cut a wide or narrow path. The cutting is done with a tool bit, usually of high-speed steel. Fly cutters are generally held and driven in a collet, and used in a vertical or horizontal milling machine.

MULTIPURPOSE CUTTING TOOL. Figure C-33 shows a multipurpose cutting tool. If you had only one tool bit, it might be ground as shown. One end would be ground

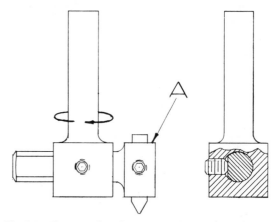

Fig. C-32. Fly cutter. If you have no circular cutting tools at hand, you can do nearly as well by using a homemade fly cutter in either a horizontal or vertical milling machine. However, this process takes longer, of course.

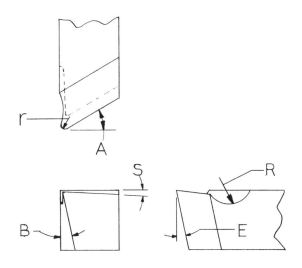

GENERAL-PURPOSE CUTTING TOOL
A 30° OR MORE.
r-OPTIONAL CUT, DEPENDING ON MATERIAL.
B-10 TO 12 DEGREES.
S- 3 TO 8 DEGREES.
E-ABOUT 12°
R-FROM 0 TO .375, DEPENDING ON MATERIAL.

CAUTION
DO NOT USE FOR
CUTTING BRONZE

Fig. C-33. Multipurpose cutting tool. If you only have one tool bit, grind it as shown.

for right-hand turning, while the other for left-hand turning. With slight grinding modifications, this type of tool will do for as much as 75 percent of all metal-cutting requirements.

COARSE-FEED FINISHING TOOL. Figure C-34 shows a coarse-feed finishing tool. Whenever a large surface requires finishing you can use a much wide tool, which can be operated with a much coarser feed.

Because its cutting lip is slanted into the cut, it causes the chip to curl tightly and roll ahead of the tool. In doing so, it continuously wipes off the tiny metallic adhesions along the tool's cutting edge that usually cause a rough surface, especially on steels.

This tool works well without coolants. The quality of the surface smoothness is equal to that done with a rounded-nose tool, which requires a much finer feed. Generally, .003 left on the diameter is enough for a good file finish.

HEAVY-HOGGING CUTTING TOOL. For heavy hogging cuts, a tool shaped as in Fig. C-35 is generally used. The tool's point, because of the great heat generated, is always the first area of failure. To minimize this problem as much as possible, the back clearance (B) is quite small. A larger, more rounded point (r) will not burn as soon, but its increase will also invite chatter. The idea is to strike a happy medium suitable to the job at hand.

In heavy hogging the leading, or cutting, edge does not

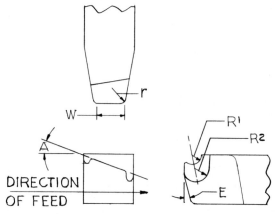

FLAT-NOSED FINISHING TOOL
W-.25 IN. OR, TWICE THE FEED RATE.
r-3 TIMES THE DEPTH OF THE CUT.
A-15 TO 25 DEGREES.
E-ABOUT 12°.
R¹
R² NEED BE ONLY ABOUT 4 TIMES THE DEPTH OF THE CUT TO BE.

Fig. C-34. Coarse-feed finishing tool. If you need to finish-cut a large surface, whether flat or round, use a tool ground as shown.

dull so rapidly. Instead, the curling chip will abrade a groove into the top of the tool just back of the cutting edge. As this groove deepens the chip curls tighter, increasing the machine's cutting load. In resharpening the tool, most of the worn groove mark must be ground off.

DULLING OF OF A CUTTING TOOL. Figure C-36 shows how a cutting tool can become dull by sliding over the work

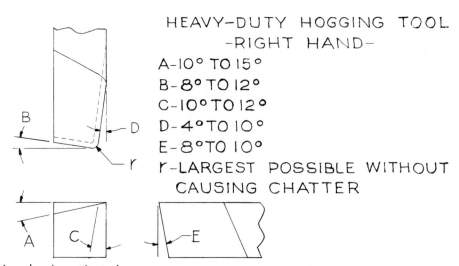

HEAVY-DUTY HOGGING TOOL
-RIGHT HAND-
A-10° TO 15°
B-8° TO 12°
C-10° TO 12°
D-4° TO 10°
E-8° TO 10°
r-LARGEST POSSIBLE WITHOUT CAUSING CHATTER

Fig. C-35. Heavy-hogging cutting tool.

without cutting, but merely glazing the surface. These results are very much the same with all metal-cutting tools, whether they are used in a lathe, drill press, shaper, or planer. Yes, even a file can become dull in this way. The use of sulphur-based cutting oils will permit any cutting tool, except a file, to shave over a much greater surface area without glazing.

Figure C-36A shows how a tool shaves with its very edge and does not split the metal ahead of the edge. However, if a tool is permitted to ride the surface without cutting, its cutting clearance soon wears away to a zero angle. The longer it slides over the work, the wider F becomes, eventually completely resisting any further cutting. This situation is possible especially when you are using a soap-water coolant.

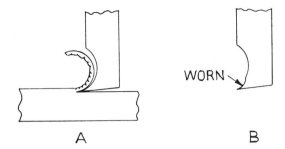

Fig. C-37. Metal splitting.

self. This phenomenon is more pronounced in heavier cutting. In observing a magnified, very slow motion movie, of a cutting operation in steel (A), actual splitting was not detected. Yet, in all cases, after prolonged cutting, it can be seen that the tool did not dull, wearing off its cutting edge. Instead, the surface just back of the cutting edge (B) becomes hollowed out, by the curling chip's pressure.

This example proves that the metal does split apart just ahead of the tool's cutting edge. As the groove wears progressively deeper, it causes the chip to curl into an even tighter coil, which, in turn increases the cutting load on the machine, the work, and the cutting tool. The only way to remedy this condition is to resharpen the tool by grinding away the eroded surface.

RUBBER-TURNING TOOL. In turning rubberlike materials, an entirely different shape of cutting tool is required, as shown in Fig. C-38. The tool is **L** shaped,

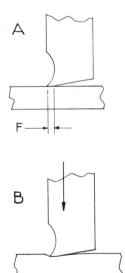

Fig. C-36. Dulling of a cutting tool.

In these cases the tendency is to force the tool into the work until the tool will cut again. However, when this force becomes great enough, as shown in B, the cutting tool will suddenly break through the glazed surface, gouging in too deeply. As in the case of large-thread finishing and in many other types of work, this sudden gouge often will break off the cutting tool, as well as ruin the work.

Always shave dry, or use a cutting oil. Then dress up the surface using soap water (emulsified oil) for the last cut or two.

METAL SPLITTING. Figure C-37 attempts to show that a cutting tool, theoretically, splits the metal ahead of it-

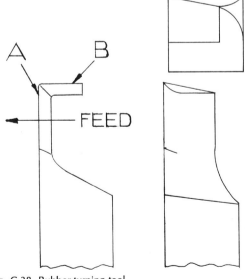

Fig. C-38. Rubber-turning tool.

producing a square or rectangular cross-sectioned chip, depending on the amount of feed and the hardness (Durometer) of the material being cut. Section A parts the material, while the foot of the tool (B) separates the chip from the work.

If you are dealing with smaller work, the substance can be frozen in liquid nitrogen, then handled much the same as a piece of metal. However, time also plays a big part in such cases.

RUBBER-SLITTING TOOL. Soft rubberlike materials cannot be cut as readily as steel or iron. However, much can be accomplished by using a thin bladelike cutting tool, as shown in Fig. C-39. Its top leading edge is always at a nega-

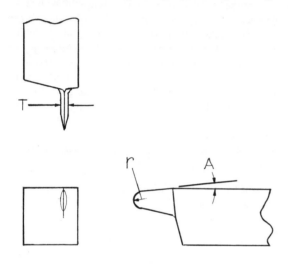

RUBBER-SLITTING TOOL
T—SHOULD BE QUITE THIN .020~.060 IN.
r—ABOUT ONE-HALF OF BLADE WIDTH.
A—SLANT ANGLE MUST ALWAYS BE NEGATIVE.

Fig. C-39. Rubber-slitting tool.

tive rake (A) to prevent lifting of the work. Although this tool cuts only with its point it should be honed smoothly all around. The smoothness lessens the heat-producing friction.

RADIUS FORM-CUTTING TOOL, EXTERNAL. Figure C-40 shows a general-purpose radius form-cutting tool. Most form tools are sharpened by grinding the top face only lest it lose its shape. Because the tool is flat, having no rake, it produces a rough, torn surface, especially when it is used on steel.

To produce a smooth formed surface, the excess metal first must be roughed away. Then the works rotation is slowed down. In using the form-cutting tool, a comparatively slower rotational speed is used, together with a sulphur-based cutting oil. Only few metals will not result in smooth formed surfaces, high-speed steel being one.

The radius can be ground in a machine or off hand. To measure the radius, hold a smooth dowel of the appropriate diameter in the arc and view it against the light emitting from a north window. A light smear of Prussian blue paste on the gaging dowel will also reveal the arc's correctness.

This type of radius forming tool will also function very effectively for internal rounding. The only difference is that, internal rounding requires more clearance toward the back side of the tool.

All form tools generally work best when they are used either upside down with the work rotating in reverse, or on the back side of the work with the job rotating in the conventional direction and the tool positioned upside down.

TYPICAL HONED FINISHING TOOL. Figure C-41 shows a typical honed finishing tool. As an example, an acme-thread finishing tool is illustrated. By honing away the marks from the grinding wheel, the tool will produce a superior finish. Because these types of tools have no top rake, they must be used in a comparatively slow work-revolving process, except in the cutting of brass or bronze.

Grinding the tool on the periphery of the wheel results in a hollowed-out surface. Most generally, only the cutting edges need to be honed.

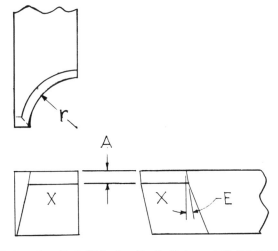

RADIUS FORM TOOL-EXTERNAL
r-GROUND TO THE DESIRED CURVE OR SHAPE.
X-SECONDARY CLEARANCE.
A-EFFECTIVE CUTTING AREA.
E-10 DEGREES OR MORE.

Fig. C-40. Radius form-cutting tool, external. One of the many types of external radius cutting tools is shown. It is used in cutting all metals. Position the tool slightly below the axial center of the work, or above center when you are cutting with the work and rotating in reverse.

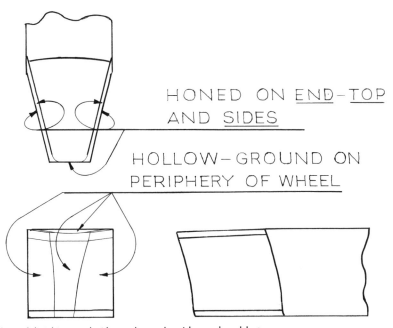

HONED ON END-TOP AND SIDES

HOLLOW-GROUND ON PERIPHERY OF WHEEL

Fig. C-41. Typical honed finishing tool. Always hone the sides and end last.

49

D

DEEP-DRAWING

PROCEDURE. The forming of sheet-metal shells by stretching and/or compressing using a die and a press is known as deep-drawing. It can be done using a variety of procedures. The process involves many types of forms or dies. In every case, however, you must adhere to certain principles. Knowing what takes place and why certainly lessens your efforts in this respect.

In deep drawing, a correctly shaped and sized piece of sheet metal, called the *blank*, is held between two rings (not necessarily round)—an upper and a lower. The ring around the punch is known as the *pressure ring, pressure pad,* or *stripper ring.* The part the blank is drawn through is always known as the *draw ring.* (See Fig. D-1.)

At the start of the press ram's downward movement, the blank is confined between the draw ring and the pressure ring. As the ram continues to move down, the blank contacts the top of the punch. As the downward movement continues, the punch begins to enter into the draw ring, carrying the blank along with it. Simultaneously the pressure pad, resting on four posts, bears down on the die cushion plate, which also moves downward.

The die cushion, which is no more than a larger cylinder and piston, is filled with compressed air. The amount of air pressure in it is controlled and regulated to match correctly the required amount of squeeze on the blank.

In the process of stretching and forming, several interesting things take place in the blank, as well as the die parts. In attempting to force a larger disc of metal through a comparatively smaller hole to form something resembling a cup, you quickly discover that many ugly wrinkles develop, even after a comparatively short draw. If the downward pressure and movement continues, the blank resists flowing through the draw ring because of the wrinkles, which in turn suddenly ruptures the work.

Using the two mentioned rings to hold the blank flat at all times helps to prevent wrinkles, although this method in itself is not the solution to all wrinkling problems, nor is it the rings' sole function. Several other factors must also be taken into account.

For example, let us picture that a round, flat-bottomed pot (shell) is to be drawn. This shell is to be roughly 6 inches in diameter and 3 inches in depth. Because the walls are each 3 inches long, add 3 inches to both sides of the 6-inch bottom diameter, totaling 12 inches, approximately the blank's diameter.

Since very little if any stretching action takes place in the flat 6-inch bottom, the blank can be pictured as a large, flat washer with a 6-inch hole and a 12-inch outside diameter. All the material outside the 6-inch diameter must be changed or somehow reduced before it will pass through

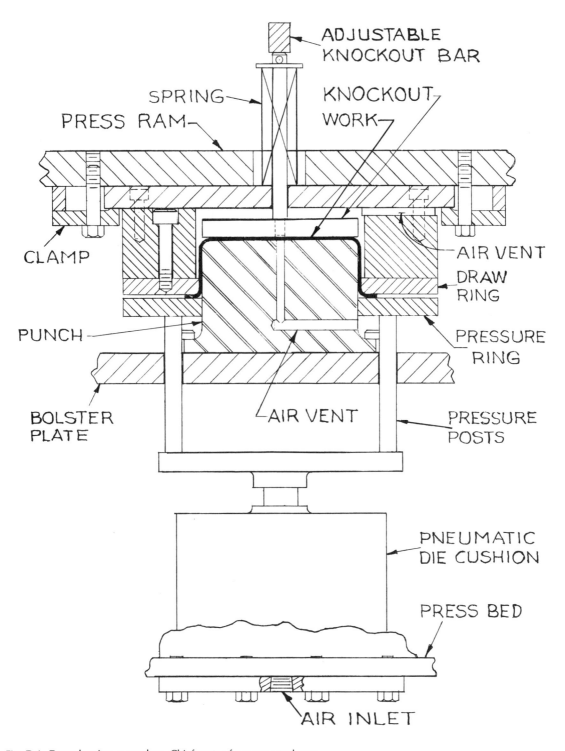

Fig. D-1. Deep-drawing, procedure. Chief parts of a press are shown.

the 6-inch draw rings' opening without wrinkling. This reduction commonly and quite easily is accomplished by controlling the plastic flow of the metal, before and as it passes through the draw ring.

What happens is this: the lubricated blank is centrally positioned atop the pressure ring. The top of the pressure ring is slightly above the nose of the punch, which is fastened to the press' bolster plate. The die's draw ring is fastened to, and rides up and down with, the press ram. The pressure ring around the punch is supported by four rods of equal length that are equally spaced around the punch. The rods operate atop a pressure plate, which is part of the die cushion. The die cushion base is bolted to the bed of the press and operates on the same principle as a cylinder and piston, which it truly is. By introducing controlled amounts of air pressure into the die cushion cylinder, the piston can be regulated to exert just enough pressure to lightly squeeze the blank between the draw and pressure rings. The holding pressure is quite constant during the full downward movement of the press ram, thus allowing the blank's flange to compress into itself before it passes over the draw ring's radius, without wrinkling.

To help clarify this action in the blank, the blank can be marked off as shown in Fig. D-2, using any number of equally spaced radiating lines. A noncircular blank can be scribed into equally spaced squares.

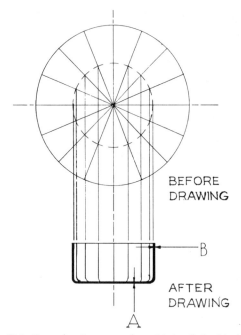

BEFORE DRAWING

B

AFTER DRAWING

A

Fig. D-2. Deep-drawing, procedure. Mark off the blank as shown.

After you have drawn the flat blank into a shell, you will notice that the radiating lines have become parallel to one another, but only along the vertical wall. This occurrence proves that the large (washer) blank did compress into itself. Also, scribing a series of equally spaced circles on the blank will show how much elongation has taken place in the drawing process.

If some doubts still exist regarding this phenomenon, satisfy yourself by measuring the wall thickness of the shell. Starting near its bottom you will find that the wall thickness increases as the shell becomes longer. However, in long draws this condition changes because of the so-called *ironing process.*

The amount of wall thickening will vary because of the metal's characteristics and the design of the die, as well as the amount of clearance between the punch and die. The general recommendation is to add 8 to 10 percent of the blank's thickness to the clearance space between the punch and the draw ring, for wall thickening.

Thus far, however, the wrinkling problems have not been totally eliminated. To do so, you must consider the following factors:

☐ The type of material being worked.
☐ The temper of the material.
☐ The thickness of the material.
☐ The blank's size and shape.
☐ The draw rings' radius.
☐ The thickness of the pressure ring.
☐ The amount of hold-down pressure on the blank.
☐ If the hold-down pressure be increased or decreased and at what points (for draws other than cylindrical).
☐ The type of lubricant used.
☐ The depth of the draws.
☐ The type of material used for the draw ring.
☐ The speed rate of the draw.

These are some of the more important points you should consider, even when you are designing comparatively simple draw dies. Any number of variations can be and are made as the size, shape, and depth of draw change. The metal itself, being either soft or springy, will make a difference, especially in the type of material you use for the draw ring. Draw rings are often made of meehanite, aluminum bronze, hardened steels, and cast irons. Unhardened steel will often do quite well, but for a very limited number of draws.

The blank, while being drawn over the rounded edge (radius) of the draw ring, does not draw more satisfactorily over a larger radius, contrary to some beliefs. You must bend the structure of the blank's metal beyond its yield point, or make it work and move around internally before it will take on the desired shape. If you draw it over a large radius, the metal is not disrupted internally enough to allow the imaginary pie shapes to compress together and almost invariably will cause wrinkling, especially in thin materials. Quite frequently, after many pieces have been run off, the draw ring's radius becomes too large from wear and wrinkling begins. To correct this fault, reduce the draw radius by facing some metal off the draw ring, then reblending the radius.

Sometimes instead of having one larger radius, the draw ring is beveled at 45°. The two corners are then slightly rounded. This method provides two sharper, but shorter, bends, and causes the material to be bent, worked, or *kneaded* twice as it passes through the draw ring.

Many types of metals will lend themselves to deep drawing, up to a point. Those that are more ductile will draw more favorably. Some metals that might be soft to start quickly will take on a work hardness in the drawing process. In these cases, the work must be annealed before you can carry out further drawing operations, otherwise the work will rupture almost immediately. Also, once the drawing begins, do not stop the action until you reach the stroke's bottom. Any midway hesitation tends to harden the work at the stopping point, inviting rupturing at that point if and when the drawing is resumed in the same piece.

The blank must always be held between the pressure and draw rings, even if the work ends up with only a very narrow flange at the end of the finish draw.

There are times when the blank must be made larger for better gripping. However, the draw becomes more difficult because of this oversized flange area. To get around this problem, a series of cutouts, known as *darts* (Fig. D-3) are cut into the blank. Darts allow for a freer flow of metal, while not compressing the outermost flange areas.

For rectangular, square, or odd cross-sectional draws, the corners of the blank must be cut at right angles to the corners' centerlines. Measuring diagonally, the flange lengths at the corners should be only 50 to 60 percent as long as the flange lengths on the straight sides, but they can vary.

It is sometimes advisable to develop the blank's outline as it pertains to the particular job, material being drawn, and die. It is not always possible to build a blanking die before you have developed fully the drawing process. Up until then the blanks should be cut out by hand. Remember to always scribe the outline of the blank you are about to draw onto the next proposed piece of stock, for reference.

The thickness of the pressure ring is all-important. When you are drawing comparatively thin materials, the work has a great tendency to wrinkle. Instead of compressing together, the thin material wants to climb over itself. It does not compress into itself as readily as does a heavier-gage material. This undesirable action requires a much thicker pressure ring than you might have planned to use.

In a cylindrical-shaped cross-sectional draw, the lifting pressure of the compressing metal is more nearly uniform, completely around. However, in rectangular or odd-shaped draws where some of the sides are straight, there is practically no, if any, thickening of the metal in its straight portions. The thickening takes place only at and near to the corners, often pushing the metal out into the adjacent straight sections, as shown by S in Fig. D-4.

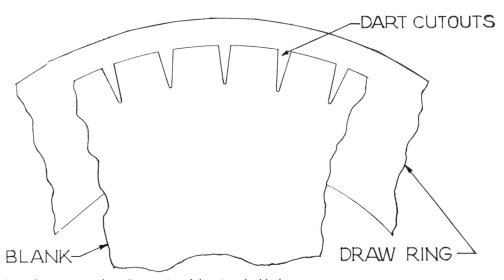

Fig. D-3. Deep-drawing, procedure. Cut a series of darts into the blank.

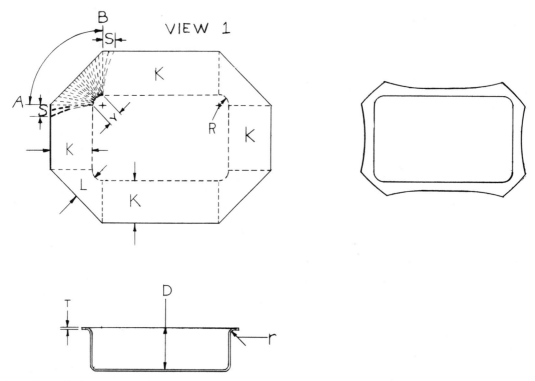

Fig. D-4. Drawn blank's action. Thickening takes place only at and near to the corners in rectangular or odd-shaped draws. Often, the process pushes the metal out into the adjacent straight sections.

In the drawing process, the corners represent a pie shape which compresses together, or into itself. The resistance of the material to compression is very great. The material will try to escape into the path of least resistance, such as holes, grooves, or deep scratches which might be present on the face of either the pressure or draw rings. If no such roughness is present, the tendency of the drawn material is to lift or bend the pressure ring in its attempt to resist being compressed.

The important point, then, is to allow only enough space between the pressure and draw rings, which is the thickness of the blank. The blank must not be pinched so tightly as to restrict its flow, nor should it be so free as to cause wrinkles. The outer dimensions of both the pressure and draw rings must always be large enough to cover the blank completely.

In a cylindrical draw, where the pressures are more nearly equal all around, the problems are much smaller. As the press ram, carrying the draw ring, moves downward it contacts the blank. The blank, resting on the pressure ring, is in turn pushed downward. The ease or firmness with which the pressure ring supports the blank's down-

ward travel is controlled by the amount of air pressure in the die cushion cylinder. As was mentioned previously, the blank's flange becomes thicker as its pie-shaped segments are drawn in and compressed together. With a pneumatic die cushion the holding pressure can be controlled so that it remains fairly constant from the start to the end of the draw stroke.

It should also be mentioned that using coil compression springs to maintain the pressure on the pressure ring is not very practical, except for comparatively short draws.

For deeper draws, unusually long springs would be required. Even then, the spring method would be of little value because, as the draw deepens, the springs become more compressed. Toward the end of the draw, the blank will be squeezed so tightly it will refuse to flow, resulting in a ruptured shell.

In draw work other than cylindrical, on the noncurving sides, the blank's movement must be retarded, or made to flow more nearly at the same rate as the slower or curving areas.

At least three retarding methods can be used. The face of the draw or pressure ring can be spotted by grinding away very shallow amounts in the necessary areas, thus allowing for a slightly looser grip on the blank at specific points, especially at the corners where the metal thickens. Across the straight areas, the blank should be held more firmly.

Another retarding method is to bolt on heavy-enough reinforcing bars to the back side of the pressure ring. It is also customary to place narrow shims of the required thickness midway between the bars' fastening bolts, or where needed. Upon tightening the bolts, the pressure ring will distort just enough in the correct places to properly regulate the flow of the blank material.

Perhaps the more commonly used flow-retarding method is known as *beading*. In this method, a flat-bottomed groove, like a long key seat, is milled into the face of the draw ring. A hardened strip of metal, representing a key, is fitted into the groove and fastened with screws from the underside. The hardened key *bead* is rounded transversely along its top. The top of the bead projects above the face of the die ring and is in alignment with a slightly wider groove cut into the face of the pressure ring. The pressure ring's groove edges are also transversely rounded. When the draw ring presses down on the blank, it forms a bead in the blank's flange. By having to negotiate over this bead, the flow of the blank material is retarded considerably.

In drawing almost any material thinner than .020 inch thick, the beading method can cause wrinkles unless the bead fits exactly and leaves no crevices for the thin material to sneak into and start wrinkling.

DRAWN BLANKS' ACTION. Figure D-4 is an attempt to show how and why a flat metallic blank takes on the shapes that it does, both during and after being deep-drawn. View No. 1 shows a flat blank as it might be cut to form a rectangular shell. The four sides (K) need to be only slightly longer than the shell is deep. The four corners (L) are cut to approximately 60 percent of the sides' lengths. As the metal is drawn over the sides of the rectangular punch, the sides merely bend over the radius of the draw ring, traveling at practically the same speed as the press ram.

Each of the four corners, however, represents 90° pie-cut sections from A to B. To enter through the draw ring without wrinkling, the corner pie cuts must be squeezed, or compressed, together. So, the corner area will be only as wide as are the arcs at Y. The corner's resistance to compression will cause it to push itself outward into the straight side sections, as indicated by S.

As the material in the corners increases in thickness, it also increases in length. Knowing this action, you purposely cut the corners' flange width at least 40 percent narrower than the flange widths on the straight sides. By doing

so you reduce the compressing corner area, which in turn reduces the chance of wrinkling. It also lessens the amount of stress at the bottom corners of the drawn shell, at which points the work ruptures first. The corner flanges need only to be long enough to remain supported between the draw and pressure rings when you are reaching the bottom of the stroke.

It is interesting to note that a certain ratio exists between the blank's thickness, the amount of radius at R, and the draw ring radius (r) in relation to the depth of the draw. Often, the best ratio combinations can be found only through experimental development, to suit the particular material being worked.

Because the corner areas of the blank (A to B) must compress into the much narrower area at Y, the shell's corner wall becomes thicker by about 9 percent.

The type of lubricant used in deep-draw work varies with the job at hand. It might be a thin or a heavy mixture of lubricating oil, mixed with white lead; a heavy high-viscosity lubricating oil; special, commercially produced deep-draw oil; or a thick cream made of Ivory soap chips whipped in hot water. Use whichever proves best.

The practice is to always build the finish draw die first. From there you must go backward, building as many dies as are required to bring about the proper finished result.

Cut out, by hand, the general outline of the proposed blank and try forming the shell in the finish die. Chances are the work will come out quite unsatisfactory. However, it will show where the blank's dimensions need to be changed, as well as other useful information needed for building the dies for the preliminary draws. The whole idea is to build only as few dies as are necessary.

IRONING. Figures D-5 through D-8 show a method of drawing long, thin-walled shells of aluminum and other soft metals. This method is sometimes known as the *ironing* process.

A flat blank slightly greater in weight than will be the weight of the finished shell is nested in the first draw die (Fig. D-3). The punches are hardened to approximately 58 Rc and ground and polished to better than 6 micro-inch rms. The dies are made very hard, in the area of 63 to 65 Rc. The throats of the dies have a comparatively narrow land. Better finishes on the work can be had by polishing the punches and die throats transversely using crocus cloth, followed by jeweler's rouge. Usually, the crocus cloth is sufficient.

The polishing is usually a long, slow process. The punches should be made .001 inch smaller in diameter at their working end, tapering larger toward the shank end. Tapering enables the drawn shell to be stripped off the

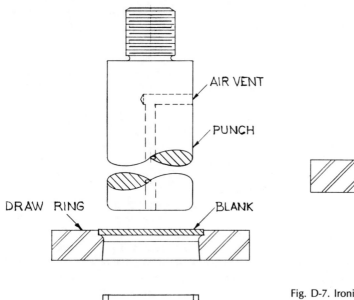

AIR VENT

PUNCH

DRAW RING   BLANK

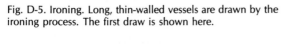

Fig. D-5. Ironing. Long, thin-walled vessels are drawn by the ironing process. The first draw is shown here.

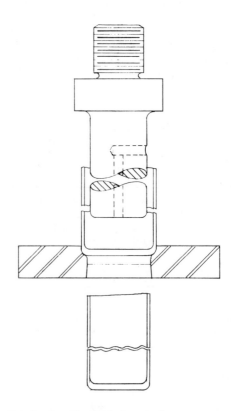

Fig. D-7. Ironing. The third draw is shown.

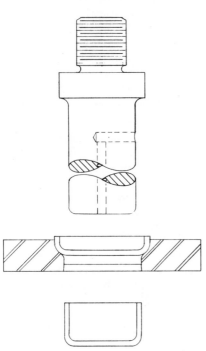

Fig. D-6. Ironing. The second draw is shown.

Fig. D-8. Ironing. The finish draw is shown.

punch easily. The underside of the die holder is provided with two opposing, lightly spring-loaded jaws. These jaws spread apart when the work is pushed through, then come together, but do not touch the punch, at the end of the stroke. During the return punch movement, the shell is stripped off.

The shell's bottom thickness remains the same throughout the drawing operations. It can, however, be faced off on a stub mandrel or coined, or squeezed out, at some stage approaching the finish draw operations.

The amount of reduction at each drawing stage depends on the material being worked. The amount of reduction is reduced as the shell becomes progressively thinner.

Also, the work might require annealing from time to time, between draws.

DIES

SIMPLE DRAW DIE. Figure D-9 shows the simplest type of draw die. This method works quite well, especially when only a small number of pieces are desired. The punch and die do not necessarily need to be hardened in every case.

One of the most difficult die-making conditions arises when only small lots of certain items are wanted. To produce many thousands or millions of pieces warrants the expenditure of the required time, effort, and money to produce a first-class die. However, to produce small lots of any item requires not only die-making skill and knowledge, but also a practical sense of ingenuity and improvization. It is safe to say that, no matter what types of dies are concerned, there are certain mechanical and physical principles that must be followed in every case.

For example, the simple draw die in Fig. D-9 embodies most of the principles required to produce a comparatively shallow, cylindrical shell. If you must hold the inside diameter, the draw ring must be bored to the punch diameter, plus two blank thicknesses, plus about 9 percent for each wall thickening. Or add 18 percent of the blank's thickness to the bore's diameter. The counterbore (T) in the die (A) is equal to the blank's thickness. The diameter of the counterbore is equal to the blank's diameter.

The draw radius (R) is made to suit, and depends on the hardness and thickness of the blank. It is often a good practice to start with a small radius, then increase it gradually until the shell stops rupturing.

The hold down ring (B) is turned to fit into a counterbore in the die for a positive centering of the punch (P). It is held down by four equally spaced screws.

The punch is pushed through in an arbor press. The punch can also be shouldered to limit its entry to any desired depth.

Note: A too-large radius in the draw ring often will do more harm than good.

DRAW AND TRIM DIE. Figure D-10 shows a combination type of draw and trim die. Quite frequently, most drawn work calls for trimming to a specific length.

These dies are commercially produced, of course. However, when the work is of some unusual material, shape, or size, other methods of trimming must be employed, even if they are somewhat unorthodox in their design.

The illustration gives an idea of how this type of die operates. Both operations are performed in the same press stroke.

Dimension X of the draw ring (R) governs the location of the cutoff. Both the punch (P) and the material it draws through the draw ring are too large in diameter to pass through the cutoff ring (D).

As the press ram continues its advance, the work material becomes more tightly pressed against the hard, sharp corners of the bore in the cutoff ring, thereby causing the scrap to be severed from the workpiece.

PINCH-TRIM DRAW DIE. Figure D-11 shows a case where several draws were grouped closely together. With the drawing difficulties encountered in such cases, the finished configuration of the work was such that the trimming method shown was devised and successfully used in conjunction with the final drawing operation. The spacing of

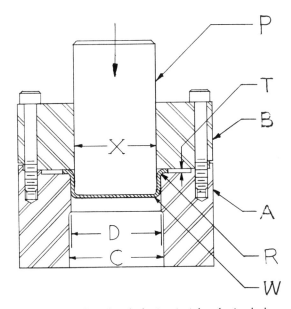

Fig. D-9. Simple draw die. The basic principles of a simple draw die are shown.

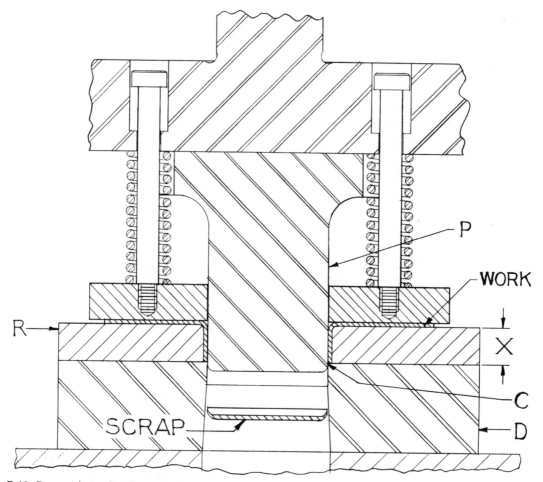

Fig. D-10. Draw and trim die. This method of drawing and trimming can be used if necessary.

the draws, their depths, and their diameters called for tolerances of plus or minus .001 inch.

After the cups, an integral part of the shell, were simultaneously drawn to slightly more than full depth, the work was placed over the anvil of the die (D) in the shown position. The hold-down ring (C) was spring loaded and would contact and hold the work firmly against the die while the punch (P) pushed the cup bottom in a reverse draw into the die. When the punch reached the die's cutting edge (E) the bottom of the cup was pinch-trimmed to the exact specified length (X).

At times, piercing the drawn bottoms will help in furthering a draw. The hole in the onstretched bottom gives the metal a freer flow over the end of the punch. As the metal is drawn, the diameter of the punched hole increases proportionately. However, because of the hole-punching the hole's edge becomes harder and more brittle. Tiny

cracks are introduced around the hole in the process. The hardness and minute cracks usually result in rupturing the work in the final draws. Thereupon, it often becomes advisable to ream out the punched holes before redrawing, to avoid splitting.

TRIMMING DIE. Figure D-12 shows another method used to trim off thin-drawn necks to the required length. The complete trim die consists of three parts.

☐ A—The outside sleeve with a tapered interior.
☐ B—The tapered (collet type) interior cutting core.
☐ C—The anvil.

The three die parts are made of tool steel, hardened between 57 and 59 Rc. The cutting off can be done in an arbor press by simply pressing down on the sleeve (A). This action causes the colletlike cutter (B) to become smaller in diameter at its bottom, while at the same time presses the work down on the anvil (C).

The movement of the sleeve's cutting edges across the top of the anvil, needs to be only slightly more than the thickness of the material in process.

The cutting sleeve's taper is a 14° 30′ included angle.

SECTIONAL DIE. Figure D-13 shows a simple sectional die, made for stamping out ornamental simitars of a light-gage metal. The handle is made separately and attached

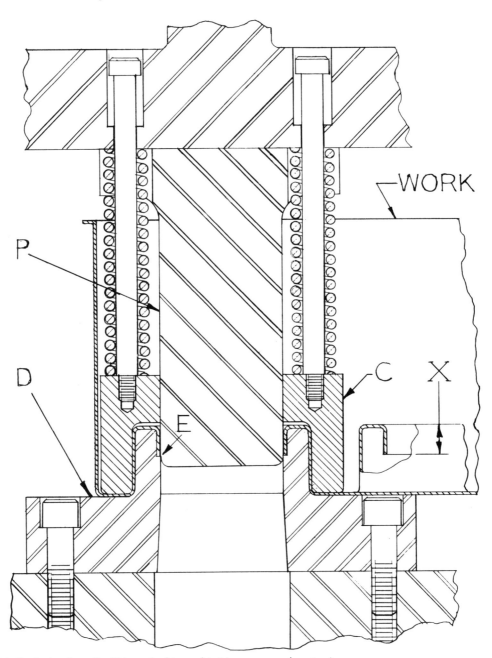

Fig. D-11. Pinch-trim draw die. This method is used to trim a reverse draw to size.

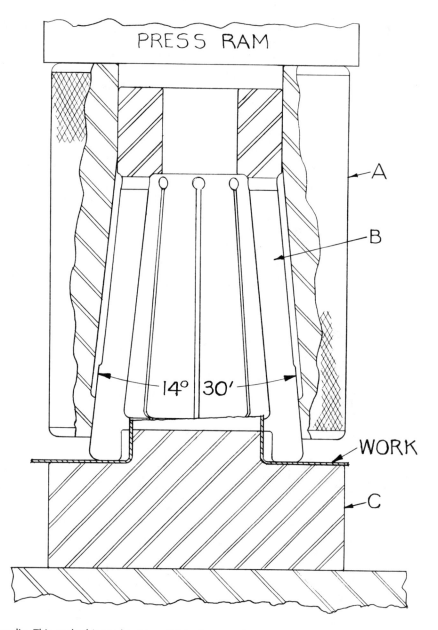

PRESS RAM

14° 30'

A

B

WORK

C

Fig. D-12. Trimming die. This method is used to trim off thin-drawn necks.

later. The stripper plate as well as the stop gaging pin purposely have been omitted from this illustration.

To begin with, scribe a complete layout of the punch on a smooth, flat plate, with the center of each arc center-punched. Then align the punch blank to register properly with the layout and screw the blank to the plate. Clamp the plate to the face plate of a lathe. True-up each center mark on the face plate with a pointed rod and indicator. Turn and bore the punch to grinding dimensions. Fasten random pieces of metal opposite the cutting, so you can measure the diameter.

Turn the die sections (C^2 and B^2) to grinding size in a four-jaw chuck. Use a fly cutter to cut the notch and clearance in the hilt section (D) to size. Assemble the sections

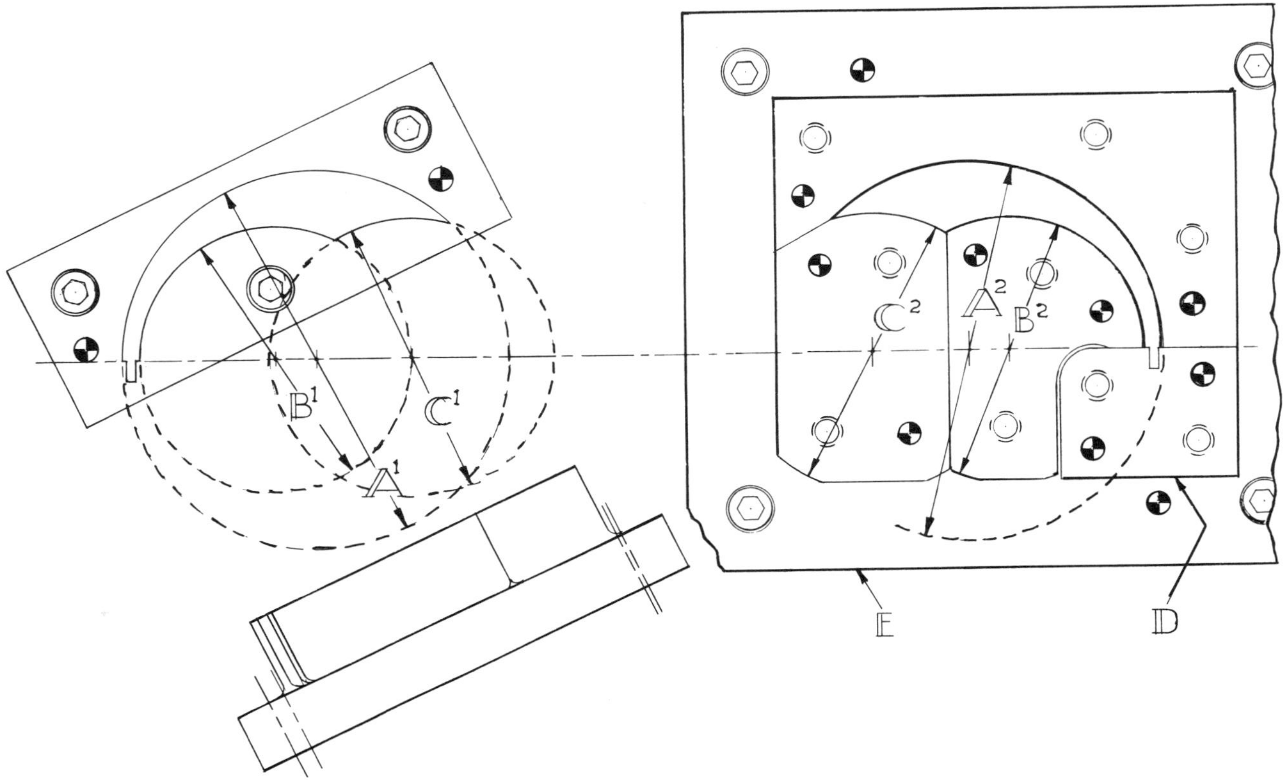

Fig. D-13. Sectional die. The construction of a simple sectional die is shown.

around the punch and scribe them off, dividing them into their most suitable proportions and fits. Trim off the sides of the sections where needed. Then drill and ream the dowel pin holes or tap the screw holes.

After hardening and grinding, again fit the die sections more closely around the punch. Use strips of cellophane for uniform clearances between the punch and die.

Clamp the die sections to the base plate (E), the screw holes having been made at least .025 larger than the diameter of the screws to allow final movement and positioning of the sections before dowel pinning.

In the final grinding of the assembled die face, elevate the die shoe approximately .030 inch, one end at a time, on the surface grinder table. Grinding off, at a shallow slant, about one-third the distance from each end of the die's face decreases the amount of sudden-load impact on the die.

Because the punch's face is flat, the stamping will come out flat. In cases where the requirements call for the stock to remain flat, the die's face must also remain flat, while the punch face must be slanted off, instead.

IMPACT-EXTRUSION DIE. Figure D-14 is a general illustration of an impact-extrusion type of die. Sometimes it is also known as a *percussion die*. This type of die is mainly used in the production of containers such as toothpaste tubes, beer cans, and electronic parts.

These dies consist mainly of a punch having a round or varied cross section and a comparatively shallow, dish-shaped die. The die's cross section conforms to that of the punch, the die being larger, of course, to the extent of the desired wall thickness of the extruded metal.

The stock (blank) is merely a flat slug resembling a dime, quarter, or silver dollar, depending on the volume of material required. The slug is positioned centrally in the concavity of the die. The punch, almost at the end of its stroke, bears down on the slug, causing the slug material to splash outwardly. However, because the die walls turn upward, the splash is compelled to turn upward, also. The amount of space between the punch's diameter and the die's vertical walls determines the thickness of the shell's wall.

Impact extrusion works on the displacement principle,

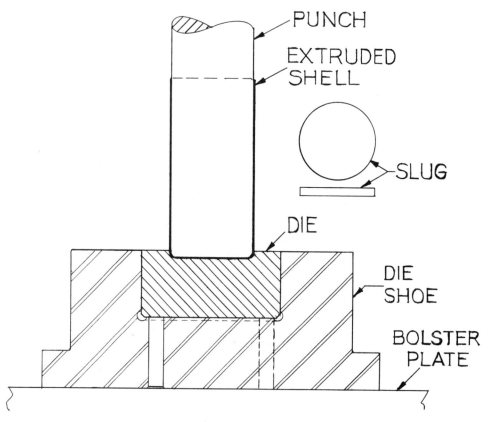

Fig. D-14. Impact-extrusion die. The principles of an extrusion die are shown.

much like pressing a smaller glass tumbler into a larger tumbler that is partially filled with a liquid. The liquid represents the slug. The downward pressure of the smaller tumbler on the liquid causes the liquid to spread by radiating outwardly. However, because the spreading is controlled by the vertical walls of the larger tumbler, the liquid, like the metal, has no other choice but to follow the path of least resistance, which is upward. It thus forms a closed-bottom tube shape.

Impact extrusion is an interesting process, especially when it is fully automated. This type of die is capable of producing many shells per minute. Of course, it works easiest with softer materials such as aluminum, zinc, copper, and lead. Impact extrusion is usually done in a much heavier press, exerting tremendous pressures.

PERFORATING DIES. Clearance between punches and dies will vary according to the materials being perforated, as well as the hardness of the material, its thickness, and purchase.

For steel, the general rule for punch and die clearance is up to 10 percent of the metal's thickness. It is 2 percent for harder materials. Brass and paper dies, however, need very little, to no clearance. For blanking paper it is often desirable to make the die very hard, in the range of 60 Rc or harder, while the punch needs to be only tough, or about 40 to 44 Rc.

In fitting a punch into a die where there is to be no clearance, grind the die to size. Machine the punch .002 to .004 inch larger than the die's dimension. Then set up both items in the press. Using a long enough bar (lever), bring down the ram and punch on the die. While maintaining a steady downward pressure with the bar, use a heavy enough mallet atop the ram to force the punch into the die. Shear off the excess metal around the punch. After removing the thin, sheared chip, the die and punch is ready for use.

For resharpening, remove the punch and peen its end with a light hammer to swell it out slightly. Grind off the die's face enough to remove the dull edge. Then reassemble the punch and die in the machine and force the punch through the die as before.

Although paper is a comparatively soft material, it is also somewhat abrasive. Because paper does not fracture in the blanking as do most metals, it must be cut all the way through in every case. If clearance is allowed, the paper will not cut completely through. Instead, it will partially hang up between the punch and die. Thus, it becomes routine to frequently resharpen paper-cutting punches and dies.

DRILLS

DRILL-GRINDING, STANDARD. It is interesting to know

that perhaps no other cutting tool is called upon to withstand more punishment and severe use than the drill. The common twist drill was developed over a long span of time. It performs most favorably, under most conditions, when it is sharpened and used correctly.

Figure D-15A shows the standard grinding angles of the drill's lips. Because the drill always cuts a cone, the 12° angle (back of the lip) applies only to the drill's outer periphery. Because the cone's diameter becomes smaller as it approaches its center, the back clearance angle must be steeper.

The steeper angle is reached by holding the drill at 59° to the grinding wheel's surface. The cutting end is supported between the thumb and index finger of the left hand, while the shank end is held and manipulated with the right hand (assuming you are right handed).

As the grinding begins, partially rotate the drill while simultaneously lowering the shank end. Without making any body movements, withdraw the drill from the grinding wheel and rotate it one-half of a revolution. Again press the drill against the wheel and repeat the same manipulation and twisting on the second lip.

The correctness of the grinding can be judged by the two lips' juncture angle, which should be about 45° (Fig. D-15A).

Although the lips' cutting angles might have been held, their widths might not be nearly the same. If not, the drill will cut oversize proportionate to the amount of difference in the lip widths. The lip widths can be measured with a scale, in a pinch.

The center point, or nib, of all drills does practically no cutting at all. Actually, as the drill rotates and is pressed into the work, it merely forces its way through. However, the amount of force required to push a drill into the work can be reduced considerably by thinning its nib, as illustrated by the shaded portion of the drill point in Fig. D-15B.

To thin the drill's nib, simply grind away the back sides of the lip clearance area by using the periphery and corner of the grinding wheel. In doing so, you introduce a more positive cutting rake to the drill's point, instead of the usual very negative rake.

DRILL-GRINDING, FLAT BOTTOM. Figure D-16 shows a method of flat-bottom drill-grinding. Begin by grinding off the drill's point, at 90° to the drill's axial centerline. Then, thin the nib as shown at A, which at the same time will result in straight cutting edges. The cutting edges should be parallel to one another. Follow this procedure by grinding the secondary clearance angle of about 15° to 20°, as shown at B. Next, using a square, grind the primary clearance angle of 7° to 9°. Both cutting edges should be of

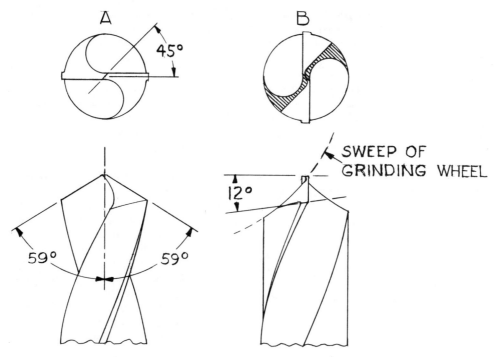

Fig. D-15. Drill-grinding, standard. Methods of correctly hand-sharpening a metal cutting drill are shown.

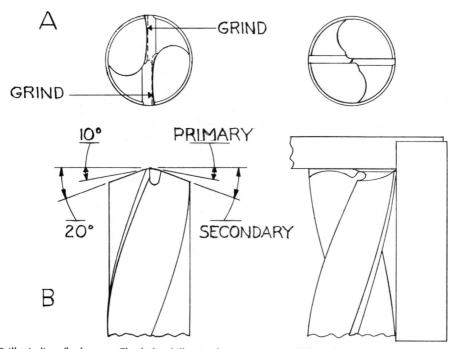

Fig. D-16. Drill-grinding, flat bottom. Check the drill point for squareness with lips of the same lengths, as shown.

the same height and at 90° to the drill's axial centerline.

Remember that a flat-bottom drill has no pilot. Therefore, it can be used only after a hole of the same diameter has been at least partially drilled.

OFF-HAND DRILL-GRINDING. Figure D-17 shows a method of grinding larger drills (over 1 inch in diameter) off-hand on the side of the grinding wheel. This method is especially handy when no drill-sharpening equipment is available. More often, it is used when the wheel's periphery is too narrow to grind a wider drill lip with single swipes. After checking the lips' angles, hold the drill in both hands. Then present it to the flat face of the wheel to either follow or correct the previously ground angles.

Note: Do not change your stance until both sides have been ground.

It is often a good practice to try out the drill by drilling into the work slightly past the angled point of the drill, while observing the widths of the two emerging chips. Chalk or otherwise mark the flute of the lip that cuts the heaviest chip. Remove the drill, then grind the marked cutting lip.

In a drill-grinding machine, the lip widths always come out much more uniform, of course.

DRILL-GRINDING GAGE, STANDARD. Figure D-18

shows a simple, drill-point grinding gage. This type of gage has the proper lip angle, and shows the comparative widths of the lips.

A bevel protractor set at 59° will very nearly serve the same purpose.

DRILL POINT FOR TOUGHER METALS. Figure D-19 shows a twist drill sharpened especially for drilling tougher metals. For example, some types of stainless steels require that the drill be ground more pointed, downwardly.

The 59° lip angles remain. However, instead of the standard 12° back clearance angle (Fig. D-15), increase it to 17° or 18°. In doing so, the cutting edge becomes too thin; therefore, the flutes' helix angle must also be decreased by 5° to 6°. This type of drill point bites into tough metals more readily.

DRILL'S RAKE ANGLE FOR BRONZE. Figure D-20 shows a drill ground for drilling holes in metals such as brass and especially bronze. Lucite and plexiglass also require a lesser cutting-rake angle.

For drilling into bronze, you absolutely must reduce the cutting rake to 0° or to slightly negative (B). It is dangerous to drill bronze with a twist drill, which has a positive rake angle (A).

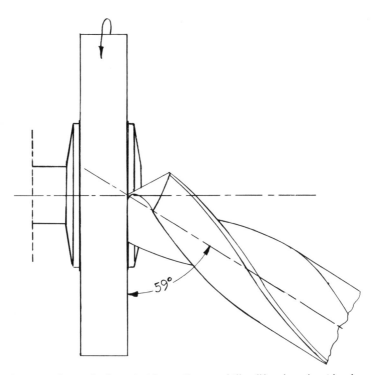

Fig. D-17. Off-hand drill-grinding. Use this method to grind larger-diameter drills off-hand on the side of a grinding wheel.

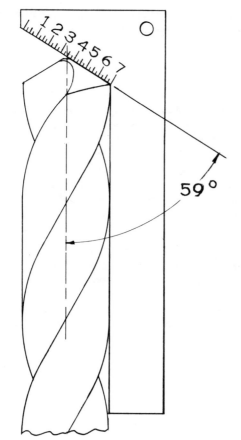

59°

Fig. D-18. Drill-grinding gage, standard.

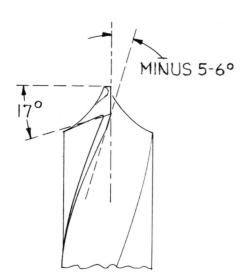

MINUS 5-6°

17°

Fig. D-19. Drill point for tougher metals.

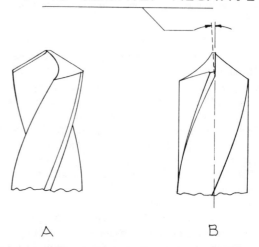

A   B

Fig. D-20. Drill's rake angle for bronze. A twist drill (A) and the correct rake angle for bronze (B) are shown.

DRILL GROUND AS A COUNTERSINK. Figure D-21 shows a twist drill ground as an 82° countersink, for flat-head screws. Short, stubby, worn-out drills are especially handy for this procedure. It is advisable to grind off the cutting edge to a 0° or slightly negative cutting rake, just as needed for drilling bronze.

DRILL GROUND FOR SPHERICAL FORMING. Figure D-22 shows a twist drill ground to a spherical point, for machining smaller ball sockets. The radius gage is made by boring out a washer to the required diameter, then cutting the washer into two 180° sections.

The spherical drill point can be quite easily ground off-hand. First, rough-grind the general outline. Then flat-grind

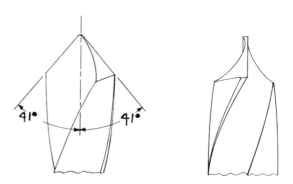

41°   41°

Fig. D-21. Drill ground as a countersink.

66

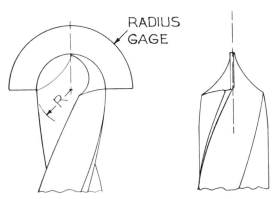

Fig. D-22. Drill ground for spherical forming. Use this method of grinding drills for forming internal spheres.

Fig. D-23. Drill prepared for hole-sizing.

the inside of each flute. The two cutting lips should be ground fairly parallel to each other, although not necessarily in line with the drill's axial center. The radii are both ground according to the radius gage, as closely as possible.

Test the final finishing of the drill's spherical end by cutting into the work. Then test the cut surface by pressing a gage or ball lightly smeared with Prussian blue against

the cut spherical surface. Mark the high points on the rounded drill end, then grind or hone them off.

DRILL PREPARED FOR HOLE-SIZING. Figure D-23 shows how a number or letter drill can be used very effectively as a hole-sizing reamer. This procedure is especially handy for work with shorter, small holes. The previously

Table D-1. Drill Sizes by Numbers and Letters.

DR.NO.	DIA.	DR.NO.	DIA.	DR.NO.	DIA.	LETTER	DIA.
80	.0135	53	.0595	26	.147	A	.234
79	.0145	52	.0635	25	.1495	B	.238
78	.016	51	.067	24	.152	C	.242
77	.018	50	.070	23	.154	D	.246
76	.020	49	.073	22	.157	E	.250
75	.021	48	.076	21	.159	F	.257
74	.0225	47	.0785	20	.161	G	.261
73	.024	46	.081	19	.166	H	.266
72	.025	45	.082	18	.1695	I	.272
71	.026	44	.086	17	.173	J	.277
70	.028	43	.089	16	.177	K	.281
69	.0292	42	.0935	15	.180	L	.290
68	.031	41	.096	14	.182	M	.295
67	.032	40	.098	13	.185	N	.302
66	.033	39	.0995	12	.189	O	.316
65	.035	38	.1015	11	.191	P	.323
64	.036	37	.104	10	.1935	Q	.332
63	.037	36	.1065	9	.196	R	.339
62	.038	35	.110	8	.199	S	.348
61	.039	34	.111	7	.201	T	.358
60	.040	33	.113	6	.204	U	.368
59	.041	32	.116	5	.2055	V	.377
58	.042	31	.120	4	.209	W	.386
57	.043	30	.1285	3	.213	X	.397
56	.0465	29	.136	2	.221	Y	.404
55	.052	28	.1405	1	.228	Z	.413
54	.055	27	.144				

drilled hole must run true, of course, and no more than .004 to .006 inch should be left in the hole for sizing with the drill.

TRUE STARTING OF DRILLS IN AN ENGINE LATHE.

When you are drilling in an engine lathe, it is not always necessary to first center-drill the work, unless very small diameter holes are to be drilled. Ordinarily, all that is required is some steadying of the drill point with the back end of the tool holder, or a like piece, as shown in Fig. D-24. The drill's cutting lips must be positioned up and down (or parallel) to the steadying surface.

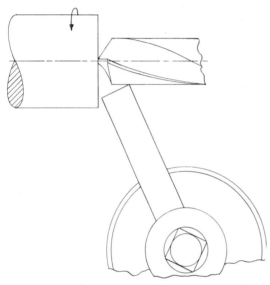

Fig. D-24. True starting of drills in an engine lathe. This method makes it unnecessary to always use a center drill.

Slowly screw the cross feed inward against the side of the drill as it begins to cut. Then release the pressure slowly as the drill enters further into the work.

HOLE-TRANSFERRING.

Figure D-25 shows a rapid method of transferring hole locations by using the pointed, shank end of the smaller drills as a center punch.

Before drilling, these center-point markings must be enlarged by regular center-punching.

Caution! Do not strike the glass-hardened drill point with anything harder than bronze, brass, or aluminum.

DRILLING PUNCHED LAYOUTS ACCURATELY.

Figure D-26 shows a good method of center-punching and

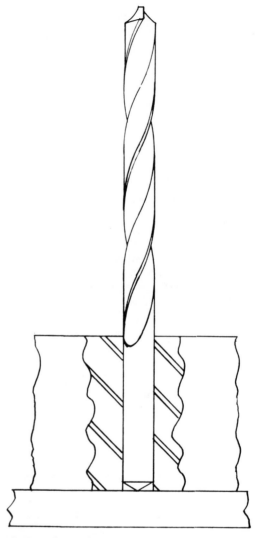

Fig. D-25. Hole-transferring. Use this method of transferring holes when the proper-diameter punch is not available.

center-drilling for more precise hole locations.

To accurately lay out hole locations is one thing, but to accurately drill a hole in that location is something else. Figure D-26A, shows the two intersecting layout lines, which can be from .002 to .003 inch wide. Using a magnifying glass and a sharp prick punch, lightly punch the line's intersecting point. Then scan the punch mark through the glass to see if the punch bottom registers in the center of both lines, as shown in B. If not, punch the mark again, tilting the punch in the direction that needs correcting. Strike

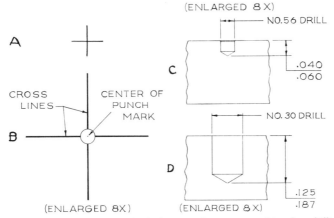

Fig. D-26. Drilling punched layouts accurately. A method of accurately center-punching then drilling precisely in that location is shown.

the punch lightly with a lightweight object, then enlarge the punch mark with a regular, sharp-pointed center punch.

The punched location is drilled in with a longer, small-diameter drill, about a No. 56, as shown at C. Only drill to about the depth shown. The drill should, preferably, be no larger than the diameter of the punch mark.

Next, the hole is made larger, as shown in D. For this step, use about a No. 30 drill and go to the depth shown. The enlarged hole now will serve as a pilot for a much larger drill. Using the described method, holes can be drilled within .002 inch F.I.R. of the laid-out location.

ACCURATE DEEP-HOLE DRILLING. Regardless of how precisely a drill is sharpened, it is still practically impossible to drill a perfectly straight hole to any greater depth. However, long, clean, straight holes can be made if proper steps are followed. Using properly sized and ground tools, holes more than 3 feet long can be drilled, finished, and running true, to within .001 inch F.I.R. or better.

A few sequential operations must be adhered to in every case. Each step is controlled, leaving nothing to chance.

No doubt, the engine lathe is the machine that is better suited for the long hole-drilling operations. They also can be done nearly as well in a radial drill press. The type of machine would depend on the shape and size of the job and the accuracy desired.

In the lathe, the work is gripped and driven, preferably in a chuck, although it could be supported and driven by other means also. The outer, or free, end of the work must be supported in a steady rest.

The plan is to drill and finish-ream a .750-inch-diameter hole, through a bar of steel 3 feet in length. The hole's

runout must be within plus or minus .001 inch F.I.R.

Thus, in Fig. D-27A, using a long enough engine lathe, the work is faced-off and center-drilled.

Next, as at B, drill an 11/16-inch-diameter hole, approximately 5 inches deep. If the bottom of the hole shows a runout, as it usually does, it will not matter at this stage.

Using a small boring tool, counterbore the drilled hole to a .716- to .720-inch diameter and 1 1/4 to 1 1/2 inches deep, as at C. This step pilots the following tool, which is a .722-inch-diameter end-cutting reamer, giving it a very true start. (See Fig. D-28.)

Ream the drilled hole with the .722-inch reamer, down to where a part of the hole's bottom is cut out, as at D. Next, make the center of the hole's bottom run true again by drilling into the bottom with the point of a .722-inch drill, as at E. However, do not drill into the bottom more than 3/32 to 1/8 inch deep.

After the hole bottom has been recentered, go back to the 11/16-inch-diameter drill. The hole is drilled in an additional 5 inches or so, as at F.

The .722-inch-diameter end-cutting reamer is used here next, as at G. Also, cut a small amount from the hole's bottom.

Again, to keep the 11/16-inch drill from straying too widely, the hole's bottom must be recentered with the .722-inch drill, as at H. Repeat the 11/16-inch-diameter drilling, the end-reaming, and recentering as often as is required to reach the entire length of the hole.

Counterbore the front end of the hole to a .746- to .748-inch pilot diameter, 1 1/4 to 1 1/2 inches deep, as at I.

Ream the entire length of the hole with the .750-inch-diameter end-cutting reamer, as at J.

69

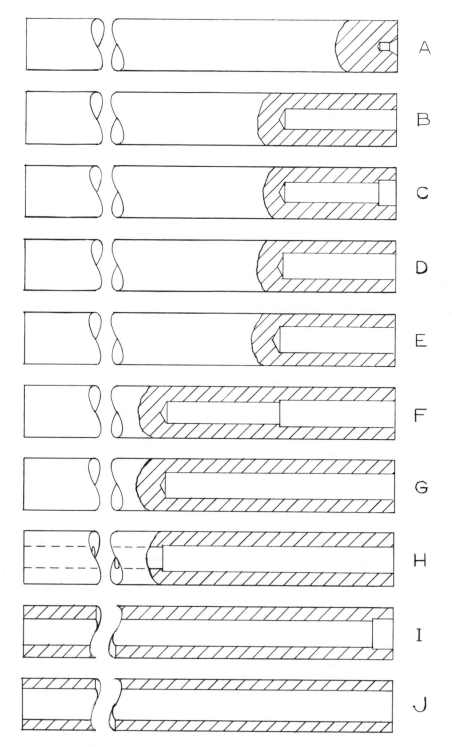

Fig. D-27. Accurate deep-hole drilling. You can precisely drill and ream unusually straight, deep holes with this method.

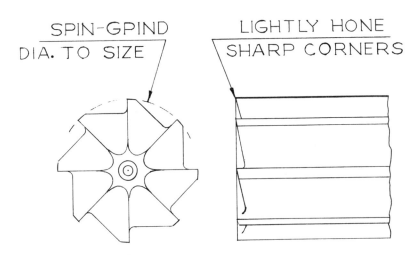

SPIN-GPIND
DIA. TO SIZE

LIGHTLY HONE
SHARP CORNERS

Fig. D-28. Deep-hole drills and reamers. Longer, straight-fluted reamers are ground to cut on their front ends only.

Note: Be sure to apply a generous amount of sulphur-based cutting oil to the entire drilling and reaming operations.

Generally, the straight, deep-hole drilling process requires the following tools:

☐ Center drill.
☐ Primary hole drill.
☐ Small-diameter boring tool.
☐ First end-cutting reamer.
☐ Recentering drill, of the same diameter as the first end-cutting reamer.
☐ Second end-cutting reamer for hole finishing.

DEEP-HOLE DRILLS AND REAMERS. For deep-hole drilling and reaming, longer shanks are silver (hard) soldered to the drills and reamers. These tools can be any of the high-speed steel types, which are usually found in the shops.

Reamers of the longer, straight-fluted types are preferred, but they must be modified for their intended purpose. These reamers are ground to cut on their front ends only (Fig. D-28). The outside diameter is spun ground, meaning it has no peripheral cutting edges. Also, the outside diameter should taper back to a smaller diameter by approximately .0001 per inch.

The reamer's front end is ground square to its axial centerline, having no angled leading edges (in other words, having sharp 90° corners). However, the corners are hand-honed lightly to prevent their flaking away under the cut.

For the shank extensions, use either a carbon steel drill rod or a ground hot- or cold-rolled mild steel rod. If you choose carbon steel, do not plunge it into oil or water to cool the hot joint. The rod's diameter should be a few thousandths of an inch smaller than the diameter of the tool, for which it is intended.

Turn the drill or reamer shank down to one-half its diameter (Fig. D-29). Next, drill the rod using two drills, one for drilling, the other for sizing the hole. The hole needs to be only 1 1/2 times deeper than the hole's diameter.

Whatever the drilled and turned diameters of the two mating parts, they should fit together quite closely, having no more than .0005 to .001 inch of play. Even if no play (clearance) is allowed, upon heating the hollow piece will expand much more than will the solid rod. Also, the thinner the solder is, the stronger will be the joint.

Before joining, thoroughly rinse the hole and the turned shank in carbon tetrachloride or acetone to remove any oil films. Then generously paint both parts with a "Handy and

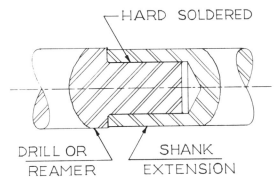

HARD SOLDERED

DRILL OR REAMER

SHANK EXTENSION

Fig. D-29. Deep-hole drills and reamers. Turn the drill or reamer shank down to half its diameter.

Harman'' silver soldering flux. Slip a ring of silver solder over the turned shank diameter before you insert it into the hole in the extension rod.

The rod should be held upright in a vise while a reduced acetylene flame is played around the joint. When the extension rod and the tool's shank become sufficiently hot, the ring of solder will melt, flowing in and around the inside of the joint. Maintain a slight downward pressure on the drill or reamer until it has cooled slightly.

Butt-welded extensions, to small-diameter drills etc., have been quite successfully accomplished using the welding unit of a metal cutting bandsaw. This process is very much like butt-welding the two saw ends together.

SPADE DRILL. When a greater amount of metal must be removed from a hole, a spade drill (Fig. D-30) can be made and used for the purpose.

High-speed steel is used for the cutting blade. After

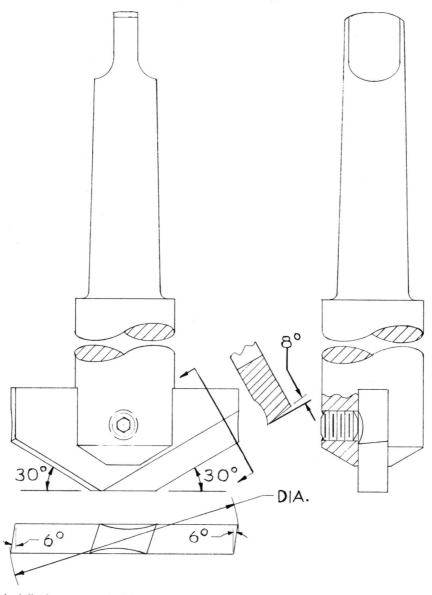

Fig. D-30. Spade drill. The way a spade drill is made used in a lathe is shown.

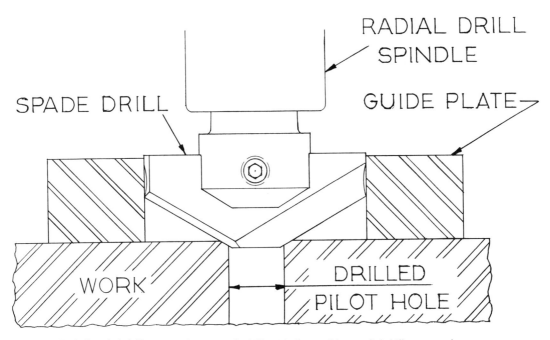

Fig. D-31. Spade drill, radial drill press. A larger spade drill might be used in a radial drill press as shown.

machining, the blade must be hardened and ground, of course. The tapered shank enables you to use the spade drill in a drill press or in the tail-stock spindle of an engine lathe. If the blade is quite large, provisions should be made to prevent the shank from rotating in its socket. For this purpose, a lathe dog is clamped around the shank while the dog's tail rests against some solid part of the machine, for example the compound rest of the lathe. In every case, a smaller-diameter pilot hole must be drilled through the work, first.

Allowances should be made in the rough boring, since close diameter dimensions cannot be held with this type of drill. Its main purpose is stock removal.

SPADE DRILL, RADIAL DRILL PRESS. Figure D-31 shows how a larger spade drill is used for gouging out larger-diameter holes in radial drill-press work. It becomes necessary to pilot the spade drill at least until it enters into the work, past its slanting cutting lips. For this purpose, a thick enough guide plate bored to the drill's cutting diameter is located centrally with the drilled pilot hole. The guide plate is fastened to the work by clamping or bolting.

With a moderate rate of feed, holes 4 to 6 inches in diameter can be drilled through quite readily.

HOLLOW DRILLS FOR SOFT MATERIALS. Figure D-32

shows a hollow drill as used for cutting holes through rubber and other soft, nonmetallic materials.

The drill consists of a short length of steel pipe tapered

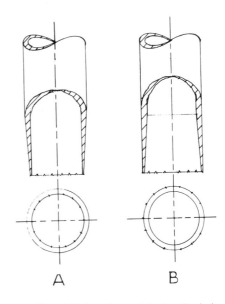

A   B

Fig. D-32. Hollow drills for soft materials. A method of producing holes through rubber and other soft, nonmetallic materials is shown.

either inside or outside, depending on what is wanted, a hole or a slug. Figure D-32B shows the tool as it would be shaped for hole drilling, while A shows how the tool is shaped for cutting out round slugs.

Note that the sharp bottom end of the tool is burred, using the sharpened edge of a somewhat heavier tool bit for the purpose. The slight burrs act as do the teeth in a saw.

The tool does not need to be hardened, and is always rotated as in a drill press. Always rest the work on wood, or such. Heating and friction can be minimized by brushing lubricating oil into and around the tool before cutting.

ESTIMATING

ESTIMATING SHOP WORK. The time required to perform any machining job can be estimated quite closely if a step-by-step procedure is followed. Do not become disappointed, however, if your estimations are not 100 percent correct. They seldom are.

Whatever the job may be, estimate one operation at a time. Then, add together these amounts of time to get the total estimated time for the whole job. However, the time the job takes also will depend on the the type and condition of the shop's equipment, as well as the skill of the person doing the job.

First, break the job down into its various operations, whether it be turning, boring, milling, or drilling. Jot down the length of time required to do each individual operation.

Second, assuming the shop's equipment is in good condition and the best man is chosen for the job, use 80 percent of his total time as the standard for machining the part.

Third, determine the number of like pieces to be made. If you are making two or more of the same piece, you can reduce the overall time per piece by 30 percent or more.

In every case, the person doing the estimating should be a first-class mechanic. His experience in these matters is valuable. If, however, a person with lesser shop experience does the estimating, he can resort to the tables on feeds and speeds as shown in the American Machinist or Machinery Handbook.

For milling machine cutters, each tooth should cut at least .006 inch. If the cutter has 30 teeth, then $30 \times 006 = .180$ inch represents the distance the work travels for each revolution of the cutter. The distance will depend on the size of the work, its material, as well as the cutter's material.

EXTRUSION

EXTRUSION OF METALS. Figure E-1 is an illustration of an extrusion die. The extrusion of metals, as well as nonmetallic materials, is very much like squirting toothpaste out of the squeezed tube. The shape of the tube's nozzle shapes the emerging material.

In extruding metals, the cylinder holding the metal to be extruded, the plunger and die, are made very heavy to prevent bursting.

Some metals can be forced through the die while they are cold, while other metals must be heated before they can be forced through the die opening. To be sure, the ma-

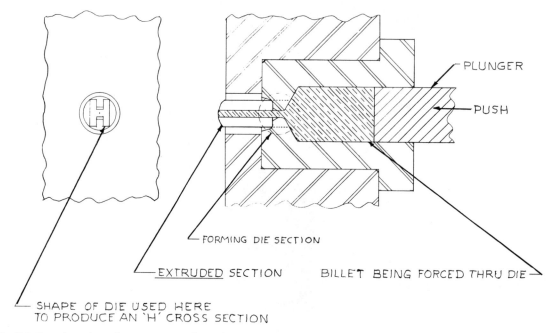

FORMING DIE SECTION

EXTRUDED SECTION　　BILLET BEING FORCED THRU DIE

SHAPE OF DIE USED HERE
TO PRODUCE AN 'H' CROSS SECTION

Fig. E-1. Extrusion of metals. An extrusion die is shown.

chine or press used for extruding is usually of tremendous proportions, having a comparatively short stroke, but exerting many tons of pressure.

Not only can infinite varieties of cross-sectional designs be extruded, but the extruded product also becomes finer grained, and consequently much stronger.

FILES

FILING AND FILE-CLEANING. Figure F-1 illustrates the better method of cleaning a file by using the corner of a soft metallic block instead of the customary, hard-bristled file brush.

You would hardly think of wiping off your razor blade with a piece of emery cloth or steel wool, and still expect it to shave like new. Yet, the same dulling condition results each time you use a hard-bristled file brush to clean your files.

You always expect your files to cut keenly and smoothly for fairly long periods of time. Finish-filing larger long shafts might require many hours of work, and the condition of the files you use is of the greatest importance.

It is also important to hold and stroke the file over the work at a greater angle to the shaft's axial centerline. This greater angle helps to prevent those metallic particles from lodging firmly in the file's teeth and marring the finish.

To clean all residue from between a file's teeth without dulling its sharp cutting edges, simply employ the sharp corners of a soft metal block. This block can be of mild steel 1 to 1 1/2 inches wide. Stroke the file with a corner of the block parallel with the file's teeth. Then wipe the file off clean with a dry, nonoily rag.

Never permit oil or grease to come in contact with the teeth of a usable file. The old practice of chalking a file is of questionable value.

FINISHING

SUPER-FINISHING. *Super-finishing* is the name of a surface finishing process developed by Chrysler Motor Corporation, which indeed finishes a surface to any degree of smoothness—from the fine ground finish down to and below 1 micro inch rms.

A fine ground surface, as illustrated in Fig. F-2B, is usually analyzed as having a smoothness of 18 micro inches rms. If this same fine ground surface is polished with fine emery cloth, it becomes only slightly smoother, but more shiny. The crests of the grinding marks are only rolled over, as shown in Fig. F-2C, instead of being cut off. Although polishing results in a brilliant surface, it is not necessarily smoother because the surface presents a multiangled condition in its roughness, reflecting the light's spectrum, much the same as a prism.

Because of the extreme smoothness resulting from the super-finishing process, the surface offers no reflecting conditions, so appears to be black. No other surface-finishing method can produce these fine results as quickly.

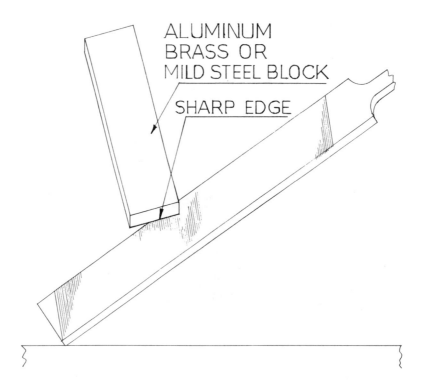

ALUMINUM BRASS OR MILD STEEL BLOCK

SHARP EDGE

Fig. F-1. Filing and file-cleaning. The better method of filing and cleaning the file is shown.

In super-finishing, a comparatively coarse stone (hone) in the area of 125 to 150 grit is used. The stone is composed of many small, hard, and sharp crystals. Rubbing it under pressure on the oily surface of the work will cut down the crests protruding through the oil film. This film consists of a mixture of mineral oil and kerosene proportioned as required.

As the grinding crests diminish in height, the stone begins to contact more oil than crests, and you will arrive at a point where the pressure of the stone against the work equals the resistance of the oil film to the stone's pressure. At this point, the stone's cutting action ceases. Continued action of the stone on the work will remove little if any more metal.

To remove more metal, you must thin out the oil more or put a greater pressure on the stone. Either of these steps will permit the stone to break through the oil film. Further cutting can continue until the stone's pressure and the oil film's resistance become equal again.

The oil in the super-finishing process serves as a cushioning lubricant, while the kerosene helps to keep the stone clean by floating away the abraded particles. This combination of liquids is known as the *coolant*, although no ap-

preciable amount of heat generation takes place in the process.

For the super-finishing process, the stone must be held rigidly when you are abrading the work surface (Fig. F-3). The stone also must be made to oscillate at a predetermined rate. The oscillating stroke of the stone is comparatively short, ranging from 1/64 to 1/4 inch. The shorter strokes are preferred.

If the oscillating stroke is too long, the oil will pile up in front of and under the stone's leading sides. This oil buildup will cause the stone—instead of resting flat or conforming to the shape of the work surface—to vary enough in its surface-contacting shape that it breaks through the oil film too soon.

It is not necessary to have great coolant pressures against the work. All that is needed is a copious flow.

The required pressure of the stone against the work surface will vary on different types of work and materials, as well as with the cross-sectional dimensions of the stone. However, the actual pressure will run in the area of 2 to 10 pounds.

In super-finishing a cylindrically shaped job (Fig. F-4) either internally or externally, the stone's surface-contacting

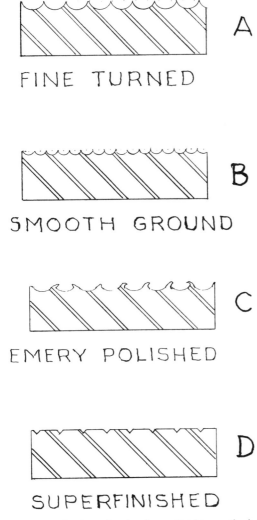

FINE TURNED — A

SMOOTH GROUND — B

EMERY POLISHED — C

SUPERFINISHED — D

Fig. F-2. Super-finishing. Results of super-finishing methods are shown.

When the stone first contacts the work, it oscillates quite rapidly over the rough surface. This action scrubs off any residue from the stone's working end left there from the previous finishing cycle, cleaning and exposing the stone's crystals and resulting in faster cutting.

In super-finishing the inside of a cylinder, the stone is rigidly held in much the same fashion as is the cutting tool in a lathe's boring bar. The bar and stone oscillate in a longitudinal direction, or parallel to the axial centerline of the cylinder. The feeding is carried on much the same as that for boring the cylinder, except that the feed rate is considerably coarser in super-finishing.

The super-finishing process differs from that of honing. In honing, long stones (hones) are used. They are pressed against the cylinder's wall by springs or by centrifugal force. As the mounted long stones of the hone rotate in the bore, they are oscillated in long and slower strokes, parallel to the cylinder's wall.

For a great many purposes, honing is very satisfactory, even though it does not produce as fine a finish as that produced by the super-finishing process. The very nature of the honing process does not lend itself to finer finishing. Although some small areas of a well-honed surface, when surface-analyzed, will fall into the low micro inch category. However, in an overall surface analysis the root mean square will rise considerably because of widely spaced scratches produced by the hone's cutting action.

In the case of super-finishing, free-moving machine parts, such as valve stems in internal combustion engines, the very smoothness of the stem's surface offers very little opportunity for any carbons to adhere. However, if carbons do adhere, do not remove them with a wire wheel. Not only does a wire wheel remove the carbons, but it also leaves many deep transverse scratches along the valve's stem. This roughed-up surface invites carbon adhesions,

dimensions remain the same. The work revolves at a comparatively low rate. The feeding progression of the stone is much the same as in the cutting of a thread in an engine lathe, with the stone representing the thread-cutting tool. Instead of being pulled along, cutting a helical groove, the stone is made to oscillate back and forth, parallel to the cylinder's axis. The oscillating stone is pulled along by the machine's feed shaft or lead screw.

The stone's oscillating rate will vary to suit, of course, again depending on the job at hand. However, the oscillation rate might run from a few strokes to several hundred per minute, or as rapidly as the mechanism will permit.

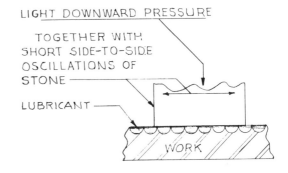

LIGHT DOWNWARD PRESSURE

TOGETHER WITH SHORT SIDE-TO-SIDE OSCILLATIONS OF STONE

LUBRICANT

WORK

Fig. F-3. Super-finishing. The correct method of using the stone is shown.

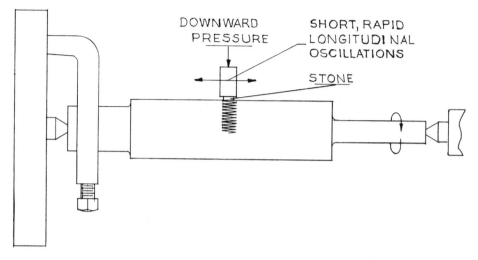

DOWNWARD PRESSURE

SHORT, RAPID LONGITUDINAL OSCILLATIONS

STONE

Fig. F-4. Super-finishing. Super-finish a cylindrically shaped job as shown.

and consequently sticky valves. The same is true in boring and honing the cylinders of an internal combustion engine. Such work was never good for any longer periods of operation. The wearing-in period was more of a wearing-out period.

A super-finished shaft will run satisfactorily inside a super-finished journal, even though they are separated by a film of oil a few millionths of an inch in thickness. The reason is that the smooth surfaces of the shaft and journal have no rough crests or irregularities to break through the

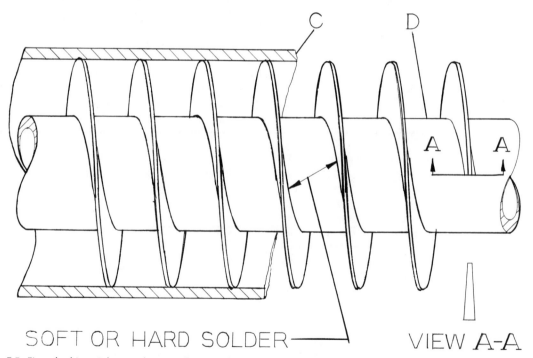

SOFT OR HARD SOLDER

VIEW A-A

Fig. F-5. Finned tubing. A heat exchanger tubing can be constructed as shown to suit certain needs.

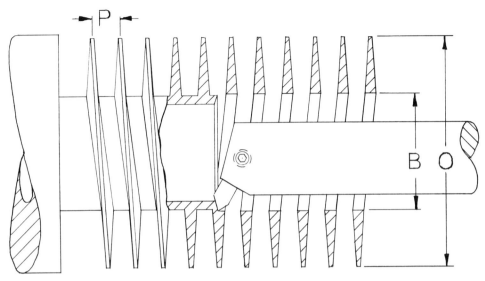

Fig. F-6. Finned tubing. Cut the fins in a lathe.

thin oil film and cause wear.

FINS

FINNED TUBING. Figure F-5 shows a novel finned tube, sometimes known as the *Serafin Tube*. Such tubes are used for cooling hot liquids—basically a heat exchanger unit. The hot liquid is conducted through the interior of tube D, while the coolant liquid is circulated around the exterior of tube D in a helical path, as directed by the attached cooling fins. The flow directions of both liquids oppose each other.

This type of tubing has several advantages. The fins, if made of brass, conduct heat rapidly. They also can be cut easily in a lathe like a thread of any desired pitch (Fig. F-6). The work then can be drilled through, leaving only a slight amount for boring. Bore B is made a bit larger than the tube's outside diameter. The larger hole permits stretching apart of the fins. The stretching-out also makes the fins cling more closely to the tube.

Before attaching the fins, sand or otherwise clean the pipe's surface thoroughly. Then wash with carbon tetrachloride or acetone before you apply the silver or soft solder flux.

Another advantage in this type of fin is that it can be screwed on over the tube, if the tube is already assembled, having no open ends.

An oxyacetylene (reduced) flame is used for the soldering. Start at the top and work downward, when possible.

G

GASKETS

GASKETS, SMALL DIAMETER. Figure G-1 shows a method of accurately cutting out smaller diameter gaskets out of rubber, neoprene, as well as other soft nonmetallic materials. First cut the material into large enough squares, then glue it onto a block of wood, as shown. Lepage's glue works quite well for this, although you also can use other glues.

Hold the wood block holding the blank in the four-jaw chuck of a lathe. Hone the thin cutting tool, shaped as shown, along its top edge and point. Then feed the tool straight into the material. Notice that the cutting tool slants downward slightly; this prevents the material from lifting off the block.

Size the diameters with a scale. It is better to cut the smallest or the inside diameter first. After cutting, you can easily peel off the material from the block and clean off the glue.

GASKET CUTTING WITH A TRAMMEL. When a larger circular gasket is required, it can be cut out with a trammel, as illustrated in Fig. G-2. Instead of the usual scriber or pencil, a specially ground, thin rubber-cutting tool is used. The cutting tool can be made from a worn-out tap or drill of any suitable diameter to fit the trammel. This tool should be ground quite thin and sharp, and honed on its front and back cutting edges, with its cutting end rounded and also sharply honed.

The soft work material is tacked onto a wooden bench or a piece of plywood. Cut out the smaller diameter first.

GEARS

SPUR GEAR, CALCULATION AND CUTTING. To acquaint you with gears and their making, four of the more common types will be described here: spur, bevel, worm, and helical. Normally, they all use the standard 14 1/2° involute tooth form.

Gears that have straight teeth cut parallel with the axis of rotation of the gear body are known as *spur gears*. You can compare spur gears with two parallel rollers whose peripheries touch, and which rotate one another by friction.

The outside diameters of these two rollers are like the pitch diameters of two mating gears. The outside diameters of the two rollers, like the pitch diameters of two gears, determine the ratio of the rollers.

However, to overcome slippage between the two rollers, you must change from a friction to a positive driving method. You do so by putting teeth on the periphery of both rollers. To accommodate the teeth, the outside di-

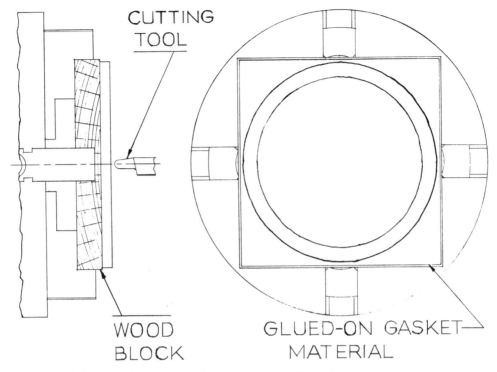

Fig. G-1. Gaskets, small diameter. You can cut washer-type gaskets readily, as shown.

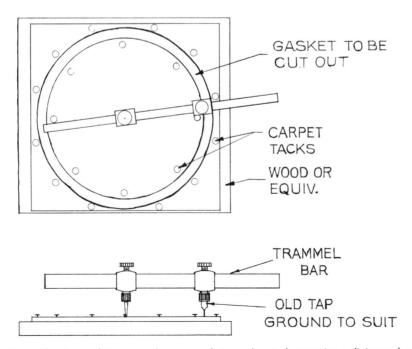

Fig. G-2. Gasket cutting with a trammel. Larger washer-type gaskets can be nicely cut using a slitting tool and a trammel.

Table G-1. Standard 14 1/2″ Involute Gear Tooth Dimensions.

DIAMETRAL PITCH	CIRCULAR PITCH	CHORDAL THICKNESS OF TOOTH ON PITCH LINE	ADDENDUM	WORKING DEPTH OF TOOTH	DEPTH OF SPACE BELOW PITCH LINE	WHOLE DEPTH OF TOOTH
0.5	6.2832	3.1416	2.0000	4.0000	2.3142	4.3142
0.75	4.1888	2.0944	1.3333	2.6666	1.5428	2.8761
1.	3.1416	1.5708	1.0000	2.0000	1.1571	2.1571
1.25	2.5133	1.2566	.8000	1.6000	.9257	1.7257
1.5	2.0944	1.0472	.6666	1.3333	.7714	1.4381
1.75	1.7952	.8976	.5714	1.1429	.6612	1.2326
2.	1.5708	.7854	.5000	1.0000	.5785	1.0785
2.25	1.3963	.6981	.4444	.8888	.5143	.9587
2.5	1.2566	.6283	.4000	.8000	.4628	.8628
2.75	1.1424	.5712	.3636	.7273	.4208	.7844
3.	1.0472	.5236	.3333	.6666	.3857	.7190
3.5	.8976	.4488	.2857	.5714	.3306	.6163
4.	.7854	.3927	.2500	.5000	.2893	.5393
5.	.6283	.3142	.2000	.4000	.2314	.4314
6.	.5236	.2618	.1666	.3333	.1928	.3595
7.	.4488	.2244	.1429	.2857	.1653	.3081
8.	.3927	.1963	.1250	.2500	.1446	.2696
9.	.3491	.1745	.1111	.2222	.1286	.2397
10.	.3142	.1571	.1000	.2000	.1157	.2157
11.	.2856	.1428	.0909	.1818	.1052	.1961
12.	.2618	.1309	.0833	.1666	.0964	.1798
13.	.2417	.1208	.0769	.1538	.0890	.1659
14.	.2244	.1122	.0714	.1429	.0826	.1541
15.	.2094	.1047	.0666	.1333	.0771	.1438
16.	.1963	.0982	.0625	.1250	.0723	.1348
17.	.1848	.0924	.0588	.1176	.0681	.1269
18.	.1745	.0873	.0555	.1111	.0643	.1198
19.	.1653	.0827	.0526	.1053	.0609	.1135
20.	.1571	.0785	.0500	.1000	.0579	.1079
22.	.1428	.0714	.0455	.0909	.0526	.0980
24.	.1309	.0654	.0417	.0833	.0482	.0898
26.	.1208	.0604	.0385	.0769	.0445	.0829
28.	.1122	.0561	.0357	.0714	.0413	.0770
30.	.1047	.0524	.0333	.0666	.0386	.0719
32.	.0982	.0491	.0312	.0625	.0362	.0674
34.	.0924	.0462	.0294	.0588	.0340	.0634
36.	.0873	.0436	.0278	.0555	.0321	.0599
38.	.0827	.0413	.0263	.0526	.0304	.0568
40.	.0785	.0393	.0250	.0500	.0289	.0539
42.	.0748	.0374	.0238	.0476	.0275	.0514
44.	.0714	.0357	.0227	.0455	.0263	.0490
46.	.0683	.0341	.0217	.0435	.0252	.0469
48.	.0654	.0327	.0208	.0417	.0241	.0449
50.	.0628	.0314	.0200	.0400	.0231	.0431
56.	.0561	.0280	.0178	.0357	.0207	.0385
60.	.0524	.0262	.0160	.0333	.0193	.0360

ameters of both rollers must be increased. The amount of increase depends on the size, as well as the number of teeth you want.

Almost any number of teeth and teeth sizes can be used, with one exception. The gear must have at least 12 teeth for a standard circular gear tooth cutter of any given size to be used and the gear to still function properly.

For gears having less than 12 teeth, either a special cutter must be used or the teeth must be shaped or broached to produce a more pronounced undercut in the tooth's profile (Fig. G-3).

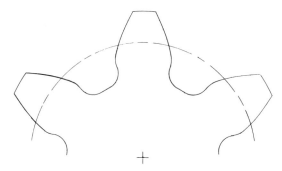

Fig. G-3. Spur gears, calculation and cutting. For gears having less than 12 teeth, shape or broach the teeth as shown to produce a more pronounced undercut in the tooth's profile.

Gear tooth sizes are generally classed in diametral pitch, which is the pitch diameter divided by the number of teeth, or the number of teeth to each inch of the pitch diameter. Although they can be larger, smaller, or in between, they generally run from 1/2 diametral pitch to 60 diametral pitches.

Refer to the spur gear index chart (Table G-1) for the number and size of the standard 14 1/2° involute tooth dimensions.

For example, let us assume that we need a pair of mating spur gears. One is to turn twice as fast as the other, or have a 2 to 1 ratio, and the gears are to carry a certain load. We choose a No. 10 diametral-pitch tooth for our example gears. The larger gear is to have 40 teeth; the smaller gear to have 20 teeth, this being a 2 to 1 ratio.

To figure out what the outside diameter of the gear blank must be to accommodate 40-10 D. P. teeth, always add 2 to the number of teeth in the gear; thus, 40 + 2 = 42. Then divide this sum by the diametral pitch of the tooth. In this case it is a No. 10 tooth; hence, 42 ÷ 10 = 4.200 inches, which is the outside diameter of the larger gear blank.

For the smaller, or 20-tooth gear, also add 2 + 20 = 22. Hence, 22 ÷ 10 = 2.200 inches, which is the outside

diameter of the smaller gear blank.

To correctly space the supporting shafts of these gears (center distance), simply add half of one gear's pitch diameter to half of the mating gear's pitch diameter (Fig. G-3). Thus, half of the smaller gear's pitch diameter equals 1 inch, and half of the larger gears pitch diameter is 2 inches. Adding the 1 inch and the 2 inches you get 3 inches, which is the gears' center distance (Fig. G-3).

The bore diameters of internal gears are calculated by subtracting 2 from the number of teeth for the gear. Instead you could add the number of teeth in both gears, then divide the sum by 2 times the diametral pitch. For example, 20 + 40 = 60; twice the 10 D. P. tooth size equals 20; hence, 60 ÷ 20 = 3 inches.

Spur gears can be cut very nicely in a horizontal, knee-and-column type of milling machine. The gear blank is placed on a mandrel, held between the centers of a universal dividing head. The dividing head is located on the table of the milling machine.

To select the proper tooth form cutters, refer to Table G-2. The shape of a tooth changes with the number of teeth in the gear. For example, the shape of a tooth in a 127-tooth gear is not exactly the same as in a 128-tooth gear. The difference is very slight, of course, but it increases as the number of teeth decrease or increase. For almost all practical purposes, these variations can be ignored, within certain limits.

Eight cutters for each diametral pitch are usually sufficient to cut all gears from 12 teeth to a rack. These eight cutters are made with the correct shape for the lowest number of teeth in their respective ranges.

For more accurate tooth shapes, it might become necessary to purchase special cutters. Half-size cutters (2 1/2, 3 1/2, etc.), which come between those listed in Table G-2, can often be purchased from stock.

From Table G-2, we select a No. 6-10 D. P. cutter for the 20-tooth gear, and a No. 3-10 D. P. cutter for the 40-tooth gear. Mount the cutter on the milling machine arbor. Select the cutting speed and feed per cutter tooth according to the type and material of the cutter and the material being cut.

The number of teeth to be cut in both of these gears permits very easy indexing. For this purpose, an index plate with any number of holes can be used. For example; the larger 40-tooth gear requires one turn of the index crank for each division, whereas the 20-tooth gear requires two turns of the index crank for each division. For other numbers of divisions, refer to Table M-1 for the standard dividing head plates.

Mistakes in indexing are very easily made. Therefore,

No. 1 cutter will cut gears from 135 teeth to a rack.
No. 2 cutter will cut gears from 55 to 134 teeth.
No. 3 cutter will cut gears from 35 to 54 teeth.
No. 4 cutter will cut gears from 26 to 34 teeth.
No. 5 cutter will cut gears from 21 to 35 teeth.
No. 6 cutter will cut gears from 17 to 20 teeth.
No. 7 cutter will cut gears from 14 to 16 teeth.
No. 8 cutter will cut gears from 12 to 13 teeth.

it is often a good idea to index and cut in very slightly, leaving division marks all the way around, then count the number of divisions. Do not count the markings.

You can now begin cutting the teeth into the blank. For more rigid cutting, the cutter's feeding should be toward the dividing head.

To centralize the cutter with the axis of the work, several methods can be used, one of which is shown in Fig. G-21. This device is put out by the Cincinnati Milling Machine Co.

Sometimes circular gear tooth cutters have a centerline on their periphery, which can be aligned with the point of the center in the dividing head.

You can also centralize the cutter with the work in the following way.

Elevate the mill table to where the gear blank almost touches the cutter. Then employ a square, standing it down on the machine's table while its blade touches either the blank or mandrel. Measure, with a scale, from both sides of the cutter's teeth to the upright square blade. The cutter will be centralized with the work when the space readings are the same on both sides (Fig. G-4).

After the cutter and work are centralized, raise the table to where the rotating cutter just begins to cut the periphery of the gear blank. Then back away the work and table enough to clear the cutter. Next, elevate the table to the full depth of the tooth. In this case, the whole depth of a No. 10 D. P. tooth is .2157 inch, including the bottom clearance (Fig. G-5).

You arrive at the working depth by dividing 2 by the diametral pitch; thus, $2 \div 10 = .200$ inch. The bottom tooth clearance is always 1/10 the thickness of the tooth at the pitch line. Our 10 D. P. tooth's thickness is .1571 inch $\div$ 10 D. P. = .0157 inch. Adding the clearance .0157 to the working depth of .200 inch equals a whole depth of .2157 inch. (Refer to Table G-1.)

SPUR GEARS, MEASUREMENT. After cutting two spaces to produce one complete tooth, we must verify the thickness of that tooth at the pitch line. The thickness of the tooth is always found by dividing the constant .15708 by the di-

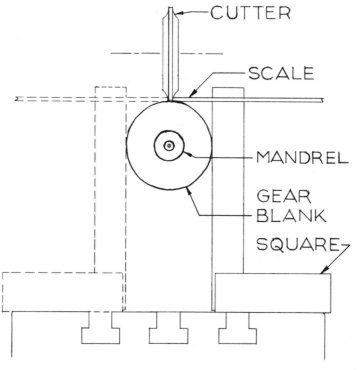

CUTTER

SCALE

MANDREL

GEAR
BLANK

SQUARE

Fig. G-4. Spur gears, calculation and cutting. Centralize the cutter with the work as shown.

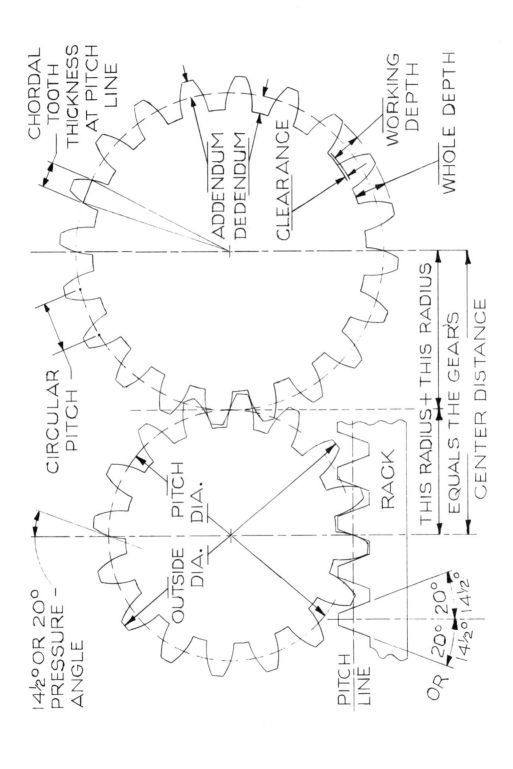

Fig. G-5. Spur gears, calculation and cutting. Detail of a No. 10 D.P. tooth is shown.

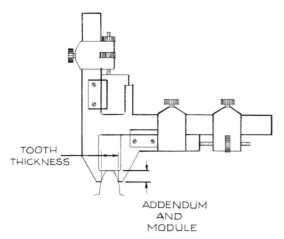

TOOTH
THICKNESS

ADDENDUM
AND
MODULE

Fig. G-6. Spur gears, calculation and cutting. Measure the tooth's thickness.

ametral pitch. Thus, .15708 ÷ 10 = .1571 inch, which represents the thickness of a No. 10 D. P. tooth.

The mating gear's teeth will not mesh, even if the gear's center distance is correct, unless the tooth's thickness is correct. To arrive at the correct tooth thickness, the thickness must be measured in one of several ways. The first and best method is by using a two-beam Vernier tooth caliper. This tool measures the tooth's thickness at a specific depth inward from the periphery of the blank (Fig. G-6) or on the pitch line. That is the reason for holding the outside diameter of a gear blank to close dimensions.

Another gaging method is to use individual gages for each pitch of tooth being cut (See Fig. G-7.)

Still another tooth-measuring method that works surprisingly well in a pinch is to lay a rod of a suitable diameter

(projecting slightly over the gear's outside diameter) into the tooth space of another gear having the same size of tooth. Then use a micrometer to measure over the rod to the periphery of the gear, opposite the rod. Add or subtract the difference between the two gear's outside diameters.

When conditions become pressing and the proper gear-tooth cutter is not readily available, you can use the fly-cutting method. (Fig. G-8.) Grind a single-point form tool to a similar-sized tooth of another gear, and hold the tool in the cross slot of a milling machine arbor, working it much the same as a circular-form tooth cutter.

The tool can be longer to project outwardly at both ends, with one end doing the roughing while the other does the finish forming. The roughing end is slightly narrower and shorter.

This method can also be used for milling infinite shapes and forms. From here on, the same procedures (except feed rate) are followed as outlined in SPUR GEARS, CALCULATION AND CUTTING.

BEVEL GEARS, LAYOUT AND CALCULATION. Bevel gears are used for transmitting rotary motion to shafts that are not parallel. Although bevel gears can be designed and

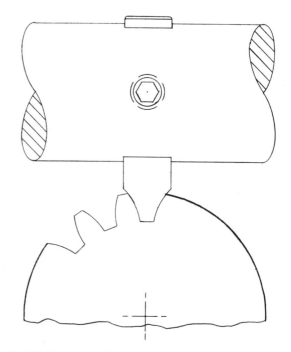

Fig. G-8. Spur gears, calculation and cutting. Use the fly-cutting method if conditions are pressing and the proper gear-tooth cutter is not available.

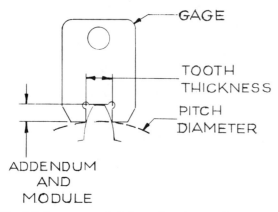

GAGE

TOOTH
THICKNESS

PITCH
DIAMETER

ADDENDUM
AND
MODULE

Fig. G-7. Spur gears, calculation and cutting. Another gaging method is shown.

cut to operate at any shaft angle, right-angled bevel gears are the most common by far. Two mating bevel gears having the same number of teeth and made to operate at right angles are often known as *miter gears*. Their cone pitch angle is always 45°, regardless of the tooth size.

In laying out a set of right-angled bevel gears, you should know the approximate load that must be carried. This measurement determines the size of the tooth, as well as the number of teeth in the gears. A example layout is shown in Fig. G-9.

In laying out bevel gears on paper, the practice is to draw two cross lines (B-B and C-C) 90° apart. Their point of intersection A is the apex of the cone's pitch angle.

Let us assume, for example, that we need a pair of miter gears having 30, No. 6 diametral pitch teeth. To find what the gears' pitch diameter will be, we divide the number of teeth by the diametral pitch of the tooth. Thus, 30 ÷ 6 = 5 inches. This procedure is similar to calculating the pitch diameters of spur gears.

Then we draw the horizontal pitch line (D-D) parallel to and 2 1/2 inches below line C-C. The 2 1/2 inches is the radius, or half the pitch diameter, of the mating gear.

Next we draw vertical lines (E-E and F-F) representing the mating gear's pitch lines. These are drawn parallel to and 2 1/2 inches from either side of the axial centerline (B-B).

Now we must calculate the length of the 45° cone's pitch radius. This is the distance from the apex point (A) to the intersection of lines D-D and E-E on one side and lines F-F and D-D on the other side. Both of these triangles will be exactly the same, of course.

Finding the length of the cone's pitch radius becomes a simple matter of calculating for the triangle's hypotenuse (Fig. T-60), or multiplying the secant of the cone's pitch angle by half of the gear's pitch diameter. For the latter method, we look into the Trig tables under 45° and we find the secant to be 1.4142 inches. We multiply this secant value by 2.500, which is one half of the pitch diameter. Thus,

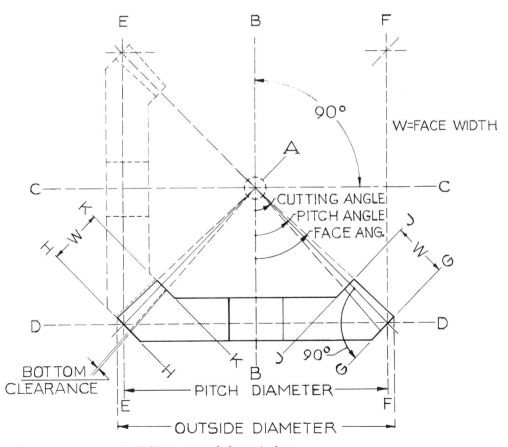

Fig. G-9. Bevel gears, layout and calculation. A sample layout is shown.

1.4142 × 2.500 = 3.535 inches. This value represents the length of the cone's pitch radius.

To find the face angle of the bevel gear, we divide the No. 6 D. P. tooth's addendum by the cone's pitch radius. Thus, .16666 ÷ 3.535 = .04711 inch. Looking into the Trig tables we find that .04711 is the sine of 2° 42′. Adding the 2° 42′ to the 45° cone pitch angle equals 47° 42′, representing the face angle.

The cutting angle, which is the addendum plus clearance, is subtracted from the 45° pitch angle. The tooth's bottom clearance is always one-tenth of the tooth's thickness. The tooth's thickness at the pitch line is always 1/2 of the circular pitch. The circular pitch of a No. 6 D. P. tooth is .5236 inch divided by 2 equals .2618 inch. Thus, .2618 ÷ 10 = .0261 inch clearance. Except for the clearance, the addendum and dedendum dimensions are exactly alike. (Refer to Table G-1.)

The No. 6 D. P. tooth's dedendum of .16666 inch is added to the clearance; thus, .1666 + .0261 = .1928 inch. This sum is then divided by the cone's pitch radius of 3.535;

thus, .1928 ÷ 3.535 = .05455 inch. Looking up this value, in the Trig tables under Sine, we find that it very closely represents 3° 7′.

By subtracting the 3° 7′ from the 45° cone pitch angle, we get 41° 53′. This number represents the root or cutting angle (Fig. G-10).

The standard gear tooth rotary cutters are made larger in diameter to include the required bottom clearance.

The outside diameter of the gear blank is found by multiplying the cosine of the cone pitch angle by twice the addendum. The addendum of a 6 D. P. tooth is .1666 inch. Twice the addendum then is .1666 × 2 = .3333 inch. The cosine for 45° is .70711 inch; thus, .70711 × .3333 = .236 inch. This value is added to the gears 5.000-inch pitch diameter; thus, 5.000 + .236 = 5.236 inches, which represents the gear blank's outside diameter (Fig. G-10).

Draw diagonal lines G-G and H-H at 90° to the cone's pitch angle. Across the intersection of the cone's pitch angle and the pitch diameter, draw lines E-E and F-F, parallel to lines G-G and H-H. Draw lines J-J and K-K. The

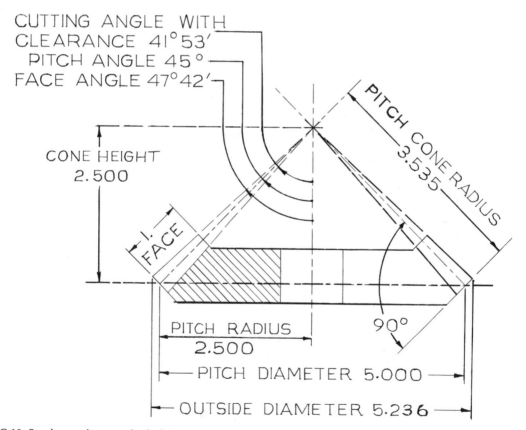

Fig. G-10. Bevel gears, layout and calculation. Dimensions are shown.

distance between these lines represents the face width (W). See Fig. G-9.

Knowing the outside diameter of the gear blank, we can now establish the gear's face width. The face width of a bevel gear is optional, but should not exceed one-third of the cone pitch radius. This proportion is better suited for cutting bevel gear teeth with a circular cutter. In our example gear, we choose to make the face width 1 inch.

When bevel gear teeth are shaped in using a single-point cutting tool, as in a bevel-gear generating machine, the width of the face is limited only by the narrowness of the cutting tool. The tooth's width, depth, and tooth space degenerate to zero at the cone's apex.

A bevel gear's blank should be turned quite closely to specifications. When the angles and diameters are held, it helps in producing the proper gear.

BEVEL GEARS, CUTTING. More recently, a method has been developed that eliminates the cut and try method of milling bevel gears and enables the operator to calculate the angle of roll and the amount of set-over.

Straight-toothed bevel gears can be cut in a milling machine when standard gear-cutting equipment is tied up or when the cone's pitch angle is out of range of the gear-cutting machine.

For example, to mill the teeth of a 30-tooth, 6 D. P., straight-toothed bevel gear with a 45° cone's pitch angle, having a tooth pressure angle of 14 1/2° (Fig. G-10), use the specifications in Table G-3.

Table G-3. Specifications for
a 30-tooth, 6 D.P. Bevel Gear.

Outside diameter of blank	= 5.236
Pitch cone radius	= 3.535
Pitch diameter at large end	= 5.000
Pitch diameter at small end	= 3.585
Circular pitch at large end	= 0.5236
Circular pitch at small end	= 0.3756
Tooth thickness and tooth space at large end	= 0.2618
Tooth thickness and tooth space at small end	= 0.1878
Whole depth of tooth at large end	= 0.3595
Whole depth of tooth at small end	= 0.2588
Addendum at large end of gear	= 0.1666
Addendum at small end of gear	= 0.1195
Dedendum and clearance at large end of gear	= 0.193
Dedendum and clearance at small end of gear	= 0.139

MILLING BEVEL GEARS

Because all of the tooth parts at the small end of the gear are in exact proportion to those at the large end, any dimensions at the small end can be obtained by multiplying the dimensions at the large end by the ratio Cs/Cr of the respective cone radii.

In the present example, $Cr = 3.535$ inches and $Cs = 3.534 - 1 = 2.535$ inches.

$$\frac{C_s}{C_r} = 0.72 \qquad [1]$$

The dimensions at the small end of the gear listed in the foregoing have been obtained by means of this procedure.

SELECTION OF SETUP

The gear blank is held on the spindle of a universal dividing head, which is aligned in the direction of the table **T**-slots of a knee-and-column type milling machine. The large end of the gear is located toward the dividing head.

Figure G-11 elevation shows the position of the gear blank with respect to the gear cutter when it is tilted at the cutting angle of 41° 53′.

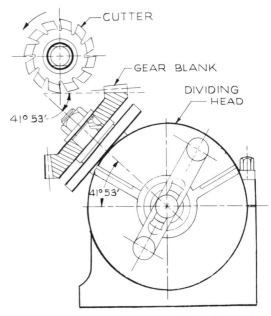

Fig. G-11. Bevel gears, cutting. The position of the gear blank with respect to the gear cutter is shown for a cutting angle of 41° 53′.

SELECTION OF BEVEL GEAR CUTTER

Best results in cutting a bevel gear tooth are obtained if the gear cutter is selected not for the number of teeth that the bevel gear is to have, but rather for the teeth of an imaginary spur gear of an entirely different diameter than the bevel gear, and calculated by means of the following formula:

$$D_1 = \frac{Pd}{\cos b} \qquad [2]$$

Where:

D_1 = Pitch diameter of an imaginary spur gear, in inches.

Pd = Pitch diameter of the bevel gear at the large end, in inches.

b = Pitch cone angle, in degrees.

Pc = Circular pitch, in inches

Nc = Number of teeth in the imaginary spur gear.

Ng = Number of teeth in the bevel gear.

Substituting the latter expressions for D_1 and Pd in formula 2, the following formula is obtained, which permits calculating the number of teeth for which the gear cutter is selected:

$$Nc = \frac{Ng}{\cos b} \qquad [3]$$

Where:

Nc = Number of teeth of the imaginary spur gear for which the gear-tooth cutter is selected.

Ng = Number of teeth in actual gear.

b = Pitch cone angle, in degrees.

In the present example, $Ng = 30$ and $b = 45°$. Hence, $Nc = 43$ teeth. Therefore, the cutter selected for the job is an arbor-mounted, high-speed steel No. 3 cutter having 6 D. P., and made for milling gears having from 35 to 54 teeth. (See Table G-2.) The same cutter can be used for milling a mating gear of the same size and pitch. However, a different cutter must be selected if the mating gear is of a different size. The teeth should preferably be milled by following the sequence of operations, as follows.

FIRST OPERATION: GASHING THE TEETH

In the first operation, gash, or rough-out, the teeth after you center the bevel-gear blank with the No. 3 gear cutter. This cutter is used in all subsequent operations (Fig. G-12).

By raising the knee, the blank is set for the depth of the cut which is 0.3595 inch equal to the whole depth at the large end of the gear. Then position each consecutive tooth for milling by plain indexing.

The number of complete turns and fractions of turns of the index crank and the circle of holes to be used for indexing are obtained by means of the following formula:

$$t = \frac{N}{D} \qquad [4]$$

where

$N = 40$
$D = 30$

the number of teeth to be cut in the bevel gear.

Hence: $t = \dfrac{40}{30} = 1\ 1/3 = 1\ 18/54$

Using the standard index plate (Table M-1) the 30-hole circle would be satisfactory for this indexing operation. However, select the 54-hole circle because it will be useful when you make the setup for the subsequent operations. Consequently, to index for each tooth, rotate the index crank one complete turn and 18 spaces on the 54-hole circle.

SECOND AND THIRD MILLING OPERATIONS

In these operations, you will mill the sides of the teeth. The width of the gashes produced by the cutter in the first operation measured at the pitch line is 0.1745 inch and 0.150 inch at the large and small ends of the gear, respectively. The correct dimensions for the finished gear are 0.2618 inch and 0.1878 inch, respectively.

In order to obtain these dimensions, an additional amount of stock must be removed on each side of the tooth space, as indicated in the shading in Fig. G-13.

DETERMINING THE ANGLE OF ROLL

To determine the angle of roll, the blank must be rotated

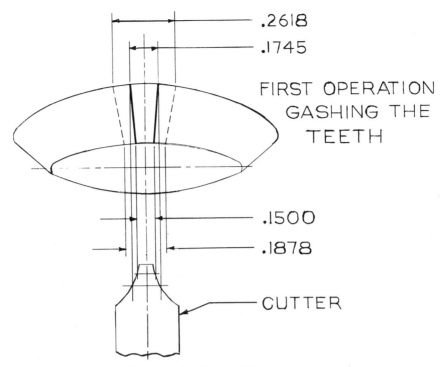

.2618

.1745

FIRST OPERATION
GASHING THE
TEETH

.1500

.1878

CUTTER

Fig. G-12. Bevel gears, cutting. Gashing the teeth is the first operation.

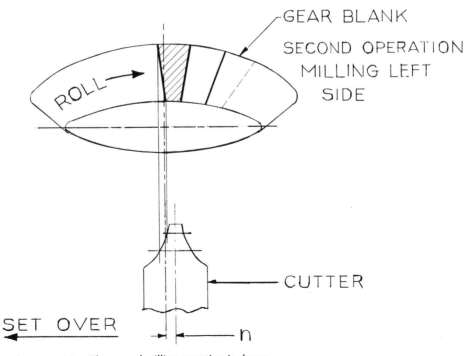

GEAR BLANK

SECOND OPERATION
MILLING LEFT
SIDE

ROLL

CUTTER

SET OVER

n

Fig. G-13. Bevel gears, cutting. The second milling operation is shown.

on its axis through an angle C in Fig. G-14, so that either line A-B or line C-D (view X, which traces the pitch line along the gear-tooth face's width) is placed in a direction parallel to the line E-F. The latter connects the points corresponding to the dimensions of the gashes (Fig. G-14) at the pitch line, at the large and small ends of the gear.

Then point A, for example, will have moved from distance d_2 to distance G from the centerline (M) in view Y. The distance (d) between points A and B in view X of Fig. G-14 will change to the distance (d) between points E and F.

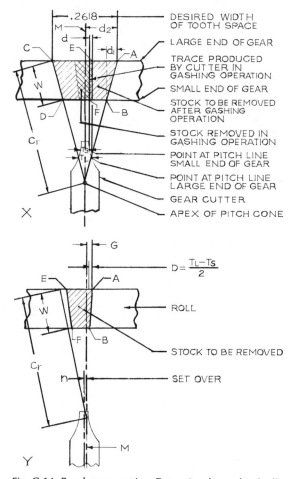

Fig. G-14. Bevel gears, cutting. Determine the angle of roll.

However, d is half the difference between the chordal thicknesses T_L and T_s of the gear cutter (Fig. G-15), corresponding to the pitch line, at the large and small ends of the gear, respectively. From the geometry of Fig. G-14 (view Y), distance G can be expressed as follows:

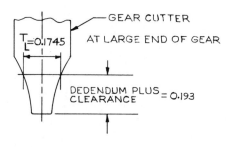

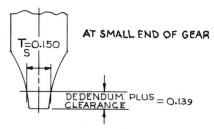

Fig. G-15. Bevel gears, cutting. Calculate the angle of roll.

$$G = c_r \times \frac{d}{w} \qquad [4]$$

$$d = \frac{T_L - T_s}{2} \qquad [5]$$

$$G = Cr \left[\frac{T_L - T_s}{2W} \right]$$

Where:

G = Distance between the centerline of the gear blank and the point at the pitch line of the gear at the large end, in inches.

C_r = Pitch cone radius, in inches.

T_L = Chordal thickness of the gear cutter tooth at the pitch line at the large end of the gear, in inches.

T_s = Chordal thickness of the gear cutter tooth at the pitch line at the small end of the gear, in inches.

W = Width of the gear-tooth face, in inches.

The amount of gear blank roll from the position in view X to that shown in view Y (Fig. G-14) is the difference between the circular distances d_2 and G of point A from centerline M of the blank. The distance d_2 is one-half of 0.2618 inch, or one-fourth of the circular pitch P_c, and the distance G is obtained from formula 4.

The corresponding angle of roll (c) in degrees is therefore obtained by dividing the difference by the pitch radius or one-half the pitch diameter of the large end of the gear, and then multiplying the result by the constant 57.3, which is the number of degrees of an arc corresponding to one radian. This relationship is expressed in the following formula:

$$C = \frac{57.3}{Pd} \left\{ \frac{P_c}{2} - \left[\frac{C_r}{W} (T_L - T_s) \right] \right\} \qquad [7]$$

Where:

C = Angle of roll, in degrees.

P_d = Pitch diameter at the large end of the gear, in inches.

P_c = Circular pitch at the large end of the gear, in inches.

C_r = Pitch cone radius at the large end of the gear, in inches.

$T_s,$
T_L = Chordal thickness of the gear cutter tooth corresponding to the pitch line at the small and large ends of the gear, respectively, in inches.

57.3 = Degrees per radian.

W = Width of the gear tooth face, in inches.

CALCULATING THE ANGLE OF ROLL

All of the values to be used in the formula are known, with the exception of the quantities of T_s and T_L. These values are obtained by direct measurement of the gear-tooth cutter you employ. Dimensions for the present example are given in Fig. G-15.

Substituting the known values in formula 7:

$$C = \frac{57.3}{5} \left\{ \frac{0.5236}{2} - \left[\frac{3.535}{1} (0.1745 - 0.150) \right] \right\}$$

$$= \frac{57.3}{5} \left[0.2618 - (3.535 \times 0.0245) \right]$$

$= 11.46 \, (0.2618 - 0.0866)$

$= 11.46 \times 0.175$

$= 2.007°$, or very nearly $2°$.

INDEXING FOR THE ANGLE OF ROLL

The angle of roll of $2°$ is obtained by plain indexing from the centered position of the blank. The number of spaces to index is obtained by dividing the angular distance between divisions by $9°$, or the angular rotation of the spindle corresponding to one turn of the index crank, thus:

$$t = \frac{2}{9} = \frac{2}{9} \times \frac{6}{6} = \frac{12}{54}$$

Index 12 spaces on the 54-hole circle, as in the case of the gashing operation.

The direction of roll is not important since the roll is reversed for milling the opposite sides of the teeth after all the teeth have been milled on one side. The only consideration is that the direction of roll and the set-over must be made in opposite directions (Fig. G-16).

DETERMINING THE SET-OVER

After you have rotated the blank on its axis to the angle C, you must set it over by an amount (N) from the centered position. This step is done to locate the blank so that the cutter will follow along the line A-B, which is now parallel to line E-F produced by the cutter (view Y, Fig. G-14). The set-over (n) is also calculated from the dimensions of the gear and cutter tooth by means of the following formula:

$$n = \frac{T_L}{2} - \frac{T_L - T_s}{2} \left(\frac{C_r}{W} \right) \qquad [8]$$

CALCULATING THE SET-OVER

Calculate the set-over n by substituting the known values in formula 8:

$$n = \frac{0.1745}{2} - \frac{(0.1745 - 0.1500) \, 3.535}{2}$$

$$= 0.0873 - \frac{0.0245 \times 3.535}{2}$$

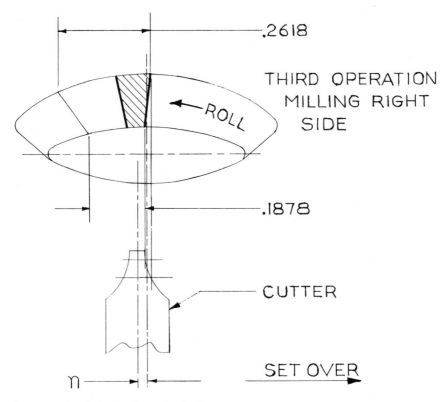

.2618

THIRD OPERATION
MILLING RIGHT
SIDE

←ROLL

.1878

CUTTER

SET OVER →

n

Fig. G-16. Bevel gears, cutting. Index for the angle of roll.

$= \quad 0.0873 - 0.01225 \times 3.535$

$= \quad 0.0873 - 0.0433$

$= \quad 0.044$ inch.

If the blank has been rolled 2° in a counterclockwise direction (when looking at the spindle end of the dividing head), move the machine table out or away from the column of the machine 0.044 inch. Conversely, if the blank has been rolled 2° in a clockwise direction (looking at the spindle end of the dividing head), move the table in toward the column of the machine 0.044 inch, to offset the work by this amount with respect to the center position used in the gashing operation.

To set for milling the opposite side of the teeth after one side has been completed, move the table twice the amount of the set over, or 0.088 inch. Roll the blank twice the angle of roll, or 4°.

After you have milled two or three complete teeth, you should measure their thickness at the pitch line at the large and small ends of the gear. These measurements should

be equal to the given tooth thickness at these ends. If not, you should check the calculations and the set-over for possible errors.

ACCURACY OF TOOTH PROFILE

The objective of this operation is to mill the gear teeth to the required thickness at the pitch line, along the face width. The tooth form, however, will not be accurate throughout the length of the tooth face, especially at the small end of the gear.

Here the flank of the teeth on the addendum part of the profile might not curve sufficiently to avoid a slight interference with the mating teeth because the gear-tooth cutter is made for a tooth form that is correct for the large end of the teeth. In any other section, it might vary as indicated by the broken lines shown in Fig. G-17.

Gears milled in accordance with the method described in the foregoing will be found to mesh satisfactorily. If necessary, however, you can remove a small amount of metal in the form of a triangle from the top of the teeth

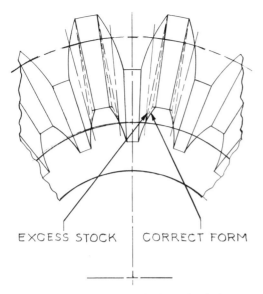

EXCESS STOCK | CORRECT FORM

Fig. G-17. Bevel gears, cutting. Make the tooth's thickness more nearly correct at the pitch line and at both its ends, as shown.

down to the pitch line at the small end, tapering off at the large end of the teeth, as indicated by the broken lines in Fig. G-17. To do so, rotate the blank through a small angle on the dividing head spindle, and then take light cuts until satisfactory meshing conditions are obtained.

This method of milling of bevel gears is especially convenient where the cone's pitch radius is unusually large and regular gear cutting equipment does not have the range to accommodate the gear to be cut.

MILLING HELICAL GEAR TEETH. *Helical gears* are gears that have the teeth cut along a helical surface. They are usually milled by using standard involute cutters of the arbor-mounted type.

In order to mill helical gears, it is necessary to rotate and at the same time feed the workpiece. One of the most generally used attachments for this type of work is the universal dividing head, which is driven from the table lead screw of the milling machine by means of change gears.

The change gears permit you to vary the ratio between the table feed rate and the revolutions per minute of the workpiece, and consequently the lead of the helical surface. The dividing-head indexing mechanism is used to space the helical teeth around the periphery of the workpiece as required.

The machine used for milling helical surfaces is usually a universal knee-and-column type of milling machine. This machine permits you to swivel the table, and consequently the workpiece located between centers of a dividing head

and tailstock, to the required angle of swivel.

The same results also can be obtained if a plain knee-type machine is employed. In this case, however, additional equipment will be required, consisting of a universal milling attachment that permits swiveling the cutter to the required angle of swivel (Fig. G-18) showing milling teeth in a rack.

When you are specifying the helix angle of helical gear teeth, the angle C (Fig. G-18) is preferred because this is also the angle used in setting up the blank for the milling operation. In other cases, as in the case of lead screws, the angle E is used to specify the helix angle of the threads. To avoid errors, it is therefore necessary to indicate clearly to which helix angle the given value should apply.

From the geometry of Fig. G-18, the following formulae are obtained:

$$E + C = 90 \qquad\qquad [9]$$
$$L = \pi D \,(\tan E) \qquad\qquad [10]$$
$$L = \pi D \,(\cot C) \qquad\qquad [11]$$

Where:

E and C = Helix angles, in degrees.
$\quad L$ = Lead of helix, in inches.
$\quad D$ = Diameter of the cylinder or blank, in inches.

If a helical gear is rolled on a plane (flat) surface, the traces of the teeth will line up in equally spaced, parallel straight lines. The axial distance (P_a) between consecutive teeth is the axial pitch; P_n is the normal pitch; and P_c is the circular pitch of the teeth. The circular pitch, normal

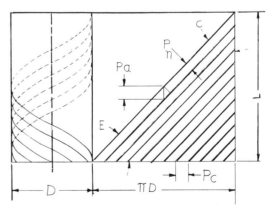

Fig. G-18. Milling helical gear teeth. Axial, circular, and normal pitches of equally spaced teeth are shown.

pitch, and axial pitch are measured as shown in Fig. G-18, at the pitch line of the gear.

The normal pitch measures the thickness of the gear cutter tooth and the tooth thickness and tooth space of the gear at the pitch line. The circular pitch is calculated by substituting the known pitch diameter of the gear for the diameter (D), and the number of teeth in the gear for N. Hence,

$$P_c = \frac{\pi P_d}{N} \qquad \textbf{[12]}$$

P_c = Circular path, in inches.

P_d = Pitch diameter of gear, in inches.

N = Number of teeth.

The normal and axial pitches (P_n and P_a) can be obtained from the circular pitch P_c and the helix angle, as follows:

$$P_n = P_c \, (\cos C) \qquad \textbf{[13]}$$
$$\text{or } P_n = P_c \, (\sin E)$$
$$\text{and } P_a = P_c \, (\tan E)$$
$$\text{or } P_a = P_c \, (\cot C)$$

Where:

P_n = Normal pitch, in inches.

P_a = Axial pitch, in inches.

P_c = Circular pitch, in inches.

and C = Helix angles, degrees.

Combining formula 12 and formula 13:

$$P_n = \frac{\pi P_d}{N \, (\cos C)} \qquad \textbf{[14]}$$

However, the normal diametral pitch is:

$$P_{nd} = \frac{N}{P_d \, (\cos C)} \qquad \textbf{[15]}$$

The diametral pitch (P_{nd}) of helical gears is specified by numerical values such as 5, 7, or 10 in the same way as the diametral pitch for spur gears. By combining formulae 14 and 15, the following normal pitch formula results:

$$P_n = \frac{\pi}{P_{nd}} \qquad \textbf{[16]}$$

This formula is similar to the formula for spur gears. In the latter, the circular pitch is the normal pitch of the helical gear teeth.

HELICAL GEARS WITH SHAFTS AT RIGHT ANGLES

Two helical gears with shafts at right angles to each other have different helix angles. Each angle is the complement of the other (Fig. G-19). Hence:

$$C_1 + C_2 = 90 \qquad \textbf{[17]}$$

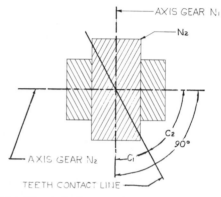

Fig. G-19. Milling helical gear teeth. Helical gears with shafts at right angles are shown.

The center distance of the gears is the subtotal of their respective pitch diameters, as expressed by solving formula 15 for P_d and applying it to each gear. The result is the following center distance formula:

$$S = \frac{1}{2P_{nd}} \left[\frac{N_1}{\cos C_1} + \frac{N_2}{\cos C_2} \right] \qquad \textbf{[18]}$$

However, from formula 18, we get:

$$C_2 = 90 - C_1$$

Therefore:

$$S = \frac{1}{2 P_{nd}} \left[\frac{N_1}{\cos C_1} + \frac{N_2}{\sin C_1} \right] \qquad \textbf{[19]}$$

Where

S = Center distance between the two gears, in inches.

P_{nd} = Normal diametral pitch of gears.

N_1, N_2 = Number of teeth in the gears.

C_1, C_2 = Helix angles of the two gears, in degrees.

HELICAL GEARS WITH PARALLEL SHAFTS

When the shafts are parallel, the angles C_1 and C_2 in formula 17 become equal, because the helix angle is the same for both gears. The center distance formula (19) changes to the following:

$$S = \frac{1}{2\,P_n\,(\cos\,C)}\,(N_1 + N_2)$$ [20]

HELICAL GEARS WITH SHAFTS AT ANGLES < 90°

Helical gears may have shafts at an angle of less than 90°. In such cases, the center distance between the meshing gears is determined by means of formula 18, as in the case of gears with shafts at right angles.

SELECTION OF THE CUTTER

Spur gear cutters for milling helical gears are selected for the hypothetical number of teeth in the section at right angles to the helix, rather than the actual number of teeth to be cut. This section is an ellipse (Fig. G-20). If the length

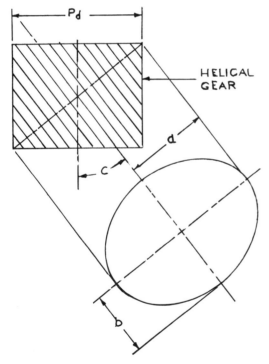

Fig. G-20. Milling helical gear teeth. The elliptical section of a helical gear is used to determine the hypothetical number of teeth for which the gear cutter is selected.

of this ellipse is divided by the normal pitch in the gear, the result is the number of teeth for which the cutter should be selected.

The major and minor axis of the ellipse (a and b, respectively) can be expressed in terms of the pitch diameter (P_d) and helix angle C, as follows (Fig. G-20).

$$a = \frac{P_d}{2\,(\cos\,C)}$$

$$b = \frac{P_d}{2}$$ [21]

However, the approximate length of the corresponding ellipse is:

$$M = \pi\,(a + b)$$ [22]

Substituting the expressions for a and b in formula 21, the following result is obtained:

$$M = \frac{P_d\,(1 + \cos\,C)}{2\,(\cos\,C)}$$

Now, by dividing M by the normal pitch P_n, the result is the hypothetical number of teeth (N_c) in the normal section:

$$N_c = \frac{M}{P_n} = \frac{\pi\,P_d\,(1 + \cos\,C)}{2\,P_n\,(\cos\,C)}$$

Where:

N_c = Hypothetical number of teeth for which gear cutter should be selected.

Using the expression for P_n obtained from formula 16 and the expression of P_d obtained by solving formula 15, the preceding formula can now be written as:

$$N_c = \frac{N\,(1 + \cos\,C)}{2\,(\cos\,C)^2}$$ [23]

This formula gives the hypothetical number of teeth that is used for selecting the gear cutter.

Another formula commonly used is:

$$N_c = \frac{N}{(\cos\,C)^3}$$ [24]

This formula is obtained by considering the radius of curvature R of the elliptical section normal to the helix (Fig. G-20) at a point corresponding to the minor axis (b). Hence:

$$R = \frac{a^2}{b} \qquad \text{[25]}$$

Substituting a and b in this formula with the expression given in formula 21:

$$R = \frac{P_d}{2 \, (\cos C)^2} \qquad \text{[26]}$$

Also:

$$2 \, \pi \, R = \frac{\pi P_d}{(\cos C)^2} \qquad \text{[27]}$$

Divide this formula by formula 15:

$$\frac{2 \, \pi \, R}{P_n} = \frac{\pi \, P_d}{P_c \, (\cos C)^3} \qquad \text{[28]}$$

However,

$$\frac{2 \, \pi \, R}{P_n} = N_c \qquad \text{[29]}$$

and

$$\frac{\pi \, P_d}{P_c} = N \qquad \text{[30]}$$

After substituting these values in formula 28, it becomes equal to formula 24. Formula 24 gives a slightly higher number of teeth than formula 23.

MILLING HELICAL GEARS FOR PARALLEL SHAFTS

Example 4: Milling a pair of helical gears for use on parallel shafts. The center distance is 8 inches. The gear ratio 2:1. The normal diametral pitch is 5. The width of the gears is 1 1/2 inches. The teeth have the same helix angle but have opposite "hands" of helix.

SELECTION OF SETUP

Helical gears are milled with the same equipment as is used in milling helical and plain milling cutters. This equipment can consist of either a universal knee-and-column type of milling machine, with a dividing head, the dividing-head driving mechanism, and an arbor to mount the gear cut-

ter; or a plain horizontal knee-and-column type of milling machine equipped with a universal milling attachment (Fig. G-18).

When the latter equipment is used, the gear cutter, rather than the machine table, is set at the angle required to place it in the plane of the tangent to the helix of the teeth to be cut. In helical gears, the value of the helix angle is calculated from or related to the pitch diameter.

NUMBER OF TEETH AND HELIX ANGLE

If N is the number of teeth in the small gear, the number of teeth in the large gear will be $2N$. Substituting in formula 19, $N = N$, $N_2 = 2N$, $P_{nd} = 5$, $C_1 = C_2 = C$, and $S = 8$ inches in the center distance. The formula as it applies in the present example is as follows:

$$8 = \frac{2N + N}{2 \times 5 \, (\cos C)}$$

or:

$$80 = \frac{3N}{\cos C}$$

In this formula, there are two unknowns: the number of teeth (N) in the small gear and the helix angle (C) of both gears. When one of these factors is assumed, the other can be calculated. The value of the helix angle can be established on the basis of the overlap, underlap, or no lap between the teeth in the gear, as measured in a direction parallel to the gear axis (Fig. G-21).

The overlap is the distance P (as in view A of Fig. G-21), by which the axial projection of the end of one tooth overlaps the beginning of the next tooth. Hence, from the geometry of view A in Fig. G-21, we get:

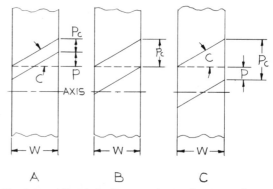

Fig. G-21. Milling helical gear teeth. Overlap (A), no lap (B), and underlap (C) between teeth in helical gears are shown.

Table G-4. 20° Involute Stub Tooth Dimensions.

THICKNESS OF TOOTH AT PITCHLINE	ADDENDUM	DEDENDUM	WHOLE TOOTH DEPTH
3/4 ———— .5236	.2500	.3125	.5625
4/5 —— .3927	.2000	.2500	.4500
5/7 ———— .3142	.1429	.1786	.3215
6/8 —— .2618	.1250	.1562	.2812
7/9 ———— .2244	.1111	.1389	.2500
8/10 —— .1963	.1000	.1250	.2250
9/11 ———— .1745	.0909	.1136	.2045
10/12 —— .1571	.0833	.1042	.1875
11/14 ———— .1440	.0773	.0968	.1741
12/14 —— .1309	.0714	.0893	.1607
13/16 ———— .1208	.0625	.0781	.1406
14/18 —— .1122	.0555	.0694	.1250
15/20 ———— .1047	.0500	.0625	.1125
16/21 —— .0982	.0476	.0595	.1071
17/22 ———— .0924	.0454	.0568	.1023
18/24 —— .0873	.0417	.0521	.0938
19/25 ———— .0827	.0400	.0500	.0900
20/26 —— .0785	.0385	.0481	.0866
21/28 ———— .0748	.0357	.0446	.0803
22/29 —— .0714	.0345	.0431	.0776
23/30 ———— .0683	.0329	.0412	.0742
24/32 —— .0654	.0313	.0391	.0704
26/35 ———— .0604	.0286	.0377	.0671
28/37 —— .0561	.0270	.0338	.0641
30/40 ———— .0524	.0250	.0313	.0600
32 42 —— .0491	.0238	.0293	.0580
34/45 ———— .0462	.0222	.0277	.0544
36/48 —— .0436	.0208	.0250	.0517
38/50 ———— .0413	.0200	.0240	.0500
40/54 —— .0393	.0185	.0231	.0470

$$P_c = W (\tan C) - P \qquad [31]$$

Where:

P_c = Circular pitch, in inches.
P = Overlap, in inches.
W = Width of the gear, in inches.
C = Helix angle, in degrees.

Expressing the overlap as a percentage (K) of the circular pitch:

$$P = K P_c$$

Formula 31 can be written thus:

$$P_c = \frac{W (\tan C)}{1 + K} \qquad [32]$$

When $K = 0$, the teeth have no lap, as in view B of Fig. G-21. When the teeth have an underlap (P), as in view

C of Fig. G-21, formula 31 changes as follows:

$$P_c = W (\tan C) + P \qquad [33]$$

Thus, in general, the conditions of overlap, no lap, and underlap of the teeth in a helical gear can be determined by means of the following formula, which is obtained by combining formulae 31, 32, and 33:

$$P_c = \frac{W (\tan C)}{1 \pm K} \qquad [34]$$

The plus sign in the denominator is used when the teeth overlap, while the minus sign is used when the teeth underlap. $K = 0$ when there is no lap. Combining formulae 12 and 15 and solving for P_c:

$$P_c = \frac{\pi}{P_{nd} (\cos C)} \qquad [35]$$

Hence, substituting this expression for P_c in formula 32 and solving for the function of C:

$$\sin C = \frac{(1 + K) \pi}{P_{nd} W} \qquad [36]$$

In the present example, $W = 1\ 1/2$ inches and $P_{nd} = 5$, and if the teeth have no lap, $K = 0$. Hence:

$$\sin C = \frac{3.1416}{5 \times 1.5}$$

$$= 0.4188$$

and:

$$C = 24° 46'$$

Substituting this value of C in the formula for this example, and solving for the number of teeth N of the small gear, the following result is obtained:

$$N = \frac{80 \times \cos 24° 46'}{3}$$

$$= \frac{80 \times 0.908}{3}$$

$$= 24.2$$

Assuming 24 teeth for the small gear, the large gear will then have $2N$, or 48, teeth. Recomputing the helix angle from center distance formula 20, the correct value of the angle C is 25° 50'. This helix angle is also the angle of swivel of the machine table.

SELECTING THE GEAR CUTTERS

If the gear cutter for the small gear is selected by means of formula 23, with $N = 24$ and $C = 25° 50'$:

$$N_c = \frac{24 (1 + \cos 25° 50')}{2 (\cos 25° 50')^2}$$

$$= \frac{24 \times 1.9}{2 \times 0.81}$$

$$= 28$$

you will find that a No. 4, 5 D. P. gear cutter (Table G-2) made to cut 26 to 34 teeth is used for cutting the teeth of the small gear.

The large gear has 48 teeth and the same helix angle as the small gear. Hence, using formula 23:

$$N_c = \frac{48 (1 + \cos 25° 50')}{2 \times (\cos 25° 50')^2}$$

$$= \frac{48 \times 1.9}{2 \times 0.81}$$

$$= 56$$

You will find that a No. 2, 5 D. P. cutter, which cuts a range of teeth from 55 to 134, should be used for milling the teeth of the large helical gear.

In this case, the same results would be obtained by determining the value of N_c by means of formula 24. Formulae 23 and 24 give results that are satisfactory under general conditions, but should be considered as an approximation subject to corrections, especially when you are milling gears to close tolerances.

COMPUTING THE LEAD

The lead is calculated by means of formula 11, using the pitch diameter of the gear and the value of the helix angle at this diameter. Combining formula 11 and formula 15:

$$L = \frac{\pi N}{P_{nd} (\sin C)} \tag{37}$$

For the small gear, $N = 24$, $P_{nd} = 5$, and $C = 25° 50'$. Hence:

$$L = \frac{3.1416 \times 24}{5 \times (\sin 25° 50')}$$

$$= \frac{3.1416 \times 24}{5 \times 0.435}$$

$$= 34.668 \text{ inches}$$

For the large gear, the lead equals 2×34.668, or 69.336, inches. See Table M-3.

CHANGE GEARS FOR THE DIVIDING-DRIVE

Because $L = 34.668$ inches, the change gears for the standard driving mechanism are calculated as follows:

$$\frac{A \times C}{B \times D} = \frac{34.668}{10} = \frac{8667}{2500}$$

This answer is simplified to the fraction 52/15. This fraction equals 3.4666, which gives a sufficiently close approximation to the calculated lead.

Gears in the dividing-head driving mechanism must be set to provide the proper combination between the direction of blank rotation and table feed, in relation to the *hand* of helix of the teeth to be milled, as in the case of milling cutters.

Helical gears for parallel shafts have helices of opposite hands. Hence, after you have milled one gear, you must alter the setup for milling the teeth of the second gear. This procedure includes transposing the above gears and reversing the direction of table swivel.

ANGLE OF TABLE SWIVEL

The angle of table swivel is the same as the helix angle of the gear teeth. It is calculated at the pitch diameter of the gear, and in the present example is $25° 50'$.

When you center the gear blank on the gear cutter, swivel the table of the machine clockwise to mill a left-hand helix, and counterclockwise to mill a right-hand helix. You must change the setup accordingly.

INDEXING

The teeth are indexed into position by plain indexing. The number of turns of the index crank to index each tooth into position for milling the small gear is:

$$t = \frac{40}{24} = 1 + \frac{16}{24}$$

and the number of turns to mill the large gear is:

$$t = \frac{40}{48} = \frac{20}{24}$$

Use the 24-hole circle in both cases.

If you use block indexing you can divide the gear into 8 blocks. After you have milled the first tooth, index the blank by turning the index crank 40/8, or 5, turns to mill a tooth spaced 45° from the first tooth. Continue this indexing until the first tooth is again in the starting position.

Now index the blank to mill the tooth following the first tooth by indexing 1 full turn and 16 spaces on the 24-hole circle. Follow this procedure by indexing 5 turns to mill each successive tooth in the blocks. Continue this indexing until all the teeth in the gear have been milled.

The same procedure is used for milling the 48 teeth in the large gear. Position each tooth by indexing 20 spaces on the 24-hole circle.

CUTTING SPEED AND FEED

The cutting speed and feed rates are selected in relation to the work and cutter materials and the type of cutter used. Gear cutters are usually made of high-speed steel and are of the form-relieved type.

MILLING HELICAL GEARS FOR SHAFTS AT RIGHT ANGLES

Example: The milling of helical gears for shafts at right angles does not present any different problems than does the milling of helical gears for parallel shafts. The two gears have different helix angles, but have the same hand of helix. The procedure used is shown in the example: Fig. G-22, which illustrates milling of the teeth of helical gears for operation on shafts at right angles. The material used is S.A.E. 3115 steel. (See Table G-5.)

SELECTION OF SETUP

The work is performed on a plain, horizontal knee-and-column type of milling machine equipped with a universal milling attachment, which permits you to swivel or tilt the cutter to the required helix angle, and a universal dividing head driven by the enclosed standard lead-driving mechanism.

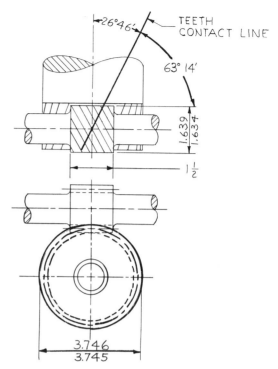

Fig. G-22. Milling helical gear teeth. Helical gears with shafts at right angles are milled as shown.

SELECTION OF GEAR CUTTER

The number of teeth for which the gear cutter should be selected is obtained from formula 21:

$$N_c = \frac{25(1 + \cos 26°46')}{2 (\cos 26° 46')^2}$$

$$= \frac{25 (1 + 0.893)}{2 (0.893)}$$

Table G-5. Specifications for Helical Gears.

GEAR SPECIFICATIONS	LARGE GEAR	SMALL GEAR
Number of teeth	25	5
Helix angle	26° 46′	63° 14′
Hand of helix	Left hand	Left hand
Normal diametral pitch	8	8
Normal pressure angle	20°	20°
Full depth of tooth	0.2696 inches	0.2696 inches
Pitch diameter	3.496-3.4955 in.	1.3888 inches
Lead at pitch diameter	21.7987 inches	2.200 inches
Center distance between gears	2.4424-2.4422 inches	

= 30

This equation indicates that the job requires the use of a No. 4-8 D. P. gear cutter made to cut a range of gear teeth from 26 to 34.

If you use formula 24, the number of teeth for which the cutter should be selected is then:

$$N_c = \frac{25}{(\cos 26° \, 46')^3}$$

$$= \frac{25}{(0.893)^3}$$

$$= 35$$

and the cutter would be a No. 3 gear cutter made to cut from 35 to 54 teeth.

ANGLE OF SWIVEL FOR THE MILLING CUTTER

The angle of swivel is the same as the helix angle. Hence,

swivel the spindle head of the universal milling attachment to the angle of 26° 46′, which can be read from the zero mark on the graduated swivel dial of the spindle head. Center the blank on the cutter by means of radial and axial lines scribed on the blank and a straightedge held against the side of the cutter.

You also can use a centering gage to increase the accuracy of the alignment (Fig. G-23). The centering gage consists of a plunger with a center point on one end and a **V** notch on the opposite end. It is held on the spindle head by means of a bracket. Adjust the plunger vertically so that the sides of the **V** notch are in contact with the periphery of the cutter. Then lock the bracket in position by means of thumb screw A. Lower the center point and lock it by means of screw B, then adjust the blank until the scribed mark is aligned with the center point.

CHANGE GEARS FOR LEAD

The lead of the large gear is 21.7987 inches. The change gears for the enclosed standard lead-driving mechanism are calculated as follows:

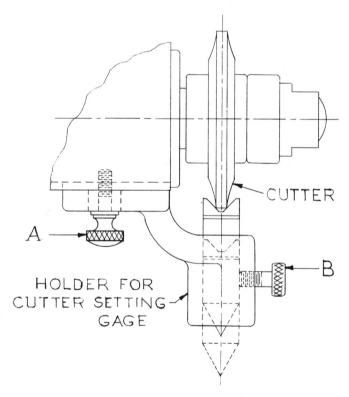

CENTERING GAGE

Fig. G-23. Milling helical gear teeth. The angle of swivel is the same as the helix angle and centering gage.

$$\frac{A \times C}{B \times D} = \frac{21.7987}{10}$$

$$= \frac{21.7987}{100000}$$

By means of continuous fractions, you will find that the common fraction 85/39 has a ratio of 2.17948, which corresponds to a lead of 21.7948 inches, or 0.0039 inches smaller than the given lead.

SELECTION OF CIRCLE OF HOLES FOR INDEXING

The number of turns t of the index crank to index 25 teeth are:

$$t = \frac{40}{25} = 1 + \frac{15}{25}$$

You will need to make one turn and 15 spaces on the 25-hole circle in the standard index plate to place each tooth in position for milling.

DEPTH OF CUT

The depth of cut is 0.2696 inches, corresponding to the full depth of the teeth. You should carry out this operation by first taking a roughing cut, followed by a finishing cut.

CUTTING FEED AND SPEED

The cutting speed and feed are selected in relation to the work and cutter materials and the type of cutter used. The cutting speed for the finishing cut is approximately 50 percent higher than that used in the roughing cut.

Cut the small gear teeth by following the same procedure as you used in milling the teeth for the large gear.

WORMS AND WORM WHEELS. Worms and worm wheels are used in drives to obtain a great reduction in speed ratio between the worm and worm wheel. The worm is the driver; the worm wheel is the driven member. This type of gearing arrangement is known as an *endless screw*. The ratio of the drive is independent of the relative pitch diameters of the worm and worm wheel.

The worm is a screw with a single thread or multiple threads, of such a form that its axial cross section is the same as that of a rack. The teeth of a worm wheel are a special form required to provide proper meshing conditions with the worm.

If the worm has a single thread, the ratio of the drive is equal to the number of teeth in the worm wheel. For a constant number of teeth in the worm wheel, the drive ratio decreases as the number of threads in the worm in-creases. With double and quadruple thread worms for example, the drive ratio becomes one-half and one-fourth of the number of teeth in the worm wheel, respectively.

In the worm, the distance between the centers of two adjacent threads is termed the *pitch*. The *lead* is the distance that any one thread advances axially in one revolution of the worm screw. Therefore, the lead and pitch in a single thread worm are equal. In double- and quadruple-thread worms, the lead is twice and four times the pitch, respectively.

CUTTING WORM WHEEL TEETH ON A MILLING MACHINE. Worms and worm wheels can be cut on a milling machine by means of thread milling cutters and hobs. The procedure used is illustrated in the following sections.

GASHING AND HOBBING A WORM WHEEL

Example: Milling a 100-tooth, left-hand worm wheel.

Pitch diameter: 7.9576 inches
Circular pitch: 0.250 inch
Full depth: 0.1716 inch
Center distance: 4.7743 inches
Gashing angle: 2° 52′
Pitch diameter of worm screw: 1.5916 inches

In cutting the teeth of a worm wheel on a milling machine, two operations are required: gashing the teeth and hobbing the teeth to the correct size and shape.

A universal milling machine equipped with a universal dividing head is used for the setup operation. Place the blank between centers of the dividing head and tailstock.

The gashing operation consists of roughing the gear teeth with an involute gear cutter having the same pitch and diameter as the worm screw. You also can use a fly cutter (Fig. G-8) for the gashing only.

Swivel the table of the machine to the gashing angle of 2° 52′ in a clockwise direction for a left-hand worm, after you align the blank on the center of the gashing cutter both crosswise and longitudinally. Then perform the gashing operation by feeding the work vertically to the depth of the teeth. It is necessary, however, to leave a sufficient amount of stock for the finishing operation.

If it is not given, you can calculate the gashing angle from the formula in Table G-6, using the known values of the lead and pitch diameter of the worm. The gashing angles for worm wheels for a variety of worms having diameters from 5/8 to 6 inches and having leads from 1/10 to 1 1/2 inch can be taken directly from the tables.

In the present worm wheel, the pitch diameter of the worm is 1.5916 inches, and the lead is 0.250 inch. Hence:

Table G-6. Gashing Angles for Worm Wheels.

LEAD OF WORM IN INCHES	NO. OF THDS PER IN. IN WORM	PITCH DIAMETER OF WORM 5/8	3/4	7/8	1	1 1/8	1 1/4	1 3/8	1 1/2	1 5/8	1 3/4	1 7/8	2	2 1/8	2 1/4	2 3/8	2 1/2
1/10	10	2°55'	2°26'	2° 5'	1°49'	1°37'	1°28'	1°20'	1°13'	1° 7'	1° 2'	58'	55'	52'	49'	46'	44'
1/9	9	3°14'	2°42'	2°19'	2° 1'	1°48'	1°37'	1°28'	1°21'	1°15'	1° 9'	1° 5'	1° 1'	57'	54'	51'	49'
1/8	8	3°38'	3° 2'	2°36'	2°17'	2° 2'	1°49'	1°39'	1°31'	1°24'	1°18'	1°13'	1° 8'	1° 4'	1° 1'	58'	54'
1/7	7	4°10'	3°28'	2°58'	2°36'	2°19'	2° 5'	1°54'	1°44'	1°36'	1°29'	1°23'	1°18'	1°14'	1° 9'	1° 6'	1° 3'
1/6	6	4°51'	4° 3'	3°28'	3° 2'	2°42'	2°26'	2°13'	2° 1'	1°52'	1°44'	1°37'	1°31'	1°26'	1°21'	1°17'	1°13'
1/5	5	5°49'	4°51'	4°10'	3°39'	3°14'	2°55'	2°39'	2°26'	2°15'	2° 5'	1°57'	1°49'	1°43'	1°37'	1°32'	1°27'
1/4	4	7°16'	6° 4'	5°12'	4°33'	4° 3'	3°39'	3°19'	3° 2'	2°48'	2°36'	2°26'	2°17'	2° 9'	2° 2'	1°55'	1°49'
2/7	3 1/2	8°17'	6°55'	5°56'	5°12'	4°37'	4°10'	3°47'	3°28'	3°12'	2°58'	2°47'	2°36'	2°27'	2°19'	2°12'	2° 5'
1/3	3	9°38'	8° 3'	6°55'	6° 3'	5°23'	4°51'	4°25'	4° 3'	3°44'	3°28'	3°14'	3° 2'	2°52'	2°42'	2°33'	2°26'
4/11	2 3/4	10°30'	8°46'	7°32'	6°36'	5°52'	5°17'	4°49'	4°25'	4° 4'	3°47'	3°32'	3°19'	3° 7'	2°57'	2°47'	2°39'
3/8	2 2/3	10°49'	9° 3'	7°46'	6°48'	6° 4'	5°27'	4°58'	4°33'	4°12'	3°54'	3°39'	3°25'	3°13'	3° 2'	2°53'	2°44'
2/5	2 1/2	11°31'	9°38'	8°17'	7°15'	6°27'	5°49'	5°17'	4°51'	4°29'	4°10'	3°53'	3°39'	3°26'	3°14'	3° 4'	2°55'
4/9	2 1/4				8° 3'	7°10'	6°27'	5°52'	5°23'	4°59'	4°37'	4°19'	4° 3'	3°46'	3°36'	3°25'	3°14'
1/2	2						7°10'	6°36'	6° 3'	5°36'	5°12'	4°51'	4°33'	4°17'	4° 3'	3°50'	3°39'
4/7	1 3/4								6°55'	6°23'	5°56'	5°32'	5°12'	4°54'	4°37'	4°23'	4°10'
2/3	1 1/2											6°27'	6° 3'	5°42'	5°23'	5° 6'	4°51'
3/4	1 1/3													6°25'	6° 3'	5°44'	5°27'
4/5	1 1/4															6° 7'	5°49'
1	1																
1 1/3	3/4																
1 1/2	2/3																

GASHING ANGLE 'G'
DIVIDE THE LEAD OF THE WORM BY THE CIRCUMFERENCE OF THE PITCH CIRCLE. THE RESULT WILL BE THE COTANGENT OF THE GASHING ANGLE.

$$\cot G = \frac{L}{3.1416\,d}$$

LEAD OF WORM IN INCHES	NO. OF THDS PER IN. IN WORM	PITCH DIAMETER OF WORM 2 5/8	2 3/4	2 7/8	3	3 1/4	3 1/2	3 3/4	4	4 1/4	4 1/2	4 3/4	5	5 1/4	5 1/2	5 3/4	6
1/10	10																
1/9	9																
1/8	8	52'	50'	48'	46'	42'	39'	36'	34'	32'							
1/7	7	1°	57'	54'	52'	48'	45'	42'	39'	37'	35'	33'					
1/6	6	1° 9'	1° 6'	1° 3'	1° 1'	56'	52'	48'	46'	43'	40'	38'	36'	35'			
1/5	5	1°23'	1°20'	1°16'	1°13'	1° 7'	1° 3'	58'	55'	52'	49'	46'	44'	42'	40'	38'	
1/4	4	1°44'	1°39'	1°35'	1°31'	1°24'	1°18'	1°13'	1° 8'	1° 4'	1° 1'	58'	55'	52'	50'	48'	46'
2/7	3 1/2	1°59'	1°54'	1°49'	1°44'	1°36'	1°29'	1°23'	1°18'	1°14'	1° 9'	1° 6'	1° 3'	1° 1'	57'	54'	52'
1/3	3	2°19'	2°13'	2° 7'	2° 2'	1°52'	1°44'	1°37'	1°31'	1°26'	1°21'	1°17'	1°13'	1° 9'	1° 6'	1° 3'	1° 1'
4/11	2 3/4	2°31'	2°25'	2°18'	2°13'	2° 2'	1°54'	1°46'	1°39'	1°34'	1°28'	1°24'	1°20'	1°16'	1°12'	1° 9'	1° 6'
3/8	2 2/3	2°36'	2°29'	2°23'	2°17'	2° 6'	1°57'	1°49'	1°43'	1°37'	1°31'	1°26'	1°22'	1°18'	1°15'	1°11'	1° 8'
2/5	2 1/2	2°47'	2°39'	2°32'	2°26'	2°14'	2° 5'	1°57'	1°49'	1°43'	1°37'	1°32'	1°28'	1°23'	1°20'	1°16'	1°13'
4/9	2 1/4	3° 5'	2°57'	2°49'	2°42'	2°30'	2°19'	2°10'	2° 2'	1°54'	1°48'	1°42'	1°37'	1°33'	1°28'	1°25'	1°21'
1/2	2	3°28'	3°19'	3°10'	3° 2'	2°48'	2°36'	2°26'	2°17'	2° 9'	2° 2'	1°55'	1°49'	1°44'	1°39'	1°35'	1°31'
4/7	1 3/4	3°58'	3°47'	3°37'	3°28'	3°12'	2°59'	2°47'	2°36'	2°27'	2°19'	2°12'	2° 5'	1°59'	1°54'	1°49'	1°44'
2/3	1 1/2	4°37'	4°25'	4°13'	4° 3'	3°44'	3°28'	3°14'	3° 2'	2°52'	2°42'	2°33'	2°26'	2°19'	2°13'	2° 7'	2° 1'
3/4	1 1/3	5°12'	4°58'	4°45'	4°33'	4°12'	3°54'	3°39'	3°25'	3°13'	3° 2'	2°53'	2°44'	2°36'	2°29'	2°23'	2°17'
4/5	1 1/4	5°32'	5°17'	5° 4'	4°51'	4°29'	4°10'	3°53'	3°39'	3°26'	3°14'	3° 4'	2°55'	2°47'	2°39'	2°32'	2°26'
1	1	6°55'	6°36'	6°19'	6° 3'	5°36'	5°12'	4°51'	4°33'	4°17'	4° 3'	3°50'	3°39'	3°28'	3°19'	3°10'	3° 2'
1 1/3	3/4			8°24'	8° 3'	7°26'	6°54'	6°27'	6° 4'	5°42'	5°23'	5° 6'	4°51'	4°37'	4°25'	4°13'	4° 2'
1 1/2	2/3				9° 3'	8°22'	7°46'	7°15'	6°49'	6°26'	6° 4'	5°44'	5°27'	5°12'	4°58'	4°45'	4°33'

$$\tan E = \frac{0.250}{3.14 \times 1.59} = .05$$

and:

$$E = 2° 52'$$

Plain indexing is used for positioning each tooth of the worm wheel. You can find the correct circle of holes on the index plate and number of turns on the index crank by means of the dividing-head indexing table (Table M-1).

$$t = \frac{40}{100} = \frac{2}{5} = \frac{12}{30}$$

Each tooth is positioned by indexing 12 spaces on the 30-hole circle of the standard plate.

For the hobbing operation, the worm wheel is held between centers but free from the dividing head driving dog, thus allowing the hob to drive the wheel while the teeth are being cut.

The worm wheel axis is at right angles to that of the worm. It is necessary, therefore, to set the table of the universal machine in the usual straight position so that the axis of the worm wheel is at right angles to the arbor on which the hob is mounted.

The hob is made for a 1/4-inch pitch, 1/4-inch lead, left-hand, single-thread worm. The diameter of the hob is 1 3/4 inches, plus 2 times the bottom of tooth clearance. The tooth clearance is always 1/10 of the pitch, which is .025 inch $\times$ 2 = .050 inch. Add that total to 1 3/4 to get 1.800 inches. The pitch diameter remains at 1.591 inches.

Adjust the workpiece so that the hob centers over the rim of the worm wheel. Lock the table of the machine in position to prevent its moving while the teeth are being hobbed. Then raise the work gradually until you obtain the proper depth.

If you must remove a large amount of stock or you need an exceptionally good finish, pass the worm wheel under the hob a number of times, bringing it into the final depth for the last revolution.

MILLING WORMS

Example: Milling a left-hand, single-thread worm for the worm wheel shown in Fig. G-24.

Outside diameter = 1.750 inches

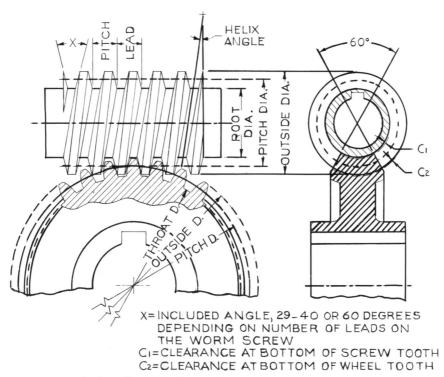

X = INCLUDED ANGLE, 29–40 OR 60 DEGREES DEPENDING ON NUMBER OF LEADS ON THE WORM SCREW
C_1 = CLEARANCE AT BOTTOM OF SCREW TOOTH
C_2 = CLEARANCE AT BOTTOM OF WHEEL TOOTH

Fig. G-24. Worms and worm wheels. Mill a left-hand, single-thread worm for the worm wheel as shown.

Pitch diameter = 1.591 inches
Lead = 0.250 inch
Pitch = 0.250 inch

You can mill the worm screw on a milling machine with thread milling cutters. Mount the cutter on the spindle of a universal spiral milling attachment (Fig. G-25) and swivel it to the helix angle of the worm threads. Place the worm blank between the centers of the dividing head and tail stock. The setup for this operation is made on a universal knee-and-column type of milling machine. The universal dividing head has a wide range divider, and is driven by means of a short lead-driving mechanism to obtain the 1/4-inch lead of the worm thread.

The thread milling cutter is selected for the given 1/4 inch pitch and 29° included angle of the worm threads. Since the worm has a single thread, you can use a thread milling cutter of stock size. This cutter will have a 1-inch hole diameter and an outside diameter of 2 5/8 inches. Swivel the cutter to an angle of 2° 52′ and then center it on the worm blank.

Worms can also be cut in a screw-cutting lathe, except that most pitches and leads in worm gearing are somewhat odd, compared to the regular pitches of screw threads. For worms, some special compounding of feed gears become necessary. Table G-7 details change gears for cutting diametral pitch threads.

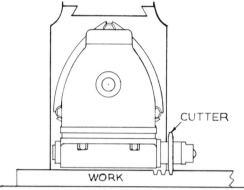

Fig. G-25. Worms and worm teeth. Place the worm blank between the centers of the dividing head and tail stock in a universal knee-and-column type of milling machine. The dividing head should have a wide-range divider.

Table G-7. Change Gears for Diametral Pitch Worms.

DIAMETRAL PITCH A	SINGLE DEPTH B	WIDTH OF TOOL POINT C	WIDTH OF TOP OF THD D	PITCH OF LATHES LEAD SCREW							
				2	3	4	5	6	7	8	10
2	1.078	.487	.526	$\frac{22}{7}$	$\frac{33}{7}$	$\frac{44}{7}$	$\frac{55}{7}$	$\frac{66}{7}$	$\frac{77}{7}$	$\frac{88}{7}$	$\frac{110}{7}$
2½	.862	.390	.421	$\frac{88}{35}$	$\frac{132}{35}$	$\frac{176}{35}$	$\frac{44}{7}$	$\frac{264}{35}$	$\frac{44}{5}$	$\frac{352}{35}$	$\frac{440}{35}$
3	.719	.325	.350	$\frac{44}{21}$	$\frac{22}{7}$	$\frac{88}{21}$	$\frac{110}{21}$	$\frac{44}{7}$	$\frac{22}{3}$	$\frac{176}{21}$	$\frac{220}{21}$
3½	.616	.278	.300	$\frac{88}{49}$	$\frac{132}{49}$	$\frac{176}{49}$	$\frac{220}{49}$	$\frac{264}{49}$	$\frac{44}{7}$	$\frac{352}{49}$	$\frac{440}{49}$
4	.540	.243	.263	$\frac{11}{7}$	$\frac{33}{14}$	$\frac{22}{7}$	$\frac{55}{14}$	$\frac{33}{7}$	$\frac{11}{2}$	$\frac{44}{7}$	$\frac{55}{7}$
5	.431	.195	.210	$\frac{44}{35}$	$\frac{66}{35}$	$\frac{88}{35}$	$\frac{22}{7}$	$\frac{132}{35}$	$\frac{22}{5}$	$\frac{176}{35}$	$\frac{44}{7}$
6	.360	.162	.175	$\frac{22}{21}$	$\frac{11}{7}$	$\frac{44}{21}$	$\frac{55}{21}$	$\frac{22}{7}$	$\frac{11}{3}$	$\frac{88}{21}$	$\frac{110}{21}$
7	.308	.139	.150	$\frac{44}{49}$	$\frac{66}{49}$	$\frac{88}{49}$	$\frac{110}{49}$	$\frac{132}{49}$	$\frac{22}{7}$	$\frac{176}{49}$	$\frac{220}{49}$
8	.270	.122	.131	$\frac{11}{14}$	$\frac{33}{28}$	$\frac{11}{7}$	$\frac{55}{28}$	$\frac{33}{14}$	$\frac{11}{4}$	$\frac{22}{7}$	$\frac{55}{14}$
9	.240	.108	.117	$\frac{44}{63}$	$\frac{22}{21}$	$\frac{88}{63}$	$\frac{110}{63}$	$\frac{44}{21}$	$\frac{22}{9}$	$\frac{176}{63}$	$\frac{220}{63}$
10	.216	.097	.105	$\frac{22}{35}$	$\frac{33}{35}$	$\frac{44}{35}$	$\frac{11}{7}$	$\frac{66}{35}$	$\frac{11}{5}$	$\frac{88}{35}$	$\frac{22}{7}$
11	.196	.088	.096	$\frac{4}{7}$	$\frac{6}{7}$	$\frac{8}{7}$	$\frac{10}{7}$	$\frac{12}{7}$	$\frac{14}{7}$	$\frac{16}{7}$	$\frac{20}{7}$
12	.180	.081	.088	$\frac{11}{21}$	$\frac{11}{14}$	$\frac{22}{21}$	$\frac{55}{42}$	$\frac{11}{7}$	$\frac{11}{6}$	$\frac{44}{21}$	$\frac{55}{21}$
14	.154	.069	.075	$\frac{22}{49}$	$\frac{33}{49}$	$\frac{44}{49}$	$\frac{55}{49}$	$\frac{66}{49}$	$\frac{11}{7}$	$\frac{88}{49}$	$\frac{110}{49}$
16	.135	.061	.066	$\frac{11}{28}$	$\frac{33}{56}$	$\frac{11}{14}$	$\frac{55}{56}$	$\frac{33}{28}$	$\frac{11}{8}$	$\frac{11}{7}$	$\frac{55}{28}$
18	.120	.054	.058	$\frac{22}{63}$	$\frac{11}{21}$	$\frac{44}{63}$	$\frac{55}{63}$	$\frac{22}{21}$	$\frac{11}{9}$	$\frac{88}{63}$	$\frac{110}{63}$
20	.108	.048	.053	$\frac{11}{35}$	$\frac{33}{70}$	$\frac{22}{35}$	$\frac{11}{14}$	$\frac{33}{35}$	$\frac{77}{70}$	$\frac{44}{35}$	$\frac{11}{7}$
24	.090	.040	.044	$\frac{11}{42}$	$\frac{11}{28}$	$\frac{11}{21}$	$\frac{55}{84}$	$\frac{33}{42}$	$\frac{11}{12}$	$\frac{22}{21}$	$\frac{55}{42}$
28	.077	.034	.038	$\frac{11}{49}$	$\frac{33}{98}$	$\frac{22}{49}$	$\frac{55}{98}$	$\frac{33}{49}$	$\frac{11}{14}$	$\frac{44}{49}$	$\frac{55}{49}$
32	.067	.030	.033	$\frac{11}{56}$	$\frac{33}{112}$	$\frac{11}{28}$	$\frac{55}{112}$	$\frac{33}{56}$	$\frac{11}{16}$	$\frac{11}{14}$	$\frac{55}{56}$
40	.054	.024	.026	$\frac{11}{70}$	$\frac{33}{140}$	$\frac{11}{35}$	$\frac{11}{28}$	$\frac{33}{70}$	$\frac{11}{20}$	$\frac{22}{35}$	$\frac{11}{14}$
48	.045	.020	.022	$\frac{11}{84}$	$\frac{11}{56}$	$\frac{11}{42}$	$\frac{55}{168}$	$\frac{33}{84}$	$\frac{11}{24}$	$\frac{11}{21}$	$\frac{55}{84}$

CUTTING DIAMETRAL-PITCH WORM SCREWS. When it becomes necessary to cut diametral-pitch worm screws for whatever the reasons and a milling machine with the required equipment is not available, then you can use a screw-cutting lathe for this purpose. However, to cut standard diametral-pitch threads, it still is necessary to provide feed gears for the lathe that will produce a screw with the desired lead.

Table G-7 shows a table of change gears for cutting diametral pitch screws. Column A shows the diametral pitch, while column B shows the corresponding depth of the thread. The third column, C, shows the width of the cutting tool at its point, while column D, shows the width of the top of the thread.

The cutting tool is the regular 29-degree included angle. A very important point to remember is that the finishing tool must be ground to exact dimensions, especially the 29-degree included angle.

If you use the three-wire method for measuring the worm's pitch diameter, you can make the point of the finishing tool slightly narrower. Never make it wider. Table G-7 also gives the pitches of the lathe's lead screws.

If, for instance, you wanted to find the gear ratio required to produce an 8 D. P. worm screw in a lathe that has a four-pitch lead screw, you first look down column A of Table G-7 to where you find 8 diametral pitch. Then look to the right until you come under lead screw pitch 4. The intersection of these two columns show the required gears to be 11 and 7: the 11-tooth gear for the stud and the 7-tooth gear for the lead screw.

Since a 7-tooth gear is too small to be practical, you must figure on larger gears. So you multiply both the 7 and 11 by 3, to get gears having 21 teeth and 33 teeth. You now have larger, workable gears. By multiplying the numerator and the denominator by the same number, you only increase the gear's diameter, you do not change the value of the fraction and the gear ratio.

GRINDING

STANDARD GRINDING-WHEEL MARKING SYSTEM. Figure G-26 shows a standard marking system chart, for identifying grinding wheels and other bonded abrasives. In case of doubt, a good rule to follow is to use a softer wheel for grinding hardened materials and a harder wheel for grinding softer materials.

THREAD-GRINDING. Most threads can be ground very precisely in a screw-cutting lathe. The requirements are a portable, tool-post grinder, a wheel-dressing fixture, and a dressing diamond. The tool post supporting the grinder rests on a wedge-shaped washer (P in Fig. G-27). The washer's periphery is graduated in degrees. By partially rotating the washer, to left or right, the grinding wheel can be tilted to match the helix angle of the thread in the work.

A screw's helix angle can be calculated by the following formula:

$$\frac{1}{P} = L$$

$$\frac{C}{D} = \pi$$

$$\frac{L}{C} = \frac{1/P}{\pi D}$$

Where:

P = Single threads per inch
L = Lead
D = Pitch diameter of work in inches
C = Pitch circumference of work in inches = πD
$\frac{L}{C}$ = Tangent of the angle

Refer to constants under tangents in the Trigonometry tables in the Appendix.

A very close angle approximation can also be made by lightly pressing a vertically positioned best-size rod (wire) into the thread groove. Partially rotate the wedge washer to left or right. Then by sighting along the face of the wheel, match its tilt angle to that of the rod held in the thread groove. The rod and the grinding wheel face should be parallel as shown by A_1 and A_2 in Fig. G-27.

Ordinarily, a comparatively soft (Alundum), fine-grit wheel is used for grinding hardened threads. The problem is to keep the wheel dressed correctly, especially for the final finishing passes.

For a finer 60° thread, dress the wheel to a sharp point. The flat at the bottom (root) of the thread develops automatically as a result of wheel wear.

To dress the wheel to the correct angles of the thread and to the screw's axial centerline, you must use a special wheel dressing fixture.

Figure G-28 shows one type of wheel-dressing fixture used for thread-grinding. This fixture is held between centers and serves quite well, except that you must take the work out of the machine each time to accommodate the fixture. After you have dressed the wheel, put the work back into the machine. You again must realign the grind-

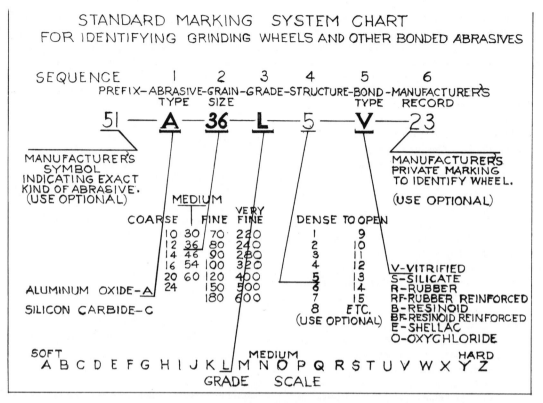

STANDARD MARKING SYSTEM CHART
FOR IDENTIFYING GRINDING WHEELS AND OTHER BONDED ABRASIVES

SEQUENCE 1 2 3 4 5 6
PREFIX – ABRASIVE – GRAIN – GRADE – STRUCTURE – BOND – MANUFACTURER'S
TYPE SIZE TYPE RECORD

51 — A — 36 — L — 5 — V — 23

MANUFACTURER'S
SYMBOL
INDICATING EXACT
KIND OF ABRASIVE.
(USE OPTIONAL)

MANUFACTURER'S
PRIVATE MARKING
TO IDENTIFY WHEEL.
(USE OPTIONAL)

MEDIUM
VERY
COARSE | FINE FINE DENSE TO OPEN

COARSE	FINE	VERY FINE		
10 30	70	220	1	9
12 36	80	240	2	10
14 46	90	280	3	11
16 54	100	320	4	12
20 60	120	400	5	13
24	150	500	6	14
	180	600	7	15
			8	ETC.

V-VITRIFIED
S-SILICATE
R-RUBBER
RF-RUBBER REINFORCED
B-RESINOID
BF-RESINOID REINFORCED
E-SHELLAC
O-OXYCHLORIDE

ALUMINUM OXIDE – A
SILICON CARBIDE – C
(USE OPTIONAL)

SOFT MEDIUM HARD
A B C D E F G H I J K L M N O P Q R S T U V W X Y Z
GRADE SCALE

EXTRACTED FROM AMERICAN STANDARD MARKINGS FOR IDENTIFYING
GRINDING WHEELS AND OTHER BONDED ABRASIVES (ASA B5.17-1958),
WITH THE PERMISSION OF THE PUBLISHER, THE AMERICAN SOCIETY OF
MECHANICAL ENGINEERS, 29 W. 39th ST., NEW YORK 18, N.Y.

Fig. G-26. Standard grinding-wheel marking system. Courtesy American Society of Mechanical Engineers.

ing wheel with the thread. Also in the case of grinding a tap, you cannot be sure that the tail stock remains set over the exact amount required to grind a slight back taper. By the time all necessary realignment is complete, it becomes necessary to re-dress the wheel once again. This process can be somewhat irritating when you are working to very close tolerances.

Figure G-29 shows a type of wheel-dressing fixture that clamps around the tail-stock spindle. It is designed so that the grinding wheel can be dressed, at will, without disrupting the work setup. After each dressing, the hinged portion of the fixture is simply swung up and back, affording no interference with the grinder's movements. The projecting shelf (L) can be swiveled to left- or right-hand thread grinding.

The shelf also supports two pads (X) having raised shoulders (Y) on their inner sides. The angles of the shoulders are fixed at 30° to the centerline separating the two shoul-

ders. The centerline, in turn, is at 90° to the axial centerline of the work.

A dressing diamond (Z) is supported in a movable block (B), which is manually pressed against the shoulders. The grinding wheel (W) is centrally positioned between the two pads. The diamond dressing is done by starting at the outer periphery of the wheel and pulling the block toward the axis of the wheel. This procedure keeps the sharp wheel edge from flaking away during the dressing procedure.

SPHERICAL O. D. GRINDING. Figure G-30 shows how spherical work can be ground to a precise curvature and diameter in one operation. Mount the work on a suitable mandrel and rotate it at a moderate speed. Set the grinding wheel spindle axis at 90° to the work's axial center. Also, the axial centers of both items must be on the same plane. To accomplish the latter, bring the wheel up and make it touch the stationary work surface (assuming it runs true).

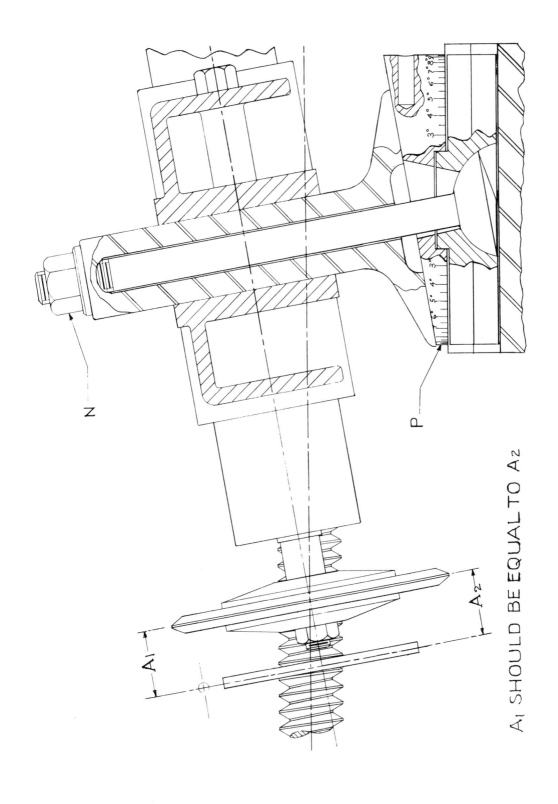

N

P

A_1

A_2

A_1 SHOULD BE EQUAL TO A_2

Fig. G-27. Thread-grinding. Threads can be ground quite precisely in a screw-cutting lathe.

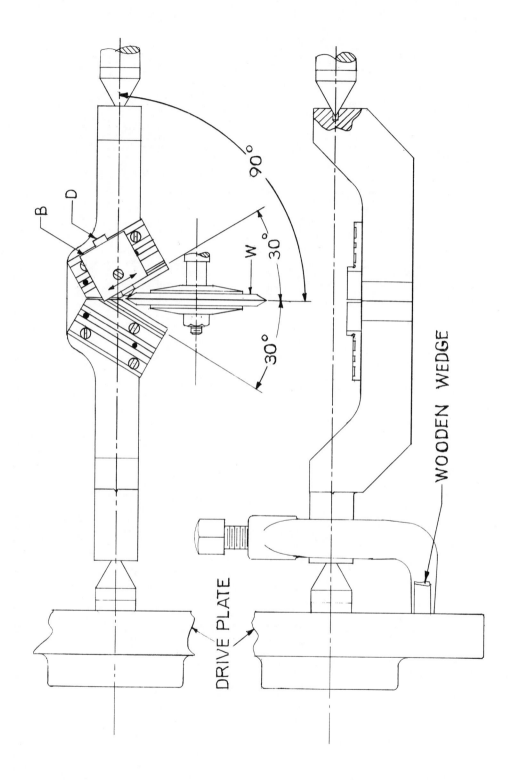

Fig. G-28. Thread-grinding. A type of wheel-dressing fixture used for thread-grinding is shown.

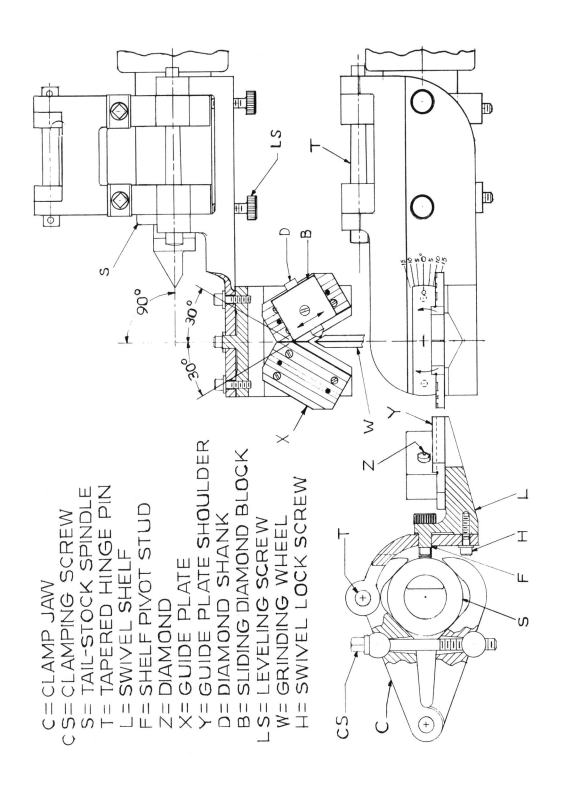

C = CLAMP JAW
CS = CLAMPING SCREW
S = TAIL-STOCK SPINDLE
T = TAPERED HINGE PIN
L = SWIVEL SHELF
F = SHELF PIVOT STUD
Z = DIAMOND
X = GUIDE PLATE
Y = GUIDE PLATE SHOULDER
D = DIAMOND SHANK
B = SLIDING DIAMOND BLOCK
LS = LEVELING SCREW
W = GRINDING WHEEL
H = SWIVEL LOCK SCREW

Fig. G-29. Thread-grinding. This type of wheel-dressing fixture clamps around the tail-stock spindle.

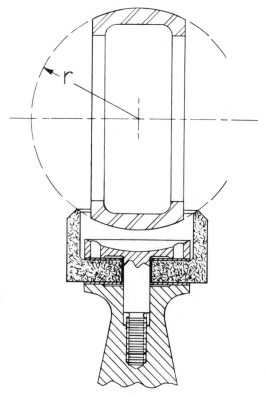

Fig. G-30. Spherical O.D. grinding. Spherical work can be readily ground to precise curvature and diameter in one operation.

Then rotate the grinding spindle by hand, then withdraw it. The marks left on the work surface will show if the wheel needs to be raised or lowered.

You can make a suitable hollow wheel by boring out a solid wheel, using a high A speed or carbide tool bit. This operation must be done at a low speed, of course.

If the work is hardened (about 60 Rc) a very soft, loose-bound grinding wheel should be used and run at 5600 to 6500 surface feet per minute. The wheel's inner diameter needs to be only approximately 10 percent greater than the chordal width of the work.

When the grinding spindle is properly set on center, up and down, the finish will show a crisscross pattern.

There is now a patented (#4,092,902) portable motorized apparatus for use in an engine lathe, for accurately generating attached spheres or spherical surfaces in soft or hardened material to within ±.0001 inch of perfect roundness to a surface smoothness of 2 or 3 rms if desired. This apparatus can be used on diameters ranging from 3/8 inch O. D. up to the capacity of the lathe—this depending on the chordal width of the spherical surface.

LENS-GRINDING METHOD. Figure G-31 shows how a lens might be ground in a lathe to a near perfect curvature, using a portable grinder.

The illustration shows a setup for grinding four lenses simultaneously on a mandrel. The glass blanks are cemented to the mandrel with hot wax.

The cup wheel must be a soft one, in the area of 100-N

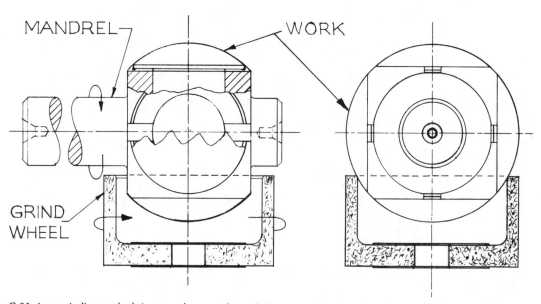

Fig. G-31. Lens-grinding method. Lens can be ground in a lathe to near perfect curvature using a portable grinder.

grain, Alundum vitrified. This wheel will leave a dull finish on glass. A thick-walled hollow lap, shaped to fit the lens' curvature, is used in conjunction with lapping abrasives and rouges to bring out perfect transparencies.

Always use a generous supply of soap water when you are grinding to keep the work cool. Soap water prevents the wax from softening and releasing the work, as well as prevents the glass from cracking.

Now available is a patented motor-driven apparatus for machining, grinding, and lapping spherical surfaces, whether metallic or nonmetallic (Pat. #4,092,902).

GRINDING SMALLER-DIAMETER BALLS. Figure G-32 shows a novel method of grinding smaller-diameter balls. This apparatus (U.S. patent #3,104,502) is a comparatively simple tool. The upper eccentric rotating plate containing the balls is urged downward by a helical coil spring. It presses the balls down against a flat abrasive belt. The grades of abrasives can be varied to suit. The abrasive belt

travels over two drum-type pulleys.

The counterbore in the upper rotating member is eccentric to the axial center of the spindle. This eccentricity causes the balls to roll over in infinite directions, while the abrasive belt helps to rotate as well as abrade the bottom side of the ball. This can be considered a *sphere-generating process*.

For ball sizing, a ball or two should be removed for measuring from time to time.

If very close tolerance is required, a larger number of balls should be processed, then graded as to their size. The size separation can be done by using two straight blades set apart about .001 inch out of parallel and slanting downward longitudinally, approximately 1°. By permitting the balls to roll down between the two blades, they will drop through, each at its respective diameter opening.

GRINDING NONMAGNETIC WORK. Figure G-33 shows a method of holding nonmagnetic materials for grinding

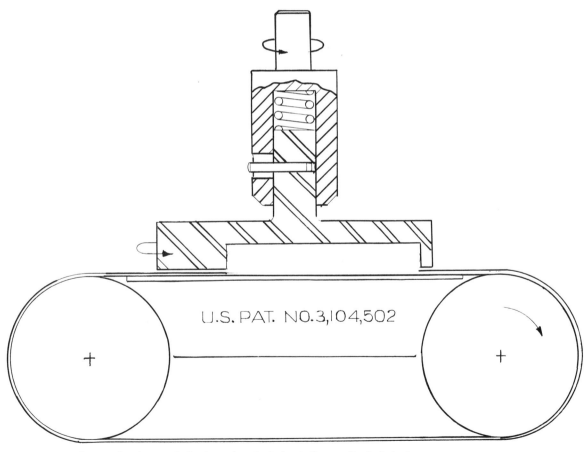

U.S. PAT. NO.3,104,502

Fig. G-32. Grinding smaller-diameter balls. A novel method of grinding smaller balls is shown.

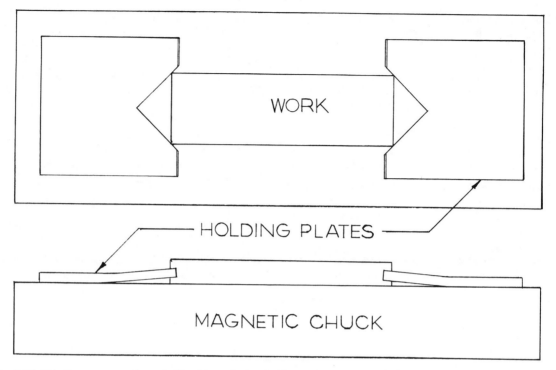

Fig. G-33. Grinding nonmagnetic work. Use this method to hold nonmagnetic materials for grinding on a magnetic chuck.

on a magnetic chuck. To prevent the work from sliding away while grinding, butt two steel plates having **V** cutouts, as shown, against the ends of the workpiece. It is more advantageous to have the **V** cutout ends bent upward from 4° to 8°. When the chuck is energized, the bent-up ends are pulled down somewhat. In doing so, a slight end pressure is exerted against the work.

The holding plates should be from 1/16 to 1/8 inch thick.

Anything less than 1/16 inch in thickness does not have quite enough magnetic attraction.

GRINDING WARPED FLAT WORK. Figure G-34 shows a good method of setting up a warped piece of metal on a magnetic chuck for flat-surface grinding. The object is to shield off the warped section of the work from the magnetic pull of the chuck. To do so, place steel shims under

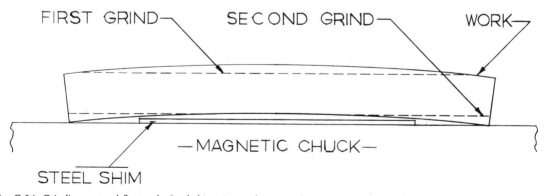

Fig. G-34. Grinding warped flat work. Steel shimming under warped open portions stops the magnetic pull of the chuck.

the elevated (warped) section of the workpiece before you energize the chuck. It is better if the shim is not allowed to touch the work. Steel shims thusly placed interrupt the magnetic downward pull where it is not wanted.

After a clean-up grind of about 80 percent on the top side, turn over the piece and shim it under any of the remaining open portions. Then, grind this second side to about 80 percent of total cleanup. Follow by turning the work over and again grinding a little more off the first side and without any shims. Repeat on the second side without shims. The more times the piece is flopped over and ground, the straighter or flatter it becomes.

HOLDING BRITTLE AND IRREGULAR WORK IN THE GRINDING VISE. Figure G-35 shows a group of irregular, crooked, and brittle pieces (W) set up in a vise for grinding. Here you use a parallel block (P) that is thick enough to support and project the pieces above the vise jaws.

Separate the pieces with narrow strips of water and oil-proof material (S), such as Cranite gasket material. These need be no more than 1/8 inch wide and thick enough to

positively separate the workpieces from one another as well as the vise jaws. Place these strips in a straight line near the work ends, as shown. The setup prevents most bending and consequently breaking of the brittle work when the vise is tightened.

After you grind the tops, turn the pieces over, with their ground side resting on the parallel block. Again insert the narrow separating strips between the pieces. Mere thumb pressure on top of the work is enough to hold the work down against the parallel block while you carefully tighten the vise.

After you finish the second side, lay the pieces flatwise on a high enough parallel block, one at a time, and grind them. The number 2 flat side is ground by resting the pieces with their first ground side down on the parallel. You can grind the ends square by gripping more than one piece at a time and rolling the vise over on its side.

THREADING-TOOL GRINDING BLOCK. Figure G-36 shows a multiangled steel block, which is sometimes used to uniformly grind thread-cutting tools. The illustration shows the block made for grinding 60° thread tools on a

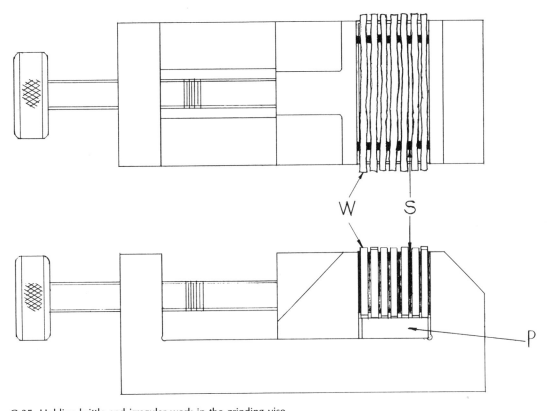

Fig. G-35. Holding brittle and irregular work in the grinding vise.

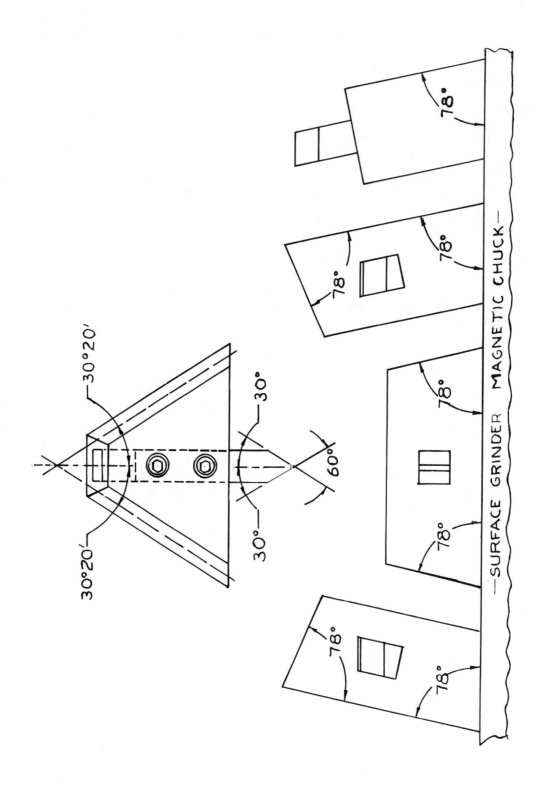

Fig. G-36. Threading-tool grinding block. Use this block when you need a threading tool to be ground exactly, such as for screws to be used for setting thread snap gages.

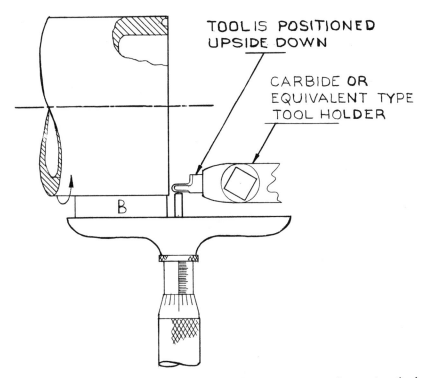

TOOL IS POSITIONED
UPSIDE DOWN

CARBIDE OR
EQUIVALENT TYPE
TOOL HOLDER

B

Fig. G-37. Tool-setting. Use this method to position a cutting tool for cutting an exact diameter into the face of the work.

surface grinder. Of course, you can make up blocks for the cutting of other threads as well. These tool-grinding blocks are especially useful when you are threading master screws for setting thread snap gages.

GROOVING

TOOL-SETTING. Figure G-37 illustrates a method of closely positioning a tool for cutting an exacting groove diameter into the face of a job.

First, the outside of the work must run true and its diameter be known. Then, if need be, you can use a riser block (B) to raise the depth micrometer far enough away to clear the tool holder. Knowing the block's thickness, the outside diameter of the work, and the groove's outside diameter, you can easily calculate what the micrometer's reading should be to give you the desired groove diameter.

The actual cutting is done with the tool positioned upside down, and rotating the work in the reverse direction. It could also be done on the back side of the work, with the tool positioned upside down and the work rotating in the conventional direction. Because it is on the front, or operator's side, the first method is much more convenient.

INDICATING

CHECKING HOLE LOCATION. Figure I-1 shows how bores in a piece of work can be precisely checked for correct locations. This method uses a vernier-type height gage in conjunction with a test indicator and precision-gage blocks. It is difficult to obtain close readings with the vernier height gage alone.

If the bores in the workpiece are quite small in diameter, fairly snug-fitting pins should be inserted into the holes. Precision-gage blocks totaling the exact required height (X) are combined, to which the test indicator is set to read zero.

Passing the indicator over the pins, then subtracting one-half the pins' diameter, will indicate the exact axial center of the bore. A combination of holes in any pattern can be checked in this fashion with the use of trigonometry. (See Fig. T-65 to 68.)

It is always better to clamp the work to a precise angle plate, whereby the work can be flopped over 90°, permitting checking from two sides. This procedure automatically forms the necessary right-angle triangles used in the calculations.

INDICATING A PUNCH MARK. Figure I-2 shows a simple, yet effective, method of trueing up center-punched work in an engine lathe. The better of the two shown methods is in illustration A. This is a comparatively light steel rod, whose one end is pointed and hardened, while its back end is center-drilled to be supported by the tail-stock center. The rod is bent into a goose neck to give it longitudinal springiness. The back end of the rod can also be held in a drill chuck, but only by a very narrow margin. The rod is test-indicated near its pointed end at X as the work is rotated manually.

Any sharp-pointed lathe center can also be used for this purpose, as shown at B. However, because a center has no springiness to constantly keep it in full engagement in the punch mark, the tail-stock spindle should be screwed out to a point where the tail-stock spindle's crank handle stops at about a 2 o'clock or 3 o'clock position. Then by hanging a light weight on the handle, you will maintain a steady inward pressure of the center against the punch mark.

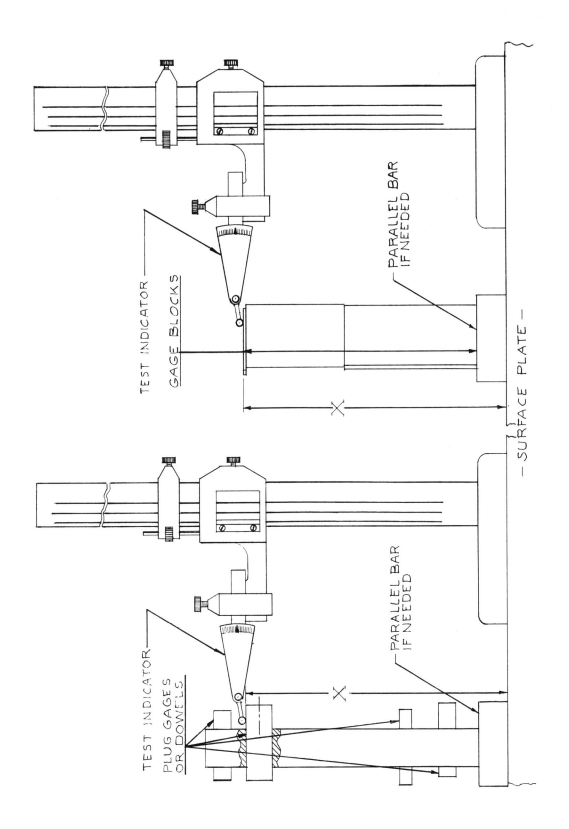

Fig. I-1. Checking hole location. Bores in a workpiece can be checked precisely for proper locations.

121

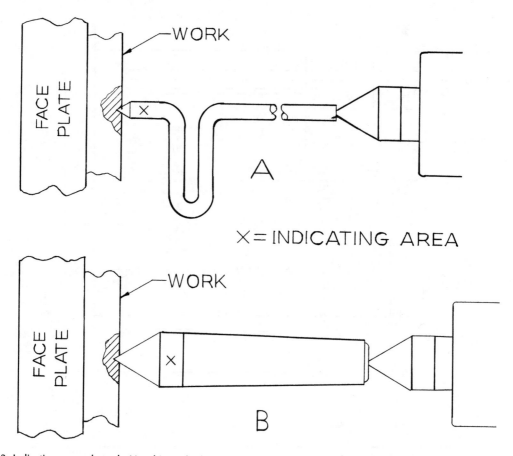

X = INDICATING AREA

Fig. I-2. Indicating a punch mark. Use this method to true up center-punched work in an engine lathe.

JAMMING

JAMMING AND GOUGING. Figure J-1 is an attempt to show why the cutting of metals in the conventional manner, especially in the lathe, is too often not as satisfactory as cutting with the tool positioned upside down and the work rotating in the reverse direction, or, if the machine's range will permit, as boring on the back side of the axial center with the tool positioned upside down and the work rotating in the forward direction.

For example, when you attempt to cut a groove of any size, shape, or depth into the face of the work, as illustrated, you almost invariably run into trouble. The instant the cutting tool begins to cut, the downward pressure on the tool also causes the tool post, the tool holder, and their supporting members to bend downward a slight amount. Not only do those items bend downward, but the type of leverage involved also tips the cutting tool into the work, as shown by A. The result is a much heavier cut than was desired, usually to a point of disaster—breaking off the cutting tool, ruining the job, or both.

As illustrated, there are several points that give (yield) more or less, under the cutting pressure. All these points help to produce the same undesirable effects. The area marked B along the cross slide acts as an additional fulcrum. With a downward pressure applied on the cutting tool, area C tends to open, thereby tipping the tool into the work even more so.

Because machines must be designed much as they are for many reasons, you can usually help ourselves around these difficulties by simply using different machining procedures. By positioning the cutting tool upside down and reversing the work rotation, the cutting results change for the better.

By reversing the cutting tool, the work rotation, or both, it becomes practically impossible for the cutting tool to gouge in under the cutting pressure. Instead, the cutting tool relieves itself very much as does a spring tool.

The principle is like using a shovel to scrape snow off a rough-surfaced sidewalk. The shovel's forward movement will stop when it strikes any roughness. Whereas, if the shovel is turned around and pulled, instead of pushed, it will slide over the roughness. Often the longitudinal carriage feed can be engaged when you are cutting into the face of the work in the reversed fashion.

The principle mentioned is involved in practically ev-

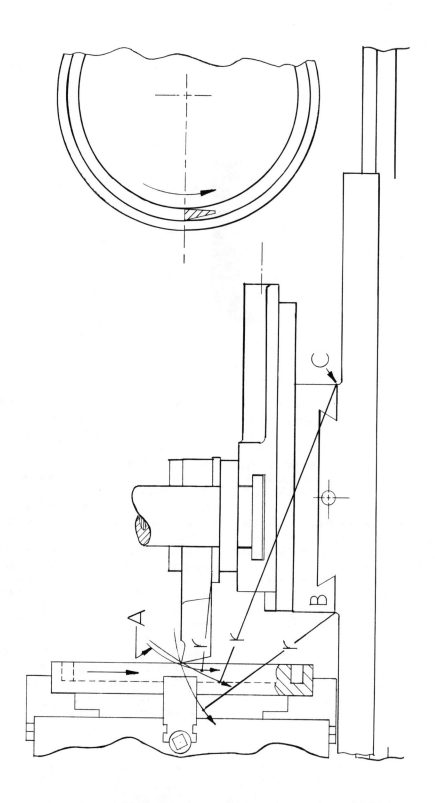

Fig. J-1. Jamming and gouging. The reason the cutting of metals, especially in a lathe, is too often not satisfactory is shown.

ery type of machining operation, whether it be round, flat, internal, or external machining. This principle always should be considered when you are planning any machining operations. The results will be a quicker and a better job, with greater satisfaction and fewer disappointments, even though the method often appears somewhat unorthodox.

JIGS AND FIXTURES

JIGS AND FIXTURES. Jigs and fixtures are designed and built for purposes of machining any number of like parts with greater accuracy, uniformity, and economy. Their designs, styles, shapes, and sizes can be almost infinite. Their types will depend on the number of like pieces to be machined, as well as the degree of accuracy required in the finished part.

Some points that you must always consider when you are designing a jig or fixture are:

☐ Does the number of parts to be machined warrant the cost of designing and building bona fide jigs and fixtures?
☐ What degree of accuracy is required in the finished part?
☐ Does the work come as a rough or partially machined item?

☐ How and from where can the part be located in the jig or fixture?
☐ Will the clamping pressure on the work cause too much distortion?
☐ Can the part be easily put into and taken out of the jig or fixture?
☐ Can the jig or fixture be easily operated by semiskilled help?
☐ Has the correct selection of bushing styles and sizes been made?
☐ Will it withstand some abuse without losing its accuracy?
☐ Are you using a drill jig? They always must stand on four legs to enable the operator to detect immediately whether the jig is setting flat on the machine table or not. Any chip beneath any one of the four legs will cause the jig to rock. A jig having only three legs will not rock when it is standing on a chip; thus, it might give the operator a false setting.

For example, let us assume we have a large number of like castings to be machined as shown in view 4 of Fig. J-2. The parts must all be interchangeable.

Before any jigs or fixtures can be designed we must figure on the best probably machining sequences (processing). In this case, we decided to mill-off the base bottom first,

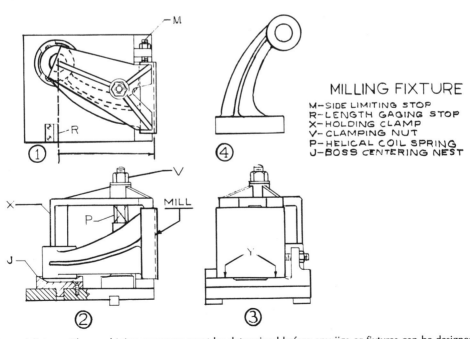

MILLING FIXTURE

M–SIDE LIMITING STOP
R–LENGTH GAGING STOP
X–HOLDING CLAMP
V–CLAMPING NUT
P–HELICAL COIL SPRING
J–BOSS CENTERING NEST

Fig. J-2. Jigs and fixtures. The machining sequence must be determined before any jigs or fixtures can be designed.

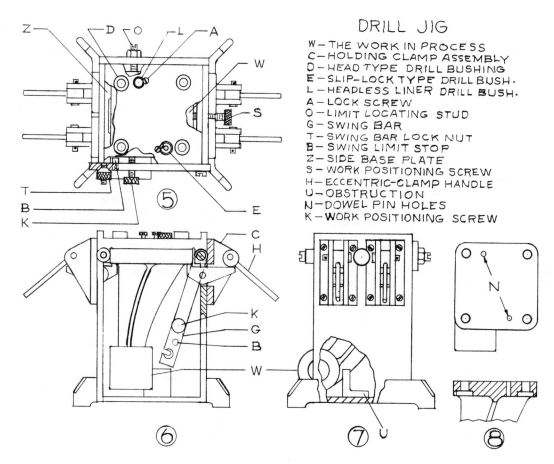

DRILL JIG

W — THE WORK IN PROCESS
C — HOLDING CLAMP ASSEMBLY
D — HEAD TYPE DRILL BUSHING
E — SLIP-LOCK TYPE DRILL BUSH.
L — HEADLESS LINER DRILL BUSH.
A — LOCK SCREW
O — LIMIT LOCATING STUD
G — SWING BAR
T — SWING BAR LOCK NUT
B — SWING LIMIT STOP
Z — SIDE BASE PLATE
S — WORK POSITIONING SCREW
H — ECCENTRIC-CLAMP HANDLE
U — OBSTRUCTION
N — DOWEL PIN HOLES
K — WORK POSITIONING SCREW

Fig. J-3. Jigs and fixtures. The machining sequence, continued.

as shown in view 2. However, to be sure the boss (W) will be in the correct position relative to the machined base, a shallow-angled cuplike nest (J) is provided. The boss rests in the cup as shown. Stud M in view 1 is provided to locate the base tangentially correct in relation to the center of the boss. The excess metal is machined off the base's bottom.

For setting up the job in the milling machine, a fixed gaging block (R) is provided for the measurement of the distance from the axial center of the cup to the machined base bottom. The base's side rests horizontally on two points (Y in view 3) to prevent rocking.

The work is held down by a clamp (X), bearing down on the boss and the top side of the base, as shown. Tighten down the clamp by a nut (V). Then mill the base bottom across in a horizontal, knee-column type of milling machine using a carbide, shell-end mill and completing the milling in one pass.

Unclamp the work by unscrewing the nut. A compressed helical coil spring (P) then lifts the loosened clamp so it can be swiveled clockwise approximately 90°, thus permitting the work to be easily removed from the fixture.

After you have deburred the sharp edges around the machined base, insert the work through the front of the drill jig (Fig. J-3, view 6) until the base contacts the back stop (O in view 5). Item U (views 6 and 7) is an obstruction positioned to prevent the operator from mistakingly inserting the work backward, into the drill jig. Screw in the right side screw (S) far enough to push the base of the work against the stop plate (Z). Raise the swinging bar (G, view 6) into place and tighten it by a nut (T). Then tighten screw K only enough to ensure that the work contacts the stop stud (O).

Next push the four clamping handles (H) downward. The clamping pressures raise and secure the work against the underside of the jig's top plate. Four clamps were chosen simply because we must assume the base to be rough and of varying thicknesses at the clamping points. The four independent clamps will better adjust to the thickness variations.

We begin by drilling through the two 3/8-inch dowel holes (N, view 8). Bore the pin-hole locations in the drill jig to receive headless liner bushings (L). Each of these holes also has a screwed-in stop-lock screw (A) alongside, as shown in view 5. Insert a removable slip-lock drill bushing (E) having a .3595-inch inside diameter into the headless liner bushing. This hole diameter will admit a 23/64-inch drill.

After you drill through both dowel pin holes, change to a removable slip-lock bushings (F) having a .3752-inch-diameter hole. Then size two dowel pin holes with a .375-inch reamer.

To help ensure against any possible work movement in the jig when you drill the larger hole, insert two .3748-inch-diameter pins into the reamed dowel holes. These pins should have knurled heads for easier insertion and removal.

These pins also should be chained to the drill jig to prevent their misplacement.

Bore the four corner bolt holes in the jig to receive head-type drill bushings (D), having a .5315-inch inside diameter. This procedure accommodates the body drill for the 1/2-inch bolts.

The job also calls for counterboring the four bolt holes, as shown in view 8. However, not all of the holes can be counterbored in the usual manner with the customary counterboring tools because of the shape of the workpiece. Therefore, a reverse type of counterboring tool must be used for at least the one hole obstructed by the boss. See simple counterboring and spot-facing tools shown in Fig. S-25, or you can use a commercially produced reverse counterboring tool, which has a detachable cutter that is attached from the underside, while the shank protrudes through the hole from above.

To lessen the work-cycle time of the drilling operation, counterbore the one obstructed hole only while the work is positioned in the drill jig. Counterbore the remaining

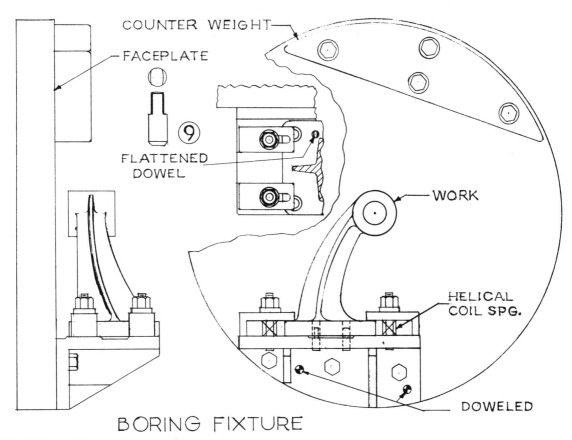

BORING FIXTURE

Fig. J-4. Jigs and fixtures. The boring fixture is shown.

three holes from the rough side in the conventional manner in another drill press.

Where the volume of production warrants, use multiple spindle drilling machines. You can preset their spindles, as well as their tables, for cutting to specific depths, at any desired spindle rotational speeds. The operator merely slides the jig from one spindle station to the next without having to reset the cutting speeds and depth for each piece.

After you have burred all machined holes with a 45° countersink, place the job atop an angle plate fixture (Fig. J-4). You can make this fixture as shown, or you can permanently bolt and dowel the angle plate to a round plate. True-up the plate on the faceplate of an engine or turret lathe.

Pressed into the top work surface of the angle plate are two .3748-inch-diameter dowel pins, located to enter into the two dowel holes in the base of the workpiece. These dowel pins need only enter into the holes in the base of the work, for a distance equal to the pin's diameter.

Grind away the upper portion of one pin on its two opposite sides as shown in view 9, for a distance equal to the pin's diameter. This type of "flattened" pin eases the loading and unloading of the workpiece into and out of the fixture.

The work, precisely aligned by the two dowel pins, is held down by four threaded studs and clamps, as shown When unscrewed, each clamp is lifted slightly by a compressed helical coil spring, thus permitting the clamp to be withdrawn, sidewise, the extent of the slot in the clamp.

For truer machining results, the whole setup must be counterbalanced. The general practice is to attach counterweights to the faceplate, diametrically opposite the loaded fixture. Shift the machine's spindle into neutral to free it from all possible drag. Then, spinning the spindle by hand will indicate whether more or less weight is needed. Move the weight either toward or away from the spindle's axial center until repeated hand spins result in the spindle's rotation coming to a stop in any random radial position.

The job is now ready for the machining of the boss. This procedure might involve boring and counterboring, facing or threading. The initial lateral gaging is done from the face of the plate or faceplate.

For the final assembling of the work with its mating part, an additional drill jig plate is required. This procedure is done during the boring of the drill jig (Fig. J-3). Insert and clamp a suitable piece of steel resembling the base of the workpiece in the drill jig. Then drill and bore the drill jig and drill plate simultaneously. Then press liners and bushings into the bores of each member. Properly locate the jig plate, in turn, by stops, and clamp it to the mating part. In this way, the same precise hole locations are drilled or reamed into the mating part to receive the dowel pins, as well as tap-drilled for the four bolt holes. This method of machining represents interchangeability.

K

KNURLING TOOL. Figure K-1 shows a common, diamond-pattern knurling tool, as used widely in most shops. This tool is held in the machine's (lathe) tool post, and at right angles to the work axis. Considerable pressure of the rollers against the work is required for knurling most metals. It is often impractical to attempt to form a full-depth knurl with just one pass over the work.

The more practical method is to screw the cross feed with the knurling tool into the revolving work. At the same time move the machine's carriage a short distance back and forth by hand. This manipulation properly aligns both rollers to form the correct size of diamond impressions. Regardless of the diameter of the work, the rollers can be made to produce the correct impressions, if started this way. Otherwise, it is common for the rollers to leave double- or half-size impressions.

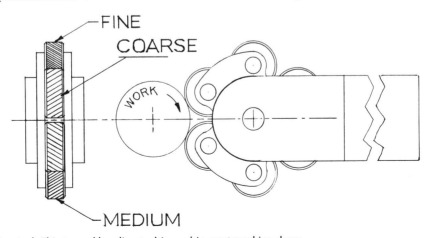

Fig. K-1. Knurling tool. This type of knurling tool is used in most machine shops.

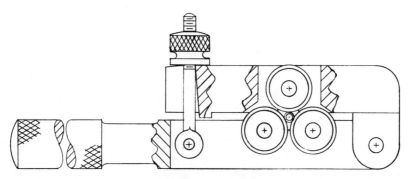

Fig. K-2. Knurling tool, hand.

When the initial pattern appears to be correct, engage the carriage feed at a comparatively fine feed rate. Screw the cross feed into the work with each back and forth pass.

Don't forget, always apply cutting oil to the work, to lubricate the tool and float away the loose metallic particles.

Never run the work too rapidly in knurling, or you will ruin the tool.

Because considerable pressure is required, it is better to complete the knurling before any other finish cuts are taken.

Finally, run a smooth file, very lightly, over the knurl.

KNURLING TOOL, HAND. Figure K-2 shows a knurling tool that is held and moved back and forth over the revolving work by hand.

The standard size of knurling rollers are used. If, however, smaller diameters of work are to be knurled, then smaller diameter knurls must be used.

LAPPING

LAPPING BLOCK. Figure L-1 shows a cast-iron lapping block. These can be round, as well as square or rectangular. The top working surface must be grooved to permit excessive lapping compound from piling up under the leading sides of the work being lapped. Always oscillate the work in a figure eight, and not always in the same area of the block.

The block also wears with use and must be resurfaced from time to time. You can resurface best by making three blocks simultaneously. Then lap each block against the two others. The surfaces of all three blocks become perfectly flat.

The same procedure can be used in finishing off 90° angle plates to perfect squareness. The angle plate lapping process is done on a perfectly flat surface. Scrape each angle plate to where it matches any of the other two plates, and vice versa.

LAPPING OUT A CURLING DIE GROOVE. Figure L-2 shows a method of smoothly finishing off the groove of a curling (beading) die by a lapping process. This smoothness is especially necessary for curling soft materials, metals, or paper.

If the surface is not smooth enough, the material will generally *hand up* instead of curling around inside the groove.

Lap A is made of iron, turned and bored to size. Round the lapping end with a form tool. You can make a simple radius gage to suit as described in Fig. R-1. Smear the curve in the radius gage lightly with Prussian blue paste. Then, trying the gage on the rounded lap end will show where any corrections need to be made. Use fine emery cloth to

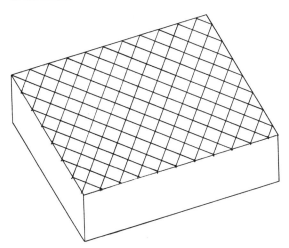

Fig. L-1. Lapping block.

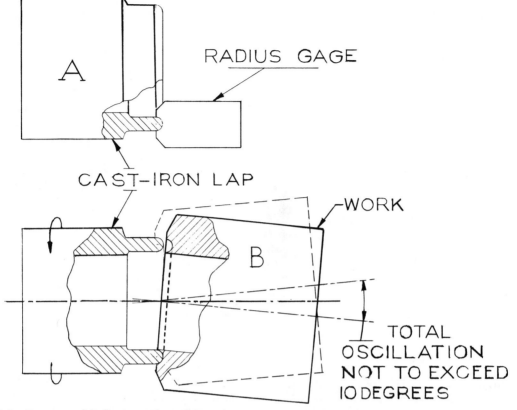

Fig. L-2. Lapping out a curling die groove. This method is used to smoothly finish off the groove of a curling die by a lapping process.

dress the lap to the correct curvature. Oscillate the emery cloth transversely across the surface as the lap revolves in the lathe.

Caution: Do not polish more than the 180° of the lap's transverse curvature.

The lap remains chucked in the lathe. Lightly smear the die groove with a comparatively fine lapping compound, and hand-press it over and engage the lap. While the lap is rotating at a moderate low speed, rock the die from side to side about 5° either side of the lap's axial center, as illustrated by B. To lessen uneven abrasion of the die, allow it to rotate approximately one-third revolution every few seconds. Every so often the lap's form should be rechecked with the radius gage, and corrections made to bring it back to proper form.

The rocking motions of the die are to prevent minute annular lines, or scratches, from developing in the groove's surface. By using a magnifying glass, inspect the die groove for surface quality. To finish the groove's surface, change

the lapping compound to a jeweler's rouge.

This surface-finishing process is slow and does require time and patience.

LAPPING SPHERICAL SURFACES. Figure L-3 shows a simple method of finishing lapping a spherical surface. For the lap you can use either a brass or iron tube faced off at both its ends. You can rotate the lap with a carpenter's bit brace by attaching a shank, or simply press it against the work and slowly rotate the lap by hand. The latter method is more tiring and considerably slower, of course. Serrate the working end of the lap by saw cuts to permit freer flow of the lapping compound. Rotate the work in either a drill press or lathe, depending on its size, but only at a moderate speed, while you press the lap against the sphere and rotate it at a moderate speed.

Because the work and lap rotate across each other's direction of rotation, they cancel out any out-of-roundness in each other. This type of action produces a perfect spherical surface.

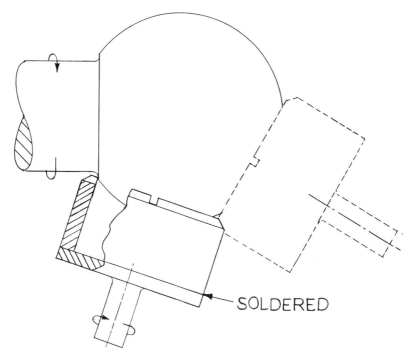

Fig. L-3. Lapping spherical surfaces. A hardened steel spherical surface can be lapped to size and roundness.

LAYOUT

HOLE LAYOUT WITH A VERNIER HEIGHT GAGE.

Figure L-4 shows a common method of laying out hole locations using a vernier height gage. There are several methods of making quite close layouts. Each depends on the shape as well as the nature of the job.

The illustration shows a workpiece being laid out after having at least two of its adjoining sides machined at 90° to each other. First paint the work with blue vitrol, or other layout dye, then clamp it to the side of a 90° angle plate or to a tool maker's knee. The angle plate with the clamped-on workpiece rests on a precise flat surface plate. The work can also be supported by a parallel bar, or the top of the work can be indicated parallel with the surface plate.

If the drawing's dimensions are given from the top and the left side of the workpiece, you merely adjust the vernier to where its flat scriber touches the top side of the work. Using a thin feeler gage, place paper or cellophane of a known thickness atop the workpiece and lightly bear the flat scriber down on the feeler. Knowing the feeler's thickness and the vernier's reading, you can now remove the vernier and lower the scriber the necessary distance plus the thickness of the feeler down to the first hole's centerline. Then scribe a line across the face of the work.

The centerline distance for the next lower set of holes is arrived at in the same way as was the first, or topmost, centerline. This procedure also involves touching the sharp-ended flat scriber on the feeler, which rests on the top side of the work. Next, again lower the scriber the required distance. By repeatedly beginning at the top to scribe each horizontal line's distance, you automatically will minimize the possibility of accumulating additional fractions of errors with each downward progression.

To scribe the intersecting cross lines, keep the workpiece clamped to the angle plate. Then carefully roll the angle plate and attached work over 90° for scribing the intersecting cross centerlines. However, if the work is perfectly square on its sides, you can roll just the workpiece itself over 90°. Then reclamp it to the angle plate. Set the vernier height gage for scribing the cross lines in the same way as described in the first scribing.

You can also scribe the line by starting from the bottom of the workpiece. This method uses measurements taken from the top surface of the parallel on which the work rests.

133

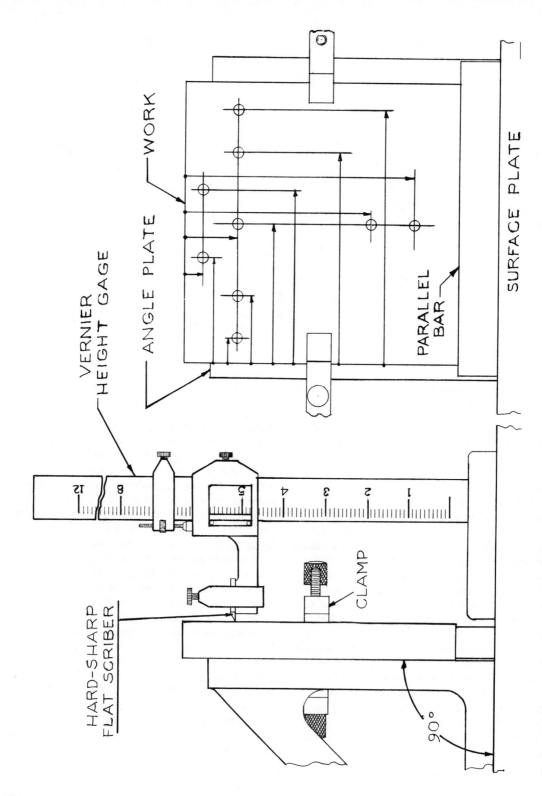

Fig. L-4. Hole layout with a vernier height gage. Hole locations can be laid out quite precisely using a sharp flat scriber in conjunction with a vernier height gage.

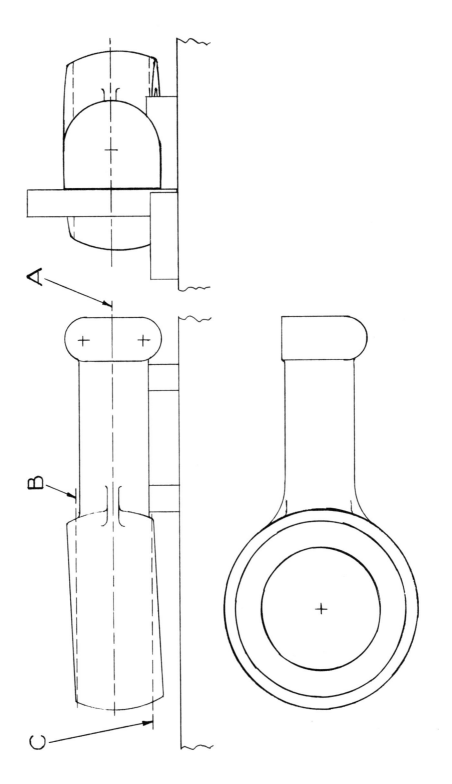

Fig. L-5. Laying out warped castings. Salvage warped castings by first scribing a line, then aligning that line with the face plate, chuck, or machine table.

It is not always necessary to use a precisely graduated vernier height gage. Instead, you can combine various sizes of precision-gage blocks to represent any specific dimension to which the scriber needs to be set.

After all the hold locations have been scribed, the next very important matter is to drill the holes exactly as laid out. For this procedure see Fig. D-26.

LAYING OUT WARPED CASTINGS. Figure L-5 shows a method of salvaging a crooked casting. In spite of some deformity, with some layout and care, the casting becomes as good as though it were symmetrical in every respect. Most castings are made having extra metal on the sides to be machined. Take advantage of this feature by laying the casting on parallels, or shims of suitable height. With the whole setup resting on a reasonably flat surface, scribe centerline A horizontally and completely around the casting. Place the parallels or shims under the area that is not to be machined, as shown.

Whether the job is to be bored in a lathe, mill, or a boring machine, set up the casting by measuring from the centerline to the face of the chuck, the machine table, or fixture.

From the horizontal centerline, scribe two more lines (B and C), both an equal distance from the scribed centerline. The sum of both spaces equal the overall finished width of the illustrated cross head.

After the boring, face-off the head to either one or both of lines B and C, in the same setup. You now have a more correctly proportioned casting that is ready for the succeeding operations.

MILLING

CLIMB-MILLING. To mill any work with the cutter rotating against the direction of feed is a most common milling practice. When you are using a slitting saw type of cutter, which has no side teeth, the results are usually quite disappointing. Because of no side teeth, the cutter has no means by which to clear itself and continue cutting in a straight line.

Although everything might have been aligned exactly, yet in a longer and deeper cut, the cutter gradually veers off to one side. If the cutting is continued, it forces the cutter past its yield point, causing it to break, as well as resulting in a ruined job.

It is often good practice to reinforce a thin cutter on each side with a heavy washer (Fig. M-1). This method does help to produce a much straighter cut, with the cutter projecting out only slightly more than the intended depth of the cut. The other alternative is to cut a very shallow groove on the first pass (cut). Then increase the depth with each succeeding cut. The first shallow cut helps to guide the following, deeper cuts. In all these instances, the tendency is for the cutter to stray, nonetheless.

If the cutter runs true and is symmetrical in every way, why does it not follow a straight line? The theory is that, in the conventional cutting practice, the cutter bottom bends trying to resist cutting. This resistance comes from starting each chip from a zero thickness and forcing each tooth to break through any glaze left on the groove's bottom by the preceding tooth. Thus, if the cutter is forced into the cut under these pressures, it naturally will bend ever so slightly and tend to veer off to one side or the other. Also, because there are no side teeth for the cutter to constantly correct itself, it continues to stray.

In *climb-milling*, or rotating the cutter with the machine's table travel, the thin cutter also flexes, not only to a lesser degree, but at a different moment. In climb-milling, the cutter's teeth are more nearly pulled straight through the cut, as compared to being pushed through, as in conventional milling practice.

In climb-milling, the work is fed into the cutter, and each tooth is presented with a fresh unglazed surface. This surface is more nearly at right angles to the tooth's cutting edge, as compared to the conventional method of starting each chip from scratch.

Climb-milling also creates a peak load on each oncoming tooth. However, here the cutter is pulled, not pushed through.

Whatever the reasons, climb-milling is far superior to conventional milling, in many cases.

Caution! The milling machine's knee, especially the table, must be snugged up fairly tight to prevent the cutter

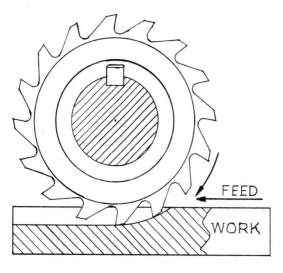

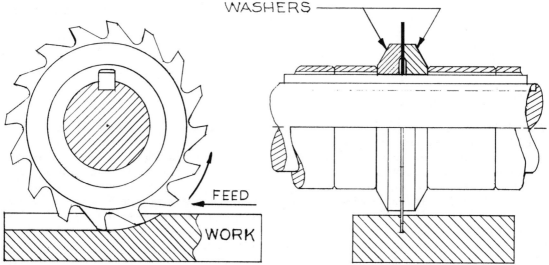

Fig. M-1. Climb-milling. Reinforce a thin cutter on each side with a heavy washer.

from pulling the work into itself. Adjust the table's tightness according to the amount of cut being made.

SLAB-MILLING THIN WORK. With some preparation beforehand, very thin pieces of work can be accurately slab-milled. Figure M-2 shows a setup in a milling machine for milling thin pieces to close dimensions.

For this procedure, prepare the support base-block (A) on which the work is to be machined. The block needs to be only thick enough so that the mill arbor amply clears the clamping nuts and bolts.

The block's width should be about 1/4 inch wider than is the work itself. Clamp the block parallel with the table's T slots, using the four drilled side holes for clamping. Using the same slab cutter as will be used for milling the work, the block is slab-milled over its entire length to ensure parallelness, both lengthwise and crosswise, but not across its entire width. Leave a narrow shoulder (B) on one side of the block. The height of the shoulder must be slightly lower than will be the finished thickness of the work.

The surface on the top of the block is somewhat wider than the workpiece, which should butt up against the shoul-

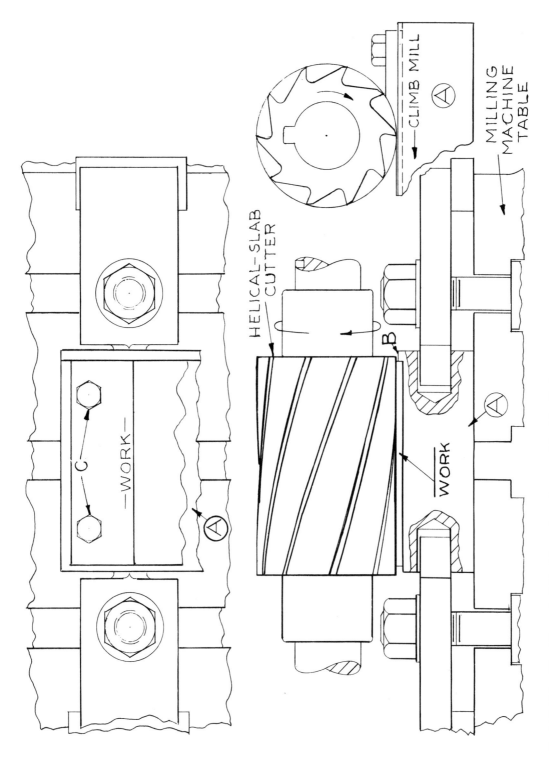

CLIMB MILL

MILLING MACHINE TABLE

HELICAL-SLAB CUTTER

B

WORK

C

WORK

Fig. M-2. Slab-milling thin work. Fairly thin work can be accurately slab-milled.

139

der. If the cutter's helix is right-handed, the block's shoulder should be toward the side of the machine's column. The workpiece is held in place by two anchoring screws (Fig. M-2C).

Begin the cutting at the free end of the work, climbmilling toward the two anchoring screws. After the piece is slab-milled to size, the hole end of the work is merely trimmed off.

MILLING MACHINE COLLET NOSE. Figure M-3 shows a standard milling-machine collet nose. These fit into the hollow tapered end of either a horizontal or vertical millingmachine spindle.

Collet C is of the push type. The tightening of the collet is done by rotating a nut (N) using a spanner wrench. The purpose of the collet nose is to hold and drive endmill cutters. The illustration shows the nose holding a boring bar. Fly cutters can also be run very nicely in the collet nose.

The lighter and smaller milling machines generally use the draw type collets. These are pulled in with a draw bar, running through the mill's spindle.

worm wheel in the dividing head is 40 to 1:

☐ Divide 40 by the number of divisions required. The result gives the number of turns or fraction of a turn of the index crank.

☐ If a fraction of a turn is required, the denominator (the lower part of the fraction) represents the circle of holes to use, while the numerator represents the number of 'spaces' in the circle over which the indexing pin must pass.

☐ Reduce the fraction to its lowest terms and multiply both parts of the fraction by the same number until the denominator equals the number of holes in any hole circle.

$$T = \frac{N}{D}$$

Where:

T = Number of complete turns or fraction of a turn of the index crank.

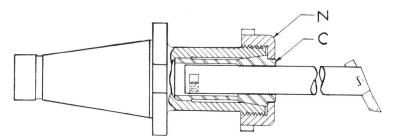
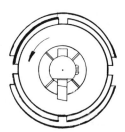

Fig. M-3. Milling machine collet nose.

CINCINNATI UNIVERSAL DIVIDING HEAD. Figure M-4 shows a standard Cincinnati universal dividing head, which is an extremely precise and useful piece of mechanism. It should always be treated with care and respect. The dividing head has many uses, not only in conjunction with the milling machine, but for many other spacing operations as well. Never neglect to lubricate the head, especially when it is in daily use. Never hammer or force any part of the dividing head.

Standard dividing heads have a 40 to 1 gear ratio, meaning that the index crank (G) must be turned 40 times to rotate the head's spindle one complete revolution.

In every case, you must divide the number of required divisions into 40. In calculating the indexing with a side plate in a standard dividing head, use the following rules to obtain the maximum number of settings for any condition of indexing. Since the ratio between the worm and

N = Number of turns of index crank for one revolution of dividing head spindle, or workpiece. Equal to 40 turns in the dividing head.

D = Number of divisions required in the workpiece.

Table M-1 shows an index table for the standard Cincinnati dividing head plate, and indicates the number of divisions that can be readily obtained with the standard head plate. If, however, the required number of divisions is not listed in the table, you must use a different or high-number side plate. Direct indexing is often used for less complicated tool room jobs because it is faster than indexing with the side plate through the 40 to 1 worm reduction.

To change the dividing head into plain index centers, turn the eccentric (located on the back side of the dividing head), disengaging the worm through a quarter of a turn.

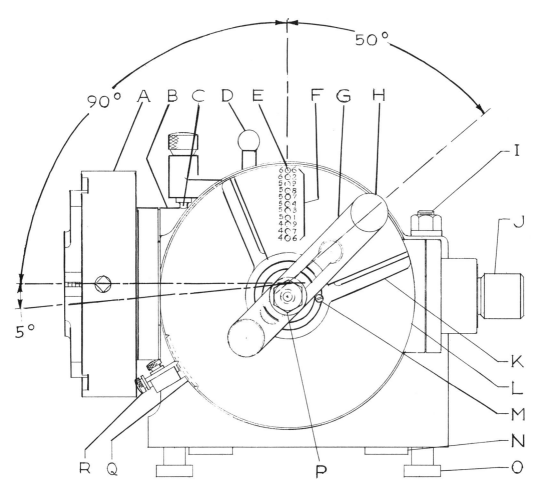

Fig. M-4. Cincinnati universal dividing head.

Then disengage the worm, and index by turning the spindle by hand.

The spindle nose (Fig. M-4B) is drilled with a 24-hole circle. It will index any number that divides evenly into this 24-hole circle.

INDEX PLATE STOP

The index plate stop (R) engages notches on the periphery of the index plate (L), preventing it from rotating. If the head is connected to the driving mechanism for a spiral or helical milling job, the index plate sector and crank rotate as a unit. For such a setup the stop must be disengaged from the plate. In other words, the stop should be engaged only when the dividing head is not connected to the power drive, as when milling spur gears, bolt heads, etc. The stop serves as a safety precaution to prevent mistakes that would occur if the plate itself were moved slightly while indexing.

The index plate stop also may be used as a guide to accurately reset work that has been removed from the dividing head for inspection, etc.

First reset the work in approximate relation with the cutter. Then withdraw the index plate stop and, with the index pin (H) engaged, rotate the crank (G) a sufficient amount to accurately position the work. Re-engage the stop into the notches on the rim of the plate.

Notch two inches of the circumference of the plate. The notches have a pitch of .060 inch. Therefore, a movement of one notice on the index plate is equivalent to 1/18460 parts of a revolution of the work.

A three-jaw chuck (A) is a standard accessory of a dividing head. Another method of holding work is between centers with a center fitting into the tapered nose of the

Table M-1. Index Table for Standard Cincinnati Head Plates.

TABLE OF DIVISIONS OBTAINABLE WITH THE STANDARD INDEX PLATE. THE PLATES ARE DRILLED ON BOTH SIDES WITH CIRCLES OF HOLES EQUALLY SPACED. THE NUMBER OF HOLES IN THE CIRCLES ARE AS FOLLOWS:

STANDARD DIVIDING HEAD PLATE
{ 1ST SIDE—24·25·28·30·34·37·38·39·41·42·43
{ 2ND SIDE—46·47·49·51·53·54·5758·59·62·66

NO.OF DIVISIONS	HOLE CIRCLE	TURNS	SPACES	NO.OF DIVISIONS	HOLE CIRCLE	TURNS	SPACES	NO.OF DIVISIONS	HOLE CIRCLE	SPACES	NO.OF DIVISIONS	HOLE CIRCLE	SPACES	NO.OF DIVISIONS	HOLE CIRCLE	SPACES	NO.OF DIVISIONS	HOLE CIRCLE	SPACES
2	ANY	20		37	37	1	3	80	24	12	148	37	10	248	62	10	460	40	4
3	24	13	8	38	38	1	2	82	41	20	150	30	8	250	25	4	464	58	5
4	ANY	10		39	39	1	1	84	42	20	152	38	10	255	51	8	470	47	4
5	ANY	8		40	ANY	1		85	34	16	155	62	16	260	39	6	472	59	5
6	24	6	16	41	41	--	40	86	43	20	156	39	10	264	66	10	480	24	2
7	28	5	20	42	42	--	40	88	66	30	160	28	7	270	54	8	490	49	4
8	ANY	5		43	43	--	40	90	54	24	164	41	10	272	34	5	496	62	5
9	54	4	24	44	66	--	60	92	46	20	165	66	16	280	28	4	500	25	2
10	ANY	4		45	54	--	48	94	47	20	168	42	10	290	58	8	510	51	4
11	66	3	42	46	46	--	40	95	38	16	170	34	8	296	37	5	520	39	3
12	24	3	8	47	47	--	40	96	24	10	172	43	10	300	30	4	528	66	5
13	39	3	3	48	24	--	20	98	49	20	176	66	15	304	38	5	530	53	4
14	49	2	42	49	49	--	40	100	25	10	180	54	12	310	62	8	540	54	4
15	24	2	16	50	25	--	20	102	51	20	184	46	10	312	39	5	560	28	2
16	24	2	12	51	51	--	40	104	39	15	185	37	8	320	24	3	570	57	4
17	34	2	12	52	39	--	30	105	42	16	188	47	10	328	41	5	580	58	4
18	54	2	12	53	53	--	40	106	53	20	190	38	8	330	66	8	590	59	4
19	38	2	4	54	54	--	40	108	54	20	192	24	5	336	42	5	600	30	2
20	ANY	2	--	55	66	--	48	110	66	24	195	39	8	340	34	4	620	62	4
21	42	1	38	56	28	--	20	112	28	10	196	49	10	344	43	5	660	66	4
22	66	1	54	57	57	--	40	114	57	20	200	30	6	360	54	6	680	34	2
23	46	1	34	58	58	--	40	115	46	16	204	51	10	368	46	5	720	54	3
24	24	1	16	59	59	--	40	116	58	20	205	41	8	370	37	4	740	37	2
25	25	1	15	60	24	--	16	118	59	20	210	42	8	376	47	5	760	38	2
26	39	1	21	62	62	--	40	120	24	8	212	53	10	380	38	4	780	39	2
27	54	1	26	64	24	--	15	124	62	20	215	43	8	390	39	4	820	41	2
28	42	1	18	65	39	--	24	125	25	8	216	54	10	392	49	5	840	42	2
29	58	1	22	66	66	--	40	130	39	12	220	66	12	400	30	3	860	43	2
30	24	1	8	68	34	--	20	132	66	20	224	28	5	408	51	5	880	66	3
31	62	1	18	70	28	--	16	135	54	16	228	57	10	410	41	4	920	46	2
32	28	1	7	72	54	--	30	136	34	10	230	46	8	420	42	4	940	47	2
33	66	1	14	74	37	--	20	140	28	8	232	58	10	424	53	5	960	24	1
34	34	1	6	75	30	--	16	144	54	15	235	47	8	430	43	4	980	49	2
35	28	1	4	76	38	--	20	145	58	16	236	59	10	432	54	5	1000	25	1
36	54	1	6	78	39	--	20				240	24	4	440	66	6			
											245	49	8	456	57	5			

spindle, in conjunction with an adjustable tail-stock center. In this case the work is rotated by a dog. The dog's tail must have no play between it and the driving member. A transverse screw in the driver is provided to tighten against the dog's tail to remove all side play.

Collets and attachments can be provided for holding work of smaller diameters.

SWIVELING THE HEAD

The spindle of the dividing head is housed in a swivel block, allowing it to be swiveled to any angle from 5° below the horizontal to 50° beyond the vertical. This arrangement permits bevel gears of any pitch angle to be milled, as well as many other types of work requiring concentrically spaced slots or holes at an angle to the centerline of the workpiece.

B   Represents the spindle nose.
C   Represents the direct indexing pin.
D   Represents the spindle clamping lever.
E   Represents the holes in the circles of holes, in the index plate.
F   Represents the number of holes in each circle of holes.
G   Represents the adjustable index crank.
H   Represents the pull-out pin, indexing knob.

I   Represents the two swivel-block tightening bolts.
J   Represents the spline shaft for the geared driving mechanism, used only when milling a helix or spiral.
K   Represents the sector arms. When you are plain-indexing a fraction of a turn, and especially when you are repeating this procedure a number of times, you use a sector, which is concentric with the index plate and crank. This procedure enables the operator to locate the index pin in the proper hole without counting the number of spaces that the pin must be moved forward for each division on the work, once he has set the sector arms for the required number of spaces. The two sector arms are set apart to include one more hole than the number of spaces to be indexed.

This factor is sometimes the source of a mistake in setting up dividing head work, and must not be overlooked.

In setting the sector, place the narrow edge of the left arm in contact with the index pin. Move the index crank the required number of spaces and then drop the crank into the corresponding hole. Next, place the right arm of the sector against the pin, and tighten the sector arms by means of lockscrew M.

L   Represents the index plate.
M   Represents the sector arm's lock screw.

Table M-2. Numbers of Holes in the Standard Plate and Fraction of Revolutions for One Space.

CIRCLE	ONE SPACE	CIRCLE	ONE SPACE
24	22'30"	46	11'44"
25	21'36"	47	11'29"
28	19'17"	49	11'1"
30	18'0"	51	10'35"
34	15'53"	53	10'11"
37	14'36"	54	10'0"
38	14'13"	57	9'28"
39	13'51"	58	9'19"
41	13'10"	59	9'9"
42	12'51"	62	8'43"
43	12'33"	66	8'11"

Table M-3. Change Gears for Cutting Approximate Angles of English Lead Helices.

CHANGE GEAR TABLE FOR CUTTING APPROX. ANGLES OF ENGLISH LEAD HELICES

DIAMETER OF WORK IN INCHES

LEAD OF HELIX INCHES	A DRIVEN	B DRIVER	C DRIVEN	D DRIVER	1/8	1/4	3/8	1/2	5/8	3/4	7/8	1	¼	½	1¾	2	2¼	2½	2¾	3	3¼	3½	3¾	4	4½	5	5½	6
2.50	27	45	20	48	8¾	17	25	32	38	43¼																		
2.78	20	45	30	48	8	15½	23	29½	35¼	40½	44¾																	
2.92	21	45	30	48	7½	15	21¾	28¼	34	39	43¼																	
3.24	27	33	19	48	6¾	13¼	19¾	25¾	31¼	36	40½	44¼																
3.70	27	33	19	42	6	11¾	17½	23	28	32½	36½	40½																
3.89	30	36	21	45	5½	11¼	16¾	22	26¾	31¼	35¼	39																
4.17	39	33	18	51	5¼	10½	15¾	20½	25¼	29½	33½	37	43¼															
4.46	39	36	21	51	4¾	9¾	14¾	19¼	23¾	27¾	31½	35	41½															
4.86	42	36	20	48	4½	9	13½	17¾	22	25¾	29½	33	39	44¼														
5.33	33	27	17	39	4	8¼	12¼	16½	20¼	23¾	27¼	30½	36½	44¼														
5.44	33	39	27	42	4	8	12	16	20	23½	26¾	30	36	41														
6.12	27	21	20	42	3½	7¼	11	14½	17¾	21	21¼	27	33	37¾	42													
6.22	33	24	19	42	3½	7	10¾	14¼	17½	20¾	23¾	26¾	32½	37¼	41½													
6.48	42	27	30	48	3¼	6¾	10¼	13½	16¾	20	23	25	31½	36¼	40¼	44¼												
6.67	30	36	--	45	3¼	6½	10½	13¼	16½	19½	22½	25¼	30¾	35¼	39½	43½												
7.29	45	27	21	48	3	6¼	9¼	12¼	15	18	20½	23½	28½	33	37	41	44¼											
7.41	51	30	17	39	3	6	9	12	14¾	17¾	20¼	22¾	28¼	32½	36½	40¼	43¾											
7.62	45	22	19	51	2¾	5¾	8¾	11½	14½	17¼	19¾	22¼	27½	32	36	39½	43											
8.33	30	39	--	36	2½	5¼	8	10½	13¼	15¾	18¼	20½	25½	29½	33½	37	40½	43½										
8.95	48	33	24	39	2½	5	7½	10	12½	14¾	17	19¼	24	28	31¾	35¾	38½	41¼	44									
9.33	42	30	24	36	2¼	4¾	7¼	9½	11¾	14	16¼	18½	23	27	30½	34	37½	40¼	43									
9.52	33	24	27	39	2¼	4½	7	9¼	11½	13¾	16	18¼	22½	26½	30	33½	36½	39½	42¼	45								
10.29	39	20	19	36	2	4¼	6½	8¾	10¾	12¾	15	17¼	21	24¾	28¼	31½	34½	37½	40	42½	45							
10.37	42	27	24	36	2	4¼	6½	8½	10½	12¾	14¾	17	20¾	24½	28	31¼	34¼	37¼	39¾	42¼	44¾							
10.50	21	45	--	20	2	4¼	6¼	8½	10½	12½	14½	16¾	20½	24¼	27¾	31	34	36¾	39½	42	44¼							
10.67	55	27	22	42	2	4	6¼	8¼	10¼	12¼	14¼	16½	20¼	24	27¼	30½	33½	36½	39	41½	43¾							
10.94	48	27	24	39	2	4	6	8¼	10¼	12	14	16¼	20	23½	26¾	30	33	35¾	38¼	40¾	43							
11.11	30	39	--	27	2	4	6	8	10	11¾	13¾	16	9¾	23	26½	29½	32½	35¼	38	40¼	42½	44¾						
11.66	36	19	24	39	1¾	3¾	5¾	7½	9½	11¼	13¼	15¾	18¾	22	25¼	28½	31¼	34	36½	39	41¼	43½						
12.00	36	39	--	30	1¾	3¾	5½	7¼	9¼	11	12¾	15	18¼	21½	24¾	27¾	30½	33¼	35¾	38	40¼	42½	44¾					
13.12	36	19	27	39	1½	3½	5¼	6¾	8½	10¼	11¾	13½	16¾	20	22¾	25¾	28¼	31	33¼	35¾	37¾	40	42	43¾				

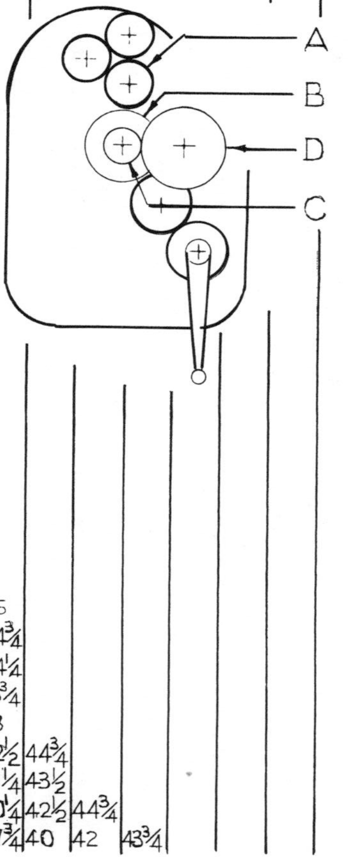

N Represents the two-**T**-slot aligning keys.

O Represents the two head-to-table anchoring bolts.

P Represents the nut used for radially setting the crank's length to match the indexing pin with the radius of the hole circle being used.

Q Represents the adjustment notches on the rim of the index plate.

R Represents the index plate stop.

Table M-2 shows a table for angular spacing. You can calculate the spacing readily, keeping in mind that one complete turn of the index crank equals 9°, one space in the 30-hole circle equals 18°, and one space in the 54-hole circle equals 10°. The tabulation in the table shows the angular movement of the dividing-head spindle for a movement of the index crank of one space in the various hole circles.

HELICAL MILLING. Just about any lead of helix can be readily cut using a universal knee-and-column type of milling machine with a dividing head and a dividing-head driving mechanism, or a plain horizontal knee-and-column type of milling machine equipped with a universal spiral milling attachment.

When you are using the spiral milling attachment, set the cutter, rather than the machine table, at the angle required to place it in the plane of the tangent to the helix to be cut.

Bear in mind that, in helical milling, the value of the helix angle is calculated from or relates to the pitch diameter of the work. Also, the angle is calculated from the axial centerline of the work. If a helical gear or cutter is rolled on a plane surface, the traces of the teeth will line up in equally spaced parallel lines.

Table M-3 shows change gears for cutting approximate angles of English lead helices, as relating to the lengths of the leads and the diameter of the work. For example, to cut a helix 4 inches in diameter and with a 25° angle, follow down the 4-inch column to 25° or to the angle nearest to 25°. In this case it is 25 1/4°. The change gears for this particular angle are 48, 36, and 18. Remember that this angle holds true only at the 4-inch pitch diameter of the work.

The standard Cincinnati enclosed driving mechanism is supplied with all plain, universal, and vertical knee-and-column milling machines as standard equipment, having a lead range of 2.5 inch to 100 inches. It is driven directly from the lead screw. For leads shorter than 2.5 inches, extra parts must be built into the machine. Consult the milling machine manufacturer for this case.

Many leads can be obtained other than those listed in the table. If you do not find a lead in the table that is close

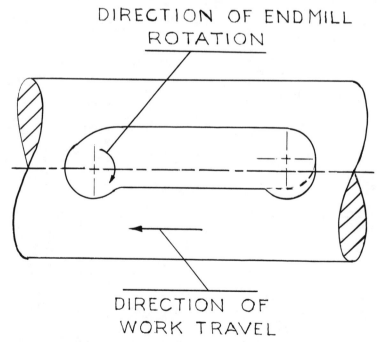

DIRECTION OF END MILL ROTATION

DIRECTION OF WORK TRAVEL

Fig.M-5. Slotting with an end mill. Using an end mill is not always satisfactory when you are cutting key seats.

enough to meet your needs, the following formula will enable you to calculate all the possibilities:

$$\frac{Lead}{10} = \frac{Driven}{Drivers} = \frac{A \times C}{B \times D}$$

SLOTTING WITH AN END MILL. Figure M-5 shows the irregular path of an end mill cutting a key seat.

At the start, a flat-bottomed hole is drilled, or usually milled out, to proper depth with a two-lip end mill, which also cuts endwise, as does a flat-bottom drill.

By engaging the longitudinal table feed, the end mill, resisting the cut, begins to pull over and away at approximately 45° to the shaft's axial centerline. The cutting be-

comes parallel with the shaft only after the cutting pressure against the end mill becomes equal with the cutting and bending resistance of the cutter. Adding to this undesirable effect is some probable sideplay in the machine's spindle, weak work support, a loose table, and too long an end mill. Everything bends more or less.

When the feed is disengaged, the cutting load lessens immediately. As the tensions relax, the end mill cuts itself back into its original centered position.

The result is a crooked and off-center slot. To avoid these results, it is better to start with an end mill that is one size smaller in diameter than the print size for the roughing cut. Then finish with the required size of end mill. Employing a shorter end mill will also reduce this discrepancy.

PIPE

AMERICAN STANDARD TAPER PIPE THREAD. Figure P-1 shows the fitting standard for an American standard taper pipe thread. The illustration is self-explanatory. The threads are always at right angles to the pipe's axial centerline. (See Table P-1.)

The standard rate of taper of the pipe thread is measured in any one of four ways: 3/4 inch per foot measured on diameter, 1/16 inch per inch, 3° 34′ included angle, or 1° 47′ from the centerline.

For sealing leaks in threaded pipe joints, various paint-

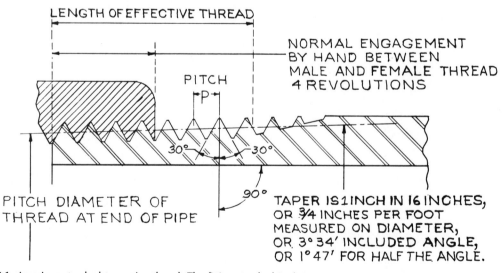

Fig. P-1. American standard taper pipe thread. The fitting standard is shown.

Table P-1. American Standard Pipe Sizes.

NOMINAL PIPE SIZE INCHES	ACTUAL OUTSIDE DIAMETER INCHES	TAP DRILL SIZE INCHES	THDS PER INCH	DISTANCE PIPE ENTERS FITTING	WALL THICKNESS			WEIGHT-LBS. PER FOOT		
					40 SCHEDULE STD.	80 EXTRA STRONG	DOUBLE EXTRA STRONG	40 SCHEDULE STD.	80 EXTRA STRONG	DOUBLE EXTRA STRONG
1/8	0.405	11/32	27	3/16	.070	.098	----	0.25	0.32	----
1/4	0.540	7/16	18	9/32	.090	.122	----	0.43	0.54	----
3/8	0.675	37/64	18	19/64	.093	.129	----	0.57	0.74	----
1/2	0.840	23/32	14	3/8	.111	.151	.307	0.86	1.09	1.714
3/4	1.050	59/64	14	13/32	.115	.157	.318	1.14	1.48	2.440
1	1.315	1 5/32	11 1/2	1/2	.136	.183	.369	1.68	2.18	3.659
1 1/4	1.660	1 1/2	11 1/2	35/64	.143	.195	.393	2.28	3.00	5.214
1 1/2	1.900	1 47/64	11 1/2	9/16	.148	.204	.411	2.72	3.64	6.408
2	2.375	2 7/32	11 1/2	37/64	.158	.223	.447	3.66	5.03	9.029
2 1/2	2.875	2 5/8	8	7/8	.208	.282	.565	5.80	7.67	13.695
3	3.50	3 1/4	8	15/16	.221	.306	.615	7.58	10.3	18.583
3 1/2	4.0	3 3/4	8	1	.231	.325	----	9.11	12.5	----
4	4.50	4 1/4	8	1 1/16	.242	.344	.690	10.8	15.0	27.451
5	5.562	5 5/16	8	1 5/32	.263	.383	.768	14.7	20.8	38.552
6	6.625	6 5/16	8	1 1/4	.286	.441	.884	19.0	28.6	53.160
8	8.625	----	8	1 15/32	.329	.510	.895	28.6	43.4	72.424
10	10.75	----	8	1 43/64	.372	.606	----	40.5	64.4	----
12	12.75	----	8	1 7/8	.414	.702	----	53.6	88.6	----
14	14.0	----	8	2	.437	.750	----	62.2	104.	----
16	16.0	----	8	2 13/64	.500	----	----	81.2	----	----

like pastes—such as red or white lead, litharge, and glycerine—are smeared over the thread or into the coupling before the male and female are screwed together.

If the joint must resist corrosion, the male thread is tinned with soft solder before the joint is permanently screwed together. However, if the pipe's operating temperature will approach a dull red heat (about 900° F) then the male thread can be tinned with hard (silver) solder. These solders come in several melting temperatures, ranging from 1050° F to 1350° F.

Because the thin coating of soft or hard solders is considerably softer than a steel or iron pipe, it will force itself, upon tightening of the joint, into any remaining crevices around the thread. The result is a very effective seal, even for the thinnest liquids or gases and under very high pressures.

Occasionally you will run into specifications listed as IPS, meaning iron pipe size. This specification originated when pipes were made of iron and were necessarily thick walled. As time passed, steel pipe making methods were developed that required much thinner walls. Because a very large number of valves, fittings, tools, and standards were already established, it would be too much of an upset to change them. Thereupon, it was decided to reduce the pipe's wall thickness from the inside, which is the reason for the odd internal dimensions of present-day pipe sizes.

PIPE-DRAWING. Pipe or tubing can be drawn to just about any diameter by being pulled through a die in a draw bench. This setup includes a hard die resting freely, radially, in a rigid holder, as illustrated in Fig. P-2.

You must first swage, or reduce in diameter, a few inches of the pipe end to permit its entry into the die. The amount will depend, of course, on the pipe's diameter. The pipe is then coated with a lithpone and shellac compound to lessen the friction and to prevent seizure.

Insert a hard internal sizing pin, usually screwed to the end of a longer shaft, into the pipe. The shaft's forward travel is limited by a stop nut threaded over the rod's tail end, which also keeps the sizing pin registering properly with the die ring. A powerful clamp grips the pipe's swaged end. The rod's stop nut, at this point, is a short distance away from its limiting member.

When the pipe is pulled by power, the rod and the siz-

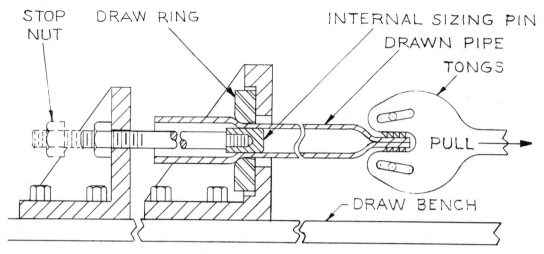

STOP NUT

DRAW RING

INTERNAL SIZING PIN

DRAWN PIPE

TONGS

PULL

DRAW BENCH

Fig. P-2. Pipe-drawing. The principles of drawing a pipe through a die in pipe-making are shown.

ing pin also advance. When the stop nut contacts the limiting member, the sizing pin registers evenly with the die ring. Consequently, the pipe's outside diameter conforms to the hole diameter of the die, while at the same time pressing in on the sizing pin, thus maintaining the drawn pipe's inside diameter.

For small-diameter tube drawing, insert a length of spring (piano) wire into the tube. Swage the tube to reduce its end diameter. Then draw both tube and wire through the die simultaneously. After drawing completely through, grip both ends of the wire in a machine and stretch them. Stretching reduces the wire's diameter, permitting its easy removal from the inside of the tube.

On the larger-diameter draws, pull the pipe completely through the die. Then saw off the swaged end.

As is characteristic of many metals, the pipe or tube takes on quite a rigid work hardness in the drawing process. Before further drawing reductions can be performed, the pipes must be furnace-annealed.

PROCESS ENGINEERING

MACHINING PROCESS ENGINEERING. To produce greater quantities of any more complex parts, which will fit and function exactly as specified, in all cases requires a considerable amount of planning.

One reason for planning is that no two or more mechanics think quite alike. Without planning, jobs requiring the efforts of many mechanics would invariably result in as many quality variations. Also, proper planning enables less expensive help to produce the same precise results at a much lower cost.

Even when full-fledged precision mechanics are employed to produce the same precise parts, each would very likely make his own interpretation of the drawing's dimensions, as well as the best procedure to follow. In every case the cost of production would be tremendous.

Therefore, it is customary to employ the knowledge of those well enough skilled in their particular fields to sketch and write up all the operational steps required to do a job from beginning to end. This procedure can be done to any extent and detail as is required.

If a variety of machinery is already set up, then the process engineer must have a list of the available machines, names, number, capacity, and location. If the machinery is not set up, then machinery suitable for the production requirements are ordered and set up on the floor, according to the machining sequence and routing sheets.

Time estimates for each machining operation are also made from the process sheet layout. The estimates dictate the number of machines that might be needed to produce some specified number of parts per hour, day, or whatever.

It is also up to the process engineer to determine and show how the part should be held and where for each machining operation; what types of holding fixtures might be best suited for each operation; what types of cutting tools are required; what jigs, tools, and gages will be needed; as well as where the machined surfaces are to be gaged from (this detail is most critical).

It is up to the tool-design division to draw and have made or ordered all specified tools, fixtures, gages, and jigs for the particular operation, as per the requests of the process engineer.

150

The whole idea of processing any part is to fully study and analyze all its dimensions. What is the part's function? Read all the drawings' notations. Determine if any tolerances can be widened or narrowed and how much. Where best might all longitudinal measurements be made from? In other words, how do you make it?

To be sure, very seldom will the first planned process layout be correct in every detail. More often than not, changes and revisions must be made along the line before the job is satisfactorily completed. Any revisions are also included in the process sheets, accordingly.

You must recognize the fact that nothing can be made perfect, especially in larger-volume production. To hold dimensions extremely close does approach near perfection, but it also raises the cost of production up and out of reach.

For an example of a machining process, let us take a gas turbine compressor disc (Figs. P-3 and P-4). The drawing might come to you as shown, but with many pertinent notes, which are not included here because of lack of space. The material, with its individual serial number stamped on its one face, comes to you as a forging. Its center is pierced through, resembling a large, thick washer.

To put together some of the thinking involved in processing such a part, you begin with the first operation, which is designated as operation No. 5. All operational numbers are in increments of 5 instead of 1,2,3, etc. This numbering method allows space for any additional operations, changes, or revisions to be inserted, without disrupting too many page and operation numbers.

OPERATION 5

Because a Bullard vertical boring mill is rigid enough, and also has provisions for supporting several cutting tools simultaneously, it was chosen for the first, or No. 5, operation.

The forged billet was placed into and trued up in the four-jaw chuck, with the part's stamped serial number on its down, or under, side. The part's serial number, like a person's birth certificate or social security number, remains with the part throughout its life.

The processing consists of two sheets for each operation. One can be considered the *talking* sheet, explaining the type of operation involved; the name, number, and location of the machine to be used, the fixture, tool, gage, and number required; and where the part should be moved to for the next operation. This is also the *routing* sheet (Fig. P-5).

The second, or mating, sheet (Fig. P-6) carries the drawn picture of that particular operation. It includes where and how much of a cut is to be made; how and where the part is to be held; and where the extent of the cutting is to be measured from. The extent and location of the cutting is usually designated by much heavier lines in the sketches.

Outside roughing dimensions shown are plus .030 inch. Inside dimensions are minus .030 inch, in the rough. These dimensions are permitted to vary up to .005 inch either way.

It is customary to rough-cut the top face first, down to the rough dimension shown. Next, the outside diameter was roughed .030 inch over the finished diameter, and down far enough to include part of the lower flange. Next, the bore was roughed out .030 inch below its finished diameter. The bore boss was rough faced to the depth shown, measured from the very top of the piece.

The contoured face cutout was roughed according to a roughing template, maintaining the contour's inner and outer rough diameters. The depth of the contoured face was roughed to the dimensions shown in the sketch.

OPERATION NO. 10

After several sequential trials and considerations, it was decided to transfer the part's serial number from its bottom face to the center of the roughed central flange's periphery. It worked out best this way, requiring fewer serial number transfers, thus eliminating numbering errors.

OPERATION NO. 15

For operation 15, a Bullard mill was chosen because of its side cutting head, which would be needed for roughing out the two flange grooves. (See Figs. P-7 and P-8.)

The top was faced off to the overall rough dimension. The outside diameter roughing was also completed. In this same setup it was decided to rough-turn the 14.030-inch shoulder diameter to the depth shown in Fig. P-8.

The bore's boss was faced to 1/2 inch below the topmost roughed surface and outwardly to approximately a 12.75-inch diameter. The second contoured face was then roughed to a depth of 1.030 inches below the topmost rough surface, using the roughing contour template for the rough gaging.

It was also decided to rough-out the two flange grooves in this setup. Two carbide cutting tools ground to the proper rough-groove width and properly spaced were mounted in reverse in the side turret. With the work rotating in reverse, the two tools were fed straight into the periphery of the work simultaneously, to the groove's rough minor diameter.

It was also decided to rough-face the top side of the upper flange to 9/16 inch from the topmost rough surface, and to the diameter shown in Fig. P-8.

Starting here it becomes a very good practice to inspect

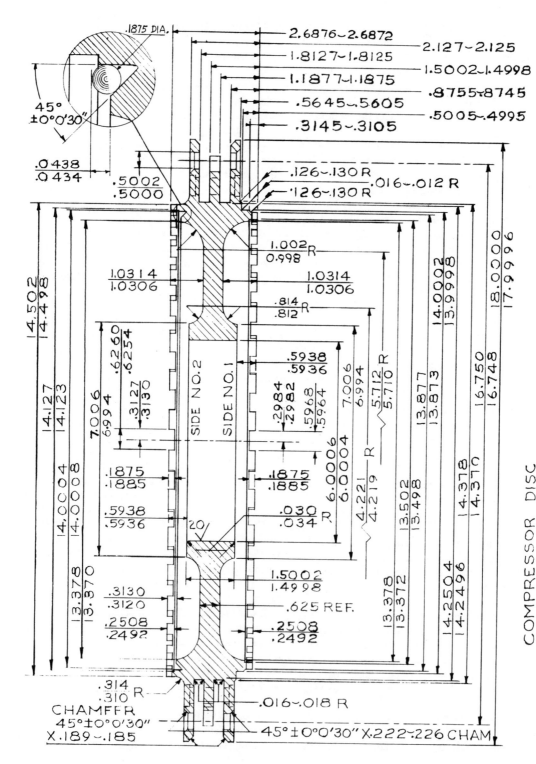

Fig. P-3. Process engineering. Gas turbine compressor disc is the example of a machining process used in this section.

COMPRESSOR DISC

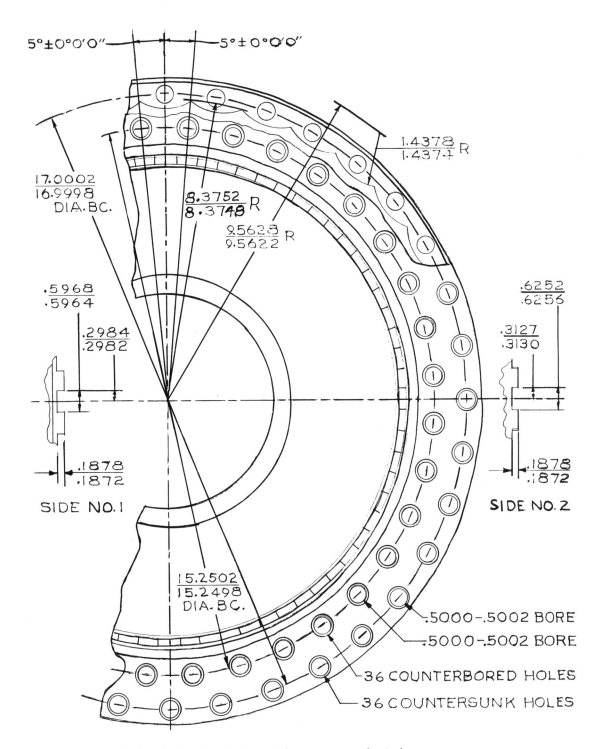

Fig. P-4. Process engineering. Another view of the gas turbine compressor disc is shown.

OPER NO.	MACH. NO. & NAME	LOC.	DESCRIPTION	FIX. NO.	TOOL NO.	GAGE NO.

First form (Fig. P-5)

DATE			CO. NAME HEAD		OPER.NO. 5 & 10	
EST. NO.					DWG. NO.	
					SHEET 1 OF 31	
PART NAME			COMPRESSOR DISC		PART NO.	

OPER NO.	MACH. NO. & NAME	LOC.	DESCRIPTION	FIX. NO.	TOOL NO.	GAGE NO.
5	BULLARD 32	A-6	ROUGH FACE	STD. 4 JAW CHUCK	T-5 BIT CARBIDE	
			ROUGH TURN		T-5-A BIT CARBIDE	G-5
			ROUGH BORE		T-5-B. BAR T-5-C BIT	G-5-A
			ROUGH CONTOUR FACE		T-5-D BIT H.S.S.	G-5-B
10	BENCH 10	A-6	STAMP SERIAL NUMBER IN CENTER OF THE PROPOSED CENTER RIBS PERIPHERY		1/8 STAMPS T-10	
			MOVE TO - A-6 - 32 BULLARD			

Fig. P-5.

DATE			CO. NAME HEAD		OPER. NO. 5 & 10	
EST. NO.					DWG. NO.	
					SHEET 2 OF 31	
PART NAME			COMPRESSOR DISC		PART NO.	

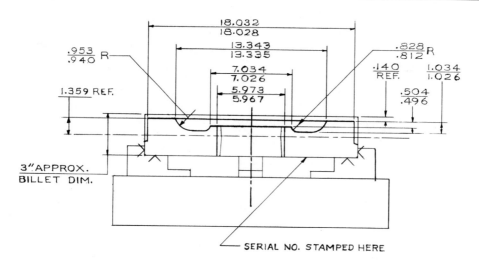

SERIAL NO. STAMPED HERE

PROC. ENG.

SCALE

Fig. P-6.

DATE	CO. NAME HEAD	OPER.NO. 15
		DWG. NO.
EST. NO.		SHEET 3 OF 31
PART NAME	COMPRESSOR DISC	PART NO.

OPER. NO.	MACH. NO. & NAME	LOC.	DESCRIPTION	FIX. NO.	TOOL NO.	GAGE NO.
15	BULLARD 32	A-6	ROUGH FACE-SECOND SIDE	4 JAW CHUCK	T-5 BIT CARBIDE	G-15
			COMPLETE O.D. ROUGHING		T-5A BIT CARBIDE	G-15A
			ROUGH CONTOUR-2ND SIDE		T-5D BIT H.S.S.	G-5B
			ROUGH-OUT THE 2 PERI-PHERAL GROOVES		T-15 2 BITS CARBIDE	G-15C G-15D
			MOVE TO-A-4 LATHE 12			

PROC. ENG.		SHEET OF

Fig. P-7.

DATE	CO. NAME HEAD	OPER.NO. 15
		DWG. NO.
EST. NO.		SHEET 4 OF 31
PART NAME	COMPRESSION DISC	PART NO.

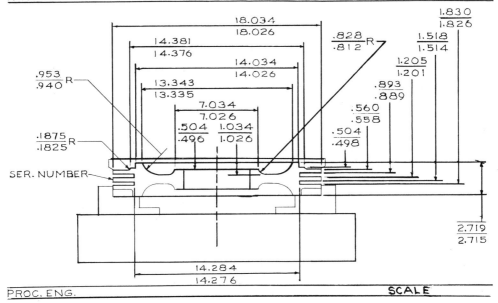

PROC. ENG.		SCALE

Fig. P-8.

the job while it is still in the machine. This step is usually done by those in quality control. Although no close dimensions were held up till now, it would, nonetheless, be extremely foolish to continue further operations if the part already is oversize or undersize at some point.

OPERATION NO. 20

For this operation we again chose a Bullard mill. The work was held in a standard four-jaw chuck. The lower section of each jaw's gripping surface was ground away enough to clear the lower flange's outside diameter. The chuck jaws must bear on the periphery of the central rib only. The work was laid into the chuck and held down by hand pressure when first tightening the jaws. The work was trued-up by indicating to within .003 inch F.I.R. (full indicator reading) the work being gripped rather lightly in the chuck to avoid excessive warpage. (See Fig. P-9.)

In each operation, the holding contact points are indicated by broad arrow heads, such as $\vee < \wedge >$.

Next was to establish, or finish, the datum surface from which all longitudinal dimensioning would be done. The datum surface is often indicated by the symbol: $\otimes$. Only after a thorough study of the job together with some preliminary processing layouts could the datum line be more favorably established.

Since we could not be sure if the two circular grooves were in the proper location longitudinally, in relation to the proposed datum surface, we could have found ourselves in a very awkward position toward the final finishing operations if we suddenly had discovered a lack of material to continue further operations. This situation could occur if the part already shows to be oversize or undersize at some point.

Therefore, to establish the datum surface more precisely, we used a pin gage No. G-20. The pin gage indicates closely enough the amount of material to be removed in finishing the datum surface to bring it more nearly in proper location, relating to the two grooves as well as the rest of the roughed-out disc.

The gage has two slidable and slightly tapering pins coupled at their outermost ends, which are moveable through holes in the gage frame and are spaced apart according to the finished groove-spacing dimensions.

By pressing the throat of the gage frame against the periphery of the two outer flanges (which were rough-turned to the same diameter), while a notched pin in the frame anvil rests down on the rough datum face, the coupled pins are urged by thumb pressure into the groove spaces. The amount of pin projection at the anvil end indicates the amount of material to be removed from the rough datum surface.

The two groove pins are slightly wedge shaped, tapering back for 1 inch from their ends to their entry into possibly varied rough groove widths and spacings.

After having established and finished the datum face, together with the 14-inch shoulder diameter, the 6-inch bore was finished to size. The bore boss was also faced to dimensions shown, measured from the datum face. The underside of the bore boss was faced off next, to dimensions shown. A double-edged radius-form tool in a boring bar was used to round off both ends of the bore, one end at a time. The last part of this operation was the finish facing of the outside of the upper flange to the depth and diameter shown, measured from the datum face.

OPERATION NO. 25

For this operation we moved to a tracer lathe equipped for contour cutting (Fig. P-11). A holding fixture was provided to maintain the trueness already in the part. The fixture was designed as shown in Fig. P-12. The work bore fit over a central pilot projection in the fixture. The pilot's diameter was .0002 inch less than the bore's finished diameter. The pilot's length needed to be no more than 1 1/4 inches. The work was pressed endwise between the pilot's shoulder and a heavy clamping washer. The washer was tightened down by four equally spaced bolts.

In this type of setup, the part runs very true with very slight, if any, run out either way. Because the contour cutting is comparatively light, it is easily supported and driven in this manner.

Special care was taken in drilling and tapping for the four bolt holes. The tapping began not less than 1/2 inch below the face of the pilot's shoulder to minimize possible fixture distortion resulting from bolt tightening.

The contoured depth was gaged from the datum face.

Note: For absolute trueness, the critical pilot's diameter and shoulder should be finish-ground after the fixture is bolted on to the lathe's faceplate.

OPERATION NO. 30

Except for the clamping washer, the same fixture and setup was used to finish the contour on side No. 2. The same contour templates were also used. (See Fig. P-13).

In this operation, the contour's depth was gaged by measuring from the face of the bore's boss through two cutouts in the clamping washer indicated by **X** in Fig. P-14. The depth of the contoured face was less critical.

OPERATION NO. 35

In this operation we permanently transferred the part's serial number from the periphery of the central rib to the web on contoured side No. 2.

DATE			CO. NAME HEAD		OPER. NO. 20		
					DWG. NO.		
EST. NO					SHEET 5 OF 31		
PART NAME			COMPRESSOR DISC		PART NO.		
OPER. NO.	MACH. NO. & NAME	LOC.	DESCRIPTION	FIX NO.	TOOL NO.	GAGE NO.	
			FINISH DATUM FACE AS PER CENTERING GAGE	4 JAW CHUCK	T-20 BIT CARBIDE	G-20	
20	BULLARD 32	A-6	ALSO FINISH DATUM DIA.		AS ABOVE	G-20A	
			FINISH BORE		T-20A T-20B BIT CARBIDE	G-20B	
			FINISH-FACE BOSSES		T-20C T-20D BIT T-20E	G-20C	
			ROUND-OFF BORE ENDS		T-20F BIT	G-20D	
			FACE TOP OF FLANGE		T-20G BIT	G-20E	
			MOVE TO-CONTOUR LATHE 12				

Fig. P-9.

DATE			CO. NAME HEAD	OPER. NO. 20
				DWG. NO.
EST. NO.				SHEET 6 OF 31
PART NAME			COMPRESSOR DISC	PART NO.

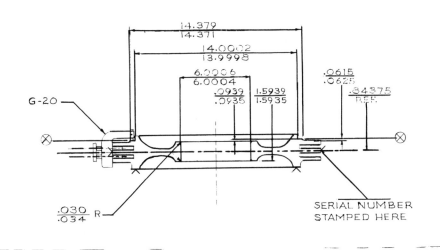

Fig. P-10.

OPER. NO. NO.	MACH. NO. & NAME	LOC.	DESCRIPTION	FIX. NO.	TOOL NO.	GAGE NO.

OPER. NO.	MACH. NO. & NAME	LOC.	DESCRIPTION	FIX. NO.	TOOL NO.	GAGE NO.
25	CONTOUR CUTTING LATHE 12	D-5	FINISH CONTOUR ON THE DATUM SIDE. THIS WILL BE SIDE NO.1	F-25 HOLDING FIXTURE	T-25 BIT CARBIDE	G-25 TEMPLATE G-25A DEPTH GA.
			MOVE TO— NO MOVE			

Fig. P-11.

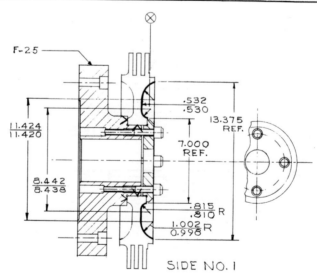

F-25

.532
.530

13.375
REF.

11.424
11.420

7.000
REF.

8.442
8.438

.815
.810 R

1.002
0.998 R

SIDE NO. 1

Fig. P-12.

DATE			CO. NAME HEAD		OPER. NO. 30 & 35		
					DWG. NO.		
EST NO.					SHEET 9 OF 31		
PART NAME			COMPRESSOR DISC		PART NO.		
OPER. NO.	MACH. NO. & NAME	LOC.	DESCRIPTION	FIX. NO.	TOOL NO.	GAGE NO.	
30	CONTOUR CUTTING LATHE 12	D-5	FINISH CONTOUR ON SIDE NO. 2	F-25 HOLD. FIX. F-25-A	T-25 BIT CARBIDE	G-25 TEMPLATE G-25A DEPTH GA.	
35	BENCH	D-5	PERMANENTLY AFFIX SERIAL NUMBER TO WEB OF SIDE 2		T-35 STENCIL		
			MOVE TO- 34 BULLARD				

Fig. P-13.

DATE		CO. NAME HEAD	OPER. NO. 30 & 35
			DWG. NO.
EST. NO.			SHEET 10 OF 31
PART NAME		COMPRESSOR DISC	PART NO.

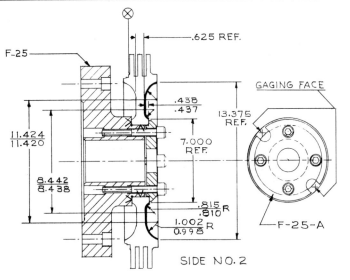

Fig. P-14.

OPERATION NO. 40

To minimize distortion, a fixture quite similar to F-30 was used for this operation. The fixture was bolted to and finished off in the Bullard mill (Fig. P-15). Here the topmost face of the work was finished to size, gaged from the datum face. The 13.500-inch-diameter counterbore, together with the counterbore's depth, was finished to size. The depth was gaged from the datum face.

With the side head, the bottommost face was finished to size, gaged from the datum face.

Because the serial number was transferred from the periphery of the central flange, the central flange's outside diameter now could be turned down to its finished diameter.

The inner sides of the two outer flanges now could be chamferred to the dimensions shown in Fig. P-16. This chamferring was gaged by two 1.500-inch dowels spaced apart the exact distance by a connecting member. The cross member, in turn, was designed to bear on the datum surface. In this way, we get the depth of both chamfers, as well as their exact relationship to the datum surface.

OPERATION NO. 45

For this operation it was again decided to employ a Bullard mill, together with a modified version of the F-25 holding fixture (Fig. P-17). However, since slightly heavier cutting is involved, together with gaging problems, it was thought best to permit the work to also rest on the datum face. This setup would minimize any springing away from the cutting tool's pressure.

The face of the top flange was finished to the dimensions shown in Fig. P-18, together with the 5/16-inch-radius fillet. The 14.500-inch diameter was also finished.

The 14.125-inch counterbore was finished to diameter and depth. The secondary, or 14.000-inch, counterbore also was finished to diameter and depth.

The annular 45° **V** groove was cut in with a single point tool to ensure that its walls were in absolute concentricity. The depth of the **V** groove was measured over a .1875-inch steel ball, gaged from the datum face. All depths in this operation were gaged from the top face of the fixture, which was in the same plane as the datum face.

OPERATION NO. 50

For milling the key slots on the No. 1 side, another holding fixture—F-50—was made. This fixture was centered and bolted onto an indexing fixture, F-50A. A horizontal, knee-column type of milling machine was chosen for this operation. (See Fig. P-19).

It was decided to locate the work by a close-fitting pilot, holding and centering the work very closely. Longitudinally the work rested on the bottom bore boss, as well as on the bottommost end of the disc.

Four strap clamps, as shown in Fig. P-20, were used to press the work downward. The strap clamps are designed to bear on the inner part of the center rib flange, to avoid distorting the two outer flanges, which at this point had finished outer surfaces. The faces of the center rib were not finished yet; therefore for they were able to withstand some slight distortion without appreciably affecting other areas of the job.

A heavy clamping washer and four bolts, as in the preceding fixtures, could also be used to ensure against any possible work movement, the four tapped bolt holes in the fixture's pilot having already been provided.

The 36 key slots were milled with an arbor-mounted staggard-tooth cutter to full depth, as gaged from the datum face. To bring the chips and burrs outward for easier burring, it was decided to cut beginning on the inside and feeding outwardly.

OPERATION NO. 55

The slots on side No. 1 were deburred.

OPERATION NO. 60

The key slots on the No. 2 side were milled in the same type of fixture (F-50) in conjunction with indexing fixture F-50-A. However, instead of the four strap clamps, the job was held down by the heavy clamping washer pressing against the bore boss. (See Figs. P-21 and P-22.)

Because the diameter of the No. 1 side was smaller, it now fit over the two keys in the fixture. The two keys located the job annularly in proper relation to the No. 1 side's slot positions. Also, the two keys prevented the work from any possible annular movement while it was being machined.

The holding fixture also supported the work against the bottommost face, to prevent the job from springing away under the cutting pressure.

A different-width, staggard-tooth cutter was used for milling the key slots in the No. 2 side. The cutter also was fed to cut from the inside outwardly, to a depth gaged from the datum face.

OPERATION NO. 65

Side No. 2's key slots were deburred.

OPERATION NO. 70

The drawing calls for 36 equally spaced scallop cutouts on

DATE		CO. NAME HEAD	OPER. NO. 40	
			DWG. NO.	
EST. NO.			SHEET 11 OF 31	
PART NAME		COMPRESSOR DISC	PART NO.	
OPER. NO.	MACH. NO. & NAME	LOC.	DESCRIPTION	FIX. NO.	TOOL NO.	GAGE NO.

OPER. NO.	MACH. NO. & NAME	LOC.	DESCRIPTION	FIX. NO.	TOOL NO.	GAGE NO.
40	BULLARD 34	A-6	FINISH TURN THE 13.875 DIA.	F-25 HOLD. FIX.	T-40 BIT CARBIDE	G-40
			FINISH 13.500 COUNTER BORE		T-40A BIT CARBIDE	G-40A
			FINISH FACE THE 13.875 DIA.		T-40B BIT CARBIDE	G-40B
			FINISH DIA. OF CENTER RIB		T-40C BIT CARBIDE	G-40C
			FINISH BOTTOM ON SIDE NO. 2		T-40D BIT CARBIDE	G-40D
			CHAMFER INSIDES OF BOTH OUTER FLANGES		T-40E BIT CARBIDE	G-40E
			MOVE TO- 35 BULLARD			

Fig. P-15.

DATE		CO. NAME HEAD	OPER. NO. 40	
			DWG. NO.	
EST. NO.			SHEET 12 OF 31	
PART NAME		COMPRESSOR DISC	PART NO.	

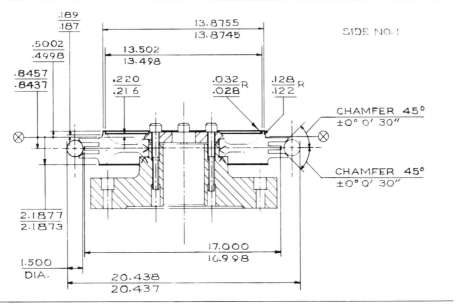

Fig. P-16.

DATE			CO. NAME HEAD				OPER. NO. 45		
EST. NO.							DWG. NO.		
							SHEET 13 OF 31		
PART NAME			COMPRESSOR DISC				PART NO.		
OPER. NO.	MACH. NO. & NAME	LOC.	DESCRIPTION			FIX. NO.	TOOL NO.		GAGE NO.
			SIDE NO. 2						
45	BULLARD 35	A-6	FINISH-FACE TOP FLANGE TO HEIGHT AND DIAMETER INCLUDING THE FILLET			F-45	T-45 CARBIDE		G-45 G-45A
			FINISH THE TWO COUNTER—BORES TO DEPTH AND DIA.				T-45A T-45B CARBIDE		G-45-B G-45-C G-45-D
			CUT THE ANNULAR V GROOVE				T-45 C CARBIDE		G-45-E G-45-F .1875 BALL
			MOVE TO – HOR. MILL 42						

Fig. P-17.

DATE		CO. NAME HEAD	OPER. NO. 45
EST. NO.			DWG. NO.
			SHEET 14 OF 31
PART NAME		COMPRESSOR DISC	PART NO.

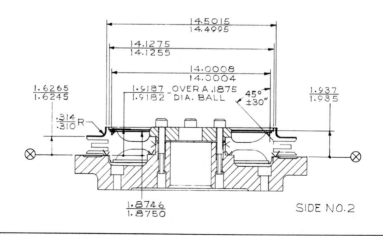

Fig. P-18.

OPER. NO.	MACH. NO. & NAME	LOC.	DESCRIPTION	FIX. NO.	TOOL NO.	GAGE NO.

OPER. NO.	MACH. NO. & NAME	LOC.	DESCRIPTION	FIX. NO.	TOOL NO.	GAGE NO.
			SIDE NO. 1			
50	HOR. MILL 42	B-4	MILL KEY CUT-OUTS ON — NO 1, DATUM, SIDE.	F-50 F-50-A	T-50	G-50 G-50-A
55	BUR BENCH	B-4	DEBURR KEY SLOTS		T-55	
			MOVE TO HOR. MILL 42			

Fig. P-19.

36 EQUALLY SPACED CUTOUTS
.5964 — .5968 WIDE
TO DEPTH SHOWN

SIDE NO. 1

.2984
.2982

.5968
.5964

.312
.310

F-50
F-50-A

INDEXING FIXTURE
36 DIV.

2 KEYS
EACH .5962 WIDE
FIXED 180° APART
TO BE USED IN
LATER OPER.

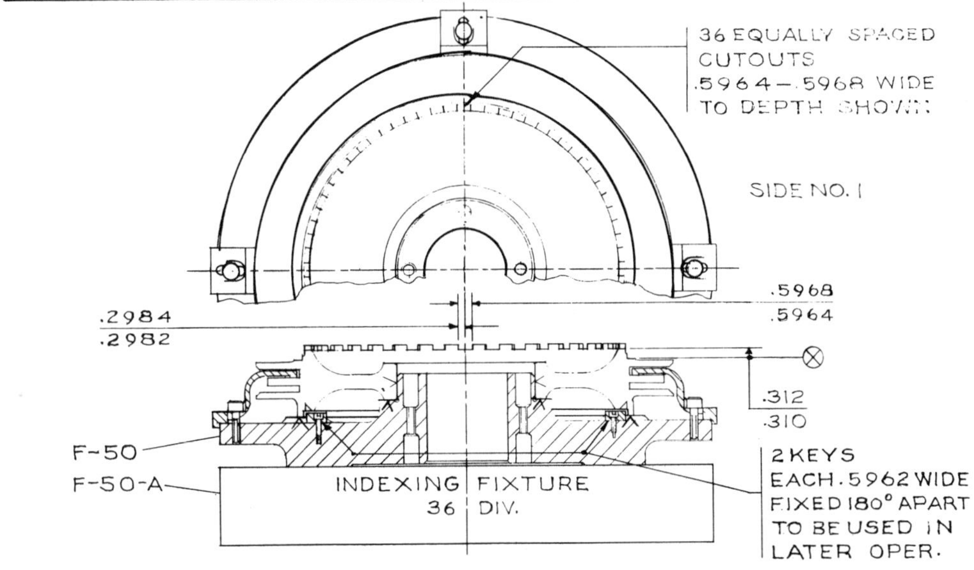

Fig. P-20.

DATE			CO. NAME HEAD		OPER.NO. 60 & 65		
					DWG. NO.		
EST. NO.					SHEET 17 OF 31		
PART NAME			COMPRESSOR DISC		PART NO.		
OPER. NO.	MACH. NO. & NAME	LOC.	DESCRIPTION	FIX. NO.	TOOL NO.	GAGE NO.	
			SIDE NO. 2				
60	HOR. MILL 42	B-4	MILL KEY CUT-OUTS ON NO. 2 SIDE	F-50 F-50-A	T-60	G-60 G-60A	
65	BUR BENCH	B-4	DEBURR KEY SLOTS ON SIDE NO. 2		T-65		
			MOVE TO VERT. MILL 12				

Fig. P-21.

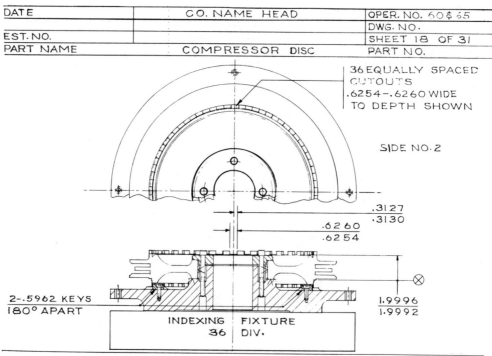

DATE		CO. NAME HEAD	OPER. NO. 60 & 65
			DWG. NO.
EST. NO.			SHEET 18 OF 31
PART NAME		COMPRESSOR DISC	PART NO.

36 EQUALLY SPACED CUTOUTS
.6254-.6260 WIDE
TO DEPTH SHOWN

SIDE NO. 2

.3127
.3130

.6260
.6254

2-.5962 KEYS
180° APART

1.9996
1.9992

INDEXING FIXTURE
36 DIV.

Fig. P-22.

the periphery of the central rib, located in exact annular relation to the milled key slots. For this purpose it was decided to use the same type of holding and indexing fixtures: F-50 and F-50A. The only exception was that two fixture keys were replaced by two longer and wider keys to engage the slots on the No. 2 side. Since the No. 2 side was of a larger diameter. To lessen the cutting load it was decided to fly-cut the scallops using a vertical, knee-column type of milling machine. (See Fig. P-23.)

The fly cutter's axial center was indicated centrally with the fixture's axial center. The machine table and work were moved longitudinally far enough to permit loading. The cutting tool in the bar was projected out far enough to cut a slightly smaller arc than the required finished radius of the cutout. The correct radius was gaged with a metal disc of the proper diameter. The disc first was smeared with a thin coat of Prussian blue, then pressed against the newly cutout surface.

After the correct radius was established, the work was moved toward the fly cutter to the point where the cutter's axial center was at the proper distance, shown in Fig. P-24, from the axial center of the work.

The depth of the cutouts can be gaged from the shoulder of the datum face. For a more positive check, however, it is better to gage diametrically across, from the bottom of one cutout to the bottom of the 180° opposite, cutout.

OPERATION NO. 75

For drilling the 72 holes, fixtures F-50 and F-50A were used. A vertical, knee-column type of milling machine was decided on for this operation because of its slidable table. (See Fig. P-25.)

The two keys in the fixture were indicated parallel with the longitudinal table travel. Next, the index turntable was swiveled one-half revolution, and the keys were indicated as before and from the same side. The test indicator must read the same on the second side as it does on the first side. At this point the cross slide was locked and the cross-feed dial set at zero.

Next, the fixture's pilot was indicated to centralize the fixture's axial center with the machine spindle's axial center. The longitudinal feed dial was set at zero.

Then the work was placed into and tightened in the fixture with its No. 1 side up. (See Fig. P-26.) The machine table was moved away from the machine spindles axial center, longitudinally, a distance equal to the radius of the inner circle of holes. In this case the distance was 7.625 inches. The 36 hole locations were all center-drilled first, followed by drilling through with a 7/16-inch twist drill.

For locating the outer circle of holes, the machine table was moved longitudinally, away from the machine's spindle axial center an additional .842 inch. This amount added to the inner radius of 7.625 inches equals 8.467 inches, which equals the cosine of this particular triangle.

Also move the machine table toward or away from the machine's column a distance equal to the sine value of the 5° angle having a radius length of 8.500 inches. In this case the sine value is .7403 inch. This position is the location of the first of the outer 36 holes. After center-drilling 36 places, each hole was drilled through using a 7/16-inch drill.

OPERATION NO. 80

The 72 holes were finish-bored in a jig-boring machine. A special holding fixture (F-80) was used for this operation. Since indexing fixtures are not always accurate enough, the hole locations were precisely located by using trigonometry, measuring rods, gage blocks, and dial test indicators. In using this method each hole was located within .0002 inch F.I.R. (See Figs. P-27 and P-28.)

OPERATION NO. 85A

To relieve the work load in the jig borer, the jig was put into a vertical, knee-column type of milling machine. Holding and indexing fixtures F-50 and F-50A were used (Fig. P-29). For the counterboring, a short, solid boring bar for cutting flat bottoms was used.

The first hole was located by indicating any one of the finished bored holes in the inner circle of holes. The remaining 35 holes were located by indexing (Fig. P-30). The depth of the counterbores were gaged from the datum face.

OPERATION NO. 85B

To counterbore the second side, the work was turned over in the same fixture. Again, one of the finished bored holes was indicated. The depth of the counterbores were gaged from the datum face.

OPERATION NO. 90A

The countersinking was done using a 45° countersink tool, which has a longer shank to permit it to flex slightly, if necessary, to follow the bored hole more closely. The countersink depth was gaged by placing a .8750-inch-diameter steel ball into the countersink, then gaging its height according to the datum face. The first hole was located by indicating. The remaining 35 hole locations were indexed into position. (See Figs. P-31 and P-32.)

OPERATION NO. 90B

To countersink the second side, the work was turned over

DATE			CO. NAME HEAD		OPER. NO.	70
					DWG. NO.	
EST. NO.					SHEET 19 OF 31	
PART NAME			COMPRESSOR DISC		PART NO.	
OPER. NO.	MACH. NO. & NAME	LOC.	DESCRIPTION	FIX. NO.	TOOL NO.	GAGE NO.
			SIDE NO. 1			
70	VERT. MILL 12	B-4	FLY-CUT THE 36 SCALLOPS	F-50 F-50-A	T-70 T-70A	G-70 G-70A
			MOVE TO VERT. MILL 13			

Fig. P-23.

DATE		CO. NAME HEAD	OPER. NO.	70
			SHEET 20 OF 31	
EST. NO.			DWG. NO.	
PART NAME		COMPRESSOR DISC	PART NO.	

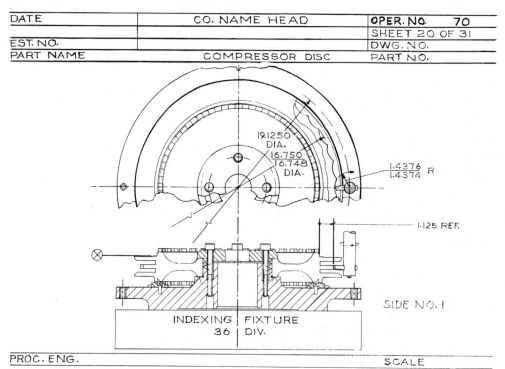

19.1250 DIA.
16.750
16.748 DIA.
1.4376
1.4374 R
1.125 REF.
SIDE NO. 1
INDEXING FIXTURE
36 DIV.

PROC. ENG.		SCALE	

Fig. P-24.

DATE	CO. NAME HEAD		OPER. NO. 75
			DWG. NO.
EST. NO.			SHEET 21 OF 31
PART NAME	COMPRESSOR DISC		PART NO.

OPER. NO.	MACH NO. & NAME		DESCRIPTION	FIX. NO.	TOOL NO.	GAGE NO.
			SIDE NO. I UP			
75	VERT. MILL 13	B-4	CENTER-DRILL AND DRILL — THRU—72—.4375 DIA. HOLES	F-50 F-50-A	T-75 T-75 A	G-75 G-75-A
			MOVE TO—JIG BORE DEPT.			

Fig. P-25.

DATE	CO. NAME HEAD		OPER. NO. 75
			DWG. NO.
EST. NO.			SHEET 22 OF 31
PART NAME	COMPRESSOR DISC		PART NO.

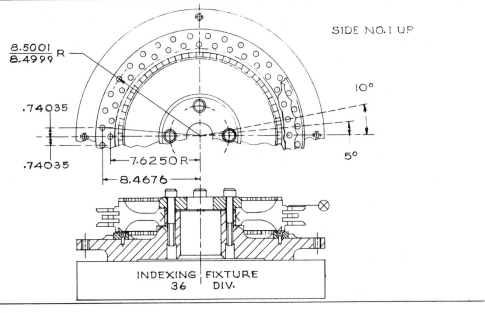

Fig. P-26.

DATE			CO. NAME HEAD		OPER. NO. 80		
					DWG. NO.		
EST. NO.					SHEET 23 OF 31		
PART NAME			COMPRESSOR DISC		PART NO.		
OPER. NO.	MACH. NO. & NAME	LOC.	DESCRIPTION	FIX. NO.	TOOL NO.	GAGE NO.
80	JIG BORER	JIG BORE DEPT.	FINISH BORE THE 72 – .5000 DIA. HOLES	F-80	T-80	G-80
			MOVE TO-12 VERT. MILL			

Fig. P-27.

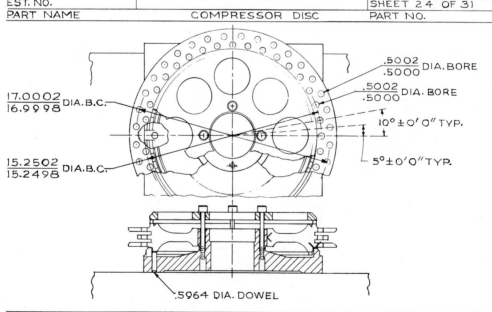

DATE	CO. NAME HEAD	OPER. NO. 80
		DWG. NO.
EST. NO.		SHEET 24 OF 31
PART NAME	COMPRESSOR DISC	PART NO.

Fig. P-28.

DATE			CO. NAME HEAD			OPER. NO. 85A & 85B		
						DWG. NO.		
EST. NO.						SHEET 25 OF 31		
PART NAME			COMPRESSOR DISC			PART NO.		
OPER. NO.	MACH. NO. & NAME	LOC.	DESCRIPTION		FIX. NO.	TOOL NO.	GAGE NO.	
85-A	VERT. MILL 13	B-4	COUNTERBORE THE INNER CIRCLE OF 36 HOLES ON — SIDE NO. 1		F-50 F-50-A	T-85-A-B	G-85-A G-85-B	
85-B	VERT. MILL 13	B-4	COUNTERBORE THE INNER CIRCLE OF 36 HOLES ON — SIDE NO. 2		F-50 F-50-A	T-85-A-B	G-85-C G-85-D	
			MOVE TO — 12 VERT. MILL					

Fig. P-29.

DATE	CO. NAME HEAD	OPER. NO. 85A & 85B
		DWG. NO.
EST. NO.		SHEET 26 OF 31
PART NAME	COMPRESSION DISC	PART NO.

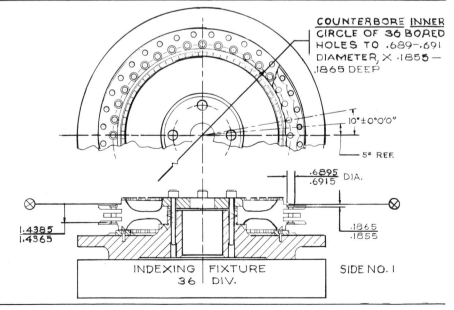

COUNTERBORE INNER CIRCLE OF 36 BORED HOLES TO .689-.691 DIAMETER, X .1855 — .1865 DEEP

10° ± 0°0'0"

5° REF.

.6895 / .6915 DIA.

1.4385 / 1.4365

.1865 / .1855

INDEXING FIXTURE 36 DIV.

SIDE NO. 1

Fig. P-30.

DATE			CO. NAME HEAD		OPER.NO.90A &90B		
					DWG. NO.		
EST. NO.					SHEET 27 OF 31		
PART NAME			COMPRESSOR DISC		PART NO.		
OPER. NO.	MACH. NO. & NAME	LOC.	DESCRIPTION	FIX. NO.	TOOL NO.	GAGE NO.
90-A	VERT. MILL	B-4	COUNTERSINK THE OUTER CIRCLE OF 36 HOLES ON — SIDE NO.2	F-50 F-50-A	T-90-A-B	G-90-B
90-B	VERT. MILL	B-4	COUNTERSINK THE OUTER CIRCLE OF 36 HOLES ON — SIDE NO.1	F-50 F-50-A	T-90-A-B	G-90-A
			MOVE TO– 38 BULLARD			

Fig. P-31.

DATE	CO. NAME HEAD	OPER. NO. 90A &90B
		DWG. NO.
EST. NO.		SHEET 28 OF 31
PART NAME	COMPRESSION DISC	PART NO.

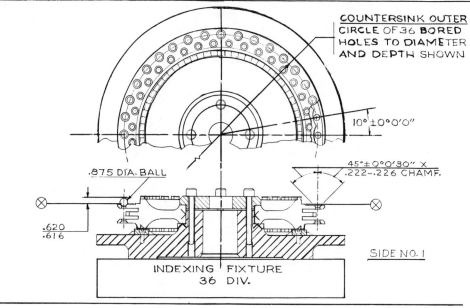

COUNTERSINK OUTER CIRCLE OF 36 BORED HOLES TO DIAMETER AND DEPTH SHOWN

10° ±0°0'0"

.875 DIA. BALL

45°±0°0'30" X .222-.226 CHAMF.

.620 .616

SIDE NO. 1

INDEXING FIXTURE 36 DIV.

Fig. P-32.

OPER. NO.	MACH NO. & NAME	LOC.	DESCRIPTION	FIX. NO.	TOOL NO.	GAGE NO.
95	BULLARD 38	A-7	FINISH OUTSIDE DIAMETER	F-95	T-90 CARBIDE T-90-A CARBIDE	G-90
			FINISH THE 4 FLANGE FACES AND BOTTOMS		T-90-B T-90-C CARBIDES	G-90-A G-90-B G-90-C G-90-D G-90-E G-90-F
			MOVE TO— BUR BENCH			
100		D-8	DEBURR ALL EXTERIOR SHARP CORNERS	F-100	T-100 T-100-A T-100-B T-100-C	
			MOVE TO— FINAL INSPEC.			

Fig. P-33.

SIDE NO. 2

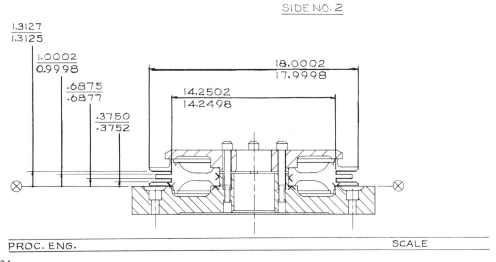

PROC. ENG.   SCALE

Fig. P-34.

in the same fixture. Again, one hole was indicated. The depth of the countersink on the second side was measured over the two .8750-inch-diameter steel balls (Fig. P-32).

OPERATION NO. 95

For the final machining operation, holding fixture F-95 was used (Fig. P-33). Even though the finish cuttings were comparatively light, a larger-diameter clamping plate, as shown in Fig. P-34, was used to hold the work more precisely and maintain the precision already in the part. The datum face of the work also bore against a face of the fixture. The clamping plate was made approximately .020 inch shallower than the distance from the upper boss' face to the extreme top of the work to ensure that the datum face was snug against the fixture.

A Bullard mill was decided on for this operation. Two carbide cutting bits, ground to the specified groove widths minus .0005 inch and spaced the specified distance apart, were mounted in reverse in the machine's side head. The tools were fed straight into the work, with the work rotating in the reverse direction, thus simultaneously finishing off the four flange walls to size and to full depth. After the bottom was reached, the feed direction was reversed to permit the tools to pick up any remaining high spots on their way back.

The gaging was done from the face of the fixture, which is in the same plane as the datum face.

This operation also included finish-grinding the flange walls, ifneed be. This step would involve removing no more than .001 to .002 inch from any side walls, using a saucer-type grinding wheel, of course.

OPERATION NO. 100

All outside corners were deburred.

OPERATION NO. 105

At this stage every machined surface, lateral and annular, should run out no more than .0002 inch F.I.R. The job is thoroughly inspected for any dimensional discrepancies. If the part passes these inspections, it moves on for several more tests such as X-ray, magnaflux, sonic test, and balance. If these are all within tolerance, the fins are assembled into the disc, then spin-tested at 10,000 rpm for a specified length of time. After disassembly, the disc is examined once more for possible diameter increase as a result of centrifical pressures. (See Fig. P-35.)

Only the final inspection group should have the widest permissable tolerances. All others must adhere to the processed dimensions, with no exceptions.

Ordinarily in processing, lateral dimensions are not

DATE			CO. NAME HEAD		OPER. NO. 105		
					DWG. NO.		
EST. NO.					SHEET 31 OF 31		
PART NAME			COMPRESSOR DISC		PART NO.		
OPER. NO.	MACH. NO. & NAME	LOC.	DESCRIPTION	FIX. NO.	TOOL NO.	GAGE NO.	
105			.THOROUGHLY INSPECT FOR ANY DIMENSIONAL DISCREPANCIES. .X-RAY .MAGNA-FLUX .SONIC TEST .BALANCE TEST .SPIN TEST AT 10,000 R.P.M. FOR 15 MIN. .REEXAMINE				
			MOVE TO BOND ROOM				

Fig. P-35.

shown in the conventional manner. Where several steps, shoulders, and faces are involved, each having some particular mating relationship with some other part, you simply cannot add together several steps or shoulders, as shown in the original drawing. There is always the possibility of accumulating too many tolerance fractions, making the part too long, or simply adding together the lower side of the tolerances, making the part too short.

Instead, each step, face, or shoulder spacing is dimensioned individually from a single point: the datum line. In this way each dimension is independent of those adjacent to it, much like machining several different diameters on a shaft, where each diameter is independent of those on either side. To obtain correct lateral spacing, the tolerances on the right side of the datum line can be whatever you wish to make them, but when you are figuring the tolerances on the left side of the datum line, you must halve them to get correct overall lateral dimensions.

R

RADIUS GAGE

RADIUS GAGE. Figure R-1 shows a good method of making a female radius gage. This system works especially well for radii of smaller dimensions. It involves drilling or reaming a hole of the desired diameter through a comparatively thin piece of flat steel, as in Fig. R-1A.

Then saw away as much of the hole as necessary, leaving only enough metal for proper depth finishing, as in B. Gage the depth by employing a dowel with the same diameter, having its one end machined flat, as in C, to the correct depth (X), as measured with a micrometer.

The amount of metal to be dressed off the female radius gage is shown in D.

REAMER

DIAMETER INCREASE OR DECREASE. Figure R-2 shows a method of increasing or decreasing the diameter of a solid reamer. Although this practice is sometimes frowned upon, it nonetheless is a very convenient sizing method for very closely fitting dowel pins, etc. This system is not recommended for reaming more than half a dozen holes after each such treatment, however.

To reduce the reamer's diameter, hold the hone as shown, stroking parallel with the flutes. Do not stroke the hone across the flutes. Stroke each flute about four times, then try the reamer for size in a like piece of metal.

To increase the reamer's diameter, use either a high-

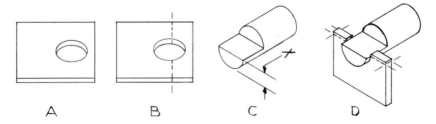

A   B   C   D

Fig. R-1. Radius gage. A good method of making a female radius gage, especially for radii of smaller dimensions is shown. Although it is not perfect, it will suffice in most cases.

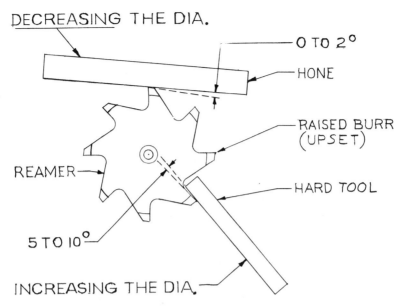

Fig. R-2. Reamer, diameter increase or decrease. This method can be used to increase or decrease a reamer's hole sizing, but it is frowned upon.

speed steel or carbide tool, pressing its dull side against the leading side of the flute's cutting edge, touching the edge as shown. After stroking each flute, a very slight burr, or upset, develops on each cutting edge, thereby increasing the reamer's diameter.

The amount of diameter increase or decrease should never exceed more than .0003 inch.

S

SCROLL-CUTTING

SCROLL-CUTTING. Scroll-cutting, depending on its size and lead, can be done on a rotary table in a vertical-type milling machine, using an end mill for the cutting tool. The rotary table is powered through an auxiliary feed shaft running parallel to the table's longitudinal feed screw. With the proper gearing combinations, almost any pitch or lead of groove can be cut (Fig. S-1).

Scrolls also can be cut in an engine lathe, using a flat-nosed tool fed across the face of the work, much the same as coarse-feeding across any facing job. However, once the cross-feed is engaged, it should remain so until the bottom of the groove has been reached.

If you start the scroll-cutting on the outside of the blank, you must continue until the tool reaches the relief in the center. Then withdraw the tool without disturbing the feed engagement.

You can control the depth of each cut with a micrometer-adjustable screw stop clamped to the ways of the lathe. This stop limits the forward movement of the carriage and consequently the tool's cutting depth. Use a roughing and a finishing tool as for cutting a square thread. Also, you can do the cutting either left- or right-handed.

SOLDERING

HARD-SOLDERING A MULTIWALLED VESSEL. An attempt to hard- (silver-) solder a simple double-walled vessel together presented more of a problem than expected. It was all caused by the thermal expansion of the materials. The job could have been done quite easily had a large enough furnace been available.

However, using an acetylene flame the two cylinders were both readily soldered to the No. 1 end plate, as shown in Fig. S-2. The second, or No. 2, end plate could also be easily soldered with the single flame torch to one of the cylinders, but not to both. Regardless of which of the two cylinders—the inner or outer—was soldered to the end plate first, the second soldering would invariably cause the first joint to break loose.

After some study it was decided to solder both cylinders to the No. 2 end plate simultaneously. This method would permit both cylinders to elongate from the heat to any length. Upon cooling, they would merely ride up and down, exerting no fracturing pressures on any of the joints.

Thus, it was decided to make a multinozzled torch in the shape of a loop. For this tool, a length of 3/8-inch copper tubing was bent around to an appropriate diameter loop,

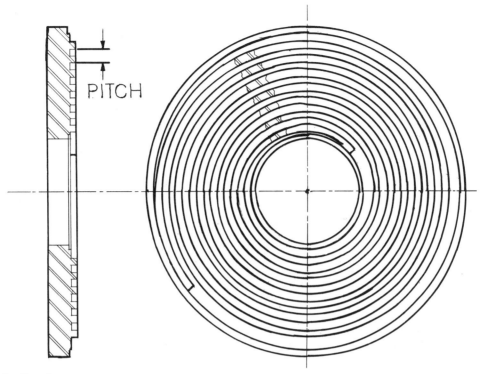

PITCH

Fig. S-1. Scroll-cutting.

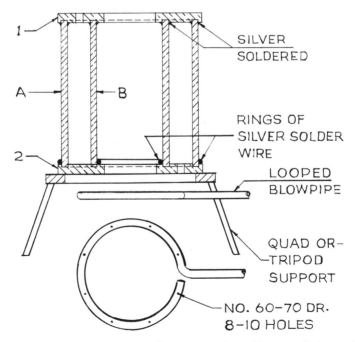

1

SILVER
SOLDERED

A

B

RINGS OF
SILVER SOLDER
WIRE

2

LOOPED
BLOWPIPE

QUAD OR-
TRIPOD
SUPPORT

NO. 60-70 DR.
8-10 HOLES

Fig. S-2. Hard-soldering a multiwalled vessel. An acetylene flame was used to solder two cylinders to the No. 1 end plate.

177

as shown. Eight to ten No. 60 holes were drilled into the loop, as shown. The long pipe's shank was stuffed with steel wool to help arrest possible flaming inside the shank.

A suitable hose coupling was soldered to the shank end to receive the screw couplings from the gas supply tank hoses. The gas ran through a manifold connecting with more than one tank of acetylene. The reason for using more than just one tank of acetylene was because the withdrawal of acetylene gas at too great a rate from a single tank creates an explosive hazard.

After washing the joints-to-be with carbon tetrachloride or acetone, a generous amount of Handy and Harman silver soldering flux was brushed into and around the joints. A ring of silver solder wire was placed around each of the two joints, as shown.

The work itself rested on a convenient stand, while the torch's height was adjustable through the use of clamps. Upon heating, the work expanded quite uniformly. The silver solder ring melted into the joints with excellent results. The separate pieces of the work all expanded and shrunk together.

Remember to always clean the joints with either carbon tetrachloride or acetone before attempting any soldering. Also remember that a thin film of solder results in a stronger joint than one with a greater amount of solder. A seam of solder only .001 to .003 inch thick is stronger than a seam .005 inch or more in thickness.

Instead of using rings of silver solder around the joints, it is sometimes more advantageous to cut the large ring into short sections after bending, especially in the case of larger-diameter work. Also bear in mind that the solder, when melted, prefers to run toward the source of the heat, in every case.

SPRINGS

FLAT SPRINGS. An infinite variety of springs can be made out of flat carbon steel spring stock. Some spring materials might contain various elements such as chromium, vanadium, etc. Flat-spring stock also can be purchased already hardened and tempered. However, this type cannot always be formed as readily without inviting breakage, as compared to forming soft, unhardened stock, especially where sharper bends are called for.

Since all flat stock has a rolling grain, it becomes most important to cut the spring blank so that all bending (flexing) when in use will be at, or nearly at, right angles to the stock's rolling grain. Never bend the stock with the grain, always across the grain.

Figure S-3 shows an example of laying out and cutting

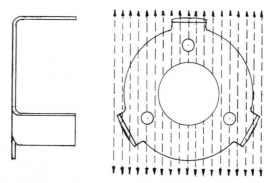

DIRECTION OF ROLLING GRAIN

Fig. S-3. Flat springs. An example of the layout and cutting of the spring blank is shown.

the spring blank so that no part of the spring will be compelled to bend parallel with the grain. Bending parallel with the grain will cause the spring to break at that point in its earliest stages of use, if not before.

For hardening and tempering of springs see Table S-1. *See also* Steels.

SPRING-COILING, HELICAL. Figure S-4 shows a method of coiling helical springs in an engine lathe. Mandrel A, around which the spring wire is wound, can be as long as the lathe's bed, and almost any diameter. However, the mandrel should always be at least 10 percent smaller in diameter than the finished spring's inside diameter. There is always a certain amount of springback, whereby the coil's diameter becomes larger after all tensions are released. The amount of diameter springback de-

Table S-1. Hardening Temperature Colors.

Degrees Centigrade/Fahrenheit		Colors
538	1000	Black Red
649	1200	Blood Red
746	1375	Low Cherry Red
774	1425	Medium Cherry Red
815	1500	Full Cherry Red
843	1550	Bright Red
898	1650	Salmon
940	1725	Orange
996	1825	Lemon
1080	1975	Light Yellow
1205	2200	White-Showing Tiny Bubbles

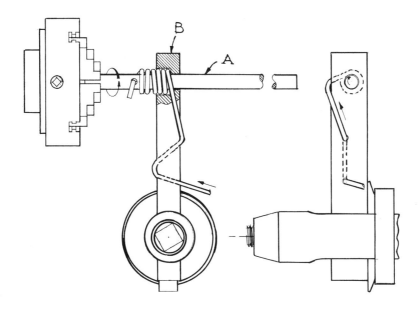

Fig. S-4. Spring-coiling, helical. Long helical springs can be coiled in an engine lathe as shown.

pends on how much tension was applied to the wire as it was pulled into the winding.

The support arm (B), which is held in the tool post, can serve two purposes. First, it can support a long, slender mandrel for winding long, smaller-diameter springs. Second, by counterboring the one side of the support arm, as shown, you can hold the diameter of the coiling to closer dimensions and produce a much more closely wound extension type of spring.

The better method of feeding the wire is through a drilled hole into the counterbore. The hole is on the top or bottom side, next to the counterbore's shoulder; the location will depend on whether the spring is to be wound left or right handed. Also, by pulling the wire around and through the holes in the support arm, you automatically set up a uniform tension, helping to retard the wire's flow.

For tight, close coiling it is customary to measure the wire's diameter. Then set the lead screw's feed rate for cutting that pitch of thread. If such a pitch setting cannot be matched, use the next coarser setting.

A hole drilled, as shown, at right angles through the mandrel is usually sufficient to drive the coiling wire. Bend over a short projecting end of the wire to prevent the wire from pulling out through the hole.

To remove the just-wound spring, disengage the spindle's drive lever or manually rotate the spindle in the reverse of the coiling direction for two or more turns. Then loosen the tool post gradually or loosen the mandrel by opening the chuck.

After all tensions have been released, cut the wire opposite the bent-over end to permit the spring and support arm to be slipped off the mandrel.

Spring-winding machines do not necessarily use mandrels to wind springs. In some, you force the wire to negotiate over grooved rollers. You can space these rollers any distance from each other to produce the desired coil diameter. Also, you can tilt them by cam action to any helix angles to produce a tight and loose spring in the same coiling.

A cutoff tool also actuated by cam action (flying shears) can be set to cut the spring to any required length, without stopping the machine.

UNIFORM COMPRESSION-LOAD SPRING. Figure S-5 shows a novel type of compression spring that in theory requires nearly the same amount of pressure to compress it slightly or fully. Because of its shape, it automatically makes its own load adjustments as it flexes.

Although this type of spring has not been fully tested, it would be safe to assume that, with some modification, it would behave as theorized. This modification would consist of either narrowing or widening the sides (A or B), to make the spring behave as stated.

This type of spring can be fairly useful for hold-down rings in deep-draw dies, where a more uniform pressure is most desirable.

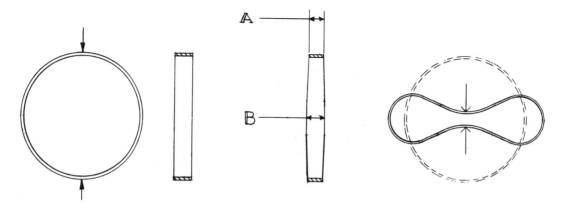

Fig. S-5. Uniform compression-load spring. This novel type of compression spring in theory requires the same amount of pressure to compress it fully or slightly.

SPHERICAL SURFACES

SPHERE-GENERATING FIXTURE, EXTERNAL. Figure S-6 shows a practical, though not the most accurate, sphere-generating fixture. The fixture fastens atop a lathe's compound rest. Also it is hand-cranked, and uses a worm screw and gear to move the cutting tool in a circular pattern. This particular fixture was designed to operate in a horizontal plane, but it can be made to function in a vertical plane as well, by merely modifying its attaching provisions.

It is customary to set the height of the tool's cutting edge on center or slightly below center by shimming under the fixture. This height is not all important. It is most important, however, to set the axial center of the turn table (P) in the exact center with the axial centerline of the work. Improper alignment in this respect will result in either an elongated or shortened sphere.

The easiest method of closely centering the fixture with the work is to have the work running perfectly true at the start.

OPERATION NO. 1

In almost every case a four-jaw chuck and the head stock center are the most convenient for the sphere turning, as will be shown in the following operations.

Figure S-7 shows a method used for center-drilling the stock. Only the tail end needs to be center-drilled at this time. The head-stock center serves as a stop to prevent the work from creeping away from the tail-stock center under heavy roughing-cut pressure.

It is also a very good idea to file a notch, marking the limit of the rough-turning, as shown in Fig. S-7. Paint or chalk markings disappear because of chip abrasion.

After you have roughed the shank, turn the work end for end. With a driving dog slipped over the shank, true-up the work reasonably close and center-drill the second end.

OPERATION NO. 2

With the chuck jaws opened, position the work between centers and drive it by the dog as shown in Fig. S-8. Turn the sphere blank down to approximately .060 inch over the sphere's finished diameter.

Then, using template number one, rough-turn the spherical end. Start near the lateral center of the sphere, using a tool ground for left-handed cutting.

Engage the carriage feed, feeding leftward, at the same time manually turning the cross-feed slide inwardly. Always guide yourself by the template, but only when the work is not rotating. A smear of Prussian blue paste in the template helps to designate the highest points in a roughed work.

When the work rotation resumes, the Prussian blue marks are difficult to see. Therefore, the practice is to lengthen these markings with a soft lead pencil or such for better visibility.

After the front spherical end is satisfactorily roughed, use template number two to bring the second curvature into proper relationship with the first.

Note: templates for this purpose can be made by boring a piece of 1/8- to 3/16-inch-thick steel plate (preferably hot rolled). Bevel the end corners of the bore, after which you can saw the washer into sections of suitable lengths.

When the spherical roughing is completed, install the sphere-generating fixture (Fig. S-6). The height of the cutting tool's edge must be fairly close with that of the work's centerline. Bolt the fixture atop the lathe's compound rest.

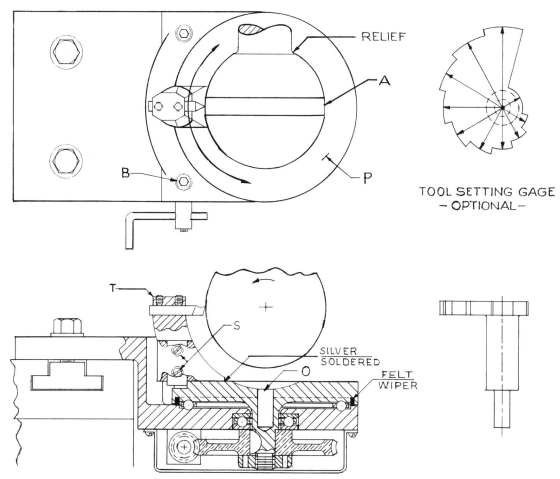

RELIEF

A

B

P

TOOL SETTING GAGE
– OPTIONAL –

T

S

SILVER
SOLDERED

O

FELT
WIPER

Fig. S-6. Sphere-generating fixture, external.

Here, to permit sweeping the cutting tool around the end of the work to more precisely center the fixture, you must back away the tail-stock center. However, before you do, the work must be gripped in the four-jaw chuck once again. Gradually tighten each jaw a little at a time, so as not to disturb the trueness of the head-stock center. Indicate the roughed spherical surface; it should run well within .001 inch F.I.R.

OPERATION NO. 3

Then, by removing screw B (Fig. S-6), disengage the worm screw from the worm wheel, thus allowing a free sweep of the cutting tool from front to back, as illustrated in Fig. S-9.

To achieve this free sweep without hitting the sphere's end, move the lathe's carriage (with fixture) far enough to the right to clear the spherical end, as shown by F in Fig. S-9.

A tiny scar is left at the points where the tool touches the work on both the front and back sides. Encircle these marks with a pencil. Rotate the work 180° and repeat the sweeping. When the tool marks register in the same spots longitudinally, you can assume the fixture is centered. Mark the cross-feed dial with chalk, then tighten the cross-slide gib to prevent accidental cross-slide movement.

Replace the regular tail-stock center by a relieved center (Fig. S-10). Turn diameter A down to the finished diameter of the sphere, or slightly below when permissible, by simply employing the tool in the fixture. Move the tool in or out by cranking the fixture turntable.

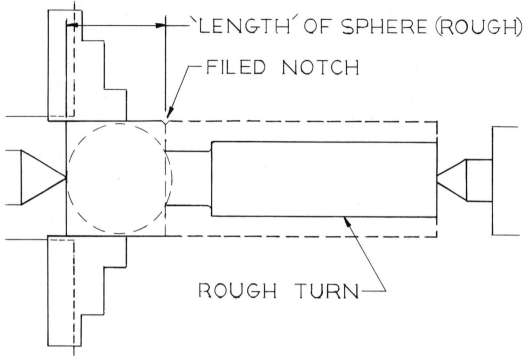

Fig. S-7. Sphere-generating fixture, external. Use this method for center-drilling the stock.

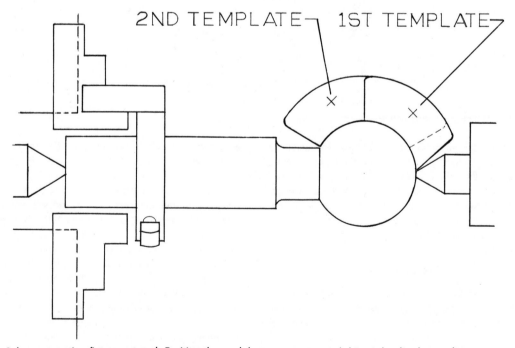

Fig. S-8. Sphere-generating fixture, external. Position the work between centers and drive it by the dog as shown.

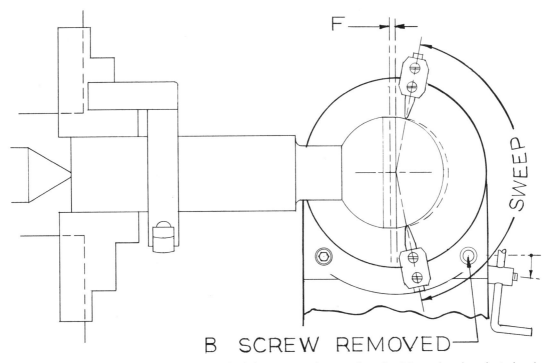

F

SWEEP

B SCREW REMOVED

Fig. S-9. Sphere-generating fixture, external. Move the lathe's carriage far enough to the right to clear the spherical end.

Caution: do not touch the cross-feed handle.

OPERATION NO. 4

For the following spherical finish turning, swivel the tool and tool post to the right as shown at C in Fig. S-10, enough to clear the tail-stock center. Set the tool's cutting radius as in B, nearly touching the turned straight diameter.

Move the carriage to the right far enough to avoid cutting too heavily. Begin cutting at the center hole. Feed to the left far enough to permit a micrometer measurement of the sphere's diameter.

If the cut is too heavy, move the carriage to the left enough to relieve the load. Never start another cut without first bringing the tool around and touching against the first finished spherical surface. Use only the carriage of the lathe for the moving.

The idea is to make a final finish cut, starting at the transverse center of the sphere and first feeding toward the center hole. Without moving anything but the fixture's feed crank, continue by cutting the left side of the sphere, feeding toward the neck as far as conditions will permit.

Generally, it becomes necessary to swivel the fixture's tool post to the left, as at D, for the final corner metal removal.

Now tighten the work in the chuck and withdraw the tail-stock center. You now may file, polish, or lap the sphere.

Figure S-6 shows an optional method of centering the fixture with the work. First, after the sphere is roughed out reasonably close, insert the setting gage into O in the center of the fixture's turntable. Secondly, extend the cutting tool to where it almost touches the annular surface of the desired radius, as indicated by the arrows. Third, continue cutting until the sphere measures within the desired diameter.

Sphere-Generating, Internal. For internal spherical boring, a tool as shown in Fig. S-11 works very nicely, especially where a smaller number of pieces are to be machined, because of the comparatively simple and quick setup that it involves.

The turntables that support the cutting tool can be rotated 360°. However, in boring ball sockets, the rotation needs to be no more than 90°—one-fourth of the circle—or less.

The rotary action is supplied through a square rod suitably bent and having a crosswise hole at each end. The hole at one end fits over a dowel pin pressed into the top of the turntable and located 45° from the cutting tool's center-

183

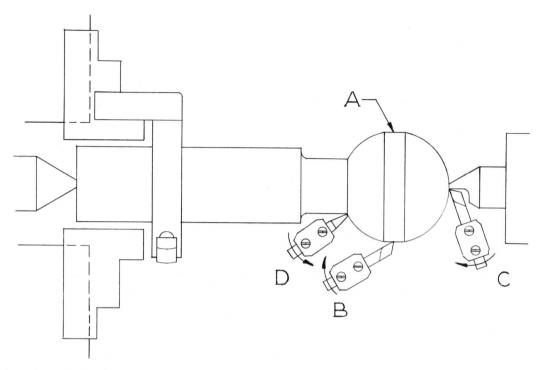

Fig. S-10. Sphere-generating fixture, external. Replace the regular tail-stock center by a relieved center.

line, while its back-end hole fits over a pin pressed into a Morse tapered shank, fitting into the tail stock. The pin also may be pressed into a short piece of steel, which in turn, is held in a drill chuck in the tail-stock spindle.

Rotating the wheel of the tail-stock spindle will cause the tool's turntable to swivel to the left or right. For work setup and cutting-tool alignment, merely lift the connecting rod off the pins to permit the turntable to be manually swiveled from side to side.

With any pointed tool bit in place, slowly advance the boring fixture into the stationary roughed-out bore of the work, while manually swiveling the turntable through a 140° to 180° arc.

When the cutting tool touches both sides of the true running bore, you can assume the boring tool to be centered with the job. A further check is to rotate the work one-half turn and repeat the manual swiveling.

If the cutting tool's edge touches the work at the same depth inward and at the same height as in the first trial, you know the tool's cutting edge is located exactly in the center of the work.

For this type of work, it is best to use a measuring gage made out of a round disc with its corners rounded. Turn its diameter equal to the finished diameter of the spherical

socket. Knowing how deep the spherical bore should be from the face of the workpiece, scribe a limit line across the gaging disc, accordingly. Generally the spherical bore is made slightly deeper, then faced off to the proper depth according to the gage.

After you have centered the fixture, the first object is to cut an arc of the required radius. This step is done by the cut-and-try method, although a tool-gaging method also could be used, pushing the cutting tool in or out to bore the required radial length.

To measure the arc, lightly smear the periphery of the gaging disc with Prussian blue paste then try it in the bore, pressing in lightly while partially rotating the disc. The blue marks will show if and where any corrections need to be made.

When you arrive at the correct curvature, then you must work on the depth of the spherical bore in relation to the face of the workpiece.

SPHERICAL FORM TOOL, INTERNAL. To form-cut an internal spherical surface like that in a ball socket, a simple tool as shown in Fig. S-12 often can be used.

Cut a round disc of high-speed steel as shown. After hardening, grind the tool round, by pressing it over a ta-

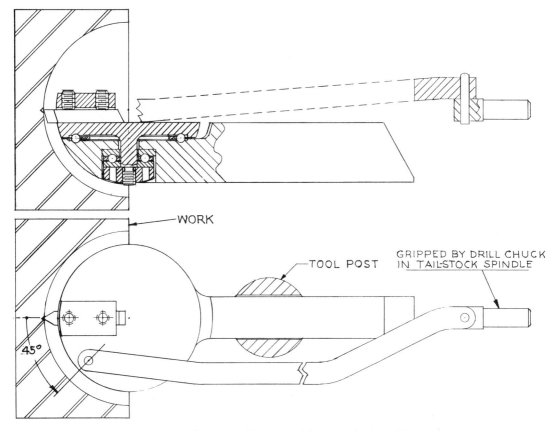

Fig. S-11. Sphere-generating, internal. Use this practical boring tool for internal spherical boring.

pered mandrel. By using eccentric bushings in the center hole, you can resharpen the front "end" of the tool as it wears away.

The tool's back end is flat so as to rest against the bottom of the **U** cutout in the shank. The shank's diameter must necessarily be quite large to prevent chatter.

Tighten the set screw on the tool after if engages the stationary work with which it centers itself. In every case,

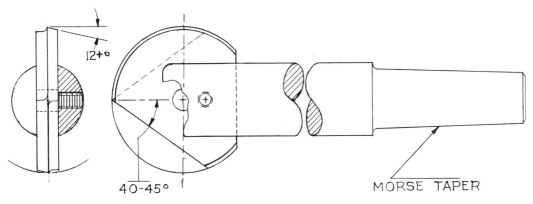

Fig. S-12. Spherical form tool, internal.

before using this tool you must rough-out the work and be sure it is true running, of course.

Shift the machine down to its lowest rotational speed and use a generous supply of sulphur-based cutting oil, especially when you are forming in steel. Use no coolant or lubricant when you are forming in iron.

Caution: Never permit the form tool to ride the surface without cutting. Doing so will dull the tool very quickly.

SPHERICAL FORMING, EXTERNAL. Figure S-13 shows the general method of producing a spherical shape with a form tool. This method is generally used in most turning machines such as engine lathes, turret lathes, and automatic screw machines.

The method's advantage is that it is quite rapid. Its disadvantage is that the results are not as good as those produced by generating the sphere. They are not as round.

The tool's cutting surface must point directly into the

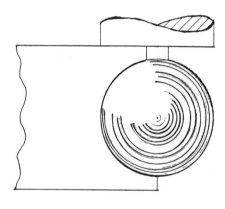

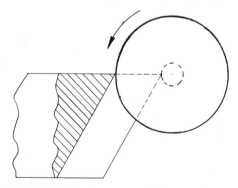

Fig. S-13. Spherical forming, external. The general method of producing spherical shapes, particularly of a smaller diameter as in engine and turret lathes, as well as in automatic screw machines is shown.

center of the work, thereby requiring additional cutting clearance. It must be of the proper shape to result in a more nearly true sphere.

You can help to eliminate chatter by cutting on the back side with the cutting tool positioned upside down or rotating the work in the reverse direction with the tool positioned upside down. The rate of cutting is governed by the rigidity of the ball's neck. As soon as the neck becomes too slender to support the cutting, the ball tends to run away or to climb over the form tool.

This type of form tool is sharpened by grinding the top surface only.

SPHERE-GENERATING IN A MILLING MACHINE, EXTERNAL. Another very good method of generating a nearly perfect sphere is shown in Fig. S-14. This method will work with just one cutting point. However, the generating process is speeded up in direct proportion to the number of cutting edges in the tool.

A setup of this kind can be worked nicely in either a horizontal or vertical milling machine. The work can be held in a dividing head chuck and rotated by power take-off of an auxiliary feed shaft. Disconnect the regular table-feed screw and lock the table to prevent any table movement. If you are working only a few pieces, you can crank the dividing head by hand.

Tilt up the dividing head spindle that is holding and turning the work to prevent cutting off the ball at the neck. This type of setup would also apply to a vertical milling machine.

In a horizontal milling machine, remove the dividing-head keys so the whole dividing head can be swiveled toward the machine's column, whatever the required amount. In a universal milling machine, swivel the table to the desired angle, instead.

SPHERICAL GENERATION. Figure S-15 shows how a spherical section can be cut into a straight shaft using a fly cutter. This type of cutting setup can be done on either a vertical or a horizontal milling machine. Of course, a multiedge cutter, such as a hollow-mill cutter, would be much more advantageous.

A motorized, portable, sphere-generating apparatus covered by a U. S. patent (#4,092,902) is capable of generating attached spherical surfaces in either hard or soft, metallic or nonmetallic, materials to within ±.0002 inch of perfect roundness, with a finish down to 3 rms on diameters ranging from about 3/8 inch up to 6 inches or up to the lathe's capacity. It is limited only by the chordal width of the arc. Here only a micrometer is needed for the gaging.

SPHERICAL GRINDING. Figure S-16 shows a very good method of grinding a spherical surface. For this method,

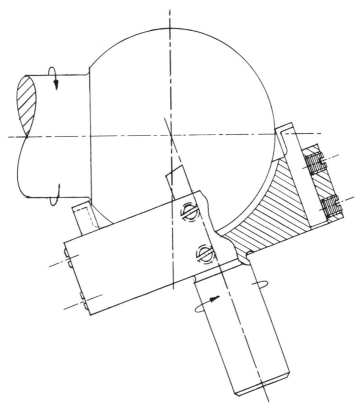

Fig. S-14. Sphere-generating in a milling machine, external. Even a milling machine can be set up to generate spherical surfaces.

use a hollow, cup type of grinding wheel. The wheel's inside diameter needs to be only about 95 percent of the sphere's diameter and of a comparatively loose bond, especially if the work is hardened.

The grinding wheel's spindle is swiveled and locked at either 90° to the work's axial centerline or as nearly to 90° as conditions will permit. The interior of the wheel should cover the complete spherical surface or as much as must be spherical.

The narrower the wheel's cutting surface is, the closer to perfection will be the spherical result.

In setting up, the wheel is rotated by power, while the true running work is stationary. As the wheel is brought up to and touches the work, it will leave a slight scar above or below the work's center. Adjust the wheel's spindle until the wheel touches the work above and below the work centerline at the same time. As soon as the actual grinding begins, you readily can determine the correctness of the alignment by the amount of sparks given off at the top and bottom of the grinding wheel. If it is centered properly, the volume of sparks should be nearly the same above as

below center. The axial centers of the work and grinding wheel must be in exactly the same plane.

Feed the wheel slowly and directly into the work. Keep the periphery of the wheel thinned from the cutting edge outward by using a carborundum stick.

You can make up your own hollow grinding wheels if some difficulty arises in attempting their purchase. You can bore a solid wheel to size with a high-speed or, preferably, a carbide tool bit much as you would bore out a piece of metal. In this case, however, the work rotation must be very slow.

STEADY RESTS

STEADY REST, ALIGNMENT. Figure S-17 shows a method of lining up work in a steady rest when there are no center holes in the work. If the work is hollow and rough, it may be aligned in several ways. In practically every case, the center in the tail-stock spindle also plays an important role.

If the work is round and has center holes in its ends,

187

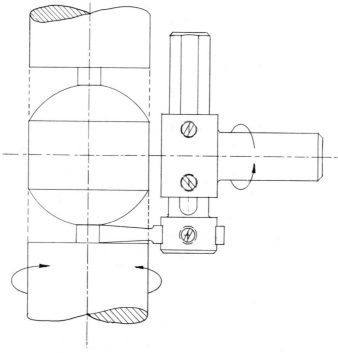

Fig. S-15. Spherical generation. A simple tool can be used to generate a spherical surface into a straight shaft.

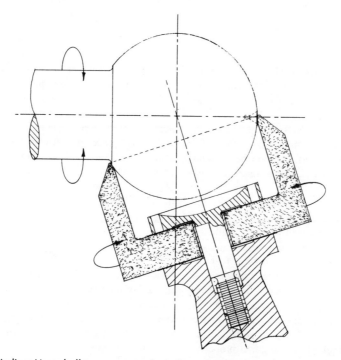

Fig. S-16. Spherical grinding. Use a hollow, cup type of grinding wheel for spherical grinding.

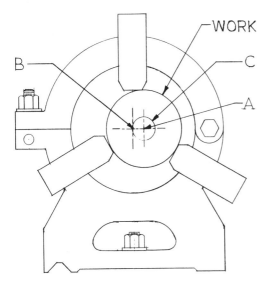

Fig. S-17. Steady rest, alignment in. When there are no center holes in the work, use this method to line up the work in a steady rest.

you merely use the tail-stock center to hold the work in the exact location, while you adjust the steady rest around the work.

However, if no center holes are present, bring the tail-stock center up close to the end of the work, but not touching. Then by holding a pencil, chalk, or scriber against the slowly rotating face of the work, draw the smallest possible circle, as in Fig. S-17C. No matter what the drawn circle's diameter happens to be, the steady rest is adjusted to where that circle's center (A) registers more centrally with the point of the tail-stock center (B).

Although it is not possible to visually set the steady rest exactly, it nonetheless is close enough for the drilling of a straight hole partially into the work. The next step is to countersink the hole with a tool bit, as shown in Fig. C-11, after which the work will be supported by the tail-stock center. You now can withdraw the steady rest.

If, as in larger work which has a rough-cored hole offering no surface on which to scribe circles, a flat piece of metal is driven, flatwise, a short distance in the cored hole, then by painting the flat piece with layout dye, chalk, or such, you can accommodate a circle. Adjust the steady rest until the smallest scribed circle registers centrally with the point of the tail-stock center. Then remove the flat piece to permit machining of the interior of the workpiece.

To align a hollow job more accurately, measure the machined bore for tapering. If the bore's diameter is the same at its front as it is in the back, you can assume that

your steady rest's lineup is good. If the bore's diameter measures less at its back end, then you must shift the work in the steady rest away from you, or toward the back of the machine. These movement directions hold true only when boring or grinding on the back side of the bore. The converse would be true when grinding or boring in the conventional manner, on the front side of the bore.

If no holes are permissible on the end of the workpiece, then you have the choice of scribing the smallest possible circle on the work's end, then aligning its center with the point of the tail-stock center. You should follow this step by indicating longitudinally along the top and side of the work, for as great a distance as possible to check for parallel with the ways.

To check your alignment further, you can smear a straightedge with a thin amount of Prussian blue paste. Then touch the straightedge across the face of the work. The blue mark left on the work will show if and in which way any corrections need to be made in the steady rest.

If the job is finish-faced, run a test indicator across the face to show if the steady rest needs adjusting and in which direction.

If the work is a lengthy shaft calling for longitudinal turning or grinding, adjust the steady rest to produce in the work the same diameters at both ends of the cut.

SPOT-TURNING LARGE SHAFTS FOR A STEADY REST. Whenever it becomes necessary to center-drill large, rough-surfaced shafts in a lathe, set up a steady rest near the shaft's free end (No. 1 in Fig. S-18). Adjust the steady rest very loosely to the shaft's diameter.

While end No. 1 rests in a steady rest, end No. 2 is gripped in a chuck. For safety's sake, keep the steady rest closed. Lubricate end No. 1 well with white or red lead and oil. Purposely set the "top" steady rest jaw a short distance from the rough shaft's surface, but do not allow it to touch the work.

Bring up the tail-stock spindle fairly close to the shaft's end, but not necessarily touching. This procedure is a mere precaution against the shaft's working loose and falling out of the chuck.

Chuck the shaft by only a narrow margin, or by a substantially wider one if narrow steel shims are used between the jaws and the shaft. Either way, the driving must also act as a universal joint.

Although the rough shaft might bounce considerably in the steady rest, there is very little, if any, bounce near the chuck jaws where the spot-turning is to be done. Therefore, you will get a fairly round turned diameter.

Only a narrow cleanup cut is taken next to the chuck jaws. This surface needs to be only wide enough to accom-

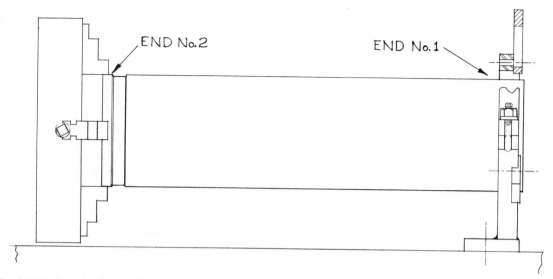

Fig. S-18. Spot-turning large shafts for a steady rest. Use this method to prepare large, rough shafts for center-drilling in a lathe.

modate the thickness of the steady-rest jaws.

Next, turn the work end for end, with end No. 2 now supported in the steady rest. True-up end No. 1 in the four-jaw chuck, while the No. 2 spot-turned end is centered in the steady rest.

Using a drill that is somewhat larger than the pilot diameter of a standard-sized center drill and is held in a drill chuck, drill a hole into the shaft to the required depth. Follow by countersinking the hole with a 60° countersink tool, or use a straightedged tool bit, as shown in Fig. C-13A, to cut the 60° countersink. The angle and the roundness of the hole need not be perfect. In the machining process, the center hole soon conforms to the shape of the hard tailstock center.

By again turning the work around, end for end, center end No. 1 in the steady rest.

On some nonround, odd-shaped jobs it might be necessary to fasten a steel ring around the work. After a light cut is taken off of the ring's periphery, the work can be supported in a steady rest, rotating with that ring.

STEADY REST, BELT CUSHION. Figure S-19 shows a simple and better method of running ''finished'' work in the steady rest. By using an oily leather belt or lubricating a new one, you can completely eliminate the possibility of marring the finish on the work. Cut out one end of the belt to receive the steady rest's clamping bolt.

Press a flat, wooden block into the opening, if it is a hollow job, to help center the work in the steady rest. Touch the tail-stock center against the rotating work, then adjust

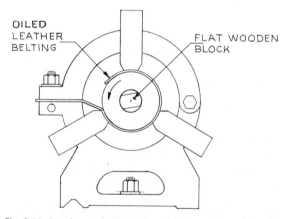

Fig. S-19. Steady rest, belt cushion. This is a simple and better method of running finished work in the steady rest without marring its finish.

the steady rest accordingly.

Although this cushioning system is a very good one, it is not recommended for heavy, prolonged cutting. Do not neglect to keep the belt well lubricated.

STEELS

STEELS, IDENTIFICATION. The matter of steels can be very confusing until you become better acquainted with some of the identification methods for them, their general usage, as well as their characteristics and the methods of processing them.

GROUP-A	GROUP-B	GROUP-C	GROUP-D
S.A.E. 1010−1035 VERY LOW CARBON	S.A.E. 1040−52100 HIGHER CARBON	TOOL STEELS INCLUDING HIGH-SPEED	STAINLESS STEELS

Fig. S-20. Steels, identification. The four basic groups of steel are shown.

All steels can be separated and placed into one of four basic groups, as shown in Fig. S-20. Each group possesses something in common, either in their composition or performance. To identify better some of these steels, the American Society of Automotive Engineers (S.A.E.), numbers them according to their carbon content. The carbon content is represented by the last two digits, and by the last three digits when the carbon content is over 1 percent. The first two digits represent other elements in the steel's composition. Steels seldom possess more than 2.5 percent carbon.

GROUP A

Group A represents those steels having the least amount of carbon, such as S.A.E. 1010. This metal is used mostly for electromagnetic purposes.

The steel possessing the next greater amount of carbon is S.A.E. 1020. This steel is used very widely, in automobile frames, bodies, wheels, etc., as well as for bridge and building girders, frying pans and water pipes, and precision tools and gages.

Because their carbon content is too low, these steels will not harden even with repeated heating and cooling. Steels must contain upwards of .35 percent carbon before they will take on some degree of hardness. These mild, or low-carbon, steels come in both the hot-rolled (H.R.S.), and the cold rolled (C.R.S.), and are designated as S.A.E. 1020 H.R.S. or 1020 C.R.S.

This mildness is most advantageous for a great many purposes. The S.A.E. 1010 through 1035 steels can be only case-hardened or hard chrome-plated. Cast iron also contains large amounts of carbon, but it is in the form known as graphite, whereas the steel's carbon is called Cementite.

GROUP B

Steels in group B, such as S.A.E. 1040 through 52100, are those possessing more than .35 percent carbon. The

higher-carbon steels can usually be recognized by the sparks they give off when they are being ground, particularly in a subdued light. These resemble a profusion of bright, yellow, bursting stars. The greater the carbon content, the greater is this bright yellow profusion.

These steels are used where hardness is required solidly through, but where no great heat will be involved in its usage—no more than 250° F.

GROUP C—TOOL STEELS

Tool steels, as such, differ from other steels mainly in their composition and consequently their performance. Tool steels do not necessarily contain greater amounts of carbon. Instead, various amounts of other elements are added (alloyed) to the molten batch of metal to make the steel behave and perform in some specific way, under some specific condition. Tool steels are made to withstand shock and higher operating temperatures, some to maintain a sharp cutting edge. Their application is extremely broad.

Most tool steels harden at temperatures of 1425° F to 1825° F, then are tempered down to the desired hardness. In use, however, they will not stand higher temperatures. Like carbon steels they begin to soften as soon as their operating temperatures climb above 350° F.

High-speed tool steels, on the other hand, contain various percentages of tungsten, as well as vanadium, cobalt, chromium, molybdenum, and manganese. This composition raises the hardening temperature to slightly above 2200° F. Also, it does not soften, even though it might operate at a red heat.

High-speed tool steels are used primarily for most types of metal-cutting tools, as well as for many higher-temperature tool applications. They can often be recognized by the sparks they give off when they are ground. These sparks resemble dark red spears with an occasional bursting star, very much like the sparks given off when you are grinding cast iron. Also, the chips from turning high-speed steels are about as brittle as dried spaghetti.

Generally tool steels other than high-speed are used for

making practically all other items that operate at a comparatively low temperature, for example, blanking and perforating punches and dies, chisels, etc. The type of tool steel to use will, of course, depend on several things, such as: How hard can it be made? Does it warp too badly? Is its quenching shrinkage excessive? Is it strong enough to carry the intended load? Is it shock-resistant? Will it wear longer than others? Will it hold a sharp cutting edge longer? Can the particular shape of the workpiece be hardened properly without cracking? Is the hardening temperature excessive? How easily can it be finished after hardening?

The many types of tool steels are alloyed with various elements to give them certain specific characteristics. However, what might be excellent for one purpose might not be at all suitable for another. Very seldom, if ever, will one type of steel be found that satisfies all of the many questions. You can obtain descriptive literature on the types and uses of the various tool steels from steel jobbers. One very good booklet identifying the many types of steels, their heat treatments, their uses and makers, can be purchased from

H. M. Halvorsen, Publisher
P. O. Box 63, Harper Station
Detroit, Michigan 48232

GROUP D—STAINLESS STEELS

There are many types of stainless steels. Their primary purpose is to resist corrosion. Because different elements, liquids, and gases have their own peculiar corrosive actions, one type of stainless cannot serve all purposes. Therefore, many types of stainless steels had to be developed, each having some particular corrosion-resisting ability to overcome some particular corrosion problem.

Although this situation might be generally true, the anticorrosion properties disappear if the stainless steel item had been subjected to high temperatures such as in welding. (Welding is used extensively in the fabrication of infinite kinds of stainless steel equipment.) The tendency is for the steel to rust along the welded seams as a result of carbon precipitation caused by the high heat. In other words, the granular structure of the metal becomes disarranged. However, if the steel has been stabilized through the addition of columbium or tantalum, its anticorrosion properties change very little, if at all, when it is subjected to higher heat.

In some types of stainless steels, the carbons can be restabilized (properly rearranged) after welding by heating to 1825° F, then plunging the work into a water bath. This same procedure is used in stress-relieving stainless steel.

Type 347 stainless steel is of a particularly unusual composition. It, no doubt, is among the more sophisticated types of stainless. It will resist corrosion against most of the stronger acids, even after having been welded.

About 50 percent of all stainless steels contain roughly 18 percent chromium and about 8 percent nickel, with various amounts of other elements added to make the steel behave in some specific way, under some specific condition. These steels are of the austenitic type and are nonmagnetic. The remainder, or the ferritic types, contain no nickel at all and are magnetic.

STEELS, HARDENING. The various groups of steels are hardened in different ways. Group A steels can be only case-hardened or hard chrome-plated. Case-hardening is done by carburizing, cyaniding, or nitriding. Perhaps the most commonly used hardening process is carburizing, which introduces a carbon monoxide gas into the steel to make it hardenable. Incidentally, all metals are porous, to a greater or lesser extent. How else would the carbon monoxide gas enter into the metals? Heating, of course, does result in making all metals less dense.

CARBURIZING LOW-CARBON STEEL

For carburizing, fill an iron or steel box with 1 1/2 inches or so of a carburizing mixture, usually a commercially produced item. Old charred bones and shoe leather work fairly well, also. Lay the work atop the mixture in the box. Then pour in more mixture, packing it firmly around the work. Cover the work with another 1 1/2 inches or so of the carburizing mixture. After firmly packing it down, place a cover over the box. Seal the seams with fireclay or wet asbestos to help contain the gas. Place the box into a furnace and heat to 1650° F to 1700° F. The gas emitted from the carburizing mixture penetrates into the work at approximately .001 inch per hour.

After the work has been carburized to the desired depth, it is removed from the box and quenched in lukewarm water. Water produces a hard surface, approaching 70 Rockwell on the C scale.

The surface of the work can also be tempered to some lower hardness by first emery-polishing a section of the work to a certain temperature or color. (See Table S-1.) If a tempering oven is available, use it instead. However, carburized items are seldom, if ever, tempered.

One nice thing about case-hardened work is that the surface can be made very hard, while its soft core eliminates the danger of it cracking.

Often, parts are made calling for case-hardening of some

of its areas only. However, when you are carburizing in the closed box, the whole workpiece is enveloped with the carburizing gas, thereby becoming hardenable all over. So, when you do not want this condition, you can separate the hard from the soft areas by at least two methods. You purposely can leave the portion that is to remain soft with slightly more stock than the planned thickness of the case hardness is to be. After carburizing, machine off the excess metal. Then reheat and quench. Only the remaining carburized portion will become hard.

The other method is to machine the work to near finished dimensions all over. Then mask off the area to be carburized with a suitable tape or masking paint. Then copper-plate the unmasked surface (which is to remain soft). Before packing the work into the carburizing box, strip off the masking. Now only the exposed, unplated area will be penetrated by the carburizing gas, while the copper-plated surface of the work is shielded from the gas. Follow this step by quenching in oil or water, depending on the hardness desired.

CYANIDING

Another very commonly used case-hardening method is cyaniding. Place the finished or very nearly finished work into a pot of molten cyanide of potassium, allowing the work to cook at 1550° F to 1650° F for as long as is required for the desired depth of case. Count on soaking one hour for every .001 inch of case depth. Follow this step by quenching in water, which produces an extremely hard surface, in the 70 Rc range.

Caution: be very careful when you are working with cyanide; it is extremely poisonous. The furnace fumes should be carried away by proper ventilation. Stand away a short distance when you are plunging the hot-cyanided work into the quenching bath. It produces a very loud report, like that of a shotgun blast, as it contacts and splashes the water.

For small, simple work, the piece can be heated with an oxyacetylene flame. Then rub a cyanide pellet over its surface, repeating as often as desired. Follow by a water quench.

HARDENING

In hardening, most steels with a higher carbon content are heated to 1425° F to 1550° F and quenched in oil, water, or air. The type of quench to use depends on the steel's carbon content, it shape, and purpose. Water quenching produces a harder result, but the chances of cracking the work also increases. Oil quenching is milder, cushioning the quenching shock.

The quenching bath is used for bringing the work up to, or very near, its maximum obtainable hardness. In every steel-hardening case, the maximum hardness must always be obtained first. Then the work is drawn (tempered) down to whatever the hardness requirement. In other words, work is not hardened up to a certain hardness. Instead, the work is hardened all the way first, then tempered back down to the desired hardness. Tempering enables the work to withstand greater amounts of shock or bending without fracturing, and still continue to be hard enough to perform its intended function.

TEMPERING

For drawing or tempering the hardness, the better practice is to use a temperature-controlled oven. Place the work into the oven immediately after quenching, before it cools down to room temperature.

The time period between removing the work from the quench bath and placing it into the warm tempering oven is a critical one. In every case the quenching bath should always be kept warm, between 150° F and 180° F.

The work in the tempering oven can become fairly soft once again if it is allowed to remain soaking long enough, even at a comparatively low temperature.

HARDENING HIGH-SPEED TOOL STEEL

In hardening high-speed tool steels it is customary to heat the metal slowly up to about 1500° F, followed by heating rapidly up to 2250° F to 2375° F, depending on the type. Quench in oil, then draw (temper) at 1100° F to 1150° F for two hours.

Hardened high-speed steel does not readily soften from heat, as does carbon steel. To anneal (resoften) hardened high-speed steel you must reheat it in a furnace up to its hardening temperature, then allow it to soak at that heat one hour for each inch of its thickness. Then shut off the furnace, permitting the work to cool with the furnace.

Another method is to transfer the hot work from the furnace and bury it in lime until cold. Either way, the annealing process usually requires most of 24 hours.

You can harden small, more simple, work by heating with an oxyacetylene flame until the surface of the work begins to show tiny bubbles. With a pot of quenching oil close at hand, immerse the work and cool it down to where it shows no more redness. However, before the work becomes cold, slowly reheat it again to a dull red, then allow it to cool off in the air. This method serves very well for hardening smaller, solid, forged boring bars. Only the cutting end needs to be hardened. Some hardness is always lost in every tempering process, but the brittleness of the work is also lessened.

HARDENING STAINLESS STEEL

Only some types of stainless steels can be hardened readily, while some can be case-hardened only. There are at least two types. The W stainless hardens by heating in a furnace to 950° F. Then instead of the customary quenching, it is removed from the furnace and allowed to cool to room temperature. This process is known as *age-hardening*. At its hardest, it will be only about 48 Rc. (See Table S-3.)

The more common types of hardenable stainless steels are in the 440 series. The 440-A contains about .40 percent carbon. The 440-B contains about .65 percent carbon, and the 440-C contains about .90 percent carbon.

For example, the 440-C is heated to 1825° F and quenched in oil or water. Its hardness can also be tempered very much like most high-carbon, high-chrome steels, which it very nearly is.

Type 440 stainless can also be case-hardened by the malcomizing process, which is very much the same as nitriding. Place the work into a furnace in the presence of ammonia gas, and heat to 850° F to 900° F. Allow the work to soak at that temperature for one hour for each .001 inch of case thickness desired. Instead of quenching, shut off the furnace, permitting the work to cool with the furnace in the presence of the ammonia gas.

Because the malcomizing temperature is comparatively low, the work is usually finished to size before malcomizing. Since the work becomes slightly larger in the process it is customary to leave the work smaller by about .0002 inch for each inch of work thickness.

Steels containing about 1 percent aluminum lend themselves more favorably to malcomizing. The surface's hardness thusly obtained sometimes runs as high as 80 Rc, and that is very, very hard.

DETERMINING THE BEST HARDENING HEATS

The correct temperatures for hardening steels are usually supplied by the steelmakers. Always adhere to their recommendations. If, however, you must find the temperature on your own, you can by using a horseshoe magnet suspended by a nonmagnetic wire from a nonmagnetic rod. Partially withdraw the hot work from the furnace, and bring the magnet close to the work to find whether it attracts the magnet.

Steels go through a period of becoming nonmagnetic when they are heated to a certain temperature. This phenomenon is known as the *calescent period*. In this period the steel is in its finest granular form for hardening.

The calescent, or nonmagnetic, period is a comparatively narrow one, having a spread of only 8° to 10°. This phenomenon also takes place in reverse as the steel cools down from a temperature above the calescent point. In this reverse direction the phenomenon is known as the *decalescent period*.

The calescent period varies with the steel's carbon content, except in the case of high-speed steel. Although the carbon content of high-speed steel is comparatively low, its calescent point is above 2200° F. Because of the rapid heat loss, the better practice is to heat the work to slightly above the calescent point, before quenching. Fairly good hardening can be done even though the temperature of the heated work is as much as 100° F below the calescent point.

It is also a good practice to take note of the calescent temperature of the different steels as they are heated. You can do so with thermocouple wires connected to a heat-recording instrument. The welded ends of the chromelalumel thermocouple wires are inserted into a small-diameter drilled hole in the test piece. The two wires are separated, using twin-holed ceramic insulators, while their free ends are connected to a temperature recording instrument. By carefully observing the rising heat, you will notice that the temperature rise in the work suddenly stops, while the furnace heat rises steadily without interruption. After a few moments, the work temperature falls back a few degrees. The temperature's hesitation is when the work is at its best hardening heat. This is the time when the hot work ceases to attract the horseshoe magnet.

The calescent point of high-speed steels is reached at temperatures between 2250° F and 2375° F, depending on the composition of the steel, which does vary.

After you know the hardening temperature of a particular steel, you can harden it properly without having to insert thermocouple wires or use magnets. Simply watch the furnace's heat-recording instruments.

In the process of determining the correct hardening heats by whatever heat-measuring devices, also carefully observe and note the color of the heated work during the calescent period, and the room lighting conditions. All these factors come in very handy for any future hardening use. (See Table S-1.)

STEEL QUENCHING BATHS

Regardless of what substance is used as the quenching medium, they all serve the same purpose, and that is to cool the hot work rapidly. When you first plunge the work into a quench bath, it might not come in contact with the quenching substance. Because the work is so hot, it boils the coolant away from itself. Thereupon, the work is actually contacted and cooled by the vapors, which separate the work from the bath's fluid. In most quenching it is customary to swirl the hot work around in a figure eight.

The oils used for quenching are of a special high flash point type to minimize their igniting as much as possible.

For some work, brine is used for the quenching. For this enough salt should be dissolved in the water to float a potato. Even molten lead is used for quenching some items. Many of these quenching mediums are often just a matter of choice. Nonetheless, all of them have different boiling points, whereby some turn into a vapor sooner than others, affording varied cooling rates.

It is usually during the quenching when the work cracks, especially if the quench medium is too cold. Tremendous internal stresses are set up during the cooling and shrinking. These stresses are generally more concentrated around inside sharp corners, such as in square holes, or where heavy sections meet with quite light sections in the same piece. Even after quenching, if the work is allowed to cool down to room temperature, sudden cracks often will develop. The better practice is always to maintain a warm quenching bath. Never permit the work to become completely cold before tempering (drawing).

TEMPERING STEELS

If no tempering furnace or oven is readily available, a heavier steel plate warmed to a dull red heat can serve the same purpose almost as well. Its thickness would depend on the thickness of the work. Heavier work will, of course, require more heat.

Lay the hardened work flat on the hot plate. Turn the work over frequently, always watching very closely for the temperature color changes in the work. This operation is performed outside of the furnace. Since you are depending on colors by which to gage your heat, you must expose the surfaces of the work by sanding or grinding away the surface oxides, at least around the more critical areas, before you do any tempering.

By frequently flopping the work over on the hot plate, you will permit the heat to enter more deeply and uniformly into the work. The final hardness can be determined reasonably close by the color of the exposed surface. Table S-2 shows the names of the heat colors for drawing.

The higher hardening heat also destroys the steel's metallurgical properties up to .020 inch deep, through decarbonization. Therefore, it is customary to leave up to .020 inch extra material on each surface for the final finish grinding.

Table S-2. Tempering Heat Colors.

Degrees Centigrade/Fahrenheit		Colors
215	420	Very Faint Yellow
221	430	Very Pale Yellow
228	440	Light Yellow
232	450	Pale Straw Yellow
238	460	Straw Yellow
241	470	Deep Straw Yellow
248	480	Dark Yellow
255	490	Yellow Brown
260	500	Brown Yellow
264	510	Spotted Red Brown
270	520	Brown Purple
277	530	Light Purple
282	540	Full Purple
288	550	Dark Purple
293	560	Full Blue
299	570	Dark Blue
316	600	Very Dark Blue
332	630	Blue Green

HARDENING TEMPERATURES BY COLORS

Even though each color and shade thereof represents a specific temperature, it is difficult to determine exact temperatures by color alone. Of course, the visual color temperature method is not as accurate as that of heat-measuring instruments. So very much depends on the observer's eyesight, his ability to distinguish colors, the amount of oxide on the workpiece, as well as the type and amount of lighting in the room. Nonetheless, quite satisfactory hardening results can be obtained by using the visual heat color method, as described in Table S-1.

HARDNESS TESTING

At this stage it is customary to test the hardness of your workpiece. For this test, the Rockwell hardness testing machine is most generally used. However, if you have no Rockwell testing machine immediately available, you can use the corner of a file with which to test the hardness of the work. The file should be comparatively new, sharp, and free of oils or grease.

Instead of holding the file by its handle, a much shorter grip on the file itself is more practical. However, you have no way of knowing what filing is supposed to feel like and what degree of hardness this feel indicates, unless, through practice, you become familiar with what a known hardness files and feels like. You must have some type of standard to go by.

The common cutting tools for high-speed steel often measure 60 to 62 Rockwell in hardness on the machine's Rockwell C scale. The hardness number is always followed by the adjoining symbol *Rc*, meaning Rockwell C scale. For softer materials, the symbol is Rb, or Rockwell B scale.

A file used in hardness testing is never sawed back and forth across the work being tested. Instead, with a firm grip, press the file down hard on the work and push it forward very slowly for a short distance, perhaps not exceeding 1/2 inch. If you felt the slightest bite (cut) you can be sure the hardness of the workpiece is between 60 and 61 Rc.

If a new file used in this way does not even begin to bite into the work after a couple of attempts, you can assume its hardness to be over 61 Rc. The varying degrees of cutting efforts are in direct proportion to the hardness of the piece being tested.

To determine just what the Rockwell hardness reading is in each case is quite impossible unless known hardnesses were file-tested beforehand, by the one doing the testing. This then, simply becomes a matter of comparison of the file's bite on a known hardness to the bite on the piece being tested.

A very good stunt for increasing your testing feel familiarity is to file-test a piece of a known hardness. In reversing the process, do the file test on the work first to estimate its hardness. Then, to verify that estimation, test that same piece in the Rockwell tester to see how close you came. This is a very good method of developing your hardness testing ability using a file.

It is also a very good idea to have on hand pieces of a known hardness, on which the bite of a file can occasionally be tried for the comparison feel test. It is fairly possible to estimate the true hardness of steels within a point or two once you have acquired the feel of the file's bit.

See Table S-3.

STRAIGHTENING

STRAIGHTENING WIRE, ROD, AND TUBING. Figure S-21 shows a simple method of straightening rods, wires, or tubing when the diameters are comparatively small and the work is not over 3 to 4 feet in length. If it happens to be tubing it is a good idea to plug the end that is gripped in the collet or chuck to prevent the tube from collapsing and pulling out.

In every case you must bend the work as it revolves. To do so, use any wooden block having a hole drilled through large enough to admit the work. Slip the block over the stationary work up to the collet or chuck. After starting the spindle and work rotation, bend the work by manually forcing it over with the wooden block. Then pull the block straight back with its hole aimed toward the tail-stock center. Depending on the crookedness of the work, the process often must be repeated two or three times.

This same principle can be used to straighten longer and heavier work by bolting the drilled wooden block atop a lathe's compound rest. After the work rotation is begun, swivel the block and compound 20° to 30° in either direction and tighten it. Then hand-crank the lathe carriage toward the tail stock.

In most cases it might be advisable to grease or oil the work before processing.

STRAIGHTENING LONG RODS, TUBING, OR WIRES. A handy method for straightening kinks and curls out of longer wire, rods, or tubes of smaller diameters is shown in Fig. S-22. A piece of bent pipe with a hole somewhat larger than the diameter of the work is held and rotated in a lathe's collet or chuck. Push the work through the bent pipe and project it out far enough to be gripped with a lathe dog, clamp, or pliers. Then pull it.

It is better to grease the work with white-lead and oil before starting it through. If the work is quite long, remove the lathe's tail stock completely.

Begin the lathe spindle rotation, while at the same time pulling the work straight-on out. The work itself does not turn.

When the work is many feet in length, you might need the help of two or more persons for additional support.

SUPPORTING WORK

STRAPPING WORK TO THE DRIVING PLATE. Figure S-23 shows a method of holding and driving work that must run true with the center hole at the one end, while internal work is to be performed on the opposite end.

It was the custom to use rawhide lacings to tie the work to the driving plate. The practice was to partially unscrew the driving plate from the spindle. After the lacing was completed, the driving plate would be fully screwed back on the spindle to tighten the lacings. In every case the outer end of the work was supported in a steady rest. This type of binding would serve as a universal joint, exerting very little, if any, bending pressure on the work.

With the gradual disappearance of leather belting along with rawhide lacings, a much easier and quicker holding method is now being used. The same results can be obtained by employing a semiflexible strap of steel (P). Position the strap, which has three holes, in front of the lathe dog. Draw it in by evenly tightening the two bolts (B). Any difference in the dog's thickness, as at S, is automatically taken care of by the flexing strap (P).

Table S-3. Hardness Comparison Chart.

DIA. IN MM OF 10MM BALL IMPRESSION AT 3000 KGM LOAD	BRINELL HARDNESS NO. IN KILOGRAMS	ROCKWELL C 120° CONE. 150 KGM LOAD	ROCKWELL B 1-16 DIAMETER BALL 100 KILOGRAM LOAD	SHORE-SCLEROSCOPE NUMBER	TENSILE STRENGTH AT 1000 PSI	DIA. IN MM OF 10MM BALL IMPRESSION AT 3000 KGM LOAD	BRINELL HARDNESS NO. IN KILOGRAMS	ROCKWELL C 120° CONE. 150 KGM LOAD	ROCKWELL B 1-16 DIAMETER BALL 100 KILOGRAM LOAD	SHORE-SCLEROSCOPE NUMBER	TENSILE STRENGTH AT 1000 PSI
2.00	946					4.50	179	9	90	28	89
2.05	898					4.55	174	8	89	28	87
2.10	857					4.60	170	7	88	27	85
2.15	817	72				4.65	166	6	87	27	83
2.20	782	70				4.70	163	5	86	26	82
2.25	744	68		100	368	4.75	159	4	84	26	81
2.30	713	66		95	351	4.80	156	3	83	25	78
2.35	683	64		91	336	4.85	153	2	82	25	77
2.40	652	62		87	323	4.90	149	1	81	24	76
2.45	627	60	⊗	84	310	4.95	147		80	24	75
2.50	600	58		81	297	5.00	146		79	23	74
2.55	578	57		78	286	5.05	143		78	23	72
2.60	555	55	120	75	275	5.10	140		77	22	70
2.65	532	53	119	73	265	5.15	134		75	22	69
2.70	512	52	118	70	256	5.20	131		72	21	67
2.75	495	51	117	67	248	5.25	128				
2.80	477	49	117	65	233	5.30	126				
2.85	460	48	116	63	230	5.35	124				
2.90	444	47	115	61	220	5.40	121				
2.95	430	45	115	59	212	5.45	118				
3.00	418	44	114	57	204	5.50	116				
3.05	402	43	114	55	196	5.55	114				
3.10	387	42	113	54	190	5.60	112				
3.15	375	41	112	53	186	5.65	109				
3.20	364	40	111	52	179	5.70	107				
3.25	351	38	111	51	173	5.75	105				
3.30	340	37	110	49	166	5.80	103				
3.35	332	36	109	48	160	5.85	101				
3.40	321	35	108	47	155	5.90	99				
3.45	311	34	108	46	150	5.95	97				
3.50	302	32	107	45	146	6.00	95				
3.55	293	31	106	44	143	6.05	94				

DIA. IN MM OF 10MM BALL IMPRESSION AT 3000 KGM LOAD	BRINELL HARDNESS NO. IN KILOGRAMS	ROCKWELL C 120° CONE. 150KGM LOAD	ROCKWELL B 1-16 DIAMETER BALL 100 KILOGRAM LOAD	SHORE-SCLEROSCOPE NUMBER	TENSILE STRENGTH AT 1000 PSI	DIA. IN MM OF 10MM BALL IMPRESSION AT 3000 KGM LOAD	BRINELL HARDNESS NO. IN KILOGRAMS	ROCKWELL C 120° CONE. 150KGM LOAD	ROCKWELL B 1-16 DIAMETER BALL 100 KILOGRAM LOAD	SHORE-SCLEROSCOPE NUMBER	TENSILE STRENGTH AT 1000 PSI
3.60	285	30	105	43	138	6.10	92				
3.65	277	29	104	42	134	6.15	90				
3.70	269	28	104	41	131	6.20	89				
3.75	262	27	103	40	129	6.25	87				
3.80	255	26	102	39	127	6.30	86				
3.85	248	25	102	39	125	6.35	84				
3.90	241	23	101	38	123	6.40	82				
3.95	235	22	99	37	120	6.45	81				
4.00	228	21	98	37	117	6.50	80				
4.05	223	20	97	36	114	6.55	79				
4.10	217	19	96	34	110	6.60	77				
4.15	212	18	96	33	107	6.65	76				
4.20	207	17	95	32	102	6.70	74				
4.25	202	16	94	31	100	6.75	73				
4.30	197	14	94	30	99	6.80	72				
4.35	192	13	93	30	97	6.85	70				
4.40	187	12	92	29	95	6.90	69				
4.45	183	10	91	29	92	6.95	68				

⊗ BEGINS TO SCRATCH GLASS AT THIS HARDNESS

SUPPORTING WORK WITH A TURNING TOOL. Figure S-24 shows a very convenient method of supporting between centers work in a lathe. Quite often it becomes necessary to lubricate or change the tail-stock center. If the work end is not yet finished, permit the cutting tool to dig lightly into the shaft's end, just before the work comes to a complete stop. Make sure the machine's rpm rate is set at its slowest. Permit the tool to scrape the shaft's face just before the dog's tail approaches the front of the lathe. Doing so results in a better holding condition. The digging in need be only a few thousandths inch deep.

SPOT FACING

SPOT-FACING AND REVERSE SPOT-FACING TOOLS. Figure S-25A shows a very convenient spot-facing and counterboring tool. It can be made up in very short order and functions beautifully. The shank consists of a steel rod slightly smaller in diameter than the hole to be machined. The rod need not be hardened for machining small lots. It is generally better to tap into the end of the rod for the set screw, which holds the cutting bit. On larger-diameter rods, you can drill the set screw holes into the side. A round hole is usually good enough to hold the bit. The flat end

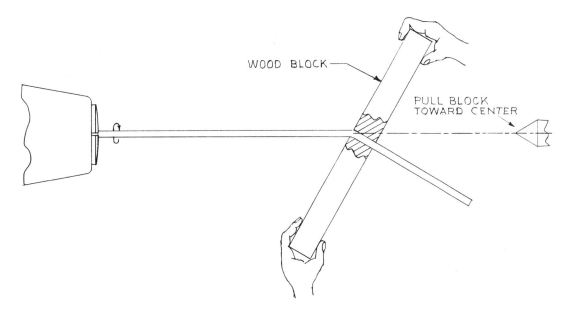

Fig. S-21. Straightening wire, rod, and tubing. Use this simple method to straighten small-diameter rods, wires, and tubing that have lengths of up to 3 feet.

of the screw pressing against the flat side of the tool bit prevents the bit from turning in its hole.

You can grind the cutting tool to any desired length, and can rotate it 180° in its hole, for reverse counterboring or spot facing.

Figure S-25B shows a solid spot-facing and counterboring tool, preferably made of high-speed steel rod. First, heat the rod with an acetylene flame to about 2200° F or when tiny bubbles appear on its surface. Then bend the rod into a sharp **L**, as shown. Heat the bent rod until the tiny bubbles appear once more. Then plunge it into a bath of quenching oil. After the hardening, you can grind the tool either off-hand or in a grinding machine. Don't forget to temper the cutting end of the tool by reheating it to a red heat for at least a few minutes.

You also can hold and drive this tool in either a drill chuck or collet.

SQUARES

MASTER SQUARE BLOCK. A great many types of gaging and measuring tools can be adjusted to extremely close tolerances, but a master square generally has no built-in adjustments. If it did have adjustments, you would still need some standard with which to compare it.

To check the squareness of a square, you easily can make up a hardened steel block, bored out for weight reduction and shaped as shown in Fig. S-26. Finish-grind the block's

bore to lightly press over some convenient-sized mandrel. Then set up the block between centers, and cylindrically grind the block's periphery over its four corners. The peripheral grinding must have no taper.

In the same setup, face-grind both ends. If the faces are slightly convex or concave, they will still average out absolutely square with the axial centerline of the block.

By placing the master square block on a precise flat surface plate, you can compare squares and check them for their accuracy. A light placed behind the square, or object

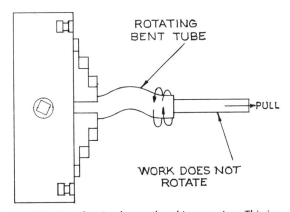

Fig. S-22. Straightening long rods, tubing, or wires. This is a handy method for straightening kinks and curls out of longer wire (up to 30 feet in length).

199

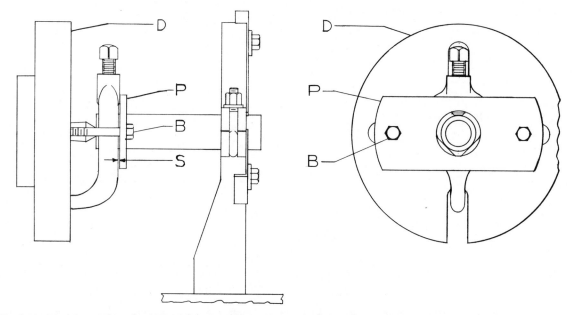

Fig. S-23. Strapping work to the driving plate. Use this method to hold work that must run true with the center hole atone end while you perform internal work at the opposite end.

being tested and the block, will show if any out-of-squareness exists. A thin smear of Prussian blue paste, smeared over the surface being checked, will also reveal if the block and work are parallel. For visual checking, it is best whenever possible to use daylight as it comes through a frosted glass window or the light from a north window. If a thin seam of light comes through between the work and the block, it will have a blue appearance,

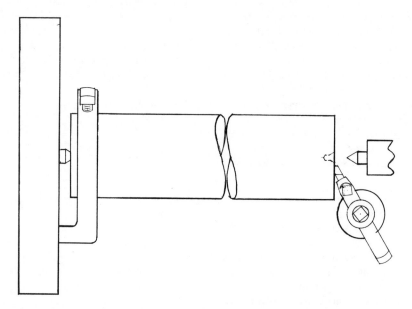

Fig. S-24. Supporting work with a turning tool. You can use this quick method of holding a shaft while you are withdrawing the tail-stock center.

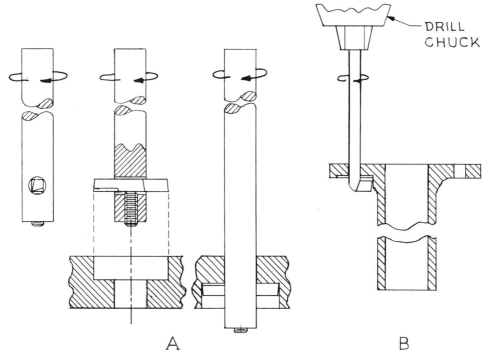

Fig. S-25. Spot-facing and reverse spot-facing tools.

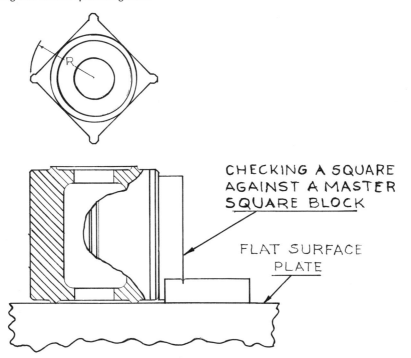

Fig. S-26. Master square block. This method is used to check the squareness of a master square.

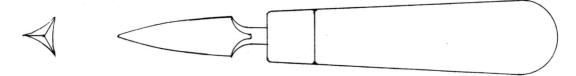

Fig. S-27. Three-cornered scraper.

representing just a few millionths of an inch of space.

SCRAPING TOOLS

THREE-CORNERED SCRAPER. Figure S-27 shows a three-cornered scraper, used for rounding-off the ends of smaller holes, burring, etc. This is a tool no machinist, tool maker, or die maker should be without.

It easily can be made up by grinding an old, worn, three-cornered file to any length or size. Hollow-grind it on the periphery of the wheel. Then finish off by honing lengthwise.

T

TAPERS

STANDARD BROWN & SHARPE TAPERS. The standard Brown & Sharpe tapers taper at the rate of .500 inch per foot, or .04166 inch per inch. This rate amounts to an included angle of 2° 23′ 10″ or 1° 11′ 35″ to the axial centerline. This rate pertains to all tapers, except for the No. 10 taper, which tapers at the rate of .5161 inch per foot, or .04301 inch per inch. (See Table T-1 and Fig. T-1.)

STANDARD MORSE TAPERS. Table T-2 shows a table of Morse taper standards. Note that each size has its own rate of taper, varying from .04988 per inch to .05263 per inch. Therefore, when you are machining a particular size of taper, always refer to the taper's table for the exact tapering rate and diameter. (See Fig. T-2.)

TURNING TAPERS. The turning of tapers in an engine lathe can be done in several ways. Which method you choose will, of course, depend on the job at hand, the size of the job, the type of equipment available, and the accuracy expected.

Generally, you will use a taper attachment, as shown in Fig. T-3, for turning a great variety of tapered work. The tapered section of a shaft being turned is shown at A. The rate of taper is governed by the amount of swiveled setting of channel G. A close-fitting, gib-adjusted block (D), slides inside of the channel of item G. The support base

(I) is sometimes attached to the lathe's carriage, while on some older and perhaps better systems the supporting base (I), is movable in a channel machined parallel to the lathe's ways, in which case an anchoring rod (K) is not required.

Ordinarily, the anchoring rod, when tightened in place by a clamp bolt (N), prevents the taper attachment from moving laterally with the carriage. Instead, the block sliding in the channel of swiveled item G and fastened to the cross slide (B) through a bolt (C), causes the cross slide, and consequently the cutting tool, to move either toward or away from the axial center of the work, thereby producing a taper.

Because the cross feed screw (E) must be removed for the tapering operation, the in-feeding of the cutting tool is done with the compound slide.

Graduations (H) on the base (I) are to be used as a general reference only. In every case you must check, measure, or gage the taper. One good, quick method of measuring the taper is shown in Figs. T-4 and T-5. Knowing the amount of taper per inch called for, mark off 1 or more inches of the taper with a scale. Then measure the diameters at each of the two markings with a micrometer, as shown in Fig. T-5. Subtract the one reading from the other to get the amount of taper for the length measured. By dividing the difference by the number of inches between the mea-

Table T-1. Standard Brown & Sharpe Tapers.

NO. OF TAPER	DIA. OF PLUG AT SMALL END	DIA. AT END OF SOCKET	STANDARD PLUG DEPTH	WHOLE LENGTH OF SHANK	DEPTH OF HOLE	END OF SOCKET TO KEYWAY	LENGTH OF KEYWAY	WIDTH OF KEYWAY	LENGTH OF TONGUE	DIAMETER OF TONGUE	THICKNESS OF TONGUE	RADIUS OF MILL FOR TONGUE	RADIUS OF TONGUE	SHANK DEPTH	TAPER PER FOOT	TAPER PER INCH
	D	A	P	B	H	K	L	W	T	d	t	R	a	S		
1	.200		15/16			15/16	3/8	.135	3/16	.170	1/8	3/16	.030	1 3/16	.500	.0416
2	.250		1 3/16			1 1/64	1/2	.166	1/4	.220	5/32	3/16	.030	1 1/2	.500	.0416
3	.312		1 1/4			1 15/32	5/8	.197	5/16	.282	3/16	3/16	.040	1 21/32	.500	.0416
4	.350	.402	1 1/2	3/4	3/8	1 13/64	11/16	.228	11/32	.320	7/32	5/16	.050	1 21/32	.500	.0416
5	.450	.523	1 3/4	2 9/32	1 7/8	1 11/16	3/4	.260	3/8	.420	1/4	5/16	.060	2 3/16	.500	.0416
6	.500	.599	2 3/8	2 31/32	2 1/2	2 9/64	7/8	.291	7/16	.460	9/32	5/16	.060	2 7/8	.500	.0416
7	.600	.725	3	3 5/8	3 1/8	2 29/32	15/16	.322	15/32	.560	5/16	3/8	.070	3 17/32	.500	.0416
8	.750	.899	3 9/16	4 1/4	3 11/16	3 29/32	1	.353	1/2	.710	11/32	3/8	.080	4 1/8	.500	.0416
9	.900	1.067	4	4 3/4	4 1/8	3 7/8	1 1/8	.385	9/16	.860	3/8	7/16	.100	4 5/8	.500	.0416
10	1.047	1.289	5 1/16	6 3/4	5 13/16	5 17/32	1 5/16	.447	21/32	1.010	7/16	1/2	.110	6 13/32	.516	.0430
11	1.250	1.530	6 3/4	7 13/16	6 7/8	6 19/32	1 5/16	.447	21/32	1.210	7/16	1/2	.130	7 15/32	.500	.0416
12	1.500	1.797	7 1/8	8 9/32	7 1/4	6 15/16	1 1/2	.510	3/4	1.460	1/2	1/2	.150	7 15/16	.500	.0416
13	1.750	2.073	7 3/4	8 29/32	7 7/8	7 9/16	1 1/2	.510	3/4	1.710	1/2	5/8	.170	8 9/16	.500	.0416
14	2.000	2.344	8 1/4	9 1/2	8 3/8	8 1/32	1 11/16	.572	27/32	1.960	9/16	3/4	.190	9 5/32	.500	.0416
15	2.250	2.616	8 3/4	10	8 7/8	8 17/32	1 11/16	.572	27/32	2.210	9/16	7/8	.210	9 21/32	.500	.0416
16	2.500	2.886	9 1/4	10 1/2	9 3/8	9	1 7/8	.635	15/16	2.450	5/8	1.	.230	10 1/4	.500	.0416

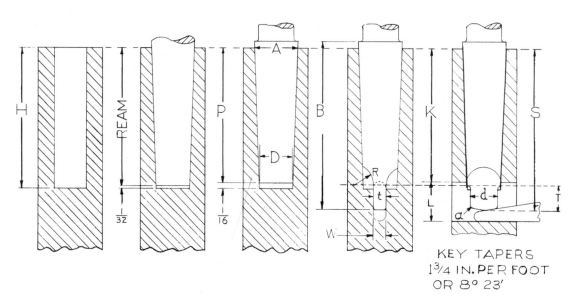

KEY TAPERS
1 3/4 IN. PER FOOT
OR 8° 23'

Fig. T-1. Standard Brown & Sharpe tapers

Table T-2. Standard Morse Tapers.

NO. OF TAPER	DIA. OF PLUG AT SMALL END	DIA. AT END OF SOCKET	STANDARD PLUG DEPTH	WHOLE LENGTH OF SHANK	DEPTH OF HOLE	END OF SOCKET TO KEYWAY	LENGTH OF KEYWAY	WIDTH OF KEYWAY	LENGTH OF TONGUE	DIAMETER OF TONGUE	THICKNESS OF TONGUE	RADIUS OF MILL FOR TONGUE	RADIUS OF TONGUE	SHANK DEPTH	TAPER PER FOOT	TAPER PER INCH	NO. OF TAPER
	D	A	P	B	H	K	L	W	T	d	t	R	a	S			
0	.252	.356	2	$2\frac{11}{32}$	$2\frac{1}{32}$	$1\frac{15}{16}$	$\frac{9}{16}$	.160	$\frac{1}{4}$	.235	$\frac{5}{32}$	$\frac{5}{32}$	.04	$2\frac{7}{32}$	.62460	.05205	0
1	.369	.475	$2\frac{1}{8}$	$2\frac{9}{16}$	$2\frac{3}{16}$	$2\frac{1}{16}$	$\frac{3}{4}$	.213	$\frac{3}{8}$	.343	$\frac{13}{64}$	$\frac{3}{16}$	.05	$2\frac{7}{16}$	.59856	.04988	1
2	.572	.700	$2\frac{9}{16}$	$3\frac{1}{8}$	$2\frac{5}{8}$	$2\frac{1}{2}$	$\frac{7}{8}$	.260	$\frac{7}{16}$	$\frac{17}{32}$	$\frac{1}{4}$	$\frac{1}{4}$	.06	$2\frac{15}{16}$	.59940	.04995	2
3	.778	.938	$3\frac{3}{16}$	$3\frac{7}{8}$	$3\frac{1}{4}$	$3\frac{1}{16}$	$1\frac{3}{16}$	.322	$\frac{9}{16}$	$\frac{23}{32}$	$\frac{5}{16}$	$\frac{9}{32}$	.08	$3\frac{11}{16}$	.60228	.05019	3
4	1.020	1.231	$4\frac{1}{16}$	$4\frac{7}{8}$	$4\frac{1}{8}$	$3\frac{7}{8}$	$1\frac{1}{4}$	.478	$\frac{5}{8}$	$\frac{31}{32}$	$\frac{15}{32}$	$\frac{5}{16}$	.10	$4\frac{5}{8}$	.62316	.05193	4
5	1.475	1.748	$5\frac{3}{16}$	$6\frac{1}{8}$	$5\frac{1}{4}$	$4\frac{15}{16}$	$1\frac{1}{2}$	.635	$\frac{3}{4}$	$1\frac{13}{32}$	$\frac{5}{8}$	$\frac{3}{8}$	.125	$5\frac{7}{8}$	.63144	.05262	5
6	2.116	2.494	$7\frac{1}{4}$	$8\frac{9}{16}$	$7\frac{3}{8}$	7	$1\frac{3}{4}$	.760	$1\frac{1}{8}$	2	$\frac{3}{4}$	$\frac{1}{2}$	.15	$8\frac{1}{4}$	.62556	.05213	6
7	2.750	3.270	10	$11\frac{5}{8}$	$10\frac{1}{8}$	$9\frac{1}{2}$	$2\frac{5}{8}$	1.135	$1\frac{3}{8}$	$2\frac{5}{8}$	$1\frac{1}{8}$	$\frac{3}{4}$	.18	$11\frac{1}{4}$	.62400	.05200	7

suring points, you will find the amount of taper per inch. The wider the spacing, the more accurate will be the reading.

After the taper rate is established, bring down the diameter to the proper size. Always check the taper before taking that last finish cut.

For the final checking of the taper, it is always best to use a bona fide female taper gage, such as the one shown

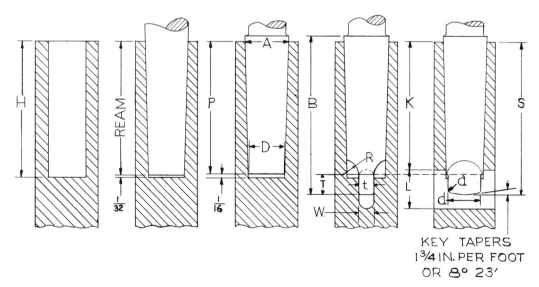

KEY TAPERS
1¾ IN. PER FOOT
OR 8° 23′

Fig. T-2. Standard Morse tapers.

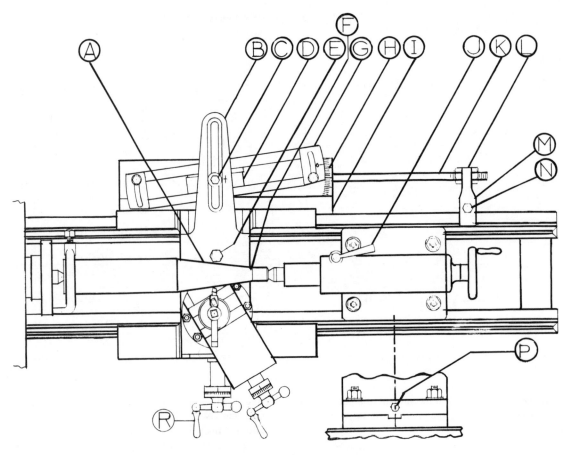

Fig. T-3. Turning tapers. The general equipment in taper-turning in a lathe is shown.

in Fig. T-6. Before trying on the female gage, lightly smear a thin, narrow stripe of Prussian blue paste along the top side of the male taper. Then rotate the work one-half revolution so that the blue smear will be on the bottom side. Slide the female gage over the top side of the male until it stops. Very lightly pressing the gage along inward and downwardly, then partially rotating the sleeve to left or right, will indicate where any corrections need to be made.

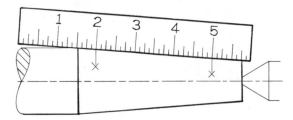

Fig. T-4. Turning tapers. One good, quick method of measuring the taper is shown.

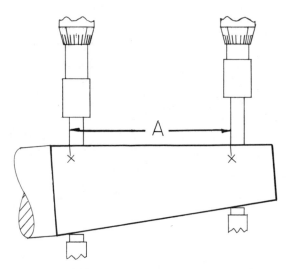

Fig. T-5. Turning tapers. Measuring a taper, continued.

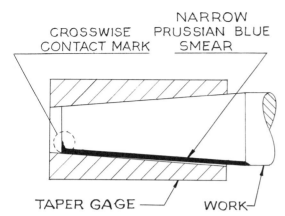

CROSSWISE
CONTACT MARK
NARROW
PRUSSIAN BLUE
SMEAR

TAPER GAGE ———

WORK

Fig. T-6. Turning tapers. Final checking of the taper should be done with a female taper gage.

The blue markings will show a crosswise smear wherever the sleeve made contact on the male taper.

TAPER CUTTING, MICROMETER MEASUREMENT

Regardless of which method you use for turning tapers, a quick and reasonably accurate method for measuring the amount of taper and its diameter is to measure with a micrometer (Figs. T-4 and T-5), along with a scale, a scriber, and a piece of chalk.

First, draw a narrow chalk mark along the entire tapered surface. Scribe the longitudinal line along the chalked line, using the scale for a straightedge (Fig. T-4).

Starting at the scribed line, divide the taper into 1, 2, 3, 4, or more inches, depending on how much of the tapered length has been turned thus far.

Carefully bring up the micrometer's spindle to one of the scribed cross lines marked **X** in Fig. T-5, with its end face resting parallel with the work surface, while the face of the mirometer's anvil contacts the work surface out of parallel on the underside. Some people prefer to position the micrometer so that its anvil is parallel with the bottom tapered surface, instead of its spindle. Write down the micrometer's reading. Then measure the second scribed cross line in the same way, also writing down the micrometer's reading.

Subtract one reading from the other. Then divide the distance (A) by the number of inches separating the two scribed cross lines. The answer is the amount of taper per inch. When that amount coincides with the taper per inch required, you can assume your taper rate to be very close.

As the turned taper's length increases, take advantage by separating the scribed cross lines as far as possible. The greater the lines' separation, the less will be your overall error.

After you have established the correct rate of taper, you must turn the taper's diameter down to whatever the print specifications call for. Never neglect to make a final taper rate check before taking that last cut, just to be sure.

Incidentally, never rely on the lathe's compound degree divisions or markings for accurate angular work.

The taper attachment shown in Fig. T-3 is an earlier design, and a good one. It offers some real advantages over many later models, and a few disadvantages as well. It is positive, offering little slack (play) between the cross and longitudinal directional movements. The only possible slack is in the sliding block's (D) fit in the channel of item G. The biggest advantage in this system is the small amount of longitudinal carriage movement required before actual tapering begins.

On many later-model lathes, the channel in item G is swiveled to the desired angle, and followed by tightening screws C and N. The attachment is then ready to cut the taper. However, because of excessive play in its linkage it requires too much carriage travel before actual tapering begins. The greatest disadvantage is that on some types of work where a taper begins or ends almost adjacent to a straight-turned section (F in Fig. T-3) where a taper is preceded by a shoulder or where a thread is cut on a tapered pipe, the one end must be supported by the tail-stock center, so the tapering is far from immediate. The lathe's carriage must begin its forward movement far enough back to make sure the cutting tool starts tapering at the predetermined point on the work. This procedure does become somewhat cumbersome.

Some older lathes, designed especially for tool room work, have two cross slides one atop the other. When uncoupled, these slides can be actuated individually, in or out by the taper attachment. The upper slide, supporting the compound and tools, can be swiveled or manipulated as required. This system is a very good one for cutting tapered threads on pipes whose end is supported by a center, and for turning the tapers on milling-machine arbors, as well as for backing-off tapered taps, cutters, etc.

Another method of turning tapers is done between centers, as in Fig. T-7. This method can only be used on shorter lengths of work or on longer work, only when the rate of taper is not too great since the limited amount of tail-stock set over also limits the steepness of the tapering. The tail-stock set over is accomplished by turning the screws (P in Fig. T-3) to the required amount of tail-stock set over.

Still another good, quick method for cutting tapers is to swivel the lathe's compound slide to the desired angle. This method is good for internal, as well as external, taper

Fig. T-7. Turning tapers. Turning a taper between centers can be done as shown.

and angle cutting. However, never depend on the degree graduations on the compound for more accurate taper work. Use taper gages or the sine bar for precise taper measurements.

NONSEIZING TAPERS. It is a fact that a tapered male plug will cling (seize) to the inside of a similar-sized female tapered bore. If the same rate of taper in both items is shallow (has a lesser angle), the clinging effect is much greater.

If both the male and female are straight, having no taper, there is no clinging.

If the tapering is increased (having a much greater angle), it becomes more difficult to press the male into the female and to make them stick together.

The shallowest angle at which nonseizing begins is about 7°, or a 14° included angle. For repeated assembly and disassembly a nonseize insurance of 30' is added to the 7° on each side, which results in a 15° included angle taper (Fig. T-8B).

Most lathe spindle noses, chucks, and collets use this angle. High-speed grinding spindle quills use a taper of 20° included angle, as shown in A in Fig. T-8. Because of the

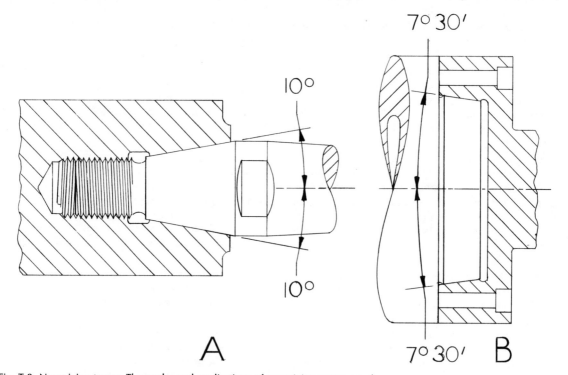

Fig. T-8. Nonseizing tapers. The angles and applications of nonseizing tapers are shown.

frequent screwing in and out of the various sizes of quills, a 20° included angle affords a more concentric seating of the quill in the grinding spindle, with less wear to both of the tapers.

TAPER-GAGING WITH PLUGS AND SLEEVES. Perhaps in no other way can the complete picture of a taper's fit be had as easily as by using the full-length engagement of a male and female taper gage. Whenever a bona fide taper gage is available, use it.

Since it is quite difficult to see or feel the closeness of a tapered fit, use smears of Prussian blue markings for the testing (Fig. T-9).

The best method is to smear a thin narrow line of Prussian blue paste along the top and length of the male taper to be tested. Rotate the male taper one-half turn to position the smear mark along the underside. Then slip the sleeve, or female, gage over the male by sliding it along the top surface of the male until it comes to an easy stop. Then with only light inward and downward pressures, partially rotate the sleeve just a few degrees in both directions.

Then carefully slide the sleeve straight off the top side of the male. Because the blue marking was smeared on lengthwise, any contacting point made by the female gage will now appear crosswise. This mark shows where and how much correction needs to be made.

To check internal tapers, thinly smear the top side of

male plug narrowly along its entire length with Prussian blue. Then slide the plug into the female, along the female's bottom surface. When the forward sliding movement stops, partially rotate the plug a few degrees to the left and right. The cross smear left in the bore, as well as on the male plug, indicates where corrections in the tapering need to be made.

Caution: Do not wiggle the plug up or down while you are trying it in the bore. Doing so will result in a false impression.

To originate a male taper, you must always use a sine bar to give you the exact angle. For this procedure refer to sine bar (Fig. T-64).

TAPPING

TAPPING SQUARE TO THE WORK FACE. A tap always wants to follow the drilled hole simply because there is less resistance in doing so. However, if the tap is permitted to start out of line with the hole, it becomes next to impossible to straighten it out. Trying to force a tap over after a few threads have been cut usually results in its breakage.

There are several methods you can use for squaring the tap with the face of the work. One of these methods is to rest the work on a drill press table while you manually rotate the tap, which is gripped in the drill chuck, until at least one or two full threads have been cut.

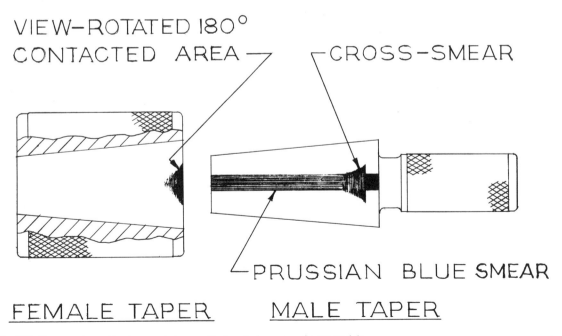

VIEW—ROTATED 180°
CONTACTED AREA
CROSS-SMEAR
PRUSSIAN BLUE SMEAR
FEMALE TAPER   MALE TAPER

Fig. T-9. Taper-gaging with plugs and sleeves. Test and closeness of a tapered fit.

Another, but slightly slower, method is to clamp the work to the faceplate of a lathe. A smaller tap can be held in a drill chuck. The chuck, in turn, is held in the tail-stock spindle.

For large taps, the tail-stock center is often used in supporting the tap's shank. To prevent tap rotation, use a lathe dog, or larger tap wrench with its one handle rested atop the compound.

There is, of course, much tapping done in large and irregular shaped sections, which do not lend themselves to clamping to any machine or fixture. Therefore, you must employ other squaring methods for cutting, at least the first two threads (Fig. T-10).

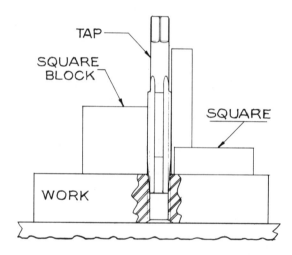

Fig. T-10. Tapping square to the work face.

Figure T-11 shows a common, commercially produced, tapping fixture. The work rests atop the base, while the tap is gripped in a vertically held tap wrench. The tap wrench spindle is at right angles to the base.

TAPPING A TRUE RUNNING THREAD. Trying to tape a smaller-diameter thread into the end of a rotating shaft invariably presented some undesirable results. Regardless of the methods used, the thread would never run true enough.

This problem was finally solved by grasping the tap wrench handle with the left hand while following the tap inward by screwing out the tail-stock center with the right hand. This, of course, is the common method of tapping holes in a lathe (Fig. T-12).

However, for true running threads, the left hand holds the wrench handle for only one-half revolution at a time,

then releases it, immediately catching the other, on-coming handle. Hold it for one-half revolution, then release it and catch the next on-coming handle.

Repeat this half-revolution catching and releasing of the wrench's handles until the tap has cut at least three to four full threads. Then the tap wrench can be gripped with both hands to complete the tapping.

It seems as though the tap follows the drilled hole, which runs out almost invariably. By manipulating the tap wrench, as mentioned, you cause it to act more as a boring tool, producing its own true bore. It works, particularly in tapping holes smaller than 1/2 inch, and in an older lathe.

TAPPING BLIND HOLES. Figure T-13 shows a cross section of a blind tapped hole. This type of tapping is very common where work must be leakproof or is simply too thick to be tapped all the way through.

Ordinarily, the effective thread depth (E) should not be less than the diameter of the screw. This one-to-one ratio can be used in steel and in places where frequent screwing in and out is not required. However, for additional security under the same conditions, the effective depth should always be up to 1 1/2 times the screw's diameter. For softer and more brittle materials, the effective thread should always be made (tapped) deeper, as much as 2 times the diameter of the screw.

Remember that the standard length of a nut is always equal to the screw's diameter. This one-to-one nut/screw ratio in steel is strong enough so that, upon excessive tightening, the standard nut will usually break the screw off before the threads in the nut are stripped.

Actual pulling tests show that holes for tapping (D) drilled as much as 25 percent larger than the screw's minor diameter are only 5 percent weaker than a full-depth thread. The larger tap drill sizes result in much easier tapping, and fewer broken taps and disappointments.

Never tap a hole that has not been either counterbored or countersunk first. In general practice, the counterbore (C) should be no smaller than the diameter of the tap's body drill, and from 1 to 1 1/2 threads deep (A). No counterboring or countersinking of a hole before tapping means very sloppy workmanship.

In Fig. T-13:

X - Designates an extra length of effective threads.

T - Designates the tapering lead produced by the starting tap.

B - Is the additional depth of the drilled hole, which should be deep enough to prevent the starting tap from striking the bottom.

By following up with a bottoming tap (one having a short

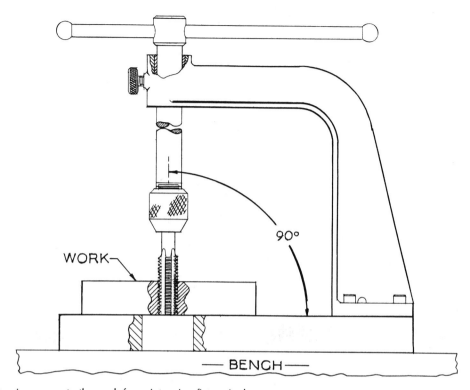

Fig. T-11. Tapping square to the work face. A tapping fixture is shown.

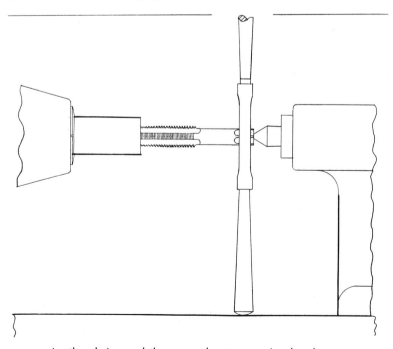

Fig. T-12. Tapping a true running thread. A worn lathe can produce true running threads.

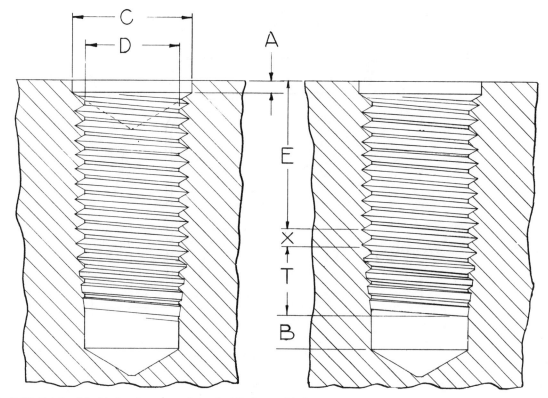

Fig. T-13. Tapping blind holes. A cross sections of a blind tapped hole.

lead), the effective threads can be made considerably deeper (longer) without increasing the total depth of the hole.

ENLARGING A TAPPED HOLE. When a tapped hole must be enlarged a few thousandths of an inch, as for hardening purposes, it can be done by first tapping the hole in the conventional manner.

Follow this step by tightly rolling or twisting a convenient length of rag and draping it over the end of the tap (Fig. T-14). The twisted rag will push the tap off-center, causing it to act as a boring tool, or reamer, and consequently producing a larger-diameter tapped hole.

Repeat the "twisted-rag" tapping until the hole acquires the required looseness. Use a bottoming tap in this enlargement effort.

TRUNCATING TAPS. Some metals are much more difficult to tap than others. Often you will get more tap breakage and work spoilage than tapped holes. One method of overcoming this difficulty is to partially grind off some of the tap's outside diameter (Fig. T-15). An older tap of the same size generally will do quite well.

The grinding can be done off-hand, with a little prac-

tice. Just make sure the back-off clearance is maintained.

Grind off, or truncate, the thread tops about 20 percent on the side. Since the tap is not compelled to cut a full-depth thread, it will turn with much less effort, thereby lessening the chance of its breakage. Follow this step by using a full-sized tap for sizing the threads.

This system has been used successfully on many types of jobs, especially when it is necessary to hand-tap small diameters in stainless steel and other tough materials.

THREADS

AMERICAN NATIONAL UNIFIED 60° THREAD, CUTTING. Figure T-16 shows an American National 60° Thread Form (Table T-3). This thread is also known as the American Standard Unified Thread (Table T-4). It was formerly known as the United States Standard Thread. The difference in names has to do with the amounts of top and bottom (crest and root) clearance; otherwise they are both alike at their pitch diameters.

Because of the sloping thread walls, the 60° thread lends itself to easy cutting with a circular form cutter in a mill-

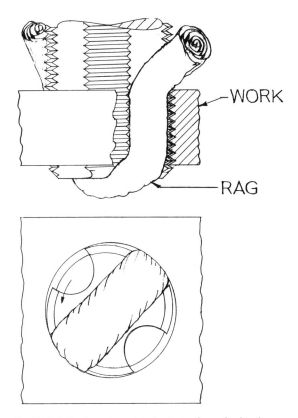

Fig. T-14. Enlarging a tapped hole. A simple method is shown.

ing machine. It can be rolled to size as in threading bolts and studs. It can be cut with a threading die, cut with a single-point tool in a screw-cutting lathe, and also ground to size very accurately.

In cutting a national form 60° thread in an engine lathe, you must first consider the pitch of the thread to be cut. If it is to be coarser than 8 threads per inch, use two tools, one for roughing and one for finishing (T-1 and T-2 in Fig. T-17). The cutting rake atop the roughing tool is rounded out to help steer the curling chip out of the thread groove.

For threading iron, brass, or bronze, the tool's top surface should always be from flat to slightly negative.

For finishing the thread, switch to form tool T-2. It is not always necessary to grind the tool's edge angles, as shown, in relation to the shank of the tool; that is, the trailing edge does not necessarily need to be parallel with the shank of the tool.

However, long practice on a very wide variety of work does favor this parallel cutting-edge-to-shank relationship. When you are cutting finer than, for example, 8 threads per inch, a roughing tool might not be necessary in every case.

The American national 60° thread can be cut in a screw-cutting lathe, using several tool-sharpening styles. The style largely depends on the thread's pitch, the material to be cut, the quality of the finish, and the fit required. Usually the amount of time allowed for cutting a thread is also a determining factor.

GROUND OFF

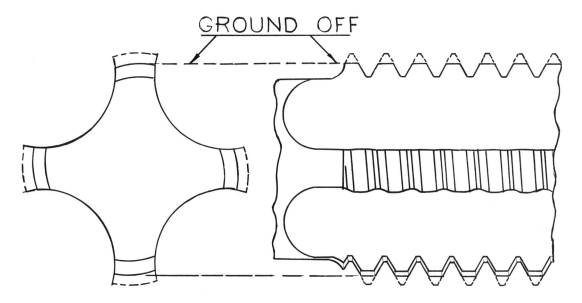

Fig. T-15. Truncating taps. Partially grind off some of the tap's outside diameter, as shown.

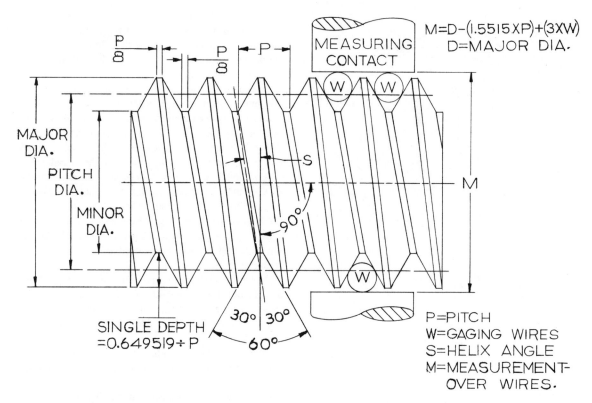

$$M = D - (1.5515 \times P) + (3 \times W)$$
$$D = MAJOR\ DIA.$$

MEASURING CONTACT

MAJOR DIA.

PITCH DIA.

MINOR DIA.

SINGLE DEPTH =0.649519 ÷ P

30° 30°

60°

90°

S

M

W W

W

P=PITCH
W=GAGING WIRES
S=HELIX ANGLE
M=MEASUREMENT-
   OVER WIRES.

Fig. T-16. American National Unified 60° thread, cutting.

Assume you are called upon to cut an external 2 5/8, 8 threads per inch, in steel. Grind a roughing tool as in T-1, its point having a .015-inch radius, with a hooked back rake on its top, to help bring out the chip.

The lathe's compound is swiveled to 29° from the screw's axial centerline. However, the tool's leading edge is set at 30°, using a thread-centering gage for the setting (Fig. T-18).

The roughing cuts are made by feeding in at 29° with the compound rest. The feeding in and cutting are stopped when the widths of the threads' tops (crests) measure slightly more than one-eighth of the threads' pitch. In 8 threads per inch, the widths of the finished crests are .0156 inch. Stop the roughing when the crest widths measure approximately .020 inch.

Use a sulphur-based cutting oil for the roughing.

Now replace the roughing tool with the finishing tool, which should be ground and honed as in T-2. Its top should be flat; its point no more than .015 wide, or slightly less than one-eighth of the thread's pitch. Its top should be pointed into, or be very slightly below, the screw's axial centerline.

The cutting tool is squared up with the screw's axial centerline, using a thread-centering gage.

Adjust the finishing tool in the thread groove to where its trailing side just starts to shave the right thread wall. At the same time, the tool's point should cut at least some of the roundness out of the bottom of the roughed-out thread groove.

For the next cut, advance the tool inward by screwing in with the compound a few thousandths of an inch. The result is usually a light shaving with the leading side of the tool on the thread's left wall.

Repeat this shaving by lesser amounts until the thread is to size. If you happen to have a female thread gage of this size, now is the time to try it on.

AMERICAN NATIONAL 60° THREAD, MEASUREMENT

If no thread gage is available, then measure your thread using three wires and a micrometer. The size (diameter) of the wires used for this purpose can be easily determined by multiplying the constant 0.57735 by the thread's pitch. The pitch in this case is .125 inch. Hence, 0.57735 × .125

Table T-3. Thread Forms, Courtesy Dercks Gage Dial.

	SCREW NO. & SIZE	THREADS PER INCH	OUTSIDE DIA. OF TAP	TAP DRILL SIZE — 75% FULL THREAD	BODY DRILL
+	0	80	.060	3-64	1-16
	1	56	.073	54	49
++	1	64	.073	53	49
+	1	72	.073	53	49
++	2	56	.086	50	44
+	2	64	.086	50	44
++	3	48	.099	47	39
+	3	56	.099	45	39
	4	32	.112	45	33
	4	36	.112	44	33
++	4	40	.112	43	33
+	4	48	.112	42	33
	5	36	.125	40	1-8
++	5	40	.125	38	1-8
+	5	44	.125	37	1-8
++	6	32	.138	36	28
	6	36	.138	34	28
+	6	40	.138	33	28
	7	30	.151	31	24
	7	32	.151	31	24
	7	36	.151	1/8	24
	8	30	.164	30	19
++	8	32	.164	29	19
+	8	36	.164	29	19
	8	40	.164	28	19
	9	24	.177	29	16
	9	30	.177	27	16
	9	32	.177	26	16

	SCREW NO. & SIZE	THREADS PER INCH	OUTSIDE DIA. OF TAP	TAP DRILL SIZE — 75% FULL THREAD	BODY DRILL
++	10	24	.190	25	11
	10	28	.190	23	11
	10	30	.190	22	11
+	10	32	.190	21	11
++	12	24	.216	16	7-32
+	12	28	.216	14	7-32
	12	32	.216	13	7-32
	14	20	.242	10	D
	14	24	.242	7	D
	16	18	.268	3	I
	16	20	.268	7-32	I
	16	22	.268	2	I
	18	18	.294	B	M
	18	20	.294	D	M
	20	16	.320	G	P
	20	18	.320	17-64	P
	20	20	.320	I	P
	22	16	.346	9-32	S
	22	18	.346	L	S
	24	16	.372	5-16	3-8
	24	18	.372	O	3-8
	26	14	.398	21-64	Y
	26	16	.398	R	Y
	28	14	.424	T	7-16
	28	16	.424	23-64	7-16
	30	14	.450	V	29-64
	30	16	.450	25-64	29-64

+ = AMERICAN NATIONAL FINE THREAD FORM
++ = AMERICAN NATIONAL COARSE THREAD FORM
AMERICAN NATIONAL FORM MACHINE SCREWS

Table T-4. American Standard United Threads.

SIZE OF TAP	COARSE THDS PER IN.	COARSE TAP DRILL	FINE THDS PER IN.	FINE TAP DRILL	EXTRA FINE THDS PER IN.	EXTRA FINE TAP DRILL
1/4	20	NO. 7	28	NO. 3	32	7/32
5/16	18	LET. F	24	LET. I	32	9/32
3/8	16	5/16	24	LET. Q	32	11/32
7/16	14	LET. U	20	25/64	28	13/32
1/2	13	27/64	20	29/64	28	15/32
9/16	12	31/64	18	33/64	24	33/64
5/8	11	17/32	18	37/64	24	37/64
1 1/16	—	—	—	—	24	41/64
3/4	10	21/32	16	11/16	20	45/64
13/16	—	—	—	—	20	49/64
7/8	9	49/64	14	13/16	20	53/64
15/16	—	—	—	—	20	57/64
1	—	—	[14]	15/16	—	—
1	8	7/8	12	59/64	20	61/64
1 1/16	—	—	—	—	18	1
1 1/8	7	63/64	[12]	1 3/64	18	1 5/64
1 3/16	—	—	—	—	18	1 9/64
1 1/4	7	1 7/64	[12]	1 11/64	18	1 3/16
1 5/16	—	—	—	—	18	1 17/64
1 3/8	6	1 7/32	[12]	1 19/64	18	1 5/16
1 7/16	—	—	—	—	18	1 3/8
1 1/2	6	1 11/32	12	1 27/64	18	1 7/16
1 9/16	—	—	—	—	18	1 1/2
1 5/8	—	—	—	—	18	1 9/16
1 11/16	—	—	—	—	18	1 5/8
1 3/4	5	1 9/16	—	—	16	1 1/16
	4 1/2	1 25/32	—	—	16	1 15/16
2 1/4	4 1/2	2 1/32				
2 1/2	4	2 1/4				
2 3/4	4	2 1/2				
3	4	2 3/4				
3 1/4	4	3				
3 1/2	4	3 1/4				
3 3/4	4	3 1/2				
4	4	3 3/4				

AMERICAN STANDARD UNIFIED THREADS. BRACKETS DENOTE S.A.E. THREAD SERIES. TAP DRILLS ALLOW APPROX. 75% FULL THREAD

= .0721 inch. This answer represents the best wire size, one that will contact the sloping thread walls at the pitch diameter (Fig. T-16).

Other wire diameters can also be used, as shown in Table T-5. This table shows the maximum and minimum wire sizes that can be used. Regardless of the wire size, however, they must always project slightly above the crests of the thread.

To find what M, (the measurement over wires) should be, resort to the formula

$$M = D - (1.5515 \times P) + (3W)$$

where

M = Measurement over wires.
D = Major, or outside diameter of screw.
P = Pitch, or the amount of axial screw travel in one revolution.

W = Diameter of measuring wires used.

The pitch in our example is: .125 inch, whereupon $1.5515 \times .125 = .1939375$ inch. This product is then subtracted from the screw's major diameter, which is 2.625 inch. Hence, $2.625 - .19393 = 2.43107$. To this add three of the wire diameters used. In this case the wire diameter is .0721. Hence, $.0721 \times 3 = .2165$. This product added to $2.43107 = 2.64758$ inches, which represents M.

Note: Loosely bind the wire ends with weak rubber bands to keep them in place while you are measuring the thread, and do not forget to cover the lathe's carriage with a cloth or whatever to protect the wires from accidentally falling and becoming lost in the chips below. You can purchase thread measuring wires. They are hardened, ground, and lapped to within five decimal places or better.

For ordinary thread cutting, the use of extremely accurate wires is not always necessary. Very handy substitutes are the shanks of new number drills.

CUTTING THE AMERICAN NATIONAL FORM THREAD

Figure T-16 shows an external American National 60° thread form, previously known as the United States Standard Thread.

The basic angle between the sides, as measured in an axial plane, is 60°. The line bisecting the 60° angle is at right angles to the axis of the screw thread.

The flat at the root and crest of the thread form is 1/8 of the pitch, or .125 times the pitch.

The single depth of the thread form is .0649519 times the pitch. The double depth of the thread form is .0649519 times 2, divided by the pitch, or .1299038 times the pitch.

To find what the bore diameter should be before threading internally, for convenience sake, keep in mind the double-depth constant .12990, or .1300. The .1300 constant is only .0001 inch greater than .1299 and much easier to remember. The .1300 double-depth constant will do for almost all American National Thread applications, with

one exception: the extremely precise thread gages.

For example, if you wish to know the depth of a 13-pitch thread, simply divide the constant .1300 by the 13-pitch thread. The answer of .100 inch is the double depth of the thread; .050 inch is the single depth.

If your screw is to be .5 inch in diameter, subtract the double depth of .100 inch from the .5-inch major diameter of the screw, to get a .400-inch drill or bore diameter for a .5-inch, 13-thread nut.

In theory these figures are quite correct but not practical. Because the cutting tool's point rounds off slightly from wear and because there are errors in the pitch and the angles, the full 100 percent thread depth cannot be used. The male and female would not engage without considerable interference. Generally, all holes to be tapped are purposely made up to 25 percent larger than the minor diameter of the tap and screw. This added clearance results in much easier tapping, with less tap breakage. The larger holes lessen the tensile strength of the mated threads by only a few percentage points.

The double-depth constant .1300 can be used for all

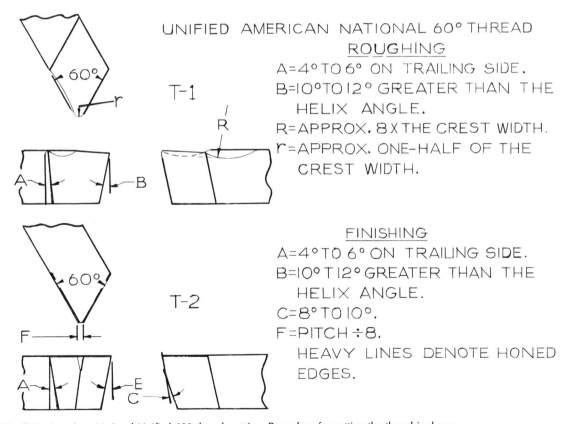

UNIFIED AMERICAN NATIONAL 60° THREAD
ROUGHING
A=4° TO 6° ON TRAILING SIDE.
B=10° TO 12° GREATER THAN THE
HELIX ANGLE.
R=APPROX. 8 X THE CREST WIDTH.
r=APPROX. ONE-HALF OF THE
CREST WIDTH.

FINISHING
A=4° TO 6° ON TRAILING SIDE.
B=10° T 12° GREATER THAN THE
HELIX ANGLE.
C=8° TO 10°.
F=PITCH ÷ 8.
HEAVY LINES DENOTE HONED
EDGES.

Fig. T-17. American National Unified 60° thread, cutting. Procedure for cutting the thread is shown.

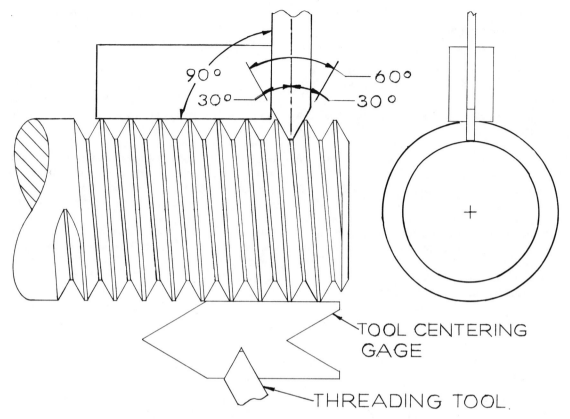

Fig. T-18. American National Unified 60° thread, cutting. Use a thread-centering gage for the setting.

larger internal threading. For example, if you must make a nut to screw over a 6-inch-diameter screw having 8 threads per inch, how much must you allow for the thread?

The double-depth constants .1299 or .1300 when divided by the pitch, 8, equal .1625 inch, so subtract this amount from the 6-inch screw's major diameter, for a bore of 5.8348 inches. Again, in theory this figure is good, but in practice this figure will not work. Allowances always must be made for variations in the cutting tool angles, for wear on the tool point, and for likely errors in the lead screw's pitch and the thread's wall angles.

Therefore, the bore in the nut is always made larger than these figures indicate. This increase might be .010 to .020 inch in the bore of the nut, for clearance. In other words, the bore should be about 5.8348 plus .010, which equals 5.844 inches. For a larger-pitch thread, the clearance should be even greater, of course.

When a single-point tool is used instead of a tap, the usual tapping clearances do not apply necessarily.

THREAD-CUTTING IN A LATHE. Thread-cutting, or

thread chasing as it is sometimes called, can be most interesting and satisfying. It can also be very frustrating if the various procedures are not followed.

Modern-day screw-cutting lathes have quick change feed and screw-cutting gear boxes, which eliminate the necessity of calculating gear ratios for almost any required thread leads. The necessary levers are merely turned or shifted into their proper positions, as indicated by the attached instruction plates, with no further calculation necessary.

Just about all lathes are geared so that, if gears having the same number of teeth are placed on both the stud and the lead screw, it will result in cutting a thread exactly the same as on the lead screw. This procedure is known as *even gearing*.

In cutting the same thread with alike gears, both the work and the lead screw rotate at the same rate. To cut a faster, or coarser, pitch thread, the lead screw must rotate faster than the work. Therefore, a larger gear must go on the stud, and a smaller gear on the lead screw.

For finer threads, the larger gear goes on the lead screw, and the smaller gear goes on the stud (Fig. T-19).

Table T-5. Wire Diameters.

THREADS PER INCH N	PITCH $P=\frac{1}{N}$	WIRE SIZES AND CONSTANTS AMERICAN NATIONAL FORM THD. WIRE SIZES		
		BEST SIZE 0.577350×P INCH	MAXIMUM 1.010363×P INCH	MINIMUM 0.505182×P INCH
4-----	0.25000	0.14434	0.25259	0.12630
4 1/2---	.22222	.12830	.22453	.11226
5----	.20000	.11547	.20207	.10104
6----	.16667	.09623	.16839	.08420
7----	.14286	.08248	.14434	.07217
7 1/2---	.13333	.07698	.13472	.06736
8----	.12500	.07217	.12630	.06315
9----	.11111	.06415	.11226	.05613
10---	.10000	.05773	.10104	.05052
11---	.09091	.05249	.09185	.04593
11 1/2-	.08696	.05020	.08786	.04393
12---	.08333	.04811	.08420	.04210
13---	.07692	.04441	.07772	.03886
14---	.07143	.04124	.07217	.03608
16---	.06250	.03608	.06315	.03157
18---	.05556	.03208	.05613	.02807
20---	.05000	.02887	.05052	.02526
24---	.04167	.02406	.04210	.02105
27---	.03704	.02138	.03742	.01871
28---	.03571	.02062	.03608	.01804
32--	.03125	.01804	.03157	.01579
36--	.02778	.01604	.02807	.01403
40--	.02500	.01443	.02526	.01263
44--	.02273	.01312	.02296	.01148
48--	.02083	.01203	.02105	.01052
56--	.01786	.01031	.01804	.00902
64--	.01562	.00902	.01579	.00789
72--	.01389	.00802	.01403	.00702
80--	.01250	.00722	.01263	.00631

If we have a lead screw with 6 threads per inch, the gears that would be required to cut 8 threads per inch would be found by multiplying both the lead screw's threads per inch and the threads per inch to be cut by the same number until it gives you the two gears you might have in your set of gears. If the answer does not match your set of gears, try a different multiplier, such as 4, 5, 6, or whatever.

If your set of gears varies by four teeth, then multiply the lead screw's thread—which in this case is 6—by 4: 6 × 4 = 24 teeth. Multiply the thread to be cut by 4 also: 8 × 4 = 32 teeth. Thereupon, you get a 24-tooth gear and a 32-tooth gear.

Because 8 is slower than 6, the larger, 32-tooth, gear goes on the lead screw, and the smaller, 24-tooth, gear goes on the stud to propel the cutting tool along at a slightly lower rate.

To cut 20 threads per inch with a 4-thread-per-inch lead screw and the gears in your set, which vary by 5 teeth, then multiply 5 teeth by 4 lead screw pitch for the stud: $5 \times 4 = 20$. Multiply 5 teeth by threads to be cut: $5 \times 20 = 100$ teeth for the lead screw.

To cut 2 threads per inch with a 4-pitch lead screw with the gears in your set varying by 4 teeth, multiply $4 \times 2 = 8$-tooth gear required for the lead scsrew; $4 \times 4 = 16$-tooth gear required for the stud. Since these two gears are too small to be practical, you must multiply both gears by some number that will give you larger gears. You can try 4 as the multiplier; whereupon, $4 \times 8 = 32$ and $4 \times 16 = 64$ as the two gears.

If the thread to be cut is slower than the pitch of the lead screw, the *driving*, or stud, *gear* will be the smaller one, while the *driven*, or lead screw, *gear* will be the larger one. The reverse is true when you are cutting threads that are faster than the pitch on the lead screw.

If you are cutting 20 threads with a 4-pitch lead screw, there might not be a 100-tooth gear available. Then you can compound the gearing by using any gears having a 2 to 1 ratio between the 20-tooth stud gear and the 100-tooth lead-screw gear. The 20-tooth stud gear must drive the large 100-tooth gear of the 2 to 1 compound, while the smaller gear drives the lead-screw 50-tooth gear.

Always remember that the *lead-screw pitch* is the thread that would be cut when gears having the same number of teeth are put on both the stud and the lead screw. When a lathe is compound geared, the stud gear drives an auxiliary gear (B in Fig. T-19) which increases or decreases the rotary motion.

Also, it is most important that the lead screw have no end play, especially when you are cutting larger-pitch threads.

LEAD AND PITCH DEFINITIONS

PITCH. The distance from a point on the screw thread to a corresponding point on the adjacent thread.

LEAD. The distance a screw advances axially in one revolution.

On a single-thread screw, the lead and pitch are exactly alike. On a double-thread screw, the lead is two times the pitch. On a triple-thread screw, the lead is three times the pitch. On a quadruple-thread screw, the lead is four times the pitch.

MEASURING THE NUMBER OF THREADS PER INCH

Figure T-20 shows a method of measuring (checking) the number of threads per inch to which the lathe's gearing

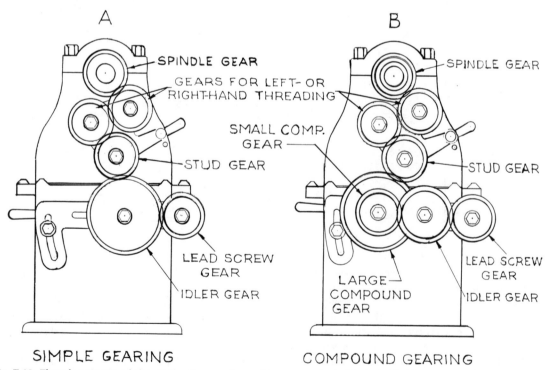

Fig. T-19. Thread-cutting in a lathe. Gear ratios are changed to cut some specific thread leads.

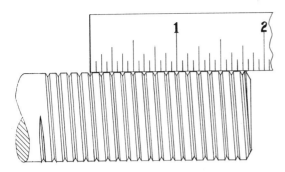

Fig. T-20. Thread-cutting in a lathe. Measure the number of threads per inch.

is set. Although there are commercially produced pitch gages for this purpose, it is very convenient to determine the number of threads per inch by simply measuring with a scale.

When a job set in a lathe is ready to be threaded, always make sure that all the gear transmission handles were shifted correctly so that the required thread pitch will result.

The first thing to do is to take a very light threading cut, just deep enough to be seen easily. Then hold a scale atop the screw, as shown, counting the number of threads in 1 inch.

Caution! Do not count the grooves. Repeat the count once more just to be sure you are cutting the right pitch.

For fine threads whose total length will only be a fraction of an inch, it is usually better to hold a pencil or scriber

on the moving tool holder or bar, permitting it to scribe the thread's pitch on the periphery of the rotating chuck or some other smooth portion of the rotating work. Whenever possible, allow the marking to continue for slightly more than 1 inch.

You then can measure the markings more easily over a 1-inch span, especially when you are cutting odd pitches of threads.

INTERNAL THREADING IN THE SCREW CUTTING LATHE

Figure T-21 shows a fast method of cutting an American National Unified 60° thread. Swivel the lathe's compound 61 percent to the axis of the work, but set the centerline of the cutting tool at right angles to the job's axial center.

For all larger-diameter internal threading, position the boring bar and cutting tool to cut on the back side of the bore, with its cutting tool positioned upside down. The boring bar enters the bore up to the limit mark (L). For all 60° threads from 8 threads per inch and coarser, first rough out the thread with a slightly rounded, hook-nose tool, 58° to 59° wide (T-1 in Fig. T-22). Feed in this roughing tool at 29°, taking as heavy a cut as the tool will stand. When you are cutting steel use a generous application of sulphur-based cutting oil.

Repeat the heavier cutting by feeding in the tool at an angle with the compound. After the point of the roughing tool has almost touched the counterbored diameter (C), change over to the 60° finishing tool (T-2 in Fig. T-22). Adjust the tool laterally until it cuts very lightly on the

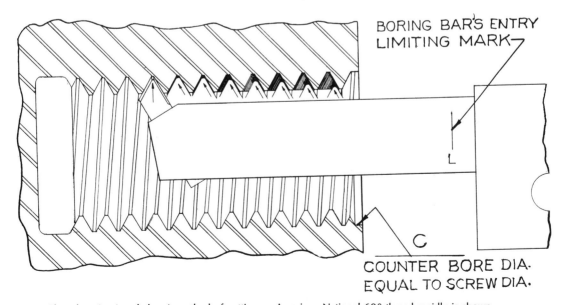

Fig. T-21. Thread-cutting in a lathe. A method of cutting an American National 60° thread rapidly is shown.

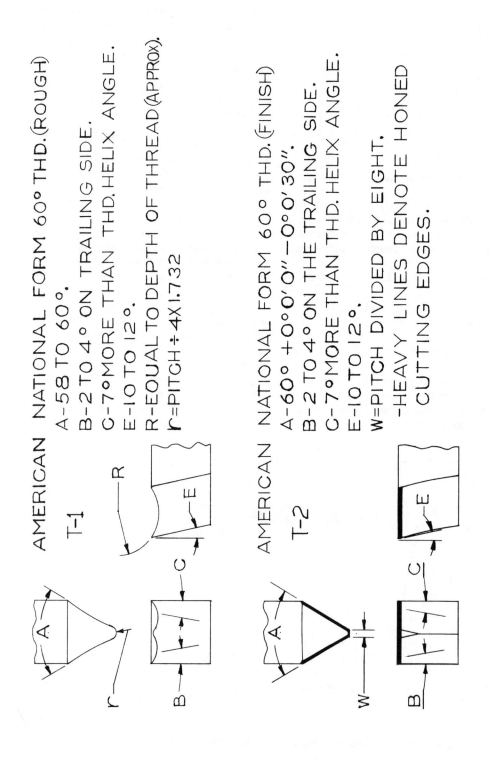

AMERICAN NATIONAL FORM 60° THD. (ROUGH)

T-1

A - 58 TO 60°.
B - 2 TO 4° ON TRAILING SIDE.
C - 7° MORE THAN THD. HELIX ANGLE.
E - 10 TO 12°.
R - EQUAL TO DEPTH OF THREAD (APPROX).
r = PITCH ÷ 4 X 1.732

AMERICAN NATIONAL FORM 60° THD. (FINISH)

T-2

A - 60° + 0° 0' 0" − 0° 0' 30".
B - 2 TO 4° ON THE TRAILING SIDE.
C - 7° MORE THAN THD. HELIX ANGLE.
E - 10 TO 12°.
W = PITCH DIVIDED BY EIGHT.
- HEAVY LINES DENOTE HONED
  CUTTING EDGES.

Fig. T-22. Thread-cutting in a lathe. First rough out the thread with a slightly rounded, hook-nose tool.

222

thread wall nearest to you, or the following side. Feed in at 61° shaving the one side of the thread until some of the bottom (root) is also cut. Mark or set the cross-feed dial to zero. Continue the cutting by feeding in at 61°, until the leading or left side of the thread shows signs of being shaved. Blow, wipe, or clean out the thread and try-in the male screw gage. If you want a more shiny finish, use a soap water coolant for the final shaves.

Using the described method of internal thread cutting, an 8-pitch thread 4 to 8 inches in diameter can be completed in not more than 10 cuts in steel, nicely and repeatedly.

THREADING BLIND INTERNALLY

Internal, as well as external, threads can be started and ended without the need to cut any relief grooves for either end of the thread (Fig. T-23).

For internal thread cutting, it is always better to cut upside down, and on the back side of the bore. Mark the top side of the bar as at A and B. The A indicates the start of the thread, while B indicates the limit of the bar's entry into the bore. The mark C is used to indicate the radial starting and stopping points of the thread.

By watching the cross-feed dial mark, synchronize lines A and B with line C to indicate when to feed the cutting tool into the thread and when to pull the tool out of the thread.

TYPES OF THREAD ENDINGS

Figure T-24 shows three of the more common methods of ending a thread cut in a screw-cutting lathe.

Pull out the tool at A at the end of each cut. This step is quite simple for a finer pitch of threads, but for larger thread cutting you must tighten the cross-feed slide, causing the tool to be pushed out as the end pressure against the tool builds up. You can control the rapidity of the push-out manually by unwinding the cross feed's screw handle. On large threads, the cross slide might be tightened to the extent where you need both hands to unwind the cross feed. This method results in a thread ending resembling that left by a circular milling cutter.

The ending of a thread in a drilled hole is shown at B. You can perform this operation very nicely if you are "quick on the draw," and then only if the lathe is equipped with a good brake. Of course, the work rotation is less rapid when you are using this system. You can drill the hole after the first cut has been made, or beforehand. In the second method, you must adjust each progressive cut to meet with the hole's diameter. Be prepared to break a threading tool occasionally.

Another very common thread ending is shown at C. This method requires no push, holes, or sudden pull outs. Always make the neck's diameter just small enough so that the threading tool will leave no marks. Any thread tool

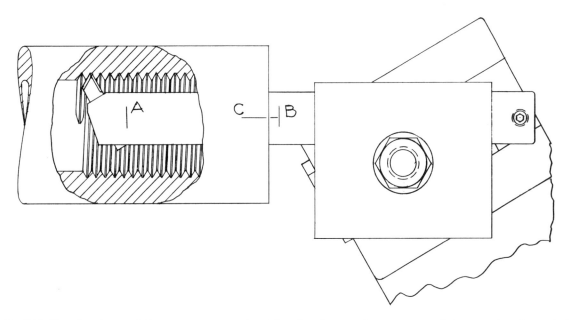

Fig. T-23. Thread-cutting in a lathe. You can start and end threads without needing to cut any relief grooves for either end of the thread, as shown.

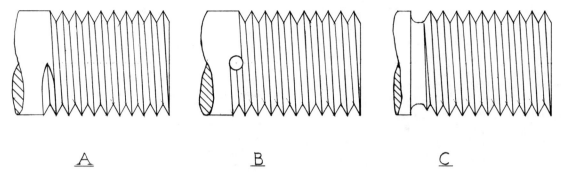

Fig. T-24. Thread-cutting in a lathe. Three methods of ending a thread cut in a screw-cutting lathe are shown.

marks around the neck invite screw breakage at that mark.

SQUARE-THREAD CUTTING

Perhaps the most simple threads to cut in the screw-cutting lathe is the square thread in (Fig. T-25). The thread groove is theoretically as wide as the thread rib. The thread groove is also as deep as it is wide, in theory.

For example, if a 4-pitch square thread is called for, in the space of 1 inch there are to be four complete threads. One complete square thread consists of one thread groove and one thread rib. Since square threads are made up of two distinct linear divisions, then 4 threads per inch multiplied by 2 equals 8 divisions. So, there are 8 divisions to the inch. Therefore, your thread-cutting tool must be 1/8 inch in width. However, because of possible errors and the necessary working clearance, the finishing tool must be at least .1255 to .1260 inch wide, giving a longitudinal clear-

ance of approximately .001 inch.

By making the thread groove .0005 inch wider, the thread's rib becomes .0005 inch narrower. Much better results can be obtained by first roughing out the thread groove with a hook-nose tool, which should be about .010 inch narrower than the finished groove width (T-1 in Fig. T-26).

In square-thread cutting it is customary to turn the end of the blank down to the screw's minor diameter, and for a width equal to the width of one thread groove.

MULTI LEAD-THREAD CUTTING

Figure T-27 shows a multiple-lead thread, which generally is used where the screw or nut travel per revolution must be increased. However, when the diameter of the work is not large enough to accommodate a coarser pitch of threads, you must cut two or more smaller threads having

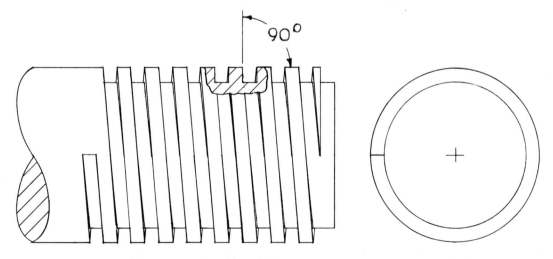

Fig. T-25. Thread-cutting in a lathe. A square thread is probably the most simple thread to cut in a lathe.

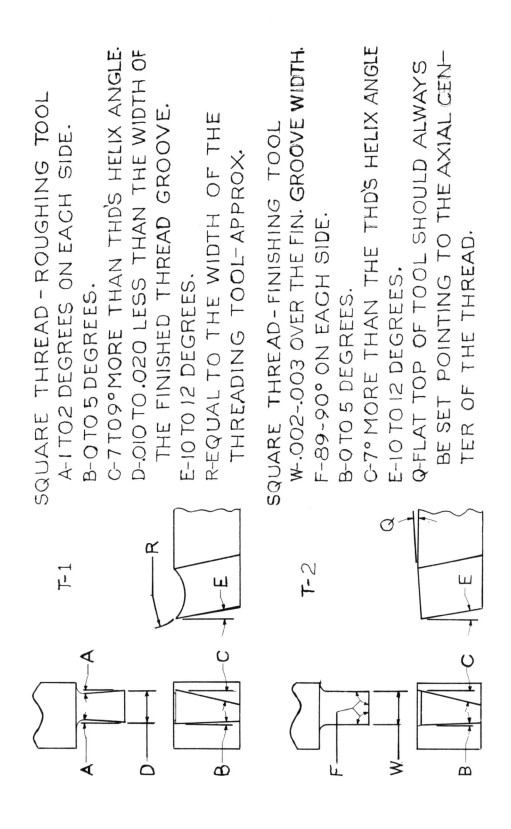

SQUARE THREAD - ROUGHING TOOL

A-1 TO 2 DEGREES ON EACH SIDE.

B-0 TO 5 DEGREES.

C-7 TO 9° MORE THAN THD'S HELIX ANGLE.

D-.010 TO .020 LESS THAN THE WIDTH OF THE FINISHED THREAD GROOVE.

E-10 TO 12 DEGREES.

R-EQUAL TO THE WIDTH OF THE THREADING TOOL-APPROX.

T-1

SQUARE THREAD - FINISHING TOOL

W-.002-.003 OVER THE FIN. GROOVE WIDTH.

F-89-90° ON EACH SIDE.

B-0 TO 5 DEGREES.

C-7° MORE THAN THE THD'S HELIX ANGLE

E-10 TO 12 DEGREES.

Q-FLAT TOP OF TOOL SHOULD ALWAYS BE SET POINTING TO THE AXIAL CENTER OF THE THREAD.

T-2

Fig. T-26. Thread-cutting in a lathe. First rough out the thread groove with a hook-nose tool to have better results for a square thread.

225

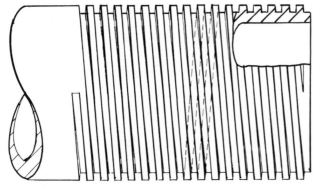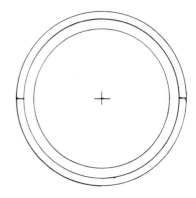

Fig. T-27. Thread-cutting in a lathe. A multiple-lead thread is shown.

a greater lead, instead of one large thread. If the rate of travel must be increased three times, cut three separate leads (of threads), or four, or whatever.

Each of these separate threads is known as a *lead*. A lead is the distance a screw advances axially in one turn.

The leads are equally spaced around the cylindrical surface of the work. You can space or divide the leads on the work surface in more than one way, depending on whether you are working with internal or external threads. After you have cut one of a two-lead thread, mark the stud gear where it is in full engagement with the spindle feed gear. Counting the number of teeth in the spindle's feed gear, mark off exactly one-half revolution on the spindle's feed gear. Now withdraw the stud gear from the spindle gear, and manually rotate the spindle exactly one-half revolution. Then reengage the stud with the spindle's feed gear. This maneuver positions the thread-cutting tool exactly halfway between the first-cut thread grooves.

In the case of a triple-lead thread, withdraw the stud gear, rotate the lathe spindle and work one-third revolution by marking and counting the teeth, then remesh the gears. In a four-lead thread, withdraw the marked-off stud gear and rotate the lathe spindle one-fourth revolution at a time, and so on.

One important matter in cutting multilead screws is the width of the cutting tool. For example, if you are called upon to cut a double-lead 4-pitch square thread, you can figure that your tool must be 2 × 4, or 1/8 inch in width. Measure the tool's width with a micrometer, making it .1255 to .1260 inch wide. If the same width of tool is used for finishing the internal thread of the mating nut, these dimensions will allow an end play of .001 to .002 inch, assuming that all other conditions are correct.

In the case of a triple-lead, four-pitch square thread, the tool must be 3 × 4 = 12, or 1/12 inch wide. Dividing the

inch by 12 equals .0833 inch. This number represents the tool's width, without clearance allowances. To allow for some end clearance, grind the tool .0843 inch wide.

Remember when you are measuring the width of the tool to hold the micrometer at nearly the same angle to the top of the tool as is the helix angle of the screw.

For a better finish and more accurate lead spacing, it is best to rough out all the thread leads first. Then go over the thread once again with the exact width and shape of tool.

For internal multilead threading, the lead spacing can be done in the same way. For external multilead threading, the work can be held between centers, with the driving dog's tail inserted into as many equally spaced holes in the driving plate as are the required number of leads.

STANDARD ACME THREAD FORM. Figure T-28 shows a standard American Acme Thread Form. The acme thread has certain advantages over the square thread. Because of its slanting walls, it can be readily milled using a circular rotary cutter. Also, the radial play between the nut and screw can be controlled by the tolerance in their pitch diameters.

In cutting an external acme thread in a screw-cutting lathe, it is customary to turn down the blank's end to a diameter equal to the minor diameter of the screw and to a width approximating one-thread groove.

Especially in larger-pitch threads, first rough out the thread using a hook-nose tool (T-1 in Fig. T-29), much like the tool used for roughing square threads. Follow the roughing by using the finishing tool (T-2 in Fig. T-29), laterally centering the end of the finishing tool with the groove's bottom width. Feed the tool straight inwardly in lessening amounts as it approaches the bottom (root) of the thread. You can buy templates for grinding and properly centering acme threading tools with the work.

Before you get too close to the bottom, however, you

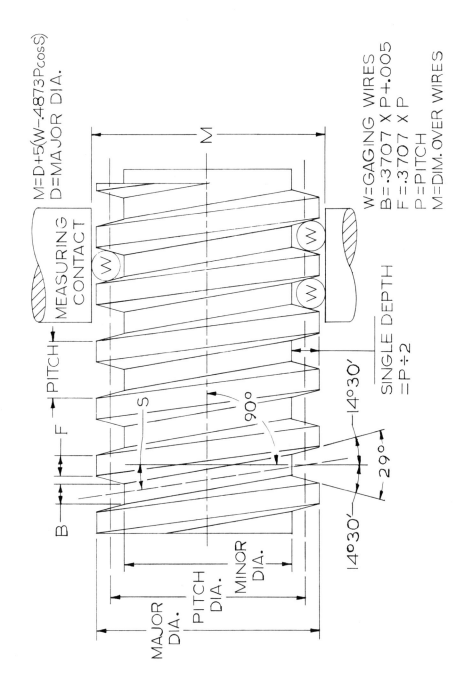

Fig. T-28. Standard Acme thread form.

ACME THREAD ROUGHING TOOL

A-1 TO 2 DEGREES ON EACH SIDE

B-0 TO .5 DEGREES.

C-7 TO 9° MORE THAN THD'S HELIX ANGLE.

D-.006 LESS THAN BOTTOM OF THREAD.

E-10 TO 12 DEGREES.

R-RADIUS OF RAKE TO APPROXIMATE WIDTH 'D'.

T-1

ACME THREAD FINISHING TOOL

B-0 TO 5 DEGREES.

C-7 TO 9° MORE THAN THD'S HELIX ANGLE.

E-10 TO 12 DEGREES.

W-TOOL SHOULD BE GROUND ACCORD-ING TO A STANDARD ACME THREAD TEMPLATE GAGE.

Q-FLAT TOP OF TOOL SHOULD ALWAYS BE SET POINTING TO THE AXIAL CENTERLINE OF THREAD.

T-2

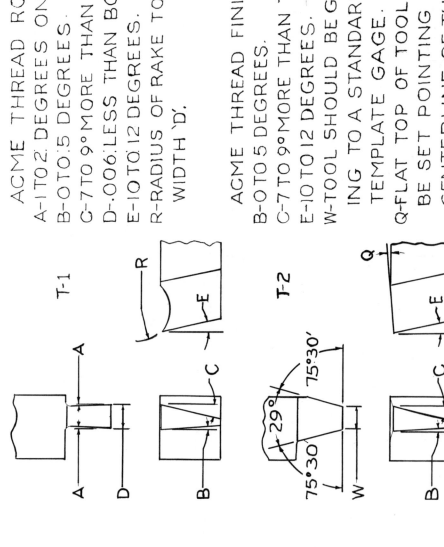

Fig. T-29. Standard Acme thread form. The cutting procedure is shown.

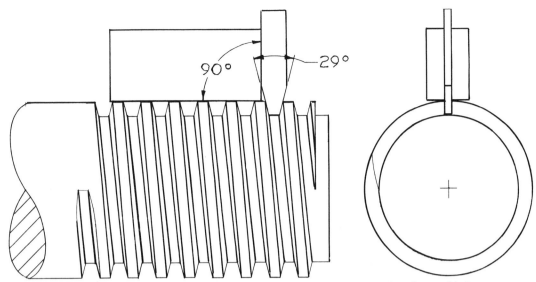

Fig. T-30. Standard Acme thread form. Check the wall angles using a square-ended block and a 29° blade.

should check the wall angles using a square-ended block and a 29° blade (Fig. T-30). The screw's pitch diameter should be checked also (Fig. T-28).

Table T-6 shows wire sizes and constants and their corresponding pitch, over which the acme thread diameter is measured.

Table T-6. Wire Sizes and Constants for Acme 29° Threads.

N-THREADS PER INCH	PITCH $P=\frac{1}{N}$	WIRE SIZES		
		BEST 0.516450P	MAXIMUM 0.650013P	MINIMUM 0.487263P
	INCH	INCH	INCH	INCH
1	1.00000	0.51645	0.65001	0.48726
1 1/3	.75000	.38734	.48751	.36545
1 1/2	.66667	.34430	.43334	.32484
2	.50000	.25822	.32501	.24363
2 1/2	.40000	.20658	.26001	.19491
3	.33333	.17215	.21667	.16242
3 1/2	.28571	.14756	.18572	.13922
4	.25000	.12911	.16250	.12182
5	.20000	.10329	.13000	.09745
6	.16667	.08608	.10834	.08121
7	.14286	.07378	.09286	.06961
8	.12500	.06456	.08125	.06091
9	.11111	.05738	.07222	.05414
10	.10000	.05164	.06500	.04873
12	.08333	.04304	.05417	.04061
14	.07143	.03689	.04643	.03480
16	.06250	.03228	.04063	.03045

For internal acme thread-cutting, it is also a good idea to counterbore the end of the nut to the screw's major diameter, and to a depth equal to the bottom width of the thread groove.

STANDARD 45° BUTTRESS THREAD, EXTERNAL.

Figure T-31 shows a standard 45° buttress thread. Because its one wall is at right angles to the screw's axis, it cannot be finish-milled in a thread-milling machine without the use of a special cutter and a universal milling attachment.

The 45° buttress thread most generally is cut in a screw-cutting lathe. This operation can be done without any particular difficulty, but because of the comparative narrowness at the bottom (root) of the thread in proportion to its depth some extra precautions are required.

Assume you must cut this thread in steel. To rough out an external buttress thread employ a rounded, hook-nose tool (T-1 in Fig. T-32) for bringing out the chip. This tool must be less than 45° wide.

Before you do any thread-roughing, be sure to tighten the cross slide so that mere friction will hold the cross slide from backing away from the cutting pressure even when all play in the cross-slide screw is backed away.

Once the cut begins, chalk-mark the cross-feed dial setting. Then remove all slack in the feed screw and nut by partially rotating the cross-feed handle in reverse until it stops. Permit enough friction in the cross slide to hold the tool in the cut. It is not uncommon to employ both hands, however, for withdrawing the tool in cases of heavier cutting. Without a tight enough cross slide, the tool will dig in too deeply and break off, when you are attempting to make a short, clean come-out.

Swivel the compound rest counterclockwise 45°. Also set the right, or 45° side of the tool at 45° to the screw's axial centerline. The roughing tool's setting is done from the machined face of the screw blank's end using a 45° blade (Fig. T-33).

Feed the tool straight into the work, taking as heavy a cut as the cutting tool will withstand. After two or more such cuts, adjust the tool's position laterally so that it now cuts on the left side of the groove. Starting near the top, feed inwardly up to the limit of the tool's capacity.

In roughing along the perpendicular thread wall, the straight-in feeding automatically results in a right-angle thread wall, while the setting of the right side of the cutting tool forms a 45° wall. Continue moving the tool laterally over to the left of the groove for an additional series of inward cuts. Feed inwardly until the tool almost touches the 45° wall. The idea is to reach the bottom of the thread, or very nearly so. *Caution.* Never try cutting with both sides

of the tool at the same time, especially in steel.

Follow this step by using a roughing tool (T-2 in Fig. T-32), align the point of this narrow, square-ended tool parallel with the screw's axis. Feed the tool inward for each cut.

To determine the approximate depth of the thread, use a slightly modified caliper. For this purpose, thin the ends of both legs to about 1/32 inch. Also bend the leg ends to the left or right to clear the thread walls. You can measure the caliper's opening by holding it diagonally on the scale, approximating the screw's helix angle (Fig. T-34).

Having established the approximate thread depth, or the minor diameter, now change over to the finishing shown at T-3 (Fig. T-35). Set this tool to rough-finish the 45° thread wall, shaving away all steps and irregularities left by the roughing cuts. Using a sulphur-based cutting oil, shave off as much as is necessary to ring the crest of the thread to within .010 inch of its finished width.

Regrind and rehone the finishing tool at this point. After a short spot-trial cut, check the 45° angle for correctness, as shown in Fig. T-33. Position a light in the back of the angle gaging for better visibility. Set the tool's angular setting by reducing the work rpm to the machine's lowest, about 6 to 8 rpm, for a 6-inch-diameter screw thread.

Using a lean mixture of soap/water coolant, make a light finish shaving cut on the 45° wall. Generally no more than two shaving cuts are required to produce a very smooth, shiny finish. Each of these cuts should also shave a slight amount of metal off the bottom of the thread.

Next insert finishing tool T-4, (Fig. T-35). Again using a sulphur-based/cutting oil, first establish the 90° wall angle, using the same block and blade as is used for checking the 45° angle. Shave the 90° side smooth over the whole length of the screw.

Here you must check for the required screw diameter to give you some idea of how much more metal must be removed. You can do so by using the three-wire method of thread measurement, as in the formula in Fig. T-31. You also can duplicate a screw plug gage of that particular size and use only one wire. In the latter case, measure from the crest of one thread over a wire resting in the thread groove on the screw's opposite side. But beware! The chances for errors are twice that of the three-wire system. Therefore, turn the screw blank's diameter closely to that of the plug you are duplicating. If in measuring the thread's diameter your micrometer reads minus .001 inch, your thread is actually minus .002 inch.

Shave the 90° wall to within .002 inch of the finished diameter using cutting oil. Here again, reduce the work rpm to its lowest, then resharpen and rehone the tool. Reset

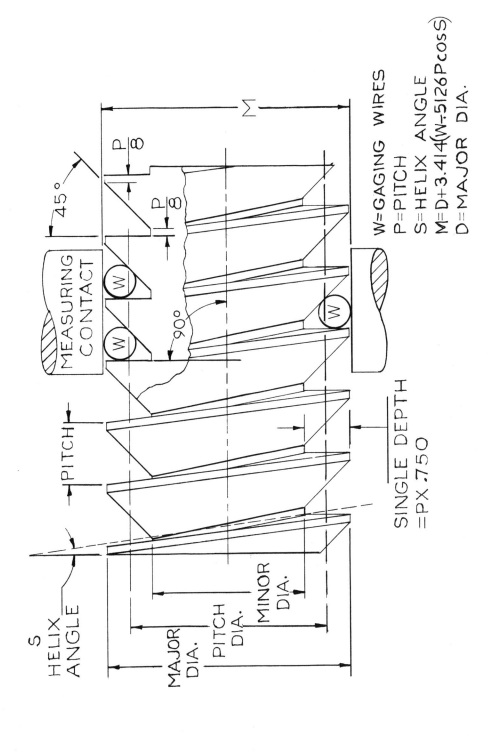

W=GAGING WIRES
P=PITCH
S=HELIX ANGLE
M=D+3.4I4(W–.5I26PcosS)
D=MAJOR DIA.

Fig. T-31. Standard 45° buttress thread (external).

231

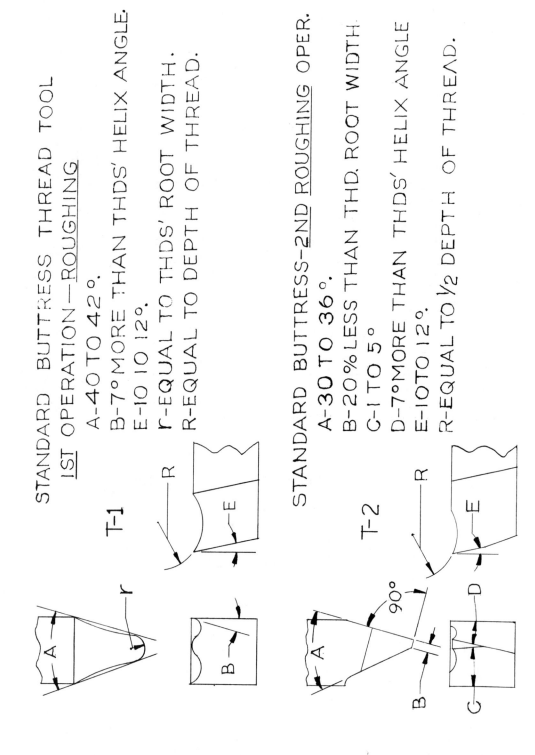

STANDARD BUTTRESS THREAD TOOL
1ST OPERATION—ROUGHING

A—40 TO 42°.
B—7° MORE THAN THDS' HELIX ANGLE.
E—10 TO 12°.
r—EQUAL TO THDS' ROOT WIDTH.
R—EQUAL TO DEPTH OF THREAD.

T-1

STANDARD BUTTRESS—2ND ROUGHING OPER.

A—30 TO 36°.
B—20% LESS THAN THD. ROOT WIDTH.
C—1 TO 5°
D—7° MORE THAN THDS' HELIX ANGLE
E—10 TO 12°.
R—EQUAL TO ½ DEPTH OF THREAD.

T-2

Fig. T-32. Standard 45° buttress thread, external. The cutting procedure is shown.

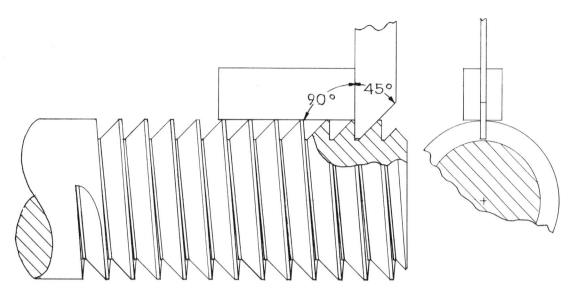

Fig. T-33. Standard 45° buttress thread, external. The roughing tool's setting is done from the machined face of the screw blank's end using the 45° blade.

it exactly. This step is often done by shaving a short spot on the end face of the screw, then switching over to a soap-water coolant, to shave off the 90° wall to size.

Caution! The finishing tools usually need resharpening after only three shaves over the thread, especially true when you are using a soap-water coolant. Never allow the finishing tool to slide over the surface without cutting a chip. The glazed surface it produces becomes more difficult and almost impossible to break through, should any additional light shaving be required to bring the thread to size.

INTERNAL 45° BUTTRESS THREAD, CUTTING. It is considerably easier to cut an internal buttress thread than it is to cut an external one. In every case, however, the cutting must be done on the back side of the bore with the cutting tool in an upside down position (Fig. T-36).

Bore the nut to the screw's minor diameter. For clearance, add 8 percent of the thread's double depth to the bore diameter. Also counterbore the nut to the screw's major diameter plus .005 inch, and to a depth equal to one-half the pitch.

The lathe's compound slide need not be set at 45°. Almost any angle over 15° will provide for all lateral tool settings and moving. The angle of the compound swivel often will depend on the types of boring bars and holders on hand. Setting the compound parallel with the axial centerline of the work is a fairly common preference.

Do the first roughing of the thread with a round-ended, hook-nose tool (T-1 in Fig. T-37). This tool should be no

more than 43° or 44° wide. Its leading, 90°, side should be aligned nearly parallel with the machined face of the nut.

Assuming the nut is of steel, we employ a sulphur-based cutting oil. Begin by making two cuts, each as deep as the tool will withstand. Then starting at the top of the thread, advance the tool forward laterally about one-half the width of the tool's nose, and feed it straight inward with each

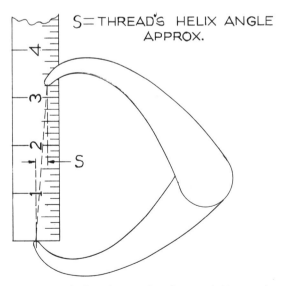

Fig. T-34. Standard 45° buttress thread, external. Measure the caliper opening.

233

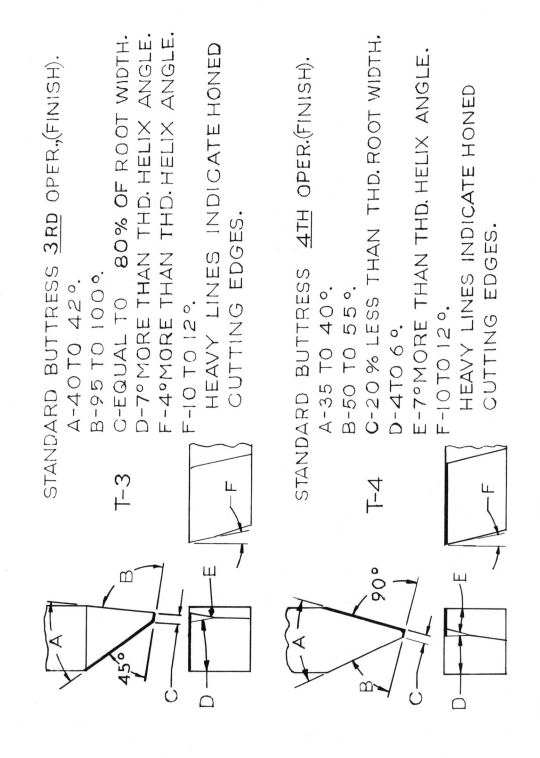

STANDARD BUTTRESS 3RD OPER., (FINISH).

A - 40 TO 42°.
B - 95 TO 100°.

T-3   C - EQUAL TO 80% OF ROOT WIDTH.
       D - 7° MORE THAN THD. HELIX ANGLE.
       F - 4° MORE THAN THD. HELIX ANGLE.
       F - 10 TO 12°.
       HEAVY LINES INDICATE HONED
       CUTTING EDGES.

STANDARD BUTTRESS 4TH OPER. (FINISH).

A - 35 TO 40°.
B - 50 TO 55°.

T-4   C - 20% LESS THAN THD. ROOT WIDTH.
       D - 4 TO 6°.
       E - 7° MORE THAN THD. HELIX ANGLE.
       F - 10 TO 12°.
       HEAVY LINES INDICATE HONED
       CUTTING EDGES.

Fig. T-35. Standard 45° buttress thread, external. The finishing operations are shown.

234

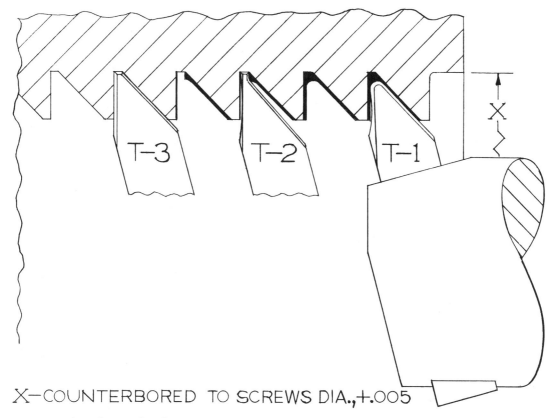

X—COUNTERBORED TO SCREWS DIA.,+.005

Fig. T-36. Internal 45° buttress thread, cutting. It is somewhat easier to cut an internal buttress thread.

cut, until the trailing side of the tool just begins to touch the 45° wall. Repeat the tool's forward advancing and inward feeding until the crests of the threads measure no less than 1/32 inch over what is to be the finished crest width.

Because of the tool's wide nose, you should still be some distance away from the thread's bottom. So change over to a much narrower, flat-ended tool (T-2 in Fig. T-37). Align this tool laterally by just touching the 90° wall. Feed straight inward for each successive cut until the tool begins to cut into the inside diameter of the counterbore at the front end of the nut. The counterbore's diameter serves as the stopping point for the thread's roughing.

For finishing the thread, use a 45° form tool (T-3 in Fig. T-38). The sides of this tool are hollow-ground on the periphery of the grinding wheel. Its top and two side edges, as well as its end, are smoothly honed. Cut upside down and on the back side to permit light cutting on the tool's three sides without difficulty. If the thread is in steel, do not neglect to use sulphurized cutting oil.

Tentatively align the leading, or 90° side of the finish-

ing tool parallel with the machined face of the nut. Bring up the tool to make it touch the stationary nut's face. Then rotate the work about 10° by hand. The work will show a shallow mark made by the cutting tool. Actually do not set the tools perfectly parallel with the face of the nut. Theoretically it might be true, but in actual practice the tool's cutting edge is not exactly on center. Also the bar springs upward and away from the cut under the cut's pressure. It, therefore, requires that certain angular compensations be made in the tool's setting beforehand to obtain the required angle. It has been found through long practice that the 90° side of the tool, when compared to the finished face of the nut, must be closer at its heel (back end) than near its point. Because of the many variables, it is practically impossible to arrive at any simple constant. However, the angle difference that this comparison indicates is about 20″.

You can test these tool settings easily. First of all, you must assume that your screw's right-angled wall is very close to 90° with the nut's axial centerline. Before trying

235

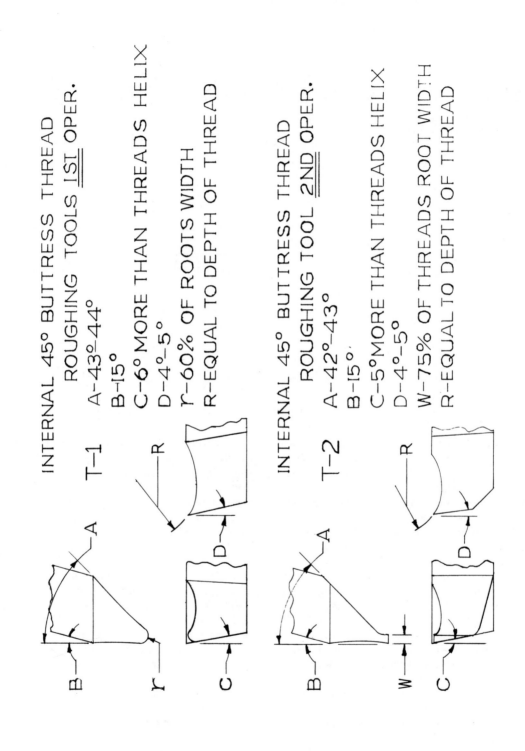

INTERNAL 45° BUTTRESS THREAD
ROUGHING TOOLS 1ST OPER.

T-1

A–43°–44°
B–15°
C–6° MORE THAN THREADS HELIX
D–4°–5°
r–60% OF ROOTS WIDTH
R–EQUAL TO DEPTH OF THREAD

INTERNAL 45° BUTTRESS THREAD
ROUGHING TOOL 2ND OPER.

T-2

A–42°–43°
B–15°.
C–5° MORE THAN THREADS HELIX
D–4°–5°
W–75% OF THREADS ROOT WIDTH
R–EQUAL TO DEPTH OF THREAD

Fig. T-37. Internal 45° buttress thread, cutting. The cutting procedure is shown.

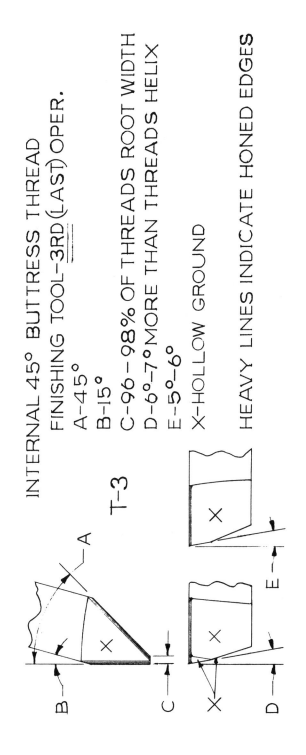

INTERNAL 45° BUTTRESS THREAD
FINISHING TOOL—3RD (LAST) OPER.

A—45°
B—15°
C—96—98% OF THREADS ROOT WIDTH
D—6°—7° MORE THAN THREADS HELIX
E—5°—6°
X—HOLLOW GROUND

HEAVY LINES INDICATE HONED EDGES

T-3

Fig. T-38. Internal 45° buttress thread, cutting. The third, and final, operation is shown.

the screw into the nut, smear its first few threads with a thin amount of Prussian blue paste. The blue impression left on the internal thread wall surfaces will show whether the angular tool setting was correct.

Begin the finishing by lightly shaving the perpendicular thread wall. Follow by feeding inwardly, also lightly cutting the 45° wall. When the finishing tool begins to cut into the counterbore, it is time to try-in the screw or plug gage.

Caution! Never force the screw into the nut if you feel the slightest "sudden" resistance. Hit the screw endwise with a lead or rawhide mallet before you urge the screw farther inward. Never fail to clean the internal threads thoroughly by blowing and wiping out all loose particles of any kind.

Run the work at or near its lowest speed, using a soap-water coolant for the last two or three shaves.

52° BUTTRESS THREAD. Figure T-39 shows a 52° buttress thread (52° included angle). This thread is almost the same as the standard 45° buttress, except that, instead of the right angle wall, this thread wall slants inward at 7°. Because of this 7° slant, it becomes possible to mill this

thread, if so desired, while the 45° wall remains at 45°.

The depth of this thread is slightly shallower than the standard buttress thread. Instead of .750 × P, it becomes .743 × P (where P = pitch). The crest and root widths remain the same as in the standard 45° buttress thread.

ROUNDED BUTTRESS THREAD, EXTERNAL CUTTING. Figure T-40 shows another type of buttress thread, which has rounded crests and roots. It is used in situations where tremendous loads must be withstood. In many respects, it is similar to the standard 45° buttress.

In cutting the external rounded buttress thread, follow nearly the same procedures as in cutting the standard 45° buttress. Because it is not as deep as the standard buttress and it has a rounded bottom, it is easier to cut.

For the first or roughing, cuts, use tool T-1 in Fig. T-41. This tool is slightly less than 45° wide. Tentatively set its left (leading) side parallel with the screw's end face. Feed this tool inwardly the same as in cutting the standard buttress thread. The object is to get to the bottom of the thread groove by the easiest possible method, even though the rough groove might be less than 45° wide. It is best to compare and duplicate the depth of the rough threads by caliper-

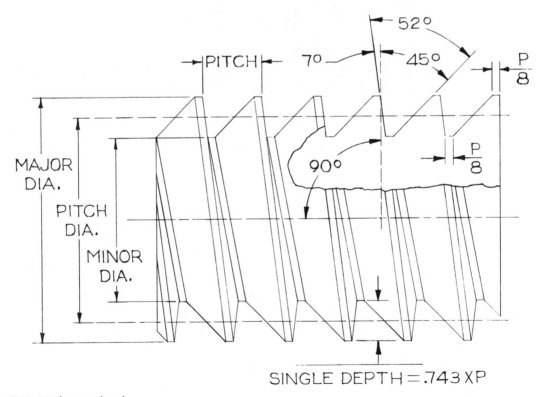

Fig. T-39. 52° buttress thread.

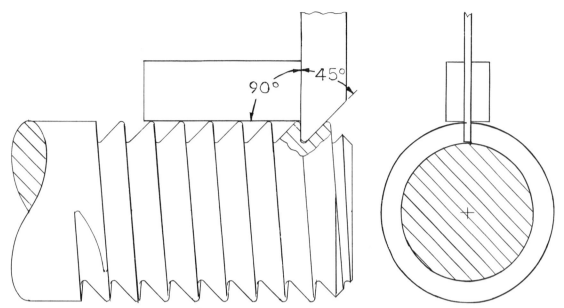

Fig. T-40. Rounded buttress thread, external cutting.

ing the male plug gage and the screw you are cutting. (See Fig. T-34.)

After you have reached the bottom, or very nearly so, begin the finishing by rounding off the crests of the thread. For this step use a form tool (Fig. T-42). This radius tool is usually set to cut off slightly more on the 90° thread wall by about .005 to .008 inch. In setting the tool's angular alignment, use the 45° blade (Fig. T-40), holding it against the screw's end face in a horizontal plane. Then bring the tool up close enough to permit the blade to enter into the tool's radius. When you hold a light below, a slight opening should show between the blade and the two inner edges of the tool, as indicated by the two Os in Fig. T-42.

Figure T-43 shows a method of grinding the crest-rounding form tool, off-hand. At A, grind the tool in a post-type grinder. First, however, grind away all unnecessary metal on the tool's working end. Roughly groove the underside of the front end on the sharp corner of a grinding wheel, breaking through the top for only a short distance.

Dress the periphery of a narrow 1/8-inch, Resinoid Bond wheel to a comparatively steep angle, as shown at B in Fig. T-43.

Grind the radius to size on the Resinoid wheel, but at a lesser angle. The wheel touches on the sharp, thin corners of the tool left from the initial rough-groove grinding. Use a template for gaging the radius, as well as for the degrees of spread (Fig. T-44).

As at C, finish the tool by honing the radius with a round

stick hone of a medium to fine grit. Honing at a slightly lesser cutting angle. Hone the straight sections using a flat, wedge-shaped hone having a rounded edge. Also hone the top side of the cutting tool.

You can check the radius of the tool by smearing a light coat of Prussian blue over a smooth tapered rod or pin. Hold the tool at right angles over the larger diameter of the pin. Slide the tool along the pin toward the pin's smaller diameter. The point where the throat of the tool's cutout touches down on the pin's surface represents the diameter or radius of the tool. You then can measure this point with a micrometer.

Feed this form tool straight inward in each succeeding cut. Use cutting oil. Continue the inward feeding and cutting until the marks on the crests from the original turning tool have almost disappeared. Then shift the machine into its lowest speed, and switch to a soap-water coolant for the last one or two finish cuts.

Then comes the finishing of both thread walls, together with the bottom of the thread. For this operation use tool T-3 in Fig. T-41. Grind and hone this tool according to a template (Fig. T-44). Tentatively align this tool's left (90°) side nearly parallel with the screw's end face. Using a low-speed and a sulphurized cutting oil, start semifinishing by shaving off the right-angled wall. The shaving should almost blend in with the rounded crest, leaving only enough for the final shaving with soap water.

Then move the tool away slightly from the 90° wall and

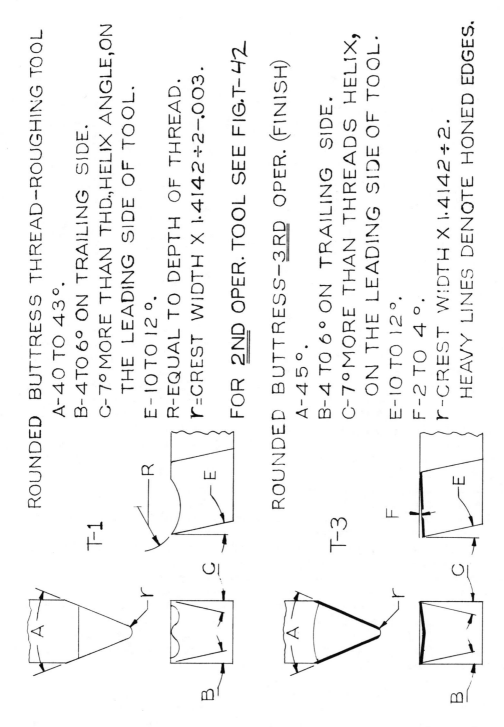

ROUNDED BUTTRESS THREAD—ROUGHING TOOL

A-40 TO 43°.

B-4 TO 6° ON TRAILING SIDE.

C-7° MORE THAN THD., HELIX ANGLE, ON THE LEADING SIDE OF TOOL.

E-10 TO 12°.

R-EQUAL TO DEPTH OF THREAD.

r=CREST WIDTH X 1.4142÷2−.003.

FOR 2ND OPER. TOOL SEE FIG.T-42

T-1

R

E

r

A

B

C

ROUNDED BUTTRESS—3RD OPER. (FINISH)

A-45°.

B-4 TO 6° ON TRAILING SIDE.

C-7° MORE THAN THREADS HELIX, ON THE LEADING SIDE OF TOOL.

E-10 TO 12°.

F-2 TO 4°.

r-CREST WIDTH X 1.4142÷2.

HEAVY LINES DENOTE HONED EDGES.

T-3

F

E

r

A

B

C

Fig. T-41. Rounded buttress thread, external cutting. The cutting procedure is shown.

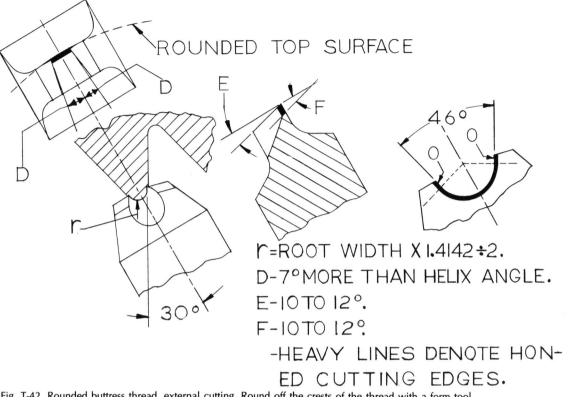

ROUNDED TOP SURFACE

r=ROOT WIDTH X 1.4142÷2.
D-7°MORE THAN HELIX ANGLE.
E-10 TO 12°.
F-10 TO 12°.
   -HEAVY LINES DENOTE HON-
   ED CUTTING EDGES.

Fig. T-42. Rounded buttress thread, external cutting. Round off the crests of the thread with a form tool.

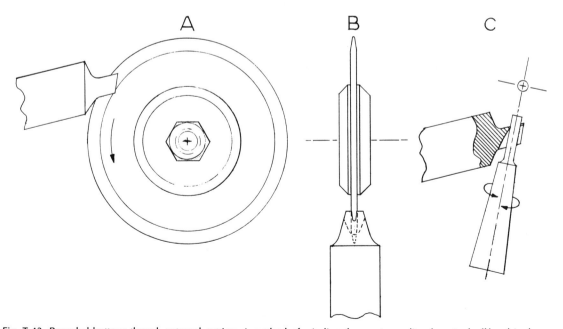

Fig. T-43. Rounded buttress thread, external cutting. A method of grinding the crest-rounding form tool off-hand is shown.

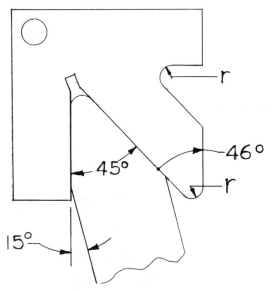

semi-finish the 45° wall. At no time should you attempt to cut with both sides of the tool at the same time. The one exception to this rule is when you are cutting external threads in brass, iron, or bronze, but never in steel. Also remove as much metal as possible from the bottom of the thread groove, while shaving the 45° side. Keep checking the wall angles with the 45° blade and square-ended block, as shown in Fig. T-40. Also caliper the minor diameter of the cut screw, to be sure it is not larger than the minor diameter of the screw plug.

The thread's size is a duplication of the male screw gage and can be closely measured by using a rod of a suitable diameter and a micrometer (Fig. T-45). In every case, the outside diameter of the screw you are cutting must be held to within .001 inch of the screw gage's outside diameter. Every .0001 inch of difference between the two multiplies the screw's diameter error by two, even though both micrometer readings are the same.

When the micrometer measurement shows the diameter of the thread to be approximately .003 inch over the gage's diameter, resharpen, rehone, and reset the tool. Now change

Fig. T-44. Rounded buttress thread, external cutting. Use a template to gage the radius and the degrees of spread.

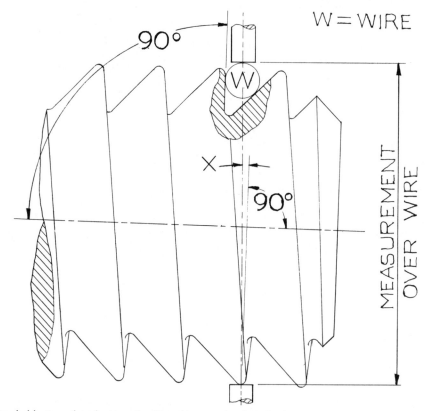

Fig. T-45. Rounded buttress thread, external cutting. Measure the thread's size.

to a soap-water coolant and shave off the 90° wall, including some of the bottom. Then, moving slightly away from the 90° side, shave off the 45° wall and some of the bottom. Check the wall angles once more, then shave the screw to size, blending the wall surface with the rounded crest.

By reversing the work rotation and using a smoother file, held in reverse fashion down against the sharp apex of the screw's first thread, you can dress off its razor sharpness.

Although the wall angles and the thread's diameter might check out according to specifications, the screw and nut, fairly likely, will not engage, but do not despair. The reason they won't is because you have a ''fat'' first half thread on the screw and a ''fat'' first and last half thread in the nut. In an external thread where each wall is cut individually, as mentioned previously, the ''fat'' thread is not as prominant. However, in internal threading the 90° side of the tool pushes away from the cut, then is pushed back in when the 45° side begins to cut, resulting in a thicker thread on the 90° wall. The thickening also develops on the 45° wall as the tool emerges out of the back end of the nut.

You must recognize the ''fat'' end threads. Then you must take a light shave or two off the first half thread in external threading, and a light shave off the first and last half threads, in internal threading. In most cases, the removal of about .005 inch of metal is sufficient.

LEFT-HAND THREAD-CUTTING. In cutting left-hand thread leads, use the same cutting tools as for cutting right-hand thread leads. However, be sure the tool has enough cutting clearance on its leading side. The cross slide does not have to be as tight for left-hand threading.

For each cut, bring the tool up closely to the rotating work, but not touching. At about two revolutions from the starting mark, engage the carriage split nut. When the starting point approaches, dig the tool into the work quite rapidly, and as deep as the tool will stand.

Then move the tool over laterally to the right, cutting on the 45° side. Feed inwardly with each cut until the crest of the thread measures approximately 1/32 inch over the finished width. Move the tool back to cut on the 90° wall, cutting until the thread's bottom is reached. Set the tool and the thread wall angles in the same manner as previously described. Chalk-mark the cross-feed screw dial, using the mark for the final finishing approaches.

Actually, despite the many details, cutting a left-hand buttress thread, whether internal or external, is quite easy, and moves along quite rapidly.

ROUNDED BUTTRESS THREAD, INTERNAL CUTTING. Cutting an internal rounded buttress thread is quite easy.

If certain steps are followed, the thread can be cut to a nice fit with the screw without having to resort to the cut-and-try method.

Always bore the nut .002 to .003 inch smaller than the diameter of the bore in the female screw gage. Doing so leaves just enough stock to smoothly finish off the crest rounding. You should also counterbore the nut .005 inch larger than the screw's outside diameter, and, to a lateral depth equal to roughly one-half the thread's pitch.

For roughing out the thread groove, use the hooked, rounded-nose tool T-1 in (Fig. T-41). Do the cutting on the back side of the bore, with the cutting tool and bar set in an upside down position. Follow practically the same procedures as in roughing out internal standard buttress threads. The roughing stops when the cutting tool cuts into the front counterbored diameter.

Then comes the finishing (rounding off) of the thread's crest. For this operation, use the same form tool as for external crest rounding (Fig. T-42). The crests are cut down to where the nut's minor diameter equals the minor diameter in the female gage. Use soap water for the last two crest-rounding cuts.

Follow this operation by semifinishing the thread walls. For this step use a tool (T-3 in Fig. 41), together with a sulphur-based cutting oil. Begin by shaving the 90° wall, but do not touch the rounded crest as yet. Continue feeding inward until the tool nearly touches the rounded crest on the 45° wall.

Resharpen the finishing tool. Then reset it according to the instructions on tool setting explained in the article on *internal 45° buttress thread cutting*. (See also Fig. T-36.)

Take a light shaving cut off the full length of the thread with the tool set to blend with the rounded crest on the 90° wall.

At this point, stop and measure the thread's diameter (Fig. T-46). This is merely the duplication of the thread's size in the female gage. For this measurement, use a standard type, Starrett inside micrometer, but instead of the regular stem extension, employ one having a spherical end (M). One homemade and soft is o.k. too.

Continue the shaving with a sulphur-based cutting oil until the micrometer shows no more than .002 inch to go.

Then, changing the coolant to soap water, shave off the thread to size. In the process, small lateral tool adjustments might be necessary to blend both thread walls with the rounded crests.

By following these instructions, as well as thinning the first and last threads in the nut, you will eliminate the back-breaking cut-and try method of screw fitting.

You can cut large diameter—5 to 6-inch diameter—

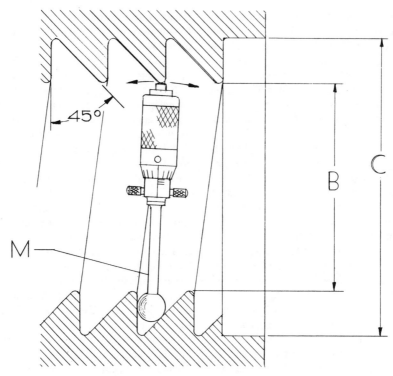

Fig. T-46. Rounded buttress thread, internal cutting. Measure the thread's diameter.

screws and nuts independent of the others, using the described procedures. Screw both together on the floor, allowing no more than .002 to Then .005 inch of play.

Cut rounded internal buttress thread in four separate operations as follows:

☐ Rough until the counterbore shows cutting.
☐ Round off the crests of the threads.
☐ Finish off by shaving the thread groove to size.
☐ Thin the thickness in the first and last threads.

METRIC THREAD-CUTTING IN A NONMETRIC TYPE LATHE. Occasionally you will be called upon to cut metric threads. These are often specified as *threads per centimeter*. A lathe having a pair of gears, one with 50 teeth and the other with 127 teeth, can cut metric threads. Mount the 127-tooth gear on the lead screw. Then figure gears for threads per centimeter the same as threads per inch.

You can find millimeter thread gears through a simple rule. First, put the 127-tooth gear on the lead screw. You can find the stud gear by multiplying the number of threads per inch in the lead screw by the pitch to be cut in millimeters, and that product by 5.

For example, to cut a 2-millimeter thread in a lathe having a four-thread-per-inch lead screw, find the stud, or driving, gear by multiplying the number of threads per inch in the lead screw by the pitch to be cut, in millimeters.

If the lead screw pitch is four, multiply the pitch by the 2-millimeter threads to be cut; thus $2 \times 4 = 8$. The 8 is multiplied by 5; thus, $8 \times 5 = 40$.

To cut one 10 mm thread with a 5-pitch lead screw, multiply $10 \times 5 \times 5 = 250$ teeth for the stud gear.

It often becomes necessary to compound the driving gears to get the required ratio with gears commonly used. The reason for the 127-tooth gear is that a millimeter is an irrational, (odd) linear measuring system, compared with the English measuring system using inches, feet, yards, etc. However, when enough of these odd millimeters are added together, somewhere along the line they must total up to a whole English number.

Looking into the millimeters-to-inches conversion tables (See Appendix) you will find that you must go as high as 127 mm before you get a rational number. Thus, the value for 127 mm is 5.0000. Now you can use this value for your metric gearing ration calculations.

TOOL POST

TOOL POST RING FOR THE LATHE. For all except quite small or very large engine lathes, a stepped tool post ring (Fig. T-47) is most useful. It eliminates the frequently slipping half-moon rockers. This slipping occurs especially in heavier cutting. Whatever tools are supported by the stepped ring are always held in a horizontal plane. The ring does have three to four elevations, in increments of 3/32 or 1/8 inch.

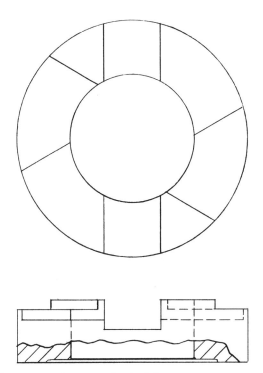

Fig. T-47. Tool post ring for the lathe.

For finer, vertical, tool adjustments, you can either pull out slightly or push in the cutting tool into the slanting slot of the tool holder. For such tools as the common cut-off tool, this type of ring always supports the blade in a non-side-slanting position.

For much heavier, turning cuts, you can place two strips of emery cloth between the ring and the compound rest to prevent slippage, while the tool holder itself is made to abut the step of the ring.

PORTABLE TOOL POST GRINDER. Figure T-48 shows a very versatile type of portable tool post grinder for use in an engine lathe. However, it also can be adapted to other machines almost as well.

This grinder is made to receive different lengths of quills, or spindles, for deeper interior grinding. It also is equipped with 1/8- to 1/4-inch diameter collets to hold and drive small-diameter mounted wheels.

Never neglect to cover the ways and carriage of the machine being used for grinding as a protection against the wheel's grit. Also, don't expect first-class results without first diamond-dressing the grinding wheel. Do not try hogging the work, make light passes only. Also don't forget to wear safety glasses when you are grinding.

Don't permit the traveling grinding wheel to come off the bore's end more than one-half the width of the wheel at either end of the grinder's lateral travel, except for checking the round diameter. This practice prevents bell mouthing.

TOOLS

TOOL FOR FORM- CUTTING FILLETS. Fillets can also be finished off nicely in an engine lathe, as well as in other turning machines. For this operation, use a form-cutting tool bit, round and set as shown in Fig. T-49. The main thing is to set the cutting tool a little below center if the work rotates in the conventional direction. Set it slightly above center, with the tool upside down, if cutting is in the reverse direction.

The top of the tool should have a rake slightly negative to zero to prevent the tool from gouging. The rotational speed of the work should be near, or at its lowest, for larger jobs, especially when you are cutting steel. Also, apply a sulphur-based cutting oil to the process.

Do not permit the tool to ride the work surface without cutting because this practice glazes the work surface and rapidly dulls the cutting tool.

TRIGONOMETRY

RIGHT-ANGLE TRIANGLES. Great many types of jobs just cannot be done correctly, if at all, without some knowledge and use of trigonometry. It is not necessary to know trigonometry from A to Z for most shop work. However, by becoming at least partially familiar with trigonometry, its application and problem solving can be of tremendous value to the precision metalworker.

Trigonometry is a system of calculating distances and angles by the use of right-angle triangles. A *right-angle triangle* is one where one of its three corners is square (90°), as shown in Fig. T-50. The square corner is often designated by a small square (X).

Trigonometry can be quite easy to understand. It can

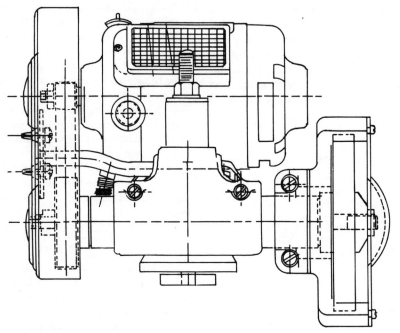

Fig. T-48. Portable tool post grinder.

also be quite complex. Bear in mind that, although there are many types of triangles, only those having a square corner are right-angle triangles, and these are what you are after.

Calculating the lengths of their sides in relation to their angles becomes impossible until you break down the triangle into one or more right-angle triangles. The right-angle triangle is the only standardized pattern that consistantly lends itself for its own calculation, as well as for the calculation of other angles and triangles.

Right-angle triangles may be up to 90° in width. However, work simplification you can break them down into one or more 45° right-angle triangles. Any amount over 45° should be treated as just another triangle and calculated from a different baseline.

Bear in mind:

☐ That every right-angle triangle has only three sides.
☐ That one of its three corners must be square (90°).
☐ That you must always have two known quantities before you will be able to calculate the third.

Of course, there had to be some standardized rules before any specific procedures governing the solution of triangles was possible. Perhaps the most important one is the square corner (Fig. T-50). There are formulas and rules

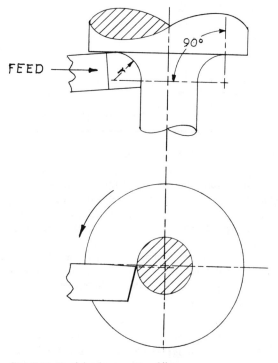

Fig. T-49. Tool for form-cutting fillets.

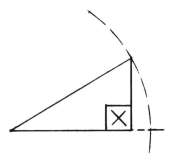

Fig. T-50. Right-angle triangles.

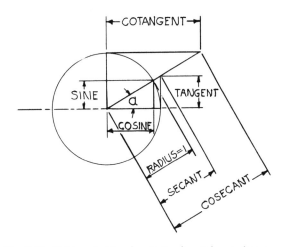

Fig. T-51. Right-angle triangles. Parts of a circle are shown.

for finding the lengths of sides, as well as the angles for every conceivable triangle that might occur. However, for most purposes, trigonometry tables, already worked out, are more convenient. They save time. They also help to eliminate the ever-possible calculation errors. See the trig tables in the Appendix.

The trig tables have been worked out using the value 1 for the lengths of the radius. The value 1 can be one of most anything, such as inches, feet, meters, or miles. For shop work, however, regard the 1 as meaning 1 inch. Therefore, in the process of solving your trig problem, where your radius happens to be greater or less than 1 inch, simply multiply whatever your dimensions are by the corresponding constants shown in the trig tables.

The trig tables show the constants for angles ranging from 0° up to and including 45°, in minutes. All angles over 45° are treated as just another triangle, and merely calculated from the adjacent baseline.

Trigonometry can be quite simple, depending on the problem at hand and the strategy used for its solution. Perhaps the most important thing about solving trig problems is your sense of logical reasoning.

Always study the problem from every angle, first. Determine which are the known quantities. Draw sketches of the problem, preferably one having a 2-inch diameter circle, which amounts to a 1-inch radius. Use a scale to measure the lengths of the sides. Also use a protractor. Determine which corner is, or can be, made square (90°).

This procedure will give you an idea whether you are on the right track or not. Often, comparatively simply problems require considerable thought and several trial layouts before you will hit on the correct procedure. Most of it then will appear to be ridiculously simple.

To be better able to recognize the sides and angles as might occur in your particular problems, study Fig. T-51. You must be acquainted well enough with the various sides of a right-angle triangle—their names, angles, and their relationship to the circle and to each other. Always remember

that the wheels of a railroad car are always tangent to the track on which they roll.

If you have but two lines radiating outwardly from a common center point, as in Fig. T-52, they are of no particular significance to you. If their degrees of spread are known, as in Fig. T-53A, it still does not offer enough information for you to work with. If an arc is drawn connecting the two radiating lines, as in Fig. T-53B, you still do not have enough information.

However, if you drop a line from the point where the slanted side intersects the arc down to the horizontal baseline, then you get a right-angle triangle, as in Fig. T-54. The dropped lines X intersects the horizontal baseline at 90°, and is known as the *sine* of the angle.

The slanting side is known first as the *hypotenuse*, then the *radius*, then the *angle*. Each definition is correct and a matter of choice, depending on the description requirements in that particular problem.

Now this pattern becomes a right angle triangle, which

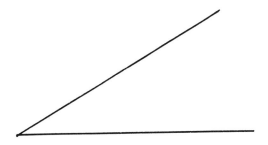

Fig. T-52. Right-angle triangles. Two lines are shown radiating outward from a common point.

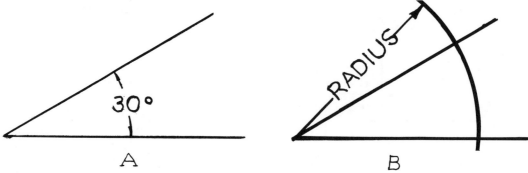

Fig. T-53. Right-angle triangles. More information on the two radiating lines is given in A and B.

readily lends itself to calculation of itself, as well as all other triangles.

THE IMAGINARY UPRIGHT BLACKBOARD. To help remove some of the ''fog'' from the trigonometry, you might compare right-angle triangles with lines drawn on an upright blackboard. Begin by drawing two lines across the center of the board, one vertical and one horizontal. The lines are at right angles to each other, or 90° apart. They divide the face of the board into four 90° sections (Fig. T-55).

Then imagine piercing a length of fine thread with two pins spaced 1 inch apart. To the thread's longer end, attach a small imaginary weight. Then stick the one pin into the board at the intersection of the horizontal and vertical lines.

With the free pin carrying the weighted thread, scribe an arc on the board, starting at the horizontal line and moving upward to the midpoint between the horizontal and vertical lines. Now the radius portion of the thread slants at 45° to the horizontal plane. It also slants at 45° from the vertical centerline (Fig. T-56). In this example, the weighted end of the thread always hangs downward, at 90°

to the horizontal centerline. This describes a 45° right-angle triangle.

At this point, do not permit yourself to become overly confused. The distance from the scribing pin down to the horizontal line is always known as the sine of the angle. However, the distance from the scribing pin to the vertical centerline can also be the sine of the angle. Both of these can also be the cosine of that angle.

Note: these likenesses happen only in the case of the 45° triangle (Fig. T-56).

If you should stop your arc-scribing even the slightest amount over 45° from the horizontal centerline, you would simply get an additional right-angle triangle, however small. The shortest side in this triangle becomes the sine; the next, and longer, side becomes the cosine.

Figures T-57 and T-58 illustrate how the sines and co-

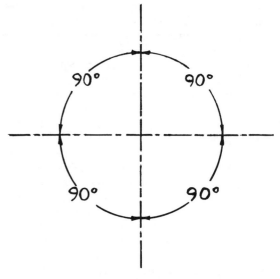

Fig. T-54. Right-angle triangles. A right-angle triangle is shown.   Fig.T-55. The imaginary upright blackboard.

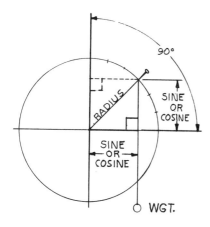

Fig. T-56. The imaginary upright blackboard. Scribe an arc on the blackboard.

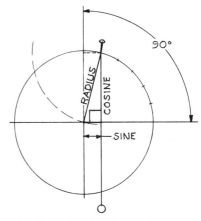

Fig. T-58. The sine and cosine change places.

sines change places as their angle increases or decreases in relation to their baselines. Also, as illustrated in Fig. T-59, the right-angle triangles can be located in any position and be of any angle. However, they all begin in the center of an imaginary circle.

CALCULATING FOR THE HYPOTENUSE. In all right-angle triangle calculations, the hypotenuse (the length of the radius or slanting side) is found by the Pythagorean theorem in four steps:

1. Multiply the sine value by itself (square it).
2. Also multiply the cosine value by itself.
3. Add the two products together.
4. Finding what number that, when multiplied by itself (extracting the square root), will result in a number equal

to the sum of those two products.

The resulting number is the hypotenuse. Fig. T-60 illustrates how this theorem works, together with the formula. This formula works for every right-angle triangle, up to and including the 90° triangle.

For example in the case of two 90° right-angle triangles combined to form a 1-inch square (Fig. T-61), we find it measures 1.41422 inches diagonally across, from sharp corner to sharp corner (A). That value (or constant) represents the hypotenuse of each of the right-angle triangles whose sides (B and C) are each 1.00000 inch long. By squaring side B you get 1.00000 inch. By squaring side C you also get 1.00000 inch. Adding the two products together you get the sum of 2. By extracting the square root of 2, you get 1.41422 inches. To satisfy yourself, multiply the constant 1.41422 by 1.41422. The result is 2.0000182084, which is very, very close to 2.

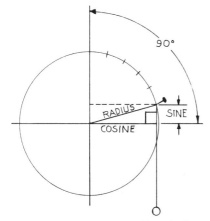

Fig. T-57. The imaginary upright blackboard. The sine and cosine change places as their angles increase or decrease in relation to their baselines.

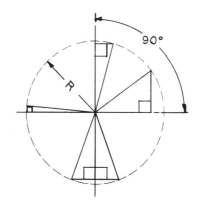

Fig. T-59. The imaginary upright blackboard. The right-angle triangles can be located in any position and be of any angle.

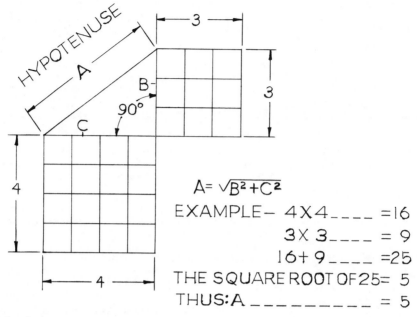

Fig. T-60. Calculating the hypotenuse.

$$A = \sqrt{B^2 + C^2}$$

EXAMPLE— 4 X 4 _ _ _ _ = 16

3 X 3 _ _ _ _ = 9

16 + 9 _ _ _ _ = 25

THE SQUARE ROOT OF 25 = 5

THUS: A _ _ _ _ _ _ _ _ = 5

Note that outside of the arc, lines B and C are both the tangent and the cotangent, while lines D and E, inside the arc, are both the sine and the cosine. Bear in mind that only in the 45° right-angle triangle do B and C have the same values. This situation is also true with lines D and E as well as with the tangent and cotangent.

THE 30° RIGHT-ANGLE TRIANGLE. In the case of the 30° right-angle triangle (Fig. T-62), the sine is always one-half as long as the radius. Interestingly enough, you can divide the circle into six equal parts with a divider caliper. After you have scribed the circle, you can step it off (divide it into six equal parts with the same divider caliper's

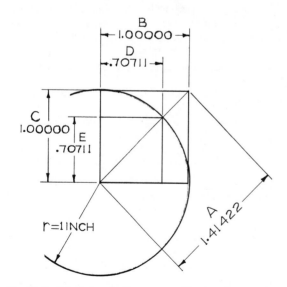

Fig. T-61. Calculating the hypotenuse. The hypotenuse of a 1-inch square can be calculated as shown.

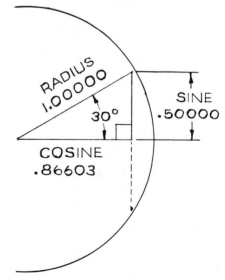

Fig. T-62. The 30° right-angle triangle. The sine of a 30° right-angle triangle is always one-half as long as the radius.

250

setting. It needs no further adjustments.

ROUND TAPERED SHAFTS.

Round tapered shafts are usually referred to as tapering either so many degrees or so many thousandths per inch. What may not always occur to you is that a round tapered shaft always consists of two separate right-angle triangles. These two triangles are positioned back to back, and are divided euqally, lengthwise, by the shaft's axial centerline (Fig. T-63).

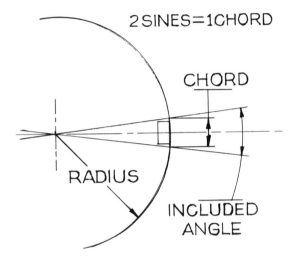

Fig. T-63. Round tapered shafts. A round tapered shaft always consists of two separate right-angle triangles positioned back to back and equally divided lengthwise by the shaft's axial centerline.

In calculating from the rate of taper per inch, calculate only one of the triangles at a time. Then multiply the sine value by 2 to get the taper's diameter at the large end. The small end's diameter is, theoretically, zero. Combining the two right-angle triangles represents the taper's included angle.

Regardless of whether the taper's large and small diameters vary by only a small fraction of an inch or by several inches, the tapering, actually and theoretically, always begins in the center of an imaginary circle.

In making male and female taper gages or parts, the male is generally made first because it is much easier to do so. The male part is then used for sizing the female taper. You can check the rate of taper on the male with a micrometer (Figs. T-4 and T-5). The difference per inch in the micrometer's readings equals the sine of that included angle. Look into the trig tables (see Appendix) where you find that same value. The place where that value is found corresponds to the amount of taper in degrees and minutes.

THE SINE BAR.

The rate, or *angle*, of taper can be checked very accurately on a sine bar (Fig. T-64) without regard to the length or diameter of the work.

The bar itself is merely a smooth, straight piece of metal of either a square or rectangular cross section, supported at each end by precise dowels. For easier calculation the dowels are made 1 inch in diameter, fixed at right angles to the bar's linear centerline and parallel to the bar's top surface and to each other.

The dowels are usually spaced 5 or 10 inches from center to center. However, most often—for the smaller tool work, etc.—this supporting dowel spacing is 5 inches.

To use the sine bar, place it on a precise flat surface plate, with one of its ends elevated by precision gage blocks. The height of this required elevation is equal to the sine of the required angle multiplied by the number of inches in the dowel spacing.

To avoid possible errors in your math, always refer to the trig tables (see Appendix) for the sine of the angle.

In the example in Fig. T-64, we are checking a 10° taper. The trig table specifies that the sine of the 10° angle is .17365 for a 1-inch radius. Since the supporting dowels are spaced 5 inches apart, the radius is 5 inches. Multiply .17365 × 5 = .86825 inch, which represents the exact amount of required bar elevation for 10°.

Check the work by laying it lengthwise atop the slanting top surface of the bar. Then pass a stand-mounted test indicator over the top of the work (A, B, C,) to indicate whether the top of the work is, or is not, parallel to the ''flat'' surface plate.

When the indicator shows no difference in its readings from A to C, you can be very sure that your workpiece tapers at exactly 10°, or .17365 per inch.

LOCATING HOLES.

A good example of the use of trigonometry is shown in the following illustrations.

Assume you have a job that calls for five bored holes equally spaced on a 2-inch-diameter circle. The set of five holes is to be located as shown in Fig. T-65 in relation to the sides of the workpiece.

If the workpiece is round, indicate the piece to centralize it with the axial center of the machine's spindle.

Then move the machine table holding the work away from the machine's column a distance of 1.0000 inch. Here drill and bore hole No. 1, which is at the top of the imaginary 2-inch circle (Fig. T-66).

For holes 5 and 2 (Fig. T-67) you must move the machine table toward the machine's column so the work will register correctly with the axial center of the boring spindle. How far and which way must you move the work from hole No. 1? Since each of the five equal divisions of a cir-

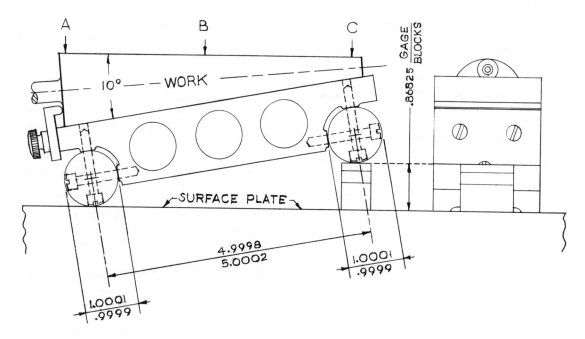

Fig. T-64. The sine bar. Use the sine bar to check the rate or angle of a taper, regardless of the diameter or length of the work.

cle equals 72°, you know that holes 5 and 2 must be located 72° from the center of hole No. 1.

However, 72° is too wide an angle for simple calculation. Also, it is not a right-angle triangle. So, instead, find how far up from the circle's center these hole locations must be. Since you are working in a 90° sector, take advantage of this fact. Subtract 72° from the vertical centerline, leaving 18°. The 18° right-angle triangle, calculated from the horizontal centerline, permits much easier figuring.

Look into the trig tables for the sine of 18° (see Ap-

pendix). You will find it to be .30902 inch. Knowing the No. 1 hole is located 1 inch above the circle's center, subtract the sine of 18° from the 1-inch vertical radius length, to get .69098 inch. This value represents the distance from the center of hole No. 1 down to the imaginary line C, running horizontally through the proposed centers of holes 5 and 2 (Fig. T-67).

Where do you go from here to locate holes 5 and 2 on the imaginary 2-inch circle? You also must find how far to the left and right of the circle's center these holes must

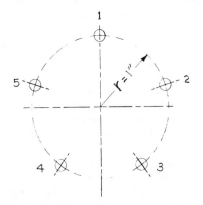

Fig. T-65. Locating holes. Locate five equally spaced holes on a 2-inch diameter circle.

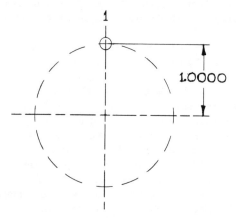

Fig. T-66. Locating holes. Drill hole no. 1 as shown.

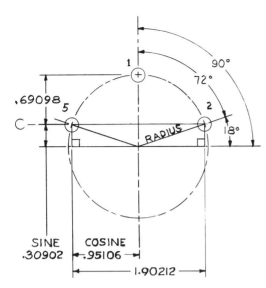

Fig. T-67. Locating holes. Locate holes no. 2 and 5 using the procedure shown.

be located. To do so, look into the trig tables for the cosine of 18°. You will find it is .95106 inch. This value locates one or both of these two holes on the 2-inch circle (Fig. T-67). To locate the second of these two holes, move the work back horizontally, 2 × .95106, or 1.90212 inch.

To locate holes 3 and 4 (Fig. T-68), continue moving the table and work toward the machine's column down to the imaginary, horizontal chord line (D). This line runs through hole locations 4 and 3. (See Fig. T-69).

You know from calculating hole locations 5 and 2 that they are both .30902 inch above the circle's horizontal centerline (Fig. T-67). Now you must find how far down from the circle's horizontal centerline holes 4 and 3 must be located. These two holes are 72° apart and in perfect symmetry with the circle's vertical centerline. To get right-angle triangles, split the 72° triangle down through the middle to get two 36° right-angle triangles. Looking into the trig tables for the cosine of 36°, you will find it to be .80902. Add this value to .30902 (the sine of the 18° angle) to get 1.11804 inches, which represents the distance the work must be moved away from horizontal line C to horizontal line D (Fig. T-68).

For the lateral location of holes 4 and 3, look into the trig tables for the sine of the 36° angle, which is .58778. This value represents the distance the work must be moved to the left or right of the vertical centerline, in order for the work to be positioned exactly on the imaginary 2-inch circle. This procedure locates one of the two holes.

To locate the second of these two holes, move the work

back, to left or right (whichever way you didn't move in the previous step), a distance of 2 × .58778, or 1.17556 inches.

For the preceding hole locating examples, a 2-inch diameter circle was chosen purposely, because, of course, a 2-inch circle has a 1-inch radius. Since all the constants found in the trig tables were also calculated on the basis of a 1-inch radius, it eliminated extra figuring, for now. If, however, the radius of your job is greater or smaller than the 1-inch illustrated example, simply multiply your radius dimensions by whatever the constant happens to be.

RAPID HOLE CALCULATOR

Figure T-70 shows a rapid boring calculator chart, for locating hole centers in a circle for the more commonly used number of holes.

PRECISE TABLE MOVEMENTS

For accurately locating hole centers, for whatever purpose, precise drilling and boring machines are generally used. They are known as *jig-boring machines*. These machines have work tables that slide in two directions only, those directions being exactly 90° to each other. Only the spindle is made to be moved up or down, not the table.

Using right-angle triangles and the worked out trigonometry tables, you can locate hole centers very accurately in the jig-boring machine.

Other machines, such as vertical and horizontal milling machines, can also be used for hole-locating purposes. Even though these machines are primarily built for heavy metal removal, they will do a splendid job for many hole-locating

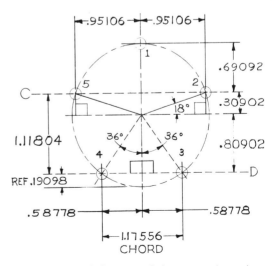

Fig. T-68. Locating holes. Locate holes no. 3 and 4 as shown.

253

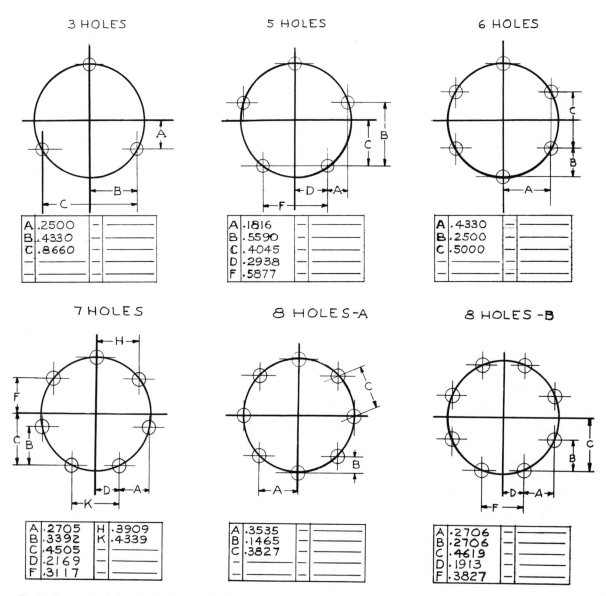

Fig. T-69. Locating holes. The horizontal chord line runs through hole locations 3 and 4.

purposes. Generally, these machines do not have the precise workmanship and measuring devices built into them.

The table movements of a precision-boring machine do not depend on the turns of their feed (translating) screws to position the work in correct relation to the spindle's axial center. In other than precision-boring machines, you can use the feed screws for locating hole centers, if the machine is not too old or if the hole-location tolerance is not finer than .001 inch.

On the other hand, a jig-boring machine is primarily built with extreme care and precision. Most of its parts have been made of seasoned and stress-relieved materials.

Also, for more precise functioning, these machines are operated in a temperature-controlled room. Their sole purpose is to precisely locate, drill, and bore holes. The locating can be done consistently within .0001 inch. The machine's table movements are precisely gaged by temperature-insulated rods of specific lengths. The table's

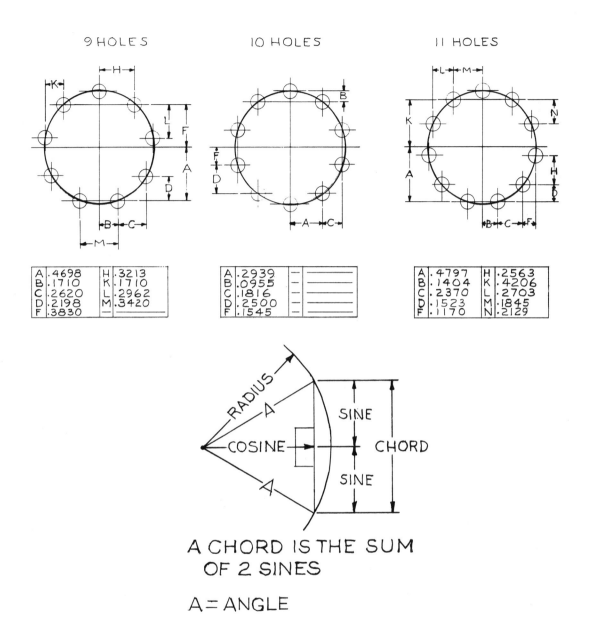

9 HOLES

A	.4698	H	.3213
B	.1710	K	.1710
C	.2620	L	.2962
D	.2198	M	.3420
F	.3830	—	

10 HOLES

A	.2939	—	
B	.0955	—	
C	.1816	—	
D	.2500	—	
F	.1545	—	

11 HOLES

A	.4797	H	.2563
B	.1404	K	.4206
C	.2370	L	.2703
D	.1523	M	.1845
F	.1170	N	.2129

A CHORD IS THE SUM
OF 2 SINES

A = ANGLE

lateral and cross-feed screws are only used for moving, but not for gaging the extent of the table's movements.

The measuring rods—one for cross, the other for lateral gaging—rest in their respective **V** channels. Each abuts their respective test-indicator stems with one of their ends while the other end abuts stops on the work table. By observing the test indicator's reading and by employing precision-gage blocks, you can make extremely precise table movements consistently.

To calculate precise table (and work) movements, trigonometry is used in almost all instances. It is a matter of solving for the lengths of sides of right-angle triangles. Trig is based on a system of constants and multipliers, and on the fact that there is always a fixed relationship (ratio) between the sides and angles of triangles. The trig tables give the constants for any degree or fraction thereof, as relating to a 1-inch radius. (See Appendix.)

The values shown in the trig tables represent a radius

255

12 HOLES

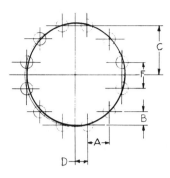

A	.2241	—	
B	.1294	—	
C	.4830	—	
D	.1294	—	
F	.2588	—	

MULTIPLY VALUE SHOWN BY DIAMETER OF CIRCLE BEING CALCULATED

Fig. T-70. Locating holes. A rapid boring calculator chart is shown.

of 1 inch. These values are usually given in five decimal places, which is closer than can be readily measured.

Because the machine's table is movable only in or out, or from side to side, you must calculate the distance and direction of the movements in straight lines in order to locate the work exactly in relation to the axial center of the machine's spindle.

In every case you must base your calculations on the known angles and other known dimensions. It, therefore, becomes more practical and simple if the triangles are broken down to 45° or less. Anything over 45° must be treated as a separate triangle and calculated from one of the other related horizontal or vertical baselines.

It does not always matter where you start the locating. These types of jobs are practically infinite in their designs, the number of hole locations, as well as their positioning. It becomes impossible to set down rigid rules of procedure, except that it is always better to figure on forward table movements only, whenever possible. Backing up should be held to a minimum, particularly when you are using the machine's feed screws for the spacing.

Of course, the better method by far for precise spacing is one using tenth indicators, measuring rods, and precision-gage blocks. In this way you know positively the exact amount of each table movement. The feed screws are merely used to push or pull the machine table, not to measure.

The precise length of the measuring rod expands and contracts in direct proportion to the surrounding room temperatures. This condition can be controlled by maintaining a constant 68° temperature in the jig-boring room and by coating the measuring rods with a heat-insulating material to prevent their expansion from warm hand contacts.

Lap the measuring rods to exact lengths by inserting each rod through a hole bored at right angles to the bottom face of an iron support block. A **V** cutout 90° to the bottom face will also serve to hold the rod square to the lap. The rod must not tilt or slant in any direction, even the slightest amount, during the lapping process.

Urge the rod downward against the lapping block and move it around in a figure eight. Place a rag or such between your hand and the rod to prevent the rod from expanding from the heat of your hand.

The rod's length must be checked from time to time in the lapping process. To do so, mount a microscope on a bench-lathe type of bed. Then, using precision-gage blocks, set the microscope's cross hair to register with the end of the gaging blocks.

By laying the rod into a **V** groove running parallel with the bed, you can view its end through the microscope to determine how closely it registers with the preset microscopes cross hair.

To depend solely on the turns of a screw for precise table movements is very much like depending on your automobile speedometer to accurately measure road distances. It is only fairly close. To measure that same road distance exactly, a precise measuring tape must be employed, instead, and then only when the weather is of a specific temperature, to prevent above-or below-normal temperatures from expanding or contracting the measuring tape.

TUBES

FLATTENING AND BENDING TUBES. What appeared to be an almost impossible tube-forming job was accomplished as shown in the following illustrations.

Attempting to partially flatten any metallic tube or ring between two plattens will usually result in a figure eight cross section. The reasons for these shapes are as follows: Beginning with A in Fig. T-71, the flat surfaces of the plattens remain flat, while the tube's points of contact changes. The contacted points, having no internal support, begin to collapse inwardly, as illustrated at B.

Because the highest point of the work is pushed inward, an ever widening area presents itself to the platten's surface, carrying with it the initially bent portion. As the squeezing continues, the tube's longitudinal cross section becomes wider (C). With nothing to support the center area,

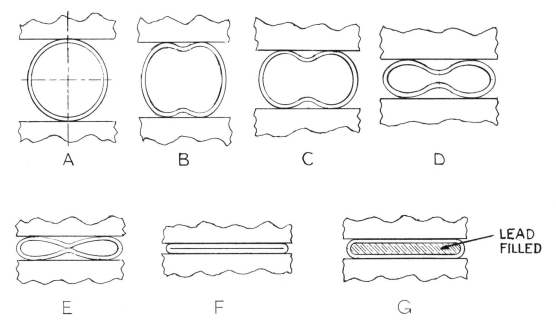

Fig. T-71. Flattening and bending tubes.

it collapses at a more rapid rate, (D and E). Only when both inside walls meet does the tube begin to flatten out again (F).

With the job at hand (Fig. T-72), it was decided to fill the tube with some suitable substance to restrict its collapsing. This fill had to be hard enough to keep the tube's center from caving in, yet be soft enough to flow under pressure. It then became a matter of displacement. After some initial experimentation with a variety of fills, it was found that lead would be the most suitable substance for the purpose.

Because the flattened tube's thickness had to be held within ±.002 inch (H in Fig. T-75), a simple thickness-limiting fixture was devised. This fixture consisted of two parallel strips of steel equal in thickness to the flattened tube's dimension. These strips were laid one on each side of the lead-filled tube (L in Fig. T-73).

Because the flat section of the tube was to be of a specific length, the flattening was done between two flat pieces of steel (P in Fig. T-73). These two pieces were equal in length to the flattened portion of the tube (D in Fig. T-73).

The transition between the flat and round sections was confined to a comparatively short length, controlled by two heavy steel sleeves (E in Fig. T-73). These sleeves also kept the tube ends from spreading out of size and shape.

The whole assembly was set into a heavy steel bending brake (press brake). The press ram was brought down un-

til the upper platten bore down on the two thickness-limiting spacers.

In this operation, the lead fill was partially forced out through both tube ends. The flattening was then complete (D in Fig. T-73).

The next step involved the transverse bending of the flattened section of the tube into a specific arc. To keep what was gained up to this point, the lead fill was allowed to remain in the tube. For this operation, a two-piece fixture was made, (Fig. T-74). The two end sleeves were also allowed to remain on the tube ends.

The tube was positioned between the two side plates of the die (P in Fig. T-74), and centered lengthwise by a scribed line on the tube, which registered with a centrally scribed line on the die. The die's (fixtures) side plates were spaced only far enough apart to admit the flattened tube. This same spacing also providing for the thickness of the punch (K).

The working surfaces of both the die and punch have a nearly 180° transverse arc cut annularly into their bending surfaces. The radii of these arcs was found by actual measurement of a worked, short filled sample of the same tube material (G in Fig. T-71).

By confining the punch and the flat of the tube between the two side plates, the tube could go nowhere except straight downward under the pressure, conforming to the annular and transverse arcs of the punch and die.

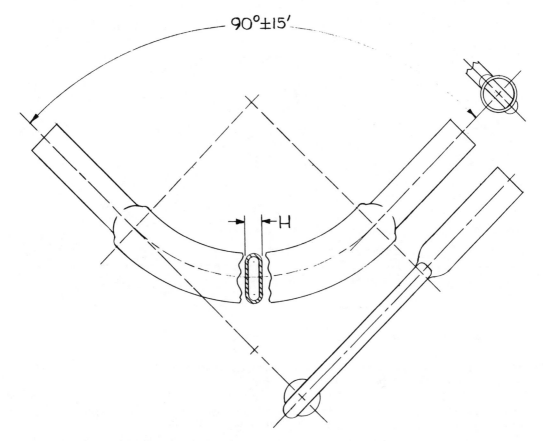

Fig. T-72. Flattening and bending tubes. Part of the procedure is shown.

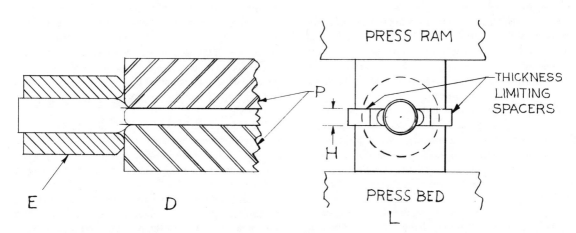

Fig. T-73. Flattening and bending tubes. Lay the strips on either side of the lead-filled tube.

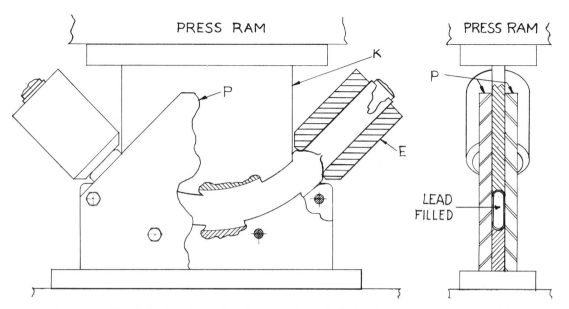

Fig. T-74. Flattening and bending tubes. A two-piece fixture can be made for bending the flattened section of the tube transversely into a specific arc.

Because the tendency of the bending tube is to spread the die's side plates, heavy **C**-clamps were employed. These were made to pinch the two side plates against the punch, but not so tight as to restrict the punch's movement. The bending of the tube into a specific arc was done in a hydraulic press. The bending fixture was designed to over-bend the tube by 1° or so, thus allowing for any slight springback during the fill's remelting.

Corrective bends up to ± 30′ then were made readily in the big bend after the lead was melted out. Correcting was done only if and when it was necessary.

This secondary (arc-forming) operation was carried out using a generous application of oil and white lead for the lubricant in the forming die. Figure T-72 shows the finished tube.

TUNGSTEN CARBIDES

TUNGSTEN CARBIDES. Tungsten carbide can be classed apart from any other type of cutting metal. Not only is it extremely hard, but it also has a high melting point. Tungsten carbide can be used for continuous high-speed cutting of hard materials. It also holds up unusually well under high-heat conditions. When high-speed steel cutting tools fail, the usual alternative is to switch over to carbide tools.

Tungsten-carbide tools are especially recommended for rapid metal removal. Tungsten carbides, of which there are many grades, can be selected to suit almost any cutting job and condition.

Because carbides are so hard, they are also quite brittle. For this reason they hold up best when they are used with a rigid cutting machine. Considerable tool breakage can also be eliminated by lessening chatter and other excessive vibrations.

Carbide tools cannot be recommended for intermittent and irregular cutting unless the cut is not too heavy and the tool is ground accordingly.

The usual cutting practice, as in a lathe, is to cut with a lighter feed and less depth. However, the work revolution can be increased up to five times, compared to cutting with high-speed steel-cutting tools.

GRINDING CARBIDES. Because of their extreme hardness, regular emery wheels will not sharpen carbide tools. Instead, they must be ground on a soft, green, silicon-carbide, vitrified-resinoid type of wheel having a 70 to 80 grit.

The better method is to grind away the steel shank of the tool on a regular grinding wheel. Then finish-grind the carbide tip on a 150-to 200-grit diamond wheel, while employing a liquid coolant. Soap water does well enough for this procedure.

The roughing of the end and side clearances of the shank should be 4° to 5° greater than the finished clearance angles of the carbide tip itself. The diamond wheel should cut the carbide only, and not the shank.

Always press the tool gently against the diamond wheel, while constantly moving the tool back and forth across the face of the wheel, while under a soap-water coolant. Avoid overheating, which can cause the carbide to crack.

Tungsten-carbide tips of various grades, shapes, and sizes, can be purchased. These can be silver soldered or copper brazed to just about any type of tool or shank to make up almost any type of cutting tool desired, even twist drills.

Carbide cutting tools cannot be ground into quite as many shapes or forms as can high-speed steel cutting tools. However, it is permissable to stray considerably from the general carbide-tool grinding practices if the tool's grinding and usage is done with a bit of care. Generally, carbide cutting tools are ground having either a negative top rake or no rake at all.

In a milling machine, where larger-diameter rotary-type cutters having carbide teeth are used, it is a good practice to include a fairly heavy flywheel on the mill's arbor fairly close to the cutter. The flywheel prevents tooth breakage by smoothening out the arbor's intermittent torque action as each of the teeth enter and leave the cut.

TANTALUM TUNGSTEN CARBIDES. Perhaps among the hardest of all metallic cutting tools are the tantalum tungsten carbides which have a melting point in the region of 4800° F. They will continue cutting metal up to the melting temperature of the tip's brazed joint. At that heat the carbide tip will fall off, of course. However, a copious flow of coolant will keep the tool's temperature below the joint's melting point.

Using carbides, you can cut cast iron, for instance, at the same speed as for the machining of brass or aluminum with high-speed steel cutting tools.

The sharpening of the tantalum tungsten carbides is done in quite the same way as in grinding the more common tungsten carbides.

ELECTRO DISCHARGE MACHINING. Tungsten carbides are also used in many types of dies. Their shaping, forming, drilling, etc. is impossible with the general run of machine tools. The material is just too hard to be machined readily. It would require costly diamond cutting tools in most cases. Together with the time involved, diamond tools would be prohibitive.

More recently electrical discharge methods of machining have been developed, which operate in reverse of the metal plating process; that is, instead of depositing metal particles on to a surface, they are electrically withdrawn.

To control the area of discharge, brass arbors are machined to the exact shape and size of the desired shape to be cut. By positioning the arbor in the exact location on the work and with the proper electrical current, the arbor will deplate the metal ahead of it. It will cut its way through the metal being worked, regardless of the metal's hardness. The area of discharge machining will follow the arbor's cross section within .0001 inch or better.

The surface of the discharged area is smooth, requiring no touch-up. The discharged metallic particles are washed away in the process by a coolant and come out as a slurry. The brass arbor, of course, also diminishes in length in the process.

It must also be mentioned that numerically controlled machines operate with punched tape inputs, specifically programmed for each application. These machines so precisely respond to the command of the punched tape that no jigs or fixtures are required for the positioning of the cutting tools. The idea of providing an electrical means of guiding machine tools has had as great an impact on manufacturing as any innovation of the past several decades.

ELECTROCHEMICAL MILLING

Although the shearing action of a sharp cutting tool is the basis for the traditional method of machining, many materials and certain designs do not lend themselves to shearing. For this reason nonconventional methods have come into vogue.

Foremost among these methods is *electrochemical milling* (E.C.M.), wherein the machine tool is not a cutting tool but the cathode of an electrolytic cell. E.C.M. can be considered an extrapolation of Michael Faraday's laws of electrolysis applied through this unique and versatile machining process, which in principle is localized electrolytic deplating.

CHEMICAL MILLING

Chemical milling is a process for stock removal based upon the chemical erosion caused by acidic or caustic solution. This method effectively achieves stress-free stock removal where conventional machining would be impossible. If proper control is exercised, extremely close tolerances can be maintained.

For more information of electrodischarge machining contact:

Cincinnati Milling Machine, Inc.
Marburg Ave.
Cincinnati, OH 45209

TURNING

TURNING LONG, BRITTLE RODS. Figure T-75 shows

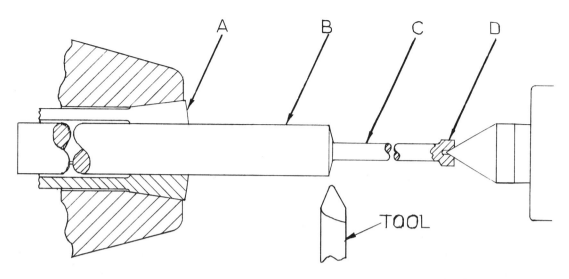

Fig. T-75. Turning long, brittle rods. The method of turning long, slender rods of brittle material is shown.

a method of turning long, slender rods of brittle materials. To start with, the stock should be straight and of a uniform diameter throughout its entire length.

Before the actual cutting begins, center-drill the work. Hold the stock (B) and drive it in the collet (A), projecting the stock out only far enough to where the finished diameter will support itself without breaking off.

The small end is supported by the tail stock center. If the turned diameter is to be quite small, you can leave a little more stock, as shown at D, to prevent the center hole from shattering. You can trim off this excess stock later.

After you have turned down to size the first projected length of stock, move back the tail stock. Again advance the stock far enough out to provide for the turning of an additional length to size.

Repeat this cutting of short sections as many times as is required to complete the required total length.

At no time should the tail-stock center fit snugly into the center hole. Instead, it should be slightly loose. The center and hole are used only to prevent the slender diameter of the rod from whipping.

TURNING SMALL-DIAMETER SHAFTS. Figure 76 shows an easy method of supporting the end of a small-diameter shaft for machining. Instead of the customary center hole, the procedure is reversed.

Since the diameter of the work is too small to receive a center hole, turn its end to a 60° point. Instead of the usually male center, use the center hole in the shank of a hardened tap held in a drill chuck.

TURNING LONG WARPING SHAFTS. To turn a long shaft straight is often more difficult to achieve than it may appear. Most types of rolled shafts contain many internal stresses. These stresses are relieved in the process of metal removal, which in turn usually results in badly warped shafts.

However, material of this kind can be turned straight by using a proven turning method. The result will be a true running shaft having very little, if any, run out.

For this turning, employ one or more steady rests, as well as the four-jaw chuck. Grip the work by a comparatively short margin, permitting it to act as a universal joint. True-up the work with even pressure by each of the four jaws. To prevent the shaft from working further into the chuck as a result of the cutting pressure, keep a blunt-nosed center in the spindle as a stop.

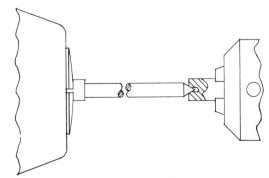

Fig. T-76. Turning small-diameter shafts. You can support a small-diameter shaft as shown.

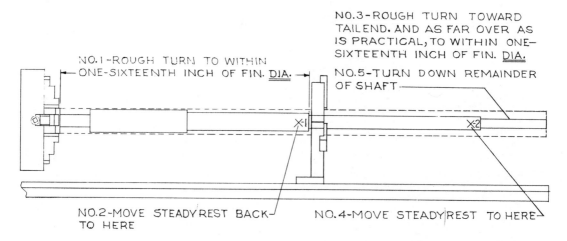

NO.3-ROUGH TURN TOWARD TAILEND. AND AS FAR OVER AS IS PRACTICAL, TO WITHIN ONE-SIXTEENTH INCH OF FIN. DIA.

NO.1-ROUGH TURN TO WITHIN ONE-SIXTEENTH INCH OF FIN. DIA.

NO.5-TURN DOWN REMAINDER OF SHAFT

NO.2-MOVE STEADY REST BACK TO HERE

NO.4-MOVE STEADY REST TO HERE

Fig. T-77. Turning long, warping shafts. You can turn a longer shaft without warping by following this procedure.

The shaft is supported in a steady rest some distance from the chuck. This distance will depend on the shaft's diameter and length, of course.

Rough-turn the shaft between the chuck and the steady rest, permitting the free end to warp as it pleases. Next, move the steady rest over to the left of the lathe's carriage to support the just-roughed portion of the shaft in the area marked X-1 in Fig. T-77.

The lathe's carriage and cutting tool are now on the right side of the steady rest. The turning proceeds using a left-hand feed direction, or toward the tail stock, and as far over as the reduced diameter of the shaft will permit without excessive chattering.

Then, move the steady rest over to the right to support the work at the right end of the second, roughed-out portion (X-2). If, after the steady-rest adjustment in its new location (the No. 1 turned surface) shows any amount of run out, true-up that section by test indicating.

Continue cutting one section at a time throughout the remaining length of the shaft, in very much the same type of procedure.

If a second steady rest is available, you can use it to support the shaft between the chuck and the rightmost steady rest, to help prevent chatter.

After roughing the full length of the shaft, reset the shaft in the four-jaw chuck by rechucking in another radial location. The shaft is now ready for the finishing cuts.

Assuming all roughed diameters are within 1/16 inch of the finished dimensions, the removal of this lesser amount of metal in the finish turning will not cut across as many stressed points. Therefore, releasing fewer stresses will result in a truer-running shaft.

WAFERS

TURNING THIN WAFERS. Figure W-1 shows a method of turning the diameters of thin wafers. Even work as thin as tissue paper can be turned without difficulty.

First, face off and recess a short piece of steel, No. 2, slightly larger than the finished diameter of the wafers. Then center-drill its back end.

Also face off and recess another piece of steel, No. 1, of the same diameter that is held in a four-jaw chuck.

First cut the material to be turned into large enough squares or whatever. Their stacked numbers may total up to as much as 12 inches. Put these blanks together in a 90° trough, acting as a **V** block. The trough can be a bent piece of sheet metal or a length of angle iron, whichever is lightest.

The trough is held up against blocks one and two while being filled with the wafer blanks. Then compress the blanks together, by screwing out the tail-stock spindle. It is better to use a ball-bearing type, or live, center for this purpose to permit the blanks to be compressed much tighter, without burning the tail-stock center.

Begin with light cuts. Continue cutting as you would in turning any solid piece of work held between centers.

This wafer-turning method of metal is a good one, among other things, for supplying experimental blanks for small draw dies. Also, by employing pot type chucks (Figs. C-17 and C-18), you can machine the faces of the wafers, if you desire.

WASHERS

THIN WASHER, TURNING AND BORING. Figure W-2 shows a method of holding thin, soft materials such as paper, aluminum, copper, etc. for accurately boring and turning. These may be washers, gaskets or whatever.

A Shows how a larger number of thin blanks can be compressed together between two steel plates, and held together by four or more bolts.
B Shows the bored work with a bolt circle cut into the face of the outer plate. This step is followed by drilling the bolt holes.
C Shows how the outside diameters can be turned to size.

For the mandrel you can use any convenient diameter of pipe or such. Hold the mandrel in a four-jaw chuck and turn it to the bore's diameter. Then slip the whole assembly on over the turned mandrel's diameter stopping against the mandrel's inner shoulder. Hold the assembly in place by pressure from a ball-bearing live center held in the

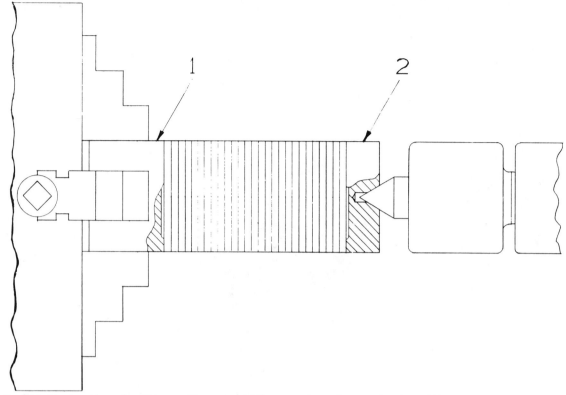

Fig. W-1. Turning thin wafers. Thin metallic or nonmetallic materials can be turned without difficulty.

machine's tail-stock spindle. A reasonably tight pressure against the outer end plate keeps the washers compressed so they can be turned as a solid piece. Both end plates also get turned down in the process, of course.

WELDMENTS

WELDMENTS. When the first boxlike structure was welded together, the bottom base plate warped so badly it became impossible to machine it. When another job of this type came along it was decided to put bends into the base plate in the opposite direction before welding. After studying the warpage in the first unit it was decided to make the bends about 5°. The bending was done in a heavy steel bending brake. Then, using a more careful welding sequence together with smaller beads of weld, the plate warped back into near perfect straightness. The amount of pull-back can be controlled by laying in or laying out additional beads of weld, if and where needed. (See Fig. W-3.)

90° ELBOW. Figure W-4 shows how a larger steel pipe was prepared for a 90° elbow. Instead of machining the

pipes to an angle of 45°, the sections were machined to an angle of 46° 30'. This is an approximation, depending on the size and number of beads to be laid down in the welding. The type of material, its thickness, and its diameter also make a difference.

We know beforehand that upon cooling, a weld will "pull." Therefore, it is often possible to determine how to prepare for a weld. You can prepare the joint so that it is crooked to start. Then allow the weld to bring it back into the desired shape. Particularly where work of this nature is repetitive, the amount of beforehand distortion can be quite satisfactorily determined.

A Shows the prepared angles of the work.
B Shows the distortion of the original preparation and the final pull-back.

MACHINING LAYOUT. It is not unusual to receive warped castings or weldments to be machined. Most of them can be machined very nicely, even though some areas might be somewhat discrepant.

Few things can be more embarrassing and disappointing than when, after some areas already have been

264

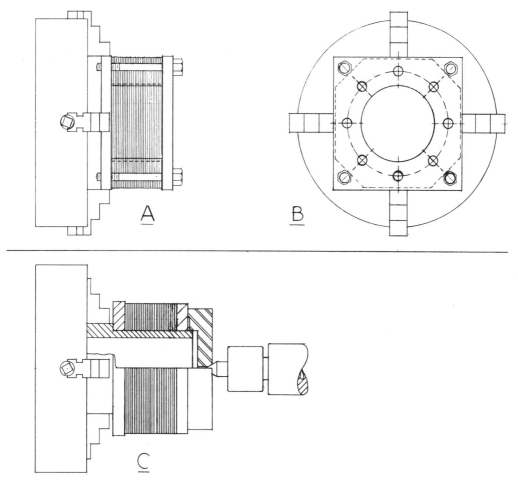

Fig. W-2. Thin washer turn and bore. Larger-diameter washers can be bored, drilled, and turned as shown.

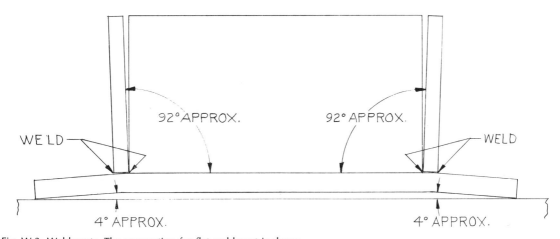

Fig. W-3. Weldments. The preparation for flat weldment is shown.

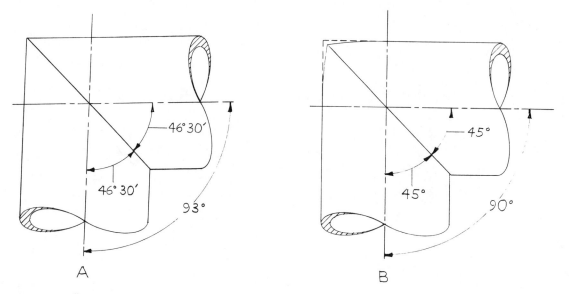

A

B

Fig. W-4. 90° elbow. Prepare tubing for a 90° welded elbow as shown.

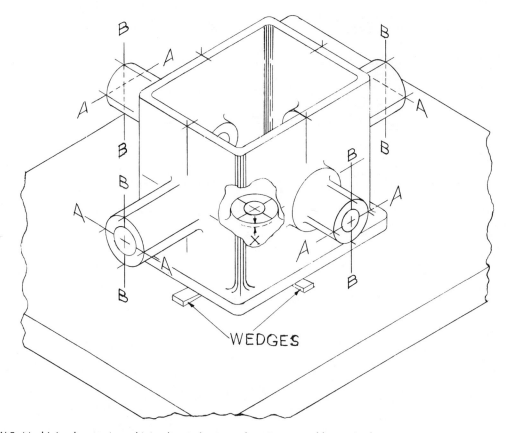

WEDGES

Fig. W-5. Machining layout. A machining layout for warped castings or weldments is shown.

266

machined, you suddenly discover the next area to be machined does not have enough stock for the finish sizing.

One good method of ensuring against this situation is to set the work on a large enough flat surface as in Fig. W-5. Then by shimming or wedging, tilt the work enough to where a trial layout will show if enough stock will be present in the necessary places to ensure a clean machined surface.

Make the layout by measuring from the flat surface plate using a surface gage and a scale. If the layout shows a shortage of material at some point, either raise, lower, or tilt the work until another trial layout proves satisfactory.

This step is followed by painting the machining areas with chalk or layout dye. Then, with the preset surface gage, scribe horizontal lines (A-A) on the four sides of the work.

If the job is of lesser proportions, roll it over 90° on its side. Make the same rough layouts as before, plus any shimming or tilting, where necessary. Line B-B is also scribed around the work.

Now, regardless of what type of machine might be chosen for the machining of the job, all you need to do to begin with is to align the work reasonably close, according to the scribed layout lines.

APPENDIX

CONVERSION OF TEMPERATURE READINGS

From Fahrenheit to Centigrade:

Subtract 32 from the Fahrenheit reading and divide by 9. Then multiply by 5.

From Centigrade to Fahrenheit:

Divide by 5, then multiply by 9. Then add 32.

WIRE AND SHEET METAL GAGES

GAGE NUMBERS	AMERICAN OR BROWN AND SHARPE	WASHBURN AND MOEN OR AMERICAN STEEL&WIRE	BIRMINGHAM OR STUBS IRON WIRE	MUSIC WIRE	IMPERIAL WIRE GAGE	U.S. STD. FOR PLATE
0000000	----	.4900	---	---	.5000	.5000
000000	.5800	.4615	---	.004	.4640	.4688
00000	.5165	.4305	.500	.005	.4320	.4375
0000	.4600	.3938	.454	.006	.4000	.4063
000	.4096	.3625	.425	.007	.3720	.3750
00	.3648	.3310	.380	.008	.3480	.3438
0	.3249	.3065	.340	.009	.3240	.3125
1	.2893	.2830	.300	.010	.3000	.2813
2	.2576	.2625	.284	.011	.2760	.2656
3	.2294	.2437	.259	.012	.2520	.2500
4	.2043	.2253	.238	.013	.2320	.2344
5	.1819	.2070	.220	.014	.2120	.2188
6	.1620	.1920	.203	.016	.1920	.2031
7	.1443	.1770	.180	.018	.1760	.1875
8	.1285	.1620	.165	.020	.1600	.1719
9	.1144	.1483	.148	.022	.1440	.1563
10	.1019	.1350	.134	.024	.1280	.1406
11	.0907	.1205	.120	.026	.1160	.1250
12	.0808	.1055	.109	.029	.1040	.1094
13	.0720	.0915	.095	.031	.0920	.0938
14	.0641	.0800	.083	.033	.0800	.0781
15	.0571	.0720	.072	.035	.0720	.0703
16	.0508	.0625	.065	.037	.0640	.0625
17	.0453	.0540	.058	.039	.0560	.0563
18	.0403	.0475	.049	.041	.0480	.0500
19	.0359	.0410	.042	.043	.0400	.0438
20	.0320	.0348	.035	.045	.0360	.0375
21	.0285	.0317	.032	.047	.0320	.0344
22	.0253	.0286	.028	.049	.0280	.0313
23	.0226	.0258	.025	.051	.0240	.0281
24	.0201	.0230	.022	.055	.0220	.0250
25	.0179	.0204	.020	.059	.0200	.0219
26	.0159	.0181	.018	.063	.0180	.0188
27	.0142	.0173	.016	.067	.0164	.0172
28	.0126	.0162	.014	.071	.0148	.0156
29	.0113	.0150	.013	.075	.0136	.0141
30	.0100	.0140	.012	.080	.0124	.0125
31	.0089	.0132	.010	.085	.0116	.0109
32	.0080	.0128	.009	.090	.0108	.0102
33	.0071	.0118	.008	.095	.0100	.0094
34	.0063	.0104	.007	.100	.0092	.0086
35	.0056	.0095	.005	.106	.0084	.0078
36	.0050	.0090	.004	.112	.0076	.0070
37	.0045	.0085	---	.118	.0068	.0066
38	.0040	.0080	---	.124	.0060	.0063
39	.0035	.0075	---	.130	.0052	-----
40	.0031	.0070	---	.138	.0048	-----

MILLIMETERS TO INCHES CONVERSION TABLE

MILLI-METERS	INCHES	MILLI-METERS	INCHES	MILLI-METERS	INCHES	MILLI-METERS	INCHES	MILLI-METERS	INCHES
1	0.0394	33	1.2992	65	2.5591	97	3.8190	129	5.0788
2	0.0787	34	1.3386	66	2.5985	98	3.8583	130	5.1182
3	0.1181	35	1.3780	67	2.6378	99	3.8977	131	5.1576
4	0.1575	36	1.4173	68	2.6772	100	3.9371	132	5.1969
5	0.1969	37	1.4567	69	2.7166	101	3.9764	133	5.2363
6	0.2362	38	1.4961	70	2.7560	102	4.0158	134	5.2757
7	0.2756	39	1.5354	71	2.7953	103	4.0552	135	5.3151
8	0.3150	40	1.5748	72	2.8347	104	4.0946	136	5.3544
9	0.3543	41	1.6142	73	2.8741	105	4.1339	137	5.3938
10	0.3937	42	1.6535	74	2.9134	106	4.1733	138	5.4332
11	0.4331	43	1.6929	75	2.9528	107	4.2127	139	5.4725
12	0.4724	44	1.7323	76	2.9922	108	4.2520	140	5.5119
13	0.5118	45	1.7717	77	3.0316	109	4.2914	141	5.5513
14	0.5512	46	1.8110	78	3.0709	110	4.3308	142	5.5907
15	0.5906	47	1.8504	79	3.1103	111	4.3702	143	5.6300
16	0.6299	48	1.8898	80	3.1497	112	4.4095	144	5.6694
17	0.6693	49	1.9291	81	3.1890	113	4.4489	145	5.7088
18	0.7087	50	1.9685	82	3.2284	114	4.4883	146	5.7481
19	0.7480	51	2.0079	83	3.2678	115	4.5276	147	5.7875
20	0.7874	52	2.0473	84	3.3071	116	4.5670	148	5.8269
21	0.8268	53	2.0867	85	3.3465	117	4.6064	149	5.8662
22	0.8662	54	2.1260	86	3.3859	118	4.6458	150	5.9056
23	0.9055	55	2.1654	87	3.4253	119	4.6851	151	5.9450
24	0.9449	56	2.2048	88	3.4646	120	4.7245	152	5.9844
25	0.9843	57	2.2441	89	3.5040	121	4.7639	153	6.0237
26	1.0236	58	2.2835	90	3.5434	122	4.8032	154	6.0631
27	1.0630	59	2.3229	91	3.5827	123	4.8426	155	6.1025
28	1.1024	60	2.3622	92	3.6221	124	4.8820	156	6.1418
29	1.1418	61	2.4016	93	3.6615	125	4.9213	157	6.1812
30	1.1811	62	2.4410	94	3.7009	126	4.9607	158	6.2206
31	1.2205	63	2.4804	95	3.7402	127	5.0001	159	6.2600
32	1.2599	64	2.5197	96	3.7796	128	5.0394	160	6.2993

1 MILLIMETER = .03937079 INCHES.

270

DECIMAL EQUIVALENTS OF FRACTIONS OF AN INCH

FRACTION	DEC. EQUIV.	FRACTION	DEC. EQUIV.	FRACTION	DEC. EQUIV.	FRACTION	DEC. EQUIV.
1/64	.015625	17/64	.265625	33/64	.515625	49/64	.765625
1/32	.03125	9/32	.28125	17/32	.53125	25/32	.78125
3/64	.046875	19/64	.296875	35/64	.546875	51/64	.796875
1/16	.0625	5/16	.3125	9/16	.5625	13/16	.8125
5/64	.078125	21/64	.328125	37/64	.578125	53/64	.828125
3/32	.09375	11/32	.34375	19/32	.59375	27/32	.84375
7/64	.109375	23/64	.359375	39/64	.609375	55/64	.859375
1/8	.1250	3/8	.3750	5/8	.6250	7/8	.8750
9/64	.140625	25/64	.390625	41/64	.640625	57/64	.890625
5/32	.15625	13/32	.40625	21/32	.65625	29/32	.90625
11/64	.171875	27/64	.421875	43/64	.671875	59/64	.921875
3/16	.1875	7/16	.4375	11/16	.6875	15/16	.9375
13/64	.203125	29/64	.453125	45/64	.703125	61/64	.953125
7/32	.21875	15/32	.46875	23/32	.71875	31/32	.96875
15/64	.234375	31/64	.484375	47/64	.734375	63/64	.984375
1/4	.2500	1/2	.5000	3/4	.7500	1	1.0000

N	$\dfrac{90}{N}$	$\dfrac{180}{N}$	$\dfrac{360}{N}$	N	$\dfrac{90}{N}$	$\dfrac{180}{N}$	$\dfrac{360}{N}$
5	18°	36°	72°	53	1°41'53"	3°23'46"	6°47'33"
6	15°	30°	60°	54	1°40'	3°20'	6°40'
7	12°51'26"	25°42'51"	51°25'43"	55	1°38'11"	3°16'22"	6°32'44"
8	11°15'	22°30'	45°	56	1°36'26"	3°12'51"	6°25'43"
9	10°	20°	40°	57	1°34'44"	3°9'28"	6°18'57"
10	9°	18°	36°	58	1°33'6"	3°6'12"	6°12'24"
11	8°10'55"	16°21'49"	32°43'38"	59	1°31'32"	3°3'3"	6°6'6"
12	7°30'	15°	30°	60	1°30'	3°	6°
13	6°55'23"	13°50'46"	27°41'32"	61	1°28'31"	2°57'3"	5°54'6"
14	6°25'43"	12°51'25"	25°42'51"	62	1°27'6"	2°54'12"	5°48'23"
15	6°	12°	24°	63	1°25'43"	2°51'26"	5°42'51"
16	5°37'30"	11°15'	22°30'	64	1°24'23"	2°48'45"	5°37'30"
17	5°17'39"	10°35'17"	21°10'35"	65	1°23'5"	2°46'9"	5°32'18"
18	5°	10°	20°	66	1°21'49"	2°43'38"	5°27'16"
19	4°44'13"	9°28'25"	18°56'50"	67	1°20'36"	2°41'12"	5°22'23"
20	4°30'	9°	18°	68	1°19'25"	2°38'49"	5°17'39"
21	4°17'9"	8°34'17"	17°8'34"	69	1°18'16"	2°36'31"	5°13'3"
22	4°5'27"	8°10'55"	16°21'49"	70	1°17'9"	2°34'17"	5°8'34"
23	3°54'47"	7°49'34"	15°39'8"	71	1°16'3"	2°32'7"	5°4'14"
24	3°45'	7°30'	15°	72	1°15'	2°30'	5°
25	3°36'	7°12'	14°24'	73	1°13'58"	2°27'57"	4°55'53"
26	3°27'42"	6°55'23"	13°50'46"	74	1°12'58"	2°25'57"	4°51'53"
27	3°20'	6°40'	13°20'	75	1°12'	2°24'	4°48'
28	3°12'51"	6°25'43"	12°51'26"	76	1°11'3"	2°22'6"	4°44'13"
29	3°6'12"	6°12'25"	12°24'50"	77	1°10'8"	2°20'16"	4°40'31"
30	3°	6°	12°	78	1°9'14"	2°18'28"	4°36'55"
31	2°54'12"	5°48'23"	11°36'46"	79	1°8'21"	2°16'43"	4°33'25"
32	2°48'45"	5°37'30"	11°15'	80	1°7'30"	2°15'	4°30'
33	2°43'38"	5°27'16"	10°54'33"	81	1°6'40"	2°13'20"	4°26'40"
34	2°38'49"	5°17'39"	10°35'18"	82	1°5'51"	2°11'42"	4°23'25"
35	2°34'17"	5°8'34"	10°17'9"	83	1°5'4"	2°10'7"	4°20'14"
36	2°30'	5°	10°	84	1°4'17"	2°8'34"	4°17'9"
37	2°25'57"	4°51'54"	9°43'47"	85	1°3'32"	2°7'4"	4°14'7"
38	2°22'6"	4°44'12"	9°28'25"	86	1°2'47"	2°5'35"	4°11'10"
39	2°18'28"	4°36'55"	9°13'51"	87	1°2'4"	2°4'8"	4°8'16"
40	2°15'	4°30'	9°	88	1°1'22"	2°2'44"	4°5'27"
41	2°11'42"	4°23'25"	8°46'50"	89	1°0'40"	2°1'21"	4°2'42"
42	2°8'34"	4°17'9"	8°34'17"	90	1°	2°	4°
43	2°5'35"	4°11'10"	8°22'20"	91	59'20"	1°58'41"	3°57'22"
44	2°2'44"	4°5'27"	8°10'54"	92	58'42"	1°57'23"	3°54'47"
45	2°	4°	8°	93	58'4"	1°56'8"	3°52'15"
46	1°57'23"	3°54'47"	7°49'33"	94	57'27"	1°54'53"	3°49'47"
47	1°54'53"	3°49'47"	7°39'34"	95	56'50"	1°53'41"	3°47'22"
48	1°52'30"	3°45'	7°30'	96	56'15"	1°52'30"	3°45'
49	1°50'12"	3°40'25"	7°20'49"	97	55'40"	1°51'20"	3°42'41"
50	1°48'	3°36'	7°12'	98	55'6"	1°50'12"	3°40'24"
51	1°45'53"	3°31'46"	7°3'32"	99	54'33"	1°49'5"	3°38'11"
52	1°43'51"	3°27'42"	6°55'23"	100	54'	1°48'	3°36'

CIRCUMFERENCES AND AREAS OF CIRCLES

CIRCUM. = DIA. X 3.14159   AREA = 3.14159 X R^2

DIAMETER IN INCHES	CIRCUM- FERENCE	AREA OF CIRCLE	DIAMETER IN INCHES	CIRCUM- FERENCE	AREA OF CIRCLE	DIAMETER IN INCHES	CIRCUM- FERENCE	AREA OF CIRCLE	DIAMETER IN INCHES	CIRCUM- FERENCE	AREA OF CIRCLE
0			4	12.5664	12.566	8	25.1327	50.265	12	37.6991	113.10
1/16	0.1964	0.0031	1/16	12.7627	12.962	1/16	25.329	51.054	1/8	38.0918	115.47
1/8	0.3927	0.0123	1/8	12.9591	13.364	1/8	25.5254	51.849	1/4	38.4845	117.86
3/16	0.5890	0.0276	3/16	13.1554	13.772	3/16	25.722	52.649	3/8	38.8772	120.38
1/4	0.7854	0.0491	1/4	13.3518	14.186	1/4	25.9181	53.456	1/2	39.2699	122.72
5/16	0.9817	0.0767	5/16	13.5481	14.607	5/16	26.115	54.269	5/8	39.6626	125.19
3/8	1.1781	0.1105	3/8	13.7445	15.033	3/8	26.3108	55.088	3/4	40.0553	127.68
7/16	1.3745	0.1503	7/16	13.9408	15.466	7/16	26.507	55.914	7/8	40.4480	130.19
1/2	1.5708	0.1964	1/2	14.1372	15.904	1/2	26.7035	56.745	13	40.8407	132.73
9/16	1.7672	0.2485	9/16	14.3335	16.349	9/16	26.8998	57.583	1/8	41.2334	135.30
5/8	1.9635	0.3068	5/8	14.5299	16.800	5/8	27.0962	58.426	1/4	41.6261	137.89
11/16	2.1598	0.3712	11/16	14.7262	17.257	11/16	27.293	59.276	3/8	42.0188	140.50
3/4	2.3562	0.4418	3/4	14.9226	17.721	3/4	27.4889	60.132	1/2	42.4115	143.14
13/16	2.5525	0.5185	13/16	15.1189	18.190	13/16	27.685	60.994	5/8	42.8042	145.80
7/8	2.7489	0.6013	7/8	15.3163	18.665	7/8	27.8816	61.862	3/4	43.1969	148.49
15/16	2.9452	0.6903	15/16	15.5116	19.147	15/16	28.078	62.737	7/8	43.5896	151.20
1	3.1416	0.7854	5	15.7080	19.635	9	28.2743	63.617	14	43.9823	153.94
1/16	3.3379	0.8866	1/16	15.9043	20.129	1/16	28.471	64.504	1/8	44.3750	156.70
1/8	3.5343	0.9940	1/8	16.1007	20.629	1/8	28.6670	65.397	1/4	44.7677	159.48
3/16	3.7306	1.1075	3/16	16.2970	21.135	3/16	28.863	66.296	3/8	45.1604	162.30
1/4	3.9270	1.2272	1/4	16.4934	21.648	1/4	29.0597	67.201	1/2	45.5531	165.13
5/16	4.1233	1.3530	5/16	16.6897	22.166	5/16	29.256	68.112	5/8	45.9458	167.99
3/8	4.3197	1.4849	3/8	16.8861	22.691	3/8	29.453	69.029	3/4	46.3385	170.87
7/16	4.5160	1.6230	7/16	17.0824	23.221	7/16	29.649	69.953	7/8	46.7312	173.78
1/2	4.7124	1.7671	1/2	17.2788	23.758	1/2	29.8451	70.882	15	47.1239	176.71
9/16	4.9087	1.9175	9/16	17.4751	24.301	9/16	30.042	71.818	1/8	47.5166	179.67
5/8	5.1051	2.0739	5/8	17.6715	24.850	5/8	30.2378	72.760	1/4	47.9093	182.65
11/16	5.3014	2.2365	11/16	17.8678	25.406	11/16	30.434	73.708	3/8	48.3020	185.66
3/4	5.4978	2.4053	3/4	18.0642	25.967	3/4	30.6305	74.662	1/2	48.6947	188.69
13/16	5.6941	2.5802	13/16	18.2605	26.535	13/16	30.827	75.622	5/8	49.0874	191.75
7/8	5.8905	2.7612	7/8	18.4569	27.109	7/8	31.0232	76.589	3/4	49.4801	194.83
15/16	6.0868	2.9483	15/16	18.6532	27.688	15/16	31.220	77.561	7/8	49.8728	197.93
2	6.2832	3.1416	6	18.8496	28.274	10	31.4159	78.540	16	50.2655	201.06
1/16	6.4795	3.3410	1/16	19.046	28.867	1/16	31.612	79.525	1/8	50.6582	204.22
1/8	6.6759	3.5466	1/8	19.2423	29.465	1/8	31.8086	80.516	1/4	51.0509	207.39
3/16	6.8722	3.7583	3/16	19.439	30.069	3/16	32.005	81.513	3/8	51.4436	210.60
1/4	7.0686	3.9761	1/4	19.6350	30.680	1/4	32.2013	82.516	1/2	51.8363	213.82
5/16	7.2649	4.2000	5/16	19.831	31.296	5/16	32.398	83.525	5/8	52.2290	217.08
3/8	7.4613	4.4301	3/8	20.0277	31.919	3/8	32.5940	84.541	3/4	52.6217	220.35
7/16	7.6576	4.6646	7/16	20.224	32.548	7/16	32.790	85.563	7/8	53.0144	223.65
1/2	7.8540	4.9087	1/2	20.4204	33.183	1/2	32.9867	86.590	17	53.4071	226.98
9/16	8.0503	5.1572	9/16	20.617	33.824	9/16	33.183	87.624	1/8	53.7998	230.33
5/8	8.2467	5.4419	5/8	20.8131	34.472	5/8	33.3794	88.664	1/4	54.1925	233.71
11/16	8.4430	5.6727	11/16	21.009	35.125	11/16	33.576	89.710	3/8	54.5852	237.10
3/4	8.6394	5.9396	3/4	21.2058	35.785	3/4	33.7721	90.763	1/2	54.9779	240.53
13/16	8.8357	6.2126	13/16	21.402	36.451	13/16	33.969	91.821	5/8	55.3706	243.98
7/8	9.0321	6.4918	7/8	21.5984	37.122	7/8	34.1648	92.886	3/4	55.7633	247.45
15/16	9.2284	6.7771	15/16	21.795	37.800	15/16	34.361	93.957	7/8	56.1560	250.95
3	9.4248	7.0686	7	21.9911	38.485	11	34.5575	95.033	18	56.5487	254.47
1/16	9.6211	7.3662	1/16	22.188	39.175	1/16	34.754	96.116	1/8	56.9414	258.02
1/8	9.8175	7.6699	1/8	22.3838	39.871	1/8	34.9502	97.205	1/4	57.3341	261.59
3/16	10.0138	7.9798	3/16	22.580	40.574	3/16	35.147	98.301	3/8	57.7268	265.18
1/4	10.2102	8.2958	1/4	22.7765	41.282	1/4	35.3429	99.402	1/2	58.1195	268.80
5/16	10.4065	8.6179	5/16	22.973	41.997	5/16	35.539	100.51	5/8	58.5122	272.45
3/8	10.6029	8.9462	3/8	23.1692	42.718	3/8	35.7356	101.62	3/4	58.9049	276.12
7/16	10.7992	9.2806	7/16	23.366	43.446	7/16	35.932	102.74	7/8	59.2976	279.81
1/2	10.9956	9.6211	1/2	23.5619	44.179	1/2	36.1283	103.87	19	59.6903	283.53
9/16	11.1919	9.9678	9/16	23.758	44.918	9/16	36.325	105.00	1/8	60.0830	287.27
5/8	11.3883	10.321	5/8	23.955	45.664	5/8	36.5210	106.14	1/4	60.4757	291.04
11/16	11.5846	10.680	11/16	24.151	46.415	11/16	36.717	107.28	3/8	60.8684	294.83
3/4	11.7810	11.045	3/4	24.3473	47.173	3/4	36.9137	108.43	1/2	61.2611	298.65
13/16	11.9773	11.416	13/16	24.544	47.937	13/16	37.110	109.59	5/8	61.6538	302.49
7/8	12.1737	11.793	7/8	24.7400	48.707	7/8	37.3064	110.75	3/4	62.0465	306.35
15/16	12.3700	12.177	15/16	24.936	49.483	15/16	37.503	111.92	7/8	62.4392	310.24

CIRCUMFERENCES AND AREAS OF CIRCLES

DIAMETER IN INCHES	CIRCUM- FERENCE	AREA OF CIRCLE	DIAMETER IN INCHES	CIRCUM- FERENCE	AREA OF CIRCLE	DIAMETER IN INCHES	CIRCUM- FERENCE	AREA OF CIRCLE	DIAMETER IN INCHES	CIRCUM- FERENCE	AREA OF CIRCLE
20	62.8319	314.16	24	75.3982	452.39	28	87.9646	615.75	32	100.531	804.25
1/8	63.2246	318.10	1/8	75.7909	457.11	1/8	88.3573	621.26	1/8	100.924	810.54
1/4	63.6173	322.06	1/4	76.1836	461.86	1/4	88.7500	626.80	1/4	101.316	816.86
3/8	64.0100	326.05	3/8	76.5763	466.64	3/8	89.1427	632.36	3/8	101.709	823.21
1/2	64.4026	330.06	1/2	76.9690	471.44	1/2	89.5354	637.94	1/2	102.102	829.58
5/8	64.7953	334.10	5/8	77.3617	476.26	5/8	89.9281	643.55	5/8	102.494	835.97
3/4	65.1880	338.16	3/4	77.7544	481.11	3/4	90.3208	649.18	3/4	102.887	842.39
7/8	65.5807	342.25	7/8	78.1471	485.98	7/8	90.7135	654.84	7/8	103.280	848.83
21	65.9734	346.36	25	78.5398	490.87	29	91.1062	660.52	33	103.673	855.30
1/8	66.3661	350.50	1/8	78.9325	495.79	1/8	91.4989	666.23	1/8	104.065	861.79
1/4	66.7588	354.66	1/4	79.3252	500.74	1/4	91.8916	671.96	1/4	104.458	868.31
3/8	67.1515	358.84	3/8	79.7179	505.71	3/8	92.2843	677.71	3/8	104.851	874.85
1/2	67.5442	363.05	1/2	80.1106	510.71	1/2	92.6770	683.49	1/2	105.243	881.41
5/8	67.9369	367.28	5/8	80.5033	515.72	5/8	93.0697	689.30	5/8	105.636	888.00
3/4	68.3296	371.54	3/4	80.8960	520.77	3/4	93.4624	695.13	3/4	106.029	894.62
7/8	68.7223	375.83	7/8	81.2887	525.84	7/8	93.8551	700.98	7/8	106.421	901.26
22	69.1150	380.13	26	81.6814	530.93	30	94.2478	706.86	34	106.814	907.92
1/8	69.5077	384.46	1/8	82.0741	536.05	1/8	94.6405	712.76	1/8	107.207	914.61
1/4	69.9004	388.82	1/4	82.4668	541.19	1/4	95.0332	718.69	1/4	107.600	921.32
3/8	70.2931	393.20	3/8	82.8595	546.35	3/8	95.4259	724.64	3/8	107.992	928.08
1/2	70.6858	397.61	1/2	83.2522	551.55	1/2	95.8186	730.62	1/2	108.385	934.82
5/8	71.0785	402.04	5/8	83.6449	556.76	5/8	96.2113	736.62	5/8	108.778	941.61
3/4	71.4712	406.49	3/4	84.0376	562.00	3/4	96.6040	742.64	3/4	109.170	948.42
7/8	71.8639	410.97	7/8	84.4303	567.27	7/8	96.9967	748.69	7/8	109.563	955.25
23	72.2566	415.48	27	84.8230	572.56	31	97.3894	754.77	35	109.956	962.11
1/8	72.6493	420.00	1/8	85.2157	577.87	1/8	97.7821	760.87	1/8	110.348	969.00
1/4	73.0420	424.56	1/4	85.6084	583.21	1/4	98.1748	766.99	1/4	110.741	975.91
3/8	73.4347	429.13	3/8	86.0011	588.57	3/8	98.5675	773.14	3/8	111.134	982.84
1/2	73.8274	433.74	1/2	86.3938	593.96	1/2	98.9602	779.31	1/2	111.527	989.80
5/8	74.2201	438.36	5/8	86.7865	599.37	5/8	99.3529	785.51	5/8	111.919	996.78
3/4	74.6128	443.01	3/4	87.1792	604.81	3/4	99.7456	791.73	3/4	112.312	1003.8
7/8	75.0055	447.69	7/8	87.5719	610.27	7/8	100.138	797.98	7/8	112.705	1010.8

0°

M	Sine	Cosine	Tan.	Cotan.	Secant	Cosec.	M
0	.00000	1.0000	.00000	Infinite	1.0000	Infinite	60
1	.00029	.0000	.00029	3437.7	.0000	3437.7	59
2	.00058	.0000	.00058	1718.9	.0000	1718.9	58
3	.00087	.0000	.00087	1145.9	.0000	1145.9	57
4	.00116	.0000	.00116	859.44	.0000	859.44	56
5	.00145	1.0000	.00145	687.55	1.0000	687.55	55
6	.00174	.0000	.00174	572.96	.0000	572.96	54
7	.00204	.0000	.00204	491.11	.0000	491.11	53
8	.00233	.0000	.00233	429.72	.0000	429.72	52
9	.00262	.0000	.00262	381.97	.0000	381.97	51
10	.00291	.99999	.00291	343.77	1.0000	343.77	50
11	.00320	.99999	.00320	312.52	.0000	312.52	49
12	.00349	.99999	.00349	286.48	.0000	286.48	48
13	.00378	.99999	.00378	264.44	.0000	264.44	47
14	.00407	.99999	.00407	245.55	.0000	245.55	46
15	.00436	.99999	.00436	229.18	1.0000	229.18	45
16	.00465	.99999	.00465	214.86	.0000	214.86	44
17	.00494	.99999	.00494	202.22	.0000	202.22	43
18	.00524	.99999	.00524	190.98	.0000	190.99	42
19	.00553	.99998	.00553	180.93	.0000	180.93	41
20	.00582	.99998	.00582	171.88	1.0000	171.89	40
21	.00611	.99998	.00611	163.70	.0000	163.70	39
22	.00640	.99998	.00640	156.26	.0000	156.26	38
23	.00669	.99998	.00669	149.46	.0000	149.47	37
24	.00698	.99997	.00698	143.24	.0000	143.24	36
25	.00727	.99997	.00727	137.51	1.0000	137.51	35
26	.00756	.99997	.00756	132.22	.0000	132.22	34
27	.00785	.99997	.00785	127.32	.0000	127.32	33
28	.00814	.99997	.00814	122.77	.0000	122.78	32
29	.00843	.99996	.00844	118.54	.0000	118.54	31
30	.00873	.99996	.00873	114.59	1.0000	114.59	30
31	.00902	.99996	.00902	110.89	.0000	110.90	29
32	.00931	.99996	.00931	107.43	.0000	107.43	28
33	.00960	.99995	.00960	104.17	.0000	104.17	27
34	.00989	.99995	.00989	101.11	.0000	101.11	26
35	.01018	.99995	.01018	98.218	1.0000	98.223	25
36	.01047	.99994	.01047	95.489	.0000	95.495	24
37	.01076	.99994	.01076	92.908	.0000	92.914	23
38	.01105	.99994	.01105	90.463	.0000	90.469	22
39	.01134	.99993	.01134	88.143	.0001	88.149	21
40	.01163	.99993	.01164	85.940	1.0001	85.946	20
41	.01193	.99993	.01193	83.843	.0001	83.849	19
42	.01222	.99992	.01222	81.847	.0001	81.853	18
43	.01251	.99992	.01251	79.943	.0001	79.950	17
44	.01280	.99992	.01280	78.126	.0001	78.133	16
45	.01309	.99991	.01309	76.390	1.0001	76.396	15
46	.01338	.99991	.01338	74.729	.0001	74.736	14
47	.01367	.99991	.01367	73.139	.0001	73.146	13
48	.01396	.99990	.01396	71.615	.0001	71.622	12
49	.01425	.99990	.01425	70.153	.0001	70.160	11
50	.01454	.99989	.01454	68.750	1.0001	68.757	10
51	.01483	.99989	.01484	67.402	.0001	67.409	9
52	.01512	.99988	.01513	66.105	.0001	66.113	8
53	.01542	.99988	.01542	64.858	.0001	64.866	7
54	.01571	.99988	.01571	63.657	.0001	63.664	6
55	.01600	.99987	.01600	62.499	1.0001	62.507	5
56	.01629	.99987	.01629	61.383	.0001	61.391	4
57	.01658	.99987	.01658	60.306	.0001	60.314	3
58	.01687	.99986	.01687	59.266	.0001	59.274	2
59	.01716	.99985	.01716	58.261	.0001	58.270	1
60	.01745	.99985	.01745	57.290	1.0001	57.299	0

| M | Cosine | Sine | Cotan. | Tan. | Cosec. | Secant | M |

89°

1°

M	Sine	Cosine	Tan.	Cotan.	Secant	Cosec.	M
0	.01745	.99985	.01745	57.290	1.0001	57.299	60
1	.01774	.99984	.01775	56.350	.0001	56.359	59
2	.01803	.99984	.01804	55.441	.0001	55.450	58
3	.01832	.99983	.01833	54.561	.0002	54.570	57
4	.01861	.99983	.01862	53.708	.0002	53.718	56
5	.01891	.99982	.01891	52.882	1.0002	52.891	55
6	.01920	.99981	.01920	52.081	.0002	52.090	54
7	.01949	.99981	.01949	51.303	.0002	51.313	53
8	.01978	.99980	.01978	50.548	.0002	50.558	52
9	.02007	.99980	.02007	49.816	.0002	49.826	51
10	.02036	.99979	.02036	49.104	1.0002	49.114	50
11	.02065	.99979	.02066	48.412	.0002	48.422	49
12	.02094	.99978	.02095	47.739	.0002	47.750	48
13	.02123	.99977	.02124	47.085	.0002	47.096	47
14	.02152	.99977	.02153	46.449	.0002	46.460	46
15	.02181	.99976	.02182	45.829	1.0002	45.840	45
16	.02210	.99975	.02211	45.226	.0002	45.237	44
17	.02240	.99975	.02240	44.638	.0002	44.650	43
18	.02269	.99974	.02269	44.066	.0002	44.077	42
19	.02298	.99974	.02298	43.508	.0003	43.520	41
20	.02326	.99973	.02327	42.964	1.0003	42.976	40
21	.02356	.99972	.02357	42.433	.0003	42.445	39
22	.02385	.99971	.02386	41.916	.0003	41.928	38
23	.02414	.99971	.02415	41.410	.0003	41.423	37
24	.02443	.99970	.02444	40.917	.0003	40.930	36
25	.02472	.99969	.02473	40.436	1.0003	40.448	35
26	.02501	.99969	.02502	39.965	.0003	39.978	34
27	.02530	.99968	.02531	39.506	.0003	39.518	33
28	.02559	.99967	.02560	39.057	.0003	39.069	32
29	.02589	.99966	.02589	38.618	.0003	38.631	31
30	.02618	.99966	.02618	38.188	1.0003	38.201	30
31	.02647	.99965	.02648	37.769	.0003	37.782	29
32	.02676	.99964	.02677	37.358	.0003	37.371	28
33	.02705	.99963	.02706	36.956	.0004	36.969	27
34	.02734	.99963	.02735	36.563	.0004	36.576	26
35	.02763	.99962	.02764	36.177	1.0004	36.191	25
36	.02792	.99961	.02793	35.800	.0004	35.814	24
37	.02821	.99960	.02822	35.431	.0004	35.445	23
38	.02850	.99959	.02851	35.069	.0004	35.084	22
39	.02879	.99958	.02880	34.715	.0004	34.729	21
40	.02908	.99958	.02910	34.368	1.0004	34.382	20
41	.02937	.59957	.02939	34.027	.0004	34.042	19
42	.02967	.99956	.02968	33.693	.0004	33.708	18
43	.02996	.99955	.02997	33.366	.0004	33.381	17
44	.03025	.99954	.03026	33.045	.0004	33.060	16
45	.03054	.99953	.03055	32.730	1.0005	32.745	15
46	.03083	.99952	.03084	32.421	.0005	32.437	14
47	.03112	.99951	.03113	32.118	.0005	32.134	13
48	.03141	.99951	.03143	31.820	.0005	31.836	12
49	.03170	.99950	.03172	31.528	.0005	31.544	11
50	.03199	.99949	.03201	31.241	1.0005	31.257	10
51	.03228	.99948	.03230	30.960	.0005	30.976	9
52	.03257	.99947	.03259	30.683	.0005	30.699	8
53	.03286	.99946	.03288	30.411	.0005	30.428	7
54	.03315	.99945	.03317	30.145	.0005	30.161	6
55	.03344	.99944	.03346	29.882	1.0005	29.899	5
56	.03374	.99943	.03375	29.624	.0006	29.641	4
57	.03403	.99942	.03405	29.371	.0006	29.388	3
58	.03432	.99941	.03434	29.122	.0006	29.139	2
59	.03461	.99940	.03463	28.877	.0006	28.894	1
60	.03490	.99939	.03492	28.636	1.0006	28.654	0

| M | Cosine | Sine | Cotan. | Tan. | Cosec. | Secant | M |

88°

M	Sine	Cosine	Tan.	Cotan.	Secant	Cosec.	M
0	.03490	.99939	.03492	28.636	1.0006	28.654	60
1	.03519	.99938	.03521	28.399	.0006	28.417	59
2	.03548	.99937	.03550	28.166	.0006	28.184	58
3	.03577	.99936	.03579	27.937	.0006	27.955	57
4	.03606	.99935	.03608	27.712	.0006	27.730	56
5	.03635	.99934	.03638	27.490	1.0007	27.508	55
6	.03664	.99933	.03667	27.271	.0007	27.290	54
7	.03693	.99932	.03696	27.056	.0007	27.075	53
8	.03722	.99931	.03725	26.845	.0007	26.864	52
9	.03751	.99930	.03754	26.637	.0007	26.655	51
10	.03781	.99928	.03783	26.432	1.0007	26.450	50
11	.03810	.99927	.03812	26.230	.0007	26.249	49
12	.03839	.99926	.03842	26.031	.0007	26.050	48
13	.03868	.99925	.03871	25.835	.0007	25.854	47
14	.03897	.99924	.03900	25.642	.0008	25.661	46
15	.03926	.99923	.03929	25.452	1.0008	25.471	45
16	.03955	.99922	.03958	25.264	.0008	25.284	44
17	.03984	.99921	.03987	25.080	.0008	25.100	43
18	.04013	.99919	.04016	24.898	.0008	24.918	42
19	.04042	.99918	.04045	24.718	.0008	24.739	41
20	.04071	.99917	.04075	24.542	1.0008	24.562	40
21	.04100	.99916	.04104	24.367	.0008	24.388	39
22	.04129	.99915	.04133	24.196	.0008	24.216	38
23	.04158	.99913	.04162	24.026	.0009	24.047	37
24	.04187	.99912	.04191	23.859	.0009	23.880	36
25	.04217	.99911	.04220	23.694	1.0009	23.716	35
26	.04246	.99910	.04249	23.532	.0009	23.553	34
27	.04275	.99908	.04279	23.372	.0009	23.393	33
28	.04304	.99907	.04308	23.214	.0009	23.235	32
29	.04333	.99906	.04337	23.058	.0009	23.079	31
30	.04362	.99905	.04366	22.904	1.0009	22.925	30
31	.04391	.99903	.04395	22.752	.0010	22.774	29
32	.04420	.99902	.04424	22.602	.0010	22.624	28
33	.04449	.99901	.04453	22.454	.0010	22.476	27
34	.04478	.99900	.04483	22.308	.0010	22.330	26
35	.04507	.99898	.04512	22.164	1.0010	22.186	25
36	.04536	.99897	.04541	22.022	.0010	22.044	24
37	.04565	.99896	.04570	21.881	.0010	21.904	23
38	.04594	.99894	.04599	21.742	.0010	21.765	22
39	.04623	.99893	.04628	21.606	.0011	21.629	21
40	.04652	.99892	.04657	21.470	1.0011	21.494	20
41	.04681	.99890	.04687	21.337	.0011	21.360	19
42	.04711	.99889	.04716	21.205	.0011	21.228	18
43	.04740	.99888	.04745	21.075	.0011	21.098	17
44	.04769	.99886	.04774	20.946	.0011	20.970	16
45	.04798	.99885	.04803	20.819	1.0011	20.843	15
46	.04827	.99883	.04832	20.693	.0012	20.717	14
47	.04856	.99882	.04862	20.569	.0012	20.593	13
48	.04885	.99881	.04891	20.446	.0012	20.471	12
49	.04914	.99879	.04920	20.325	.0012	20.350	11
50	.04943	.99878	.04949	20.205	1.0012	20.230	10
51	.04972	.99876	.04978	20.087	.0012	20.112	9
52	.05001	.99875	.05007	19.970	.0012	19.995	8
53	.05030	.99873	.05037	19.854	.0013	19.880	7
54	.05059	.99872	.05066	19.740	.0013	19.766	6
55	.05088	.99870	.05095	19.627	1.0013	19.653	5
56	.05117	.99869	.05124	19.515	.0013	19.541	4
57	.05146	.99867	.05153	19.405	.0013	19.431	3
58	.05175	.99866	.05182	19.296	.0013	19.322	2
59	.05204	.99864	.05212	19.188	.0013	19.214	1
60	.05234	.99863	.05241	19.081	1.0014	19.107	0

M	Cosine	Sine	Cotan.	Tan.	Cosec.	Secant	M

M	Sine	Cosine	Tan.	Cotan.	Secant	Cosec.	M
0	.05234	.99863	.05241	19.081	1.0014	19.107	60
1	.05263	.99861	.05270	18.975	.0014	19.002	59
2	.05292	.99860	.05299	18.871	.0014	18.897	58
3	.05321	.99858	.05328	18.768	.0014	18.794	57
4	.05350	.99857	.05357	18.665	.0014	18.692	56
5	.05379	.99855	.05387	18.564	1.0014	18.591	55
6	.05408	.99854	.05416	18.464	.0015	18.491	54
7	.05437	.99852	.05445	18.365	.0015	18.393	53
8	.05466	.99850	.05474	18.268	.0015	18.295	52
9	.05495	.99849	.05503	18.171	.0015	18.198	51
10	.05524	.99847	.05532	18.075	1.0015	18.103	50
11	.05553	.99846	.05562	17.980	.0015	18.008	49
12	.05582	.99844	.05591	17.886	.0016	17.914	48
13	.05611	.99842	.05620	17.793	.0016	17.821	47
14	.05640	.99841	.05649	17.701	.0016	17.730	46
15	.05669	.99839	.05678	17.610	1.0016	17.639	45
16	.05698	.99837	.05707	17.520	.0016	17.549	44
17	.05727	.99836	.05737	17.431	.0016	17.460	43
18	.05756	.99834	.05766	17.343	.0017	17.372	42
19	.05785	.99832	.05795	17.256	.0017	17.285	41
20	.05814	.99831	.05824	17.169	1.0017	17.198	40
21	.05843	.99829	.05853	17.084	.0017	17.113	39
22	.05872	.99827	.05883	16.999	.0017	17.028	38
23	.05902	.99826	.05912	16.915	.0017	16.944	37
24	.05931	.99824	.05941	16.832	.0018	16.861	36
25	.05960	.99822	.05970	16.750	1.0018	16.779	35
26	.05989	.99820	.05999	16.668	.0018	16.698	34
27	.06018	.99819	.06029	16.587	.0018	16.617	33
28	.06047	.99817	.06058	16.507	.0018	16.538	32
29	.06076	.99815	.06087	16.428	.0018	16.459	31
30	.06105	.99813	.06116	16.350	1.0019	16.380	30
31	.06134	.99812	.06145	16.272	.0019	16.303	29
32	.06163	.99810	.06175	16.195	.0019	16.226	28
33	.06192	.99808	.06204	16.119	.0019	16.150	27
34	.06221	.99806	.06233	16.043	.0019	16.075	26
35	.06250	.99804	.06262	15.969	1.0019	16.000	25
36	.06279	.99803	.06291	15.894	.0020	15.926	24
37	.06308	.99801	.06321	15.821	.0020	15.853	23
38	.06337	.99799	.06350	15.748	.0020	15.780	22
39	.06366	.99797	.06379	15.676	.0020	15.708	21
40	.06395	.99795	.06408	15.605	1.0C20	15.637	20
41	.06424	.99793	.06437	15.534	.0021	15.566	19
42	.06453	.99791	.06467	15.464	.0021	15.496	18
43	.06482	.99790	.06496	15.394	.0021	15.427	17
44	.06511	.99788	.06525	15.325	.0021	15.358	16
45	.06540	.99786	.06554	15.257	1.0021	15.290	15
46	.06569	.99784	.06583	15.189	.0022	15.222	14
47	.06598	.99782	.06613	15.122	.0022	15.155	13
48	.06627	.99780	.06642	15.056	.0022	15.089	12
49	.06656	.99778	.06671	14 990	.0022	15.023	11
50	.06685	.99776	.06700	14.924	1.0022	14.958	10
51	.06714	.99774	.06730	14.860	.0023	14.893	9
52	.06743	.99772	.06759	14.795	.0023	14.829	8
53	.06772	.99770	.06788	14.732	.0023	14.765	7
54	.06801	.99768	.06817	14.668	.0023	14.702	6
55	.06830	.99766	.06846	14.606	1.0023	14.640	5
56	.C6859	.99764	.06876	14.544	.0024	14.578	4
57	.06888	.99762	.06905	14.482	.0024	14.517	3
58	.06918	.99760	.06934	14.421	.0024	14.456	2
59	.06947	.99758	.06963	14.361	.0024	14.395	1
6C	.06976	.99756	.06993	14.301	1.0024	14.335	0

M	Cosine	Sine	Cotan.	Tan.	Cosec.	Secant	M

4°

M	Sine	Cosine	Tan.	Cotan.	Secant	Cosec.	M
0	.06976	.99756	.06993	14.301	1.0024	14.335	60
1	.07005	.99754	.07022	14.241	.0025	14.276	59
2	.07034	.99752	.07051	14.182	.0025	14.217	58
3	.07063	.99750	.07080	14.123	.0025	14.159	57
4	.07092	.99748	.07110	14.065	.0025	14.101	56
5	.07121	.99746	.07139	14.008	1.0025	14.043	55
6	.07150	.99744	.07168	13.951	.0026	13.986	54
7	.07179	.99742	.07197	13.894	.0026	13.930	53
8	.07208	.99740	.07226	13.838	.0026	13.874	52
9	.07237	.99738	.07256	13.782	.0026	13.818	51
10	.07266	.99736	.07285	13.727	1.0026	13.763	50
11	.07295	.99733	.07314	13.672	.0027	13.708	49
12	.07324	.99731	.07343	13.617	.0027	13.654	48
13	.07353	.99729	.07373	13.563	.0027	13.600	47
14	.07382	.99727	.07402	13.510	.0027	13.547	46
15	.07411	.99725	.07431	13.457	1.0027	13.494	45
16	.07440	.99723	.07460	13.404	.0028	13.441	44
17	.07469	.99721	.07490	13.351	.0028	13.389	43
18	.07498	.99718	.07519	13.299	.0028	13.337	42
19	.07527	.99716	.07548	13.248	.0028	13.286	41
20	.07556	.99714	.07577	13.197	1.0029	13.235	40
21	.07585	.99712	.07607	13.146	.0029	13.184	39
22	.07614	.99710	.07636	13.096	.0029	13.134	38
23	.07643	.99707	.07665	13.046	.0029	13.084	37
24	.07672	.99705	.07694	12.996	.0029	13.034	36
25	.07701	.99703	.07724	12.947	1.0030	12.985	35
26	.07730	.99701	.07753	12.898	.0030	12.937	34
27	.07759	.99698	.07782	12.849	.0030	12.888	33
28	.07788	.99696	.07812	12.801	.0030	12.840	32
29	.07817	.99694	.07841	12.754	.0031	12.793	31
30	.07846	.99692	.07870	12.706	1.0031	12.745	30
31	.07875	.99689	.07899	12.659	.0031	12.698	29
32	.07904	.99687	.07929	12.612	.0031	12.652	28
33	.07933	.99685	.07958	12.566	.0032	12.606	27
34	.07962	.99682	.07987	12.520	.0032	12.560	26
35	.07991	.99680	.08016	12.474	1.0032	12.514	25
36	.08020	.99678	.08046	12.429	.0032	12.469	24
37	.08049	.99675	.08075	12.384	.0032	12.424	23
38	.08078	.99673	.08104	12.339	.0033	12.379	22
39	.08107	.99671	.08134	12.295	.0033	12.335	21
40	.08136	.99668	.08163	12.250	1.0033	12.291	20
41	.08165	.99666	.08192	12.207	.0033	12.248	19
42	.08194	.99664	.08221	12.163	.0034	12.204	18
43	.08223	.99661	.08251	12.120	.0034	12.161	17
44	.08252	.99659	.08280	12.077	.0034	12.118	16
45	.08281	.99656	.08309	12.035	1.0034	12.076	15
46	.08310	.99654	.08339	11.992	.0035	12.034	14
47	.08339	.99652	.08368	11.950	.0035	11.992	13
48	.08368	.99649	.08397	11.909	.0035	11.950	12
49	.08397	.99647	.08426	11.867	.0035	11.909	11
50	.08426	.99644	.08456	11.826	1.0036	11.868	10
51	.08455	.99642	.08485	11.785	.0036	11.828	9
52	.08484	.99639	.08514	11.745	.0036	11.787	8
53	.08513	.99637	.08544	11.704	.0036	11.747	7
54	.08542	.99634	.08573	11.664	.0037	11.707	6
55	.08571	.99632	.08602	11.625	1.0037	11.668	5
56	.08600	.99629	.08632	11.585	.0037	11.628	4
57	.08629	.99627	.08661	11.546	1.0037	11.589	3
58	.08658	.99624	.08690	11.507	.0038	11.550	2
59	.08687	.99622	.08719	11.468	.0038	11.512	1
60	.08715	.99619	.08749	11.430	1.0038	11.474	0

| M | Cosine | Sine | Cotan. | Tan. | Cosec. | Secant | M |

85°

5°

M	Sine	Cosine	Tan.	Cotan.	Secant	Cosec.	M
0	.08715	.99619	.08749	11.430	1.0038	11.474	60
1	.08744	.99617	.08778	11.392	.0038	11.436	59
2	.08773	.99614	.08807	11.354	.0039	11.398	58
3	.08802	.99612	.08837	11.316	.0039	11.360	57
4	.08831	.99609	.08866	11.279	.0039	11.323	56
5	.08860	.99607	.08895	11.242	1.0039	11.286	55
6	.08889	.99604	.08925	11.205	.0040	11.249	54
7	.08918	.99601	.08954	11.168	.0040	11.213	53
8	.08947	.99599	.08983	11.132	.0040	11.176	52
9	.08976	.99596	.09013	11.095	.0040	11.140	51
10	.09005	.99594	.09042	11.059	1.0041	11.104	50
11	.09034	.99591	.09071	11.024	.0041	11.069	49
12	.09063	.99588	.09101	10.988	.0041	11.033	48
13	.09092	.99586	.09130	10.953	.0041	10.998	47
14	.09121	.99583	.09159	10.918	.0042	10.963	46
15	.09150	.99580	.09189	10.883	1.0042	10.929	45
16	.09179	.99578	.09218	10.848	.0042	10.894	44
17	.09208	.99575	.09247	10.814	.0043	10.860	43
18	.09237	.99572	.09277	10.780	.0043	10.826	42
19	.09266	.99570	.09306	10.746	.0043	10.792	41
20	.09295	.99567	.09335	10.712	1.0043	10.758	40
21	.09324	.99564	.09365	10.678	.0044	10.725	39
22	.09353	.99562	.09394	10.645	.0044	10.692	38
23	.09382	.99559	.09423	10.612	.0044	10.659	37
24	.09411	.99556	.09453	10.579	.0044	10.626	36
25	.09440	.99553	.09482	10.546	1.0045	10.593	35
26	.09469	.99551	.09511	10.514	.0045	10.561	34
27	.09498	.99548	.09541	10.481	.0045	10.529	33
28	.09527	.99545	.09570	10.449	.0046	10.497	32
29	.09556	.99542	.09599	10.417	.0046	10.465	31
30	.09584	.99540	.09629	10.385	1.0046	10.433	30
31	.09613	.99537	.09658	10.354	.0046	10.402	29
32	.09642	.99534	.09688	10.322	.0047	10.371	28
33	.09671	.99531	.09717	10.291	.0047	10.340	27
34	.09700	.99528	.09746	10.260	.0047	10.309	26
35	.09729	.99525	.09776	10.229	1.0048	10.278	25
36	.09758	.99523	.09805	10.199	.0048	10.248	24
37	.09787	.99520	.09834	10.168	.0048	10.217	23
38	.09816	.99517	.09864	10.138	.0048	10.187	22
39	.09845	.99514	.09893	10.108	.0049	10.157	21
40	.09874	.99511	.09922	10.078	1.0049	10.127	20
41	.09903	.99508	.09952	10.048	.0049	10.098	19
42	.09932	.99505	.09981	10.019	.0050	10.068	18
43	.09961	.99503	.10011	9.9893	.0050	10.039	17
44	.09990	.99500	.10040	9.9601	.0050	10.010	16
45	.10019	.99497	.10069	9.9310	1.0050	9.9812	15
46	.10048	.99494	.10099	9.9021	.0051	9.9525	14
47	.10077	.99491	.10128	9.8734	.0051	9.9239	13
48	.10106	.99488	.10158	9.8448	.0051	9.8955	12
49	.10134	.99485	.10187	9.8164	.0052	9.8672	11
50	.10163	.99482	.10216	9.7882	1.0052	9.8391	10
51	.10192	.99479	.10246	9.7601	.0052	9.8112	9
52	.10221	.99476	.10275	9.7322	.0053	9.7834	8
53	.10250	.99473	.10305	9.7044	.0053	9.7558	7
54	.10279	.99470	.10334	9.6768	.0053	9.7283	6
55	.10308	.99467	.10363	9.6493	1.0053	9.7010	5
56	.10337	.99464	.10393	9.6220	.0054	9.6739	4
57	.10366	.99461	.10422	9.5949	.0054	9.6469	3
58	.10395	.99458	.10452	9.5679	.0054	9.6200	2
59	.10424	.99455	.10481	9.5411	.0055	9.5933	1
60	.10453	.99452	.10510	9.5144	1.0055	9.5668	0

| M | Cosine | Sine | Cotan. | Tan. | Cosec. | Secant | M |

84°

M	Sine	Cosine	Tan.	Cotan.	Secant	Cosec.	M
0	.10453	.99452	.10510	9.5144	1.0055	9.5668	60
1	.10482	.99449	.10540	.4878	.0055	.5404	59
2	.10511	.99446	.10569	.4614	.0056	.5141	58
3	.10540	.99443	.10599	.4351	.0056	.4880	57
4	.10568	.99440	.10628	.4090	.0056	.4620	56
5	.10597	.99437	.10657	9.3831	1.0057	9.4362	55
6	.10626	.99434	.10687	.3572	.0057	.4105	54
7	.10655	.99431	.10716	.3315	.0057	.3850	53
8	.10684	.99428	.10746	.3060	.0057	.3596	52
9	.10713	.99424	.10775	.2806	.0058	.3343	51
10	.10742	.99421	.10805	9.2553	1.0058	9.3092	50
11	.10771	.99418	.10834	.2302	.0058	.2842	49
12	.10800	.99415	.10863	.2051	.0059	.2593	48
13	.10829	.99412	.10893	.1803	.0059	.2346	47
14	.10858	.99409	.10922	.1555	.0059	.2100	46
15	.10887	.99406	.10952	9.1309	1.0060	9.1855	45
16	.10916	.99402	.10981	.1064	.0060	.1612	44
17	.10944	.99399	.11011	.0821	.0060	.1370	43
18	.10973	.99396	.11040	.0579	.0061	.1129	42
19	.11002	.99393	.11069	.0338	.0061	.0890	41
20	.11031	.99390	.11099	9.0098	1.0061	9.0651	40
21	.11060	.99386	.11128	8.9860	.0062	9.0414	39
22	.11089	.99383	.11158	.9623	.0062	.0179	38
23	.11118	.99380	.11187	.9387	.0062	8.9944	37
24	.11147	.99377	.11217	.9152	.0063	.9711	36
25	.11176	.99373	.11246	8.8918	1.0063	8.9479	35
26	.11205	.99370	.11276	.8686	.0063	.9248	34
27	.11234	.99367	.11305	.8455	.0064	.9018	33
28	.11262	.99364	.11335	.8225	.0064	.8790	32
29	.11291	.99360	.11364	.7996	.0064	.8563	31
30	.11320	.99357	.11393	8.7769	1.0065	8.8337	30
31	.11349	.99354	.11423	.7542	.0065	.8112	29
32	.11378	.99350	.11452	.7317	.0065	.7888	28
33	.11407	.99347	.11482	.7093	.0066	.7665	27
34	.11436	.99344	.11511	.6870	.0066	.7444	26
35	.11465	.99341	.11541	8.6648	1.0066	8.7223	25
36	.11494	.99337	.11570	.6427	.0067	.7004	24
37	.11523	.99334	.11600	.6208	.0067	.6786	23
38	.11551	.99330	.11629	.5989	.0067	.6569	22
39	.11580	.99327	.11659	.5772	.0068	.6353	21
40	.11609	.99324	.11688	8.5555	1.0068	8.6138	20
41	.11638	.99320	.11718	.5340	.0068	.5924	19
42	.11667	.99317	.11747	.5126	.0069	.5711	18
43	.11696	.99314	.11777	.4913	.0069	.5499	17
44	.11725	.99310	.11806	.4701	.0069	.5289	16
45	.11754	.99307	.11836	8.4489	1.0070	8.5079	15
46	.11783	.99303	.11865	.4279	.0070	.4871	14
47	.11811	.99300	.11895	.4070	.0070	.4663	13
48	.11840	.99296	.11924	.3862	.0071	.4457	12
49	.11869	.99293	.11954	.3655	.0071	.4251	11
50	.11898	.99290	.11983	8.3449	1.0071	8.4046	10
51	.11927	.99286	.12013	.3244	.0072	.3843	9
52	.11956	.99283	.12042	.3040	.0072	.3640	8
53	.11985	.99279	.12072	.2837	.0073	.3439	7
54	.12014	.99276	.12101	.2635	.0073	.3238	6
55	.12042	.99272	.12131	8.2434	1.0073	8.3039	5
56	.12071	.99269	.12160	.2234	.0074	.2840	4
57	.12100	.99265	.12190	.2035	.0074	.2642	3
58	.12129	.99262	.12219	.1837	.0074	.2446	2
59	.12158	.99258	.12249	.1640	.0075	.2250	1
60	.12187	.99255	.12278	8.1443	1.0075	8.2055	0
M	Cosine	Sine	Cotan.	Tan.	Cosec.	Secant	M

M	Sine	Cosine	Tan.	Cotan.	Secant	Cosec.	M
0	.12187	.99255	.12278	8.1443	1.0075	8.2055	60
1	.12216	.99251	.12308	.1248	.0075	.1861	59
2	.12245	.99247	.12337	.1053	.0076	.1668	58
3	.12273	.99244	.12367	.0860	.0076	.1476	57
4	.12302	.99240	.12396	.0667	.0076	.1285	56
5	.12331	.99237	.12426	8.0476	1.0077	8.1094	55
6	.12360	.99233	.12456	.0285	.0077	.0905	54
7	.12389	.99229	.12485	.0095	.0078	.0717	53
8	.12418	.99226	.12515	7.9906	.0078	.0529	52
9	.12447	.99222	.12544	.9717	.0078	.0342	51
10	.12476	.99219	.12574	7.9530	1.0079	8.0156	50
11	.12504	.99215	.12603	.9344	.0079	7.9971	49
12	.12533	.99211	.12633	.9158	.0079	.9787	48
13	.12562	.99208	.12662	.8973	.0080	.9604	47
14	.12591	.99204	.12692	.8789	.0080	.9421	46
15	.12620	.99200	.12722	7.8606	1.0080	7.9240	45
16	.12649	.99197	.12751	.8424	.0081	.9059	44
17	.12678	.99193	.12781	.8243	.0081	.8879	43
18	.12706	.99189	.12810	.8062	.0082	.8700	42
19	.12735	.99186	.12840	.7882	.0082	.8522	41
20	.12764	.99182	.12869	7.7703	1.0082	7.8344	40
21	.12793	.99178	.12899	.7525	.0083	.8168	39
22	.12822	.99174	.12928	.7348	.0083	.7992	38
23	.12851	.99171	.12958	.7171	.0084	.7817	37
24	.12879	.99167	.12988	.6996	.0084	.7642	36
25	.12908	.99163	.13017	7.6821	1.0084	7.7469	35
26	.12937	.99160	.13047	.6646	.0085	.7296	34
27	.12966	.99156	.13076	.6473	.0085	.7124	33
28	.12995	.99152	.13106	.6300	.0085	.6953	32
29	.13024	.99148	.13136	.6129	.0086	.6783	31
30	.13053	.99144	.13165	7.5957	1.0086	7.6613	30
31	.13081	.99141	.13195	.5787	.0087	.6444	29
32	.13110	.99137	.13224	.5617	.0087	.6276	28
33	.13139	.99133	.13254	.5449	.0087	.6108	27
34	.13168	.99129	.13284	.5280	.0088	.5942	26
35	.13197	.99125	.13313	7.5113	1.0088	7.5776	25
36	.13226	.99121	.13343	.4946	.0089	.5611	24
37	.13254	.99118	.13372	.4780	.0089	.5446	23
38	.13283	.99114	.13402	.4615	.0089	.5282	22
39	.13312	.99110	.13432	.4451	.0090	.5119	21
40	.13341	.99106	.13461	7.4287	1.0090	7.4957	20
41	.13370	.99102	.13491	.4124	.0090	.4795	19
42	.13399	.99098	.13520	.3961	.0091	.4634	18
43	.13427	.99094	.13550	.3800	.0091	.4474	17
44	.13456	.99090	.13580	.3639	.0092	.4315	16
45	.13485	.99086	.13609	7.3479	1.0092	7.4156	15
46	.13514	.99083	.13639	.3319	.0092	.3998	14
47	.13543	.99079	.13669	.3160	.0093	.3840	13
48	.13571	.99075	.13698	.3002	.0093	.3683	12
49	.13600	.99071	.13728	.2844	.0094	.3527	11
50	.13629	.99067	.13757	7.2687	1.0094	7.3372	10
51	.13658	.99063	.13787	.2531	.0094	.3217	9
52	.13687	.99059	.13817	.2375	.0095	.3063	8
53	.13716	.99055	.13846	.2220	.0095	.2909	7
54	.13744	.99051	.13876	.2066	.0096	.2757	6
55	.13773	.99047	.13906	7.1912	1.0096	7.2604	5
56	.13802	.99043	.13935	.1759	.0097	.2453	4
57	.13831	.99039	.13965	.1607	.0097	.2302	3
58	.13860	.99035	.13995	.1455	.0097	.2152	2
59	.13888	.99031	.14024	.1304	.0098	.2002	1
60	.13917	.99027	.14054	7.1154	1.0098	7.1853	0
M	Cosine	Sine	Cotan.	Tan.	Cosec.	Secant	M

M	Sine	Cosine	Tan.	Cotan.	Secant	Cosec.	M
0	.13917	.99027	.14054	7.1154	1.0098	7.1853	60
1	.13946	.99023	.14084	.1004	.0099	.1704	59
2	.13975	.99019	.14113	.0854	.0099	.1557	58
3	.14004	.99015	.14143	.0706	.0099	.1409	57
4	.14032	.99010	.14173	.0558	.0100	.1263	56
5	.14061	.99006	.14202	7.0410	1.0100	7.1117	55
6	.14090	.99002	.14232	.0264	.0101	.0972	54
7	.14119	.98998	.14262	.0117	.0101	.0827	53
8	.14148	.98994	.14291	6.9972	.0102	.0683	52
9	.14176	.98990	.14321	.9827	.0102	.0539	51
10	.14205	.98986	.14351	6.9682	1.0102	7.0396	50
11	.14234	.98982	.14380	.9538	.0103	.0254	49
12	.14263	.98978	.14410	.9395	.0103	.0112	48
13	.14292	.98973	.14440	.9252	.0104	6.9971	47
14	.14320	.98969	.14470	.9110	.0104	.9830	46
15	.14349	.98965	.14499	6.8969	1.0104	6.9690	45
16	.14378	.98961	.14529	.8828	.0105	.9550	44
17	.14407	.98957	.14559	.8687	.0105	.9411	43
18	.14436	.98952	.14588	.8547	.0106	.9273	42
19	.14464	.98948	.14618	.8408	.0106	.9135	41
20	.14493	.98944	.14648	6.8269	1.0107	6.8998	40
21	.14522	.98940	.14677	.8131	.0107	.8861	39
22	.14551	.98936	.14707	.7993	.0107	.8725	38
23	.14579	.98931	.14737	.7856	.0108	.8589	37
24	.14608	.98927	.14767	.7720	.0108	.8454	36
25	.14637	.98923	.14796	6.7584	1.0109	6.8320	35
26	.14666	.98919	.14826	.7448	.0109	.8185	34
27	.14695	.98914	.14856	.7313	.0110	.8052	33
28	.14723	.98910	.14886	.7179	.0110	.7919	32
29	.14752	.98906	.14915	.7045	.0111	.7787	31
30	.14781	.98901	.14945	6.6911	1.0111	6.7655	30
31	.14810	.98897	.14975	.6779	.0111	.7523	29
32	.14838	.98893	.15004	.6646	.0112	.7392	28
33	.14867	.98889	.15034	.6514	.0112	.7262	27
34	.14896	.98884	.15064	.6383	.0113	.7132	26
35	.14925	.98880	.15094	6.6252	1.0113	6.7003	25
36	.14953	.98876	.15123	.6122	.0114	.6874	24
37	.14982	.98871	.15153	.5992	.0114	.6745	23
38	.15011	.98867	.15183	.5863	.0115	.6617	22
39	.15040	.98862	.15213	.5734	.0115	.6490	21
40	.15068	.98858	.15243	6.5605	1.0115	6.6363	20
41	.15097	.98854	.15272	.5478	.0116	.6237	19
42	.15126	.98849	.15302	.5350	.0116	.6111	18
43	.15155	.98845	.15332	.5223	.0117	.5985	17
44	.15183	.98840	.15362	.5097	.0117	.5860	16
45	.15212	.98836	.15391	6.4971	1.0118	6.5736	15
46	.15241	.98832	.15421	.4845	.0118	.5612	14
47	.15270	.98827	.15451	.4720	.0119	.5488	13
48	.15298	.98823	.15481	.4596	.0119	.5365	12
49	.15328	.98818	.15511	.4472	.0119	.5243	11
50	.15356	.98814	.15540	6.4348	1.0120	6.5121	10
51	.15385	.98809	.15570	.4225	.0120	.4999	9
52	.15413	.98805	.15600	.4103	.0121	.4878	8
53	.15442	.98800	.15630	.3980	.0121	.4757	7
54	.15471	.98796	.15659	.3859	.0122	.4637	6
55	.15500	.98791	.15689	6.3737	1.0122	6.4517	5
56	.15528	.98787	.15719	.3616	.0123	.4398	4
57	.15557	.98782	.15749	.3496	.0123	.4279	3
58	.15586	.98778	.15779	.3376	.0124	.4160	2
59	.15615	.98773	.15809	.3257	.0124	.4042	1
60	.15643	.98769	.15838	6.3137	1.0125	6.3924	0

M	Cosine	Sine	Cotan.	Tan.	Cosec.	Secant	M

M	Sine	Cosine	Tan.	Cotan.	Secant	Cosec.	M
0	.15643	.98769	.15838	6.3137	1.0125	6.3924	60
1	.15672	.98764	.15868	.3019	.0125	.3807	59
2	.15701	.98760	.15898	.2901	.0125	.3690	58
3	.15730	.98755	.15928	.2783	.0126	.3574	57
4	.15758	.98750	.15958	.2665	.0126	.3458	56
5	.15787	.98746	.15987	6.2548	1.0127	6.3343	55
6	.15816	.98741	.16017	.2432	.0127	.3228	54
7	.15844	.98737	.16047	.2316	.0128	.3113	53
8	.15873	.98732	.16077	.2200	.0128	.2999	52
9	.15902	.98727	.16107	.2085	.0129	.2885	51
10	.15931	.98723	.16137	6.1970	1.0129	6.2772	50
11	.15959	.98718	.16167	.1856	.0130	.2659	49
12	.15988	.98714	.16196	.1742	.0130	.2546	48
13	.16017	.98709	.16226	.1628	.0131	.2434	47
14	.16045	.98704	.16256	.1515	.0131	.2322	46
15	.16074	.98700	.16286	6.1402	1.0132	6.2211	45
16	.16103	.98695	.16316	.1290	.0132	.2100	44
17	.16132	.98690	.16346	.1178	.0133	.1990	43
18	.16160	.98685	.16376	.1066	.0133	.1880	42
19	.16189	.98681	.16405	.0955	.0134	.1770	41
20	.16218	.98676	.16435	6.0844	1.0134	6.1661	40
21	.16246	.98671	.16465	.0734	.0135	.1552	39
22	.16275	.98667	.16495	.0624	.0135	.1443	38
23	.16304	.98662	.16525	.0514	.0136	.1335	37
24	.16333	.98657	.16555	.0405	.0136	.1227	36
25	.16361	.98652	.16585	6.0296	1.0136	6.1120	35
26	.16390	.98648	.16615	.0188	.0137	.1013	34
27	.16419	.98643	.16644	.0080	.0137	.0906	33
28	.16447	.98638	.16674	5.9972	.0138	.0800	32
29	.16476	.98633	.16704	.9865	.0138	.0694	31
30	.16505	.98628	.16734	5.9758	1.0139	6.0588	30
31	.16533	98624	.16764	.9651	.0139	.0483	29
32	.16562	.98619	.16794	.9545	.0140	.0379	28
33	.16591	.98614	.16824	.9439	.0140	.0274	27
34	.16619	.98609	.16854	.9333	.0141	.0170	26
35	.16648	.98604	.16884	5.9228	1.0141	6.0066	25
36	.16677	.98600	.16914	.9123	.0142	5.9963	24
37	.16705	.98595	.16944	.9019	.0142	.9860	23
38	.16734	.98590	.16973	.8915	.0143	.9758	22
39	.16763	.98585	.17003	.8811	.0143	.9655	21
40	.16791	.98580	.17033	5.8708	1.0144	5 9554	20
41	.16820	.98575	.17063	.8605	.0144	.9452	19
42	.16849	.98570	.17093	.8502	.0145	.9351	18
43	.16878	.98565	.17123	.8400	.0145	.9250	17
44	.16906	.98560	.17153	.8298	.0146	.9150	16
45	.16935	.98556	.17183	5.8196	1.0146	5.9049	15
46	.16964	.98551	.17213	.8095	.0147	.8950	14
47	.16992	.98546	.17243	.7994	.0147	.8850	13
48	.17021	.98541	.17273	.7894	.0148	.8751	12
49	.17050	.98536	.17303	.7794	.0148	.8652	11
50	.17078	.98531	.17333	5.7694	1.0149	5.8554	10
51	.17107	.98526	.17363	.7594	.0150	.8456	9
52	.17136	.98521	.17393	.7495	.0150	.8358	8
53	.17164	.98516	.17423	.7396	.0151	.8261	7
54	.17193	.98511	.17453	.7297	.0151	.8163	6
55	.17221	.98506	.17483	5.7199	1.0152	5.8067	5
56	.17250	.98501	.17513	.7101	.0152	.7970	4
57	.17279	.98496	.17543	.7004	.0153	.7874	3
58	.17307	.98491	.17573	.6906	.0153	.7778	2
59	.17336	.98486	.17603	.6809	.0154	.7683	1
60	.17365	.98481	.17633	5.6713	1.0154	5.7588	0

M	Cosine	Sine	Cotan.	Tan.	Cosec.	Secant	M

M	Sine	Cosine	Tan.	Cotan.	Secant	Cosec.	M
0	.17365	.98481	.17633	5.6713	1.0154	5.7588	60
1	.17393	.98476	.17663	.6616	.0155	.7493	59
2	.17422	.98471	.17693	.6520	.0155	.7398	58
3	.17451	.98465	.17723	.6425	.0156	.7304	57
4	.17479	.98460	.17753	.6329	.0156	.7210	56
5	.17508	.98455	.17783	5.6234	1.0157	5.7117	55
6	.17537	.98450	.17813	.6140	.0157	.7023	54
7	.17565	.98445	.17843	.6045	.0158	.6930	53
8	.17594	.98440	.17873	.5951	.0158	.6838	52
9	.17622	.98435	.17903	.5857	.0159	.6745	51
10	.17651	.98430	.17933	5.5764	1.0159	5.6653	50
11	.17680	.98425	.17963	.5670	.0160	.6561	49
12	.17708	.98419	.17993	.5578	.0160	.6470	48
13	.17737	.98414	.18023	.5485	.0161	.6379	47
14	.17766	.98409	.18053	.5393	.0162	.6288	46
15	.17794	.98404	.18083	5.5301	1.0162	5.6197	45
16	.17823	.98399	.18113	.5209	.0163	.6107	44
17	.17852	.98394	.18143	.5117	.0163	.6017	43
18	.17880	.98388	.18173	.5026	.0164	.5928	42
19	.17909	.98383	.18203	.4936	.0164	.5838	41
20	.17937	.98378	.18233	5.4845	1.0165	5.5749	40
21	.17966	.98373	.18263	.4755	.0165	.5660	39
22	.17995	.98368	.18293	.4665	.0166	.5572	38
23	.18023	.98362	.18323	.4575	.0166	.5484	37
24	.18052	.98357	.18353	.4486	.0167	.5396	36
25	.18080	.98352	.18383	5.4396	1.0167	5.5308	35
26	.18109	.98347	.18413	.4308	.0168	.5221	34
27	.18138	.98341	.18444	.4219	.0169	.5134	33
28	.18166	.98336	.18474	.4131	.0169	.5047	32
29	.18195	.98331	.18504	.4043	.0170	.4960	31
30	.18223	.98325	.18534	5.3955	1.0170	5.4874	30
31	.18252	.98320	.18564	.3868	.0171	.4788	29
32	.18281	.98315	.18594	.3780	.0171	.4702	28
33	.18309	.98309	.18624	.3694	.0172	.4617	27
34	.18338	.98304	.18654	.3607	.0172	.4532	26
35	.18366	.98299	.18684	5.3521	1.0173	5.4447	25
36	.18395	.98293	.18714	.3434	.0174	.4362	24
37	.18424	.98288	.18745	.3349	.0174	.4278	23
38	.18452	.98283	.18775	.3263	.0175	.4194	22
39	.18481	.98277	.18805	.3178	.0175	.4110	21
40	.18509	.98272	.18835	5.3093	1.0176	5.4026	20
41	.18538	.98267	.18865	.3008	.0176	.3943	19
42	.18567	.98261	.18895	.2923	.0177	.3860	18
43	.18595	.98256	.18925	.2839	.0177	.3777	17
44	.18624	.98250	.18955	.2755	.0178	.3695	16
45	.18652	.98245	.18985	5.2671	1.0179	5.3612	15
46	.18681	.98240	.19016	.2588	.0179	.3530	14
47	.18709	.98234	.19046	.2505	.0180	.3449	13
48	.18738	.98229	.19076	.2422	.0180	.3367	12
49	.18767	.98223	.19106	.2339	.0181	.3286	11
50	.18795	.98218	.19136	5.2257	1.0181	5.3205	10
51	.18824	.98212	.19166	.2174	.0182	.3124	9
52	.18852	.98207	.19197	.2092	.0182	.3044	8
53	.18881	.98201	.19227	.2011	.0183	.2963	7
54	.18909	.98196	.19257	.1929	.0184	.2883	6
55	.18938	.98190	.19287	5.1848	1.0184	5.2803	5
56	.18967	.98185	.19317	.1767	.0185	.2724	4
57	.18995	.98179	.19347	.1686	.0185	.2645	3
58	.19024	.98174	.19378	.1606	.0186	.2566	2
59	.19052	.98168	.19408	.1525	.0186	.2487	1
60	.19081	.98163	.19438	5.1445	1.0187	5.2408	0
M	Cosine	Sine	Cotan.	Tan.	Cosec.	Secant	M

M	Sine	Cosine	Tan.	Cotan.	Secant	Cosec.	M
0	.19081	.98163	.19438	5.1445	1.0187	5.2408	60
1	.19109	.98157	.19468	.1366	.0188	.2330	59
2	.19138	.98152	.19498	.1286	.0188	.2252	58
3	.19166	.98146	.19529	.1207	.0189	.2174	57
4	.19195	.98140	.19559	.1128	.0189	.2097	56
5	.19224	.98135	.19589	5.1049	1.0190	5.2019	55
6	.19252	.98129	.19619	.0970	.0191	.1942	54
7	.19281	.98124	.19649	.0892	.0191	.1865	53
8	.19309	.98118	.19680	.0814	.0192	.1788	52
9	.19338	.98112	.19710	.0736	.0192	.1712	51
10	.19366	.98107	.19740	5.0658	1.0193	5.1636	50
11	.19395	.98101	.19770	.0581	.0193	.1560	49
12	.19423	.98095	.19800	.0504	.0194	.1484	48
13	.19452	.98090	.19831	.0427	.0195	.1409	47
14	.19480	.98084	.19861	.0350	.0195	.1333	46
15	.19509	.98078	.19891	5.0273	1.0196	5.1258	45
16	.19537	.98073	.19921	.0197	.0196	.1183	44
17	.19566	.98067	.19952	.0121	.0197	.1109	43
18	.19595	.98061	.19982	.0045	.0198	.1034	42
19	.19623	.98056	.20012	4.9969	.0198	.0960	41
20	.19652	.98050	.20042	4.9894	1.0199	5.0886	40
21	.19680	.98044	.20073	.9819	.0199	.0812	39
22	.19709	.98039	.20103	.9744	.0200	.0739	38
23	.19737	.98033	.20133	.9669	.0201	.0666	37
24	.19766	.98027	.20163	.9594	.0201	.0593	36
25	.19794	.98021	.20194	4.9520	1.0202	5.0520	35
26	.19823	.98016	.20224	.9446	.0202	.0447	34
27	.19851	.98010	.20254	.9372	.0203	.0375	33
28	.19880	.98004	.20285	.9298	.0204	.0302	32
29	.19908	.97998	.20315	.9225	.0204	.0230	31
30	.19937	.97992	.20345	4.9151	1.0205	5.0158	30
31	.19965	.97987	.20375	.9078	.0205	.0087	29
32	.19994	.97981	.20406	.9006	.0206	.0015	28
33	.20022	.97975	.20436	.8933	.0207	4.9944	27
34	.20051	.97969	.20466	.8860	.0207	.9873	26
35	.20079	.97963	.20497	4.8788	1.0208	4.9802	25
36	.20108	.97957	.20527	.8716	.0208	.9732	24
37	.20136	.97952	.20557	.8644	.0209	.9661	23
38	.20165	.97946	.20588	.8573	.0210	.9591	22
39	.20193	.97940	.20618	.8501	.0210	.9521	21
40	.20222	.97934	.20648	4.8430	1.0211	4.9452	20
41	.20250	.97928	.20679	.8359	.0211	.9382	19
42	.20279	.97922	.20709	.8288	.0212	.9313	18
43	.20307	.97916	.20739	.8217	.0213	.9243	17
44	.20336	.97910	.20770	.8147	.0213	.9175	16
45	.20364	.97904	.20800	4.8077	1.0214	4.9106	15
46	.20393	.97899	.20830	.8007	.0215	.9037	14
47	.20421	.97893	.20861	.7937	.0215	.8969	13
48	.20450	.97887	.20891	.7867	.0216	.8901	12
49	.20478	.97881	.20921	.7798	.0216	.8833	11
50	.20506	.97875	.20952	4.7728	1.0217	4.8765	10
51	.20535	.97869	.20982	.7659	.0218	.8697	9
52	.20563	.97863	.21012	.7591	.0218	.8630	8
53	.20592	.97857	.21043	.7522	.0219	.8563	7
54	.20620	.97851	.21073	.7453	.0220	.8496	6
55	.20649	.97845	.21104	4.7385	1.0220	4.8429	5
56	.20677	.97839	.21134	.7317	.0221	.8362	4
57	.20706	.97833	.21164	.7249	.0221	.8296	3
58	.20734	.97827	.21195	.7181	.0222	.8229	2
59	.20763	.97821	.21225	.7114	.0223	.8163	1
60	.20791	.97815	.21256	4.7046	1.0223	4.8097	0
M	Cosine	Sine	Cotan.	Tan.	Cosec.	Secant	M

M	Sine	Cosine	Tan.	Cotan.	Secant	Cosec.	M
0	.20791	.97815	.21256	4.7046	1.0223	4.8097	60
1	.20820	.97809	.21286	.6979	.0224	.8032	59
2	.20848	.97803	.21316	.6912	.0225	.7966	58
3	.20876	.97797	.21347	.6845	.0225	.7901	57
4	.20905	.97790	.21377	.6778	.0226	.7835	56
5	.20933	.97784	.21408	4.6712	1.0226	4.7770	55
6	.20962	.97778	.21438	.6646	.0227	.7706	54
7	.20990	.97772	.21468	.6580	.0228	.7641	53
8	.21019	.97766	.21499	.6514	.0228	.7576	52
9	.21047	.97760	.21529	.6448	.0229	.7512	51
10	.21076	.97754	.21560	4.6382	1.0230	4.7448	50
11	.21104	.97748	.21590	.6317	.0230	.7384	49
12	.21132	.97741	.21621	.6252	.0231	.7320	48
13	.21161	.97735	.21651	.6187	.0232	.7257	47
14	.21189	.97729	.21682	.6122	.0232	.7193	46
15	.21218	.97723	.21712	4.6057	1.0233	4.7130	45
16	.21246	.97717	.21742	.5993	.0234	.7067	44
17	.21275	.97711	.21773	.5928	.0234	.7004	43
18	.21303	.97704	.21803	.5864	.0235	.6942	42
19	.21331	.97698	.21834	.5800	.0235	.6879	41
20	.21360	.97692	.21864	4.5736	1.0236	4.6817	40
21	.21388	.97686	.21895	.5673	.0237	.6754	39
22	.21417	.97680	.21925	.5609	.0237	.6692	38
23	.21445	.97673	.21956	.5546	.0238	.6631	37
24	.21473	.97667	.21986	.5483	.0239	.6569	36
25	.21502	.97661	.22017	4.5420	1.0239	4.6507	35
26	.21530	.97655	.22047	.5357	.0240	.6446	34
27	.21559	.97648	.22078	.5294	.0241	.6385	33
28	.21587	.97642	.22108	.5232	.0241	.6324	32
29	.21615	.97636	.22139	.5169	.0242	.6263	31
30	.21644	.97630	.22169	4.5107	1.0243	4.6201	30
31	.21672	.97623	.22200	.5045	.0243	.6142	29
32	.21701	.97617	.22230	.4983	.0244	.6081	28
33	.21729	.97611	.22261	.4921	.0245	.6021	27
34	.21757	.97604	.22291	.4860	.0245	.5961	26
35	.21786	.97598	.22322	4.4799	1.0246	4.5901	25
36	.21814	.97592	.22353	.4737	.0247	.5841	24
37	.21843	.97585	.22383	.4676	.0247	.5782	23
38	.21871	.97579	.22414	.4615	.0248	.5722	22
39	.21899	.97573	.22444	.4555	.0249	.5663	21
40	.21928	.97566	.22475	4.4494	1.0249	4.5604	20
41	.21956	.97560	.22505	.4434	.0250	.5545	19
42	.21985	.97553	.22536	.4373	.0251	.5486	18
43	.22013	.97547	.22566	.4313	.0251	.5428	17
44	.22041	.97541	.22597	.4253	.0252	.5369	16
45	.22070	.97534	.22628	4.4194	1.0253	4.5311	15
46	.22098	.97528	.22658	.4134	.0253	.5253	14
47	.22126	.97521	.22689	.4074	.0254	.5195	13
48	.22155	.97515	.22719	.4015	.0255	.5137	12
49	.22183	.97508	.22750	.3956	.0255	.5079	11
50	.22211	.97502	.22781	4.3897	1.0256	4.5021	10
51	.22240	.97495	.22811	.3838	.0257	.4964	9
52	.22268	.97489	.22842	.3779	.0257	.4907	8
53	.22297	.97483	.22872	.3721	.0258	.4850	7
54	.22325	.97476	.22903	.3662	.0259	.4793	6
55	.22353	.97470	.22934	4.3604	1.0260	4.4736	5
56	.22382	.97463	.22964	.3546	.0260	.4679	4
57	.22410	.97457	.22995	.3488	.0261	.4623	3
58	.22438	.97450	.23025	.3430	.0262	.4566	2
59	.22467	.97443	.23056	.3372	.0262	.4510	1
60	.22495	.97437	.23087	4.3315	1.0263	4.4454	0
M	Cosine	Sine	Cotan.	Tan.	Cosec.	Secant	M

M	Sine	Cosine	Tan.	Cotan.	Secant	Cosec.	M
0	.22495	.97437	.23087	4.3315	1.0263	4.4454	60
1	.22523	.97430	.23117	.3257	.0264	.4398	59
2	.22552	.97424	.23148	.3200	.0264	.4342	58
3	.22580	.97417	.23179	.3143	.0265	.4287	57
4	.22608	.97411	.23209	.3086	.0266	.4231	56
5	.22637	.97404	.23240	4.3029	1.0266	4.4176	55
6	.22665	.97398	.23270	.2972	.0267	.4121	54
7	.22693	.97391	.23301	.2916	.0268	.4065	53
8	.22722	.97384	.23332	.2859	.0268	.4011	52
9	.22750	.97378	.23363	.2803	.0269	.3956	51
10	.22778	.97371	.23393	4.2747	1.0270	4.3901	50
11	.22807	.97364	.23424	.2691	.0271	.3847	49
12	.22835	.97358	.23455	.2635	.0271	.3792	48
13	.22863	.97351	.23485	.2579	.0272	.3738	47
14	.22892	.97344	.23516	.2524	.0273	.3684	46
15	.22920	.97338	.23547	4.2468	1.0273	4.3630	45
16	.22948	.97331	.23577	.2413	.0274	.3576	44
17	.22977	.97324	.23608	.2358	.0275	.3522	43
18	.23005	.97318	.23639	.2303	.0276	.3469	42
19	.23033	.97311	.23670	.2248	.0276	.3415	41
20	.23061	.97304	.23700	4.2193	1.0277	4.3362	40
21	.23090	.97298	.23731	.2139	.0278	.3309	39
22	.23118	.97291	.23762	.2084	.0278	.3256	38
23	.23146	.97284	.23793	.2030	.0279	.3203	37
24	.23175	.97277	.23823	.1976	.0280	.3150	36
25	.23203	.97271	.23854	4.1921	1.0280	4.3098	35
26	.23231	.97264	.23885	.1867	.0281	.3045	34
27	.23260	.97257	.23916	.1814	.0282	.2993	33
28	.23288	.97250	.23946	.1760	.0283	.2941	32
29	.23316	.97244	.23977	.1706	.0283	.2888	31
30	.23344	.97237	.24008	4.1653	1.0284	4.2836	30
31	.23373	.97230	.24039	.1600	.0285	.2785	29
32	.23401	.97223	.24069	.1546	.0285	.2733	28
33	.23429	.97216	.24100	.1493	.0286	.2681	27
34	.23458	.97210	.24131	.1440	.0287	.2630	26
35	.23486	.97203	.24162	4.1388	1.0288	4.2579	25
36	.23514	.97196	.24192	.1335	.0288	.2527	24
37	.23542	.97189	.24223	.1282	.0289	.2476	23
38	.23571	.97182	.24254	.1230	.0290	.2425	22
39	.23599	.97175	.24285	.1178	.0291	.2375	21
40	.23627	.97169	.24316	4.1126	1.0291	4.2324	20
41	.23655	.97162	.24346	.1073	.0292	.2273	19
42	.23684	.97155	.24377	.1022	.0293	.2223	18
43	.23712	.97148	.24408	.0970	.0293	.2173	17
44	.23740	.97141	.24439	.0918	.0294	.2122	16
45	.23768	.97134	.24470	4.0867	1.0295	4.2072	15
46	.23797	.97127	.24501	.0815	.0296	.2022	14
47	.23825	.97120	.24531	.0764	.0296	.1972	13
48	.23853	.97113	.24562	.0713	.0297	.1923	12
49	.23881	.97106	.24593	.0662	.0298	.1873	11
50	.23910	.97099	.24624	4.0611	1.0299	4.1824	10
51	.23938	.97092	.24655	.0560	.0299	.1774	9
52	.23966	.97086	.24686	.0509	.0300	.1725	8
53	.23994	.97079	.24717	.0458	.0301	.1676	7
54	.24023	.97072	.24747	.0408	.0302	.1627	6
55	.24051	.97065	.24778	4.0358	1.0302	4.1578	5
56	.24079	.97058	.24809	.0307	.0303	.1529	4
57	.24107	.97051	.24840	.0257	.0304	.1481	3
58	.24136	.97044	.24871	.0207	.0305	.1432	2
59	.24164	.97037	.24902	.0157	.0305	.1384	1
60	.24192	.97029	.24933	4.0108	1.0306	4.1336	0
M	Cosine	Sine	Cotan.	Tan.	Cosec.	Secant	M

M	Sine	Cosine	Tan.	Cotan.	Secant	Cosec.	M
0	.24192	.97029	.24933	4.0108	1.0306	4.1336	60
1	.24220	.97022	.24964	.0058	.0307	.1287	59
2	.24249	.97015	.24995	.0009	.0308	.1239	58
3	.24277	.97008	.25025	3.9959	.0308	.1191	57
4	.24305	.97001	.25056	.9910	.0309	.1144	56
5	.24333	.96994	.25087	3.9861	1.0310	4.1096	55
6	.24361	.96987	.25118	.9812	.0311	.1048	54
7	.24390	.96980	.25149	.9763	.0311	.1001	53
8	.24418	.96973	.25180	.9714	.0312	.0953	52
9	.24446	.96966	.25211	.9665	.0313	.0906	51
10	.24474	.96959	.25242	3.9616	1.0314	4.0859	50
11	.24502	.96952	.25273	.9568	.0314	.0812	49
12	.24531	.96944	.25304	.9520	.0315	.0765	48
13	.24559	.96937	.25335	.9471	.0316	.0718	47
14	.24587	.96930	.25366	.9423	.0317	.0672	46
15	.24615	.96923	.25397	3.9375	1.0317	4.0625	45
16	.24643	.96916	.25428	.9327	.0318	.0579	44
17	.24672	.96909	.25459	.9279	.0319	.0532	43
18	.24700	.96901	.25490	.9231	.0320	.0486	42
19	.24728	.96894	.25521	.9184	.0320	.0440	41
20	.24756	.96887	.25552	3.9136	1.0321	4.0394	40
21	.24784	.96880	.25583	.9089	.0322	.0348	39
22	.24813	.96873	.25614	.9042	.0323	.0302	38
23	.24841	.96865	.25645	.8994	.0323	.0256	37
24	.24869	.96858	.25676	.8947	.0324	.0211	36
25	.24897	.96851	.25707	3.8900	1.0325	4.0165	35
26	.24925	.96844	.25738	.8853	.0326	.0120	34
27	.24953	.96836	.25769	.8807	.0327	.0074	33
28	.24982	.96829	.25800	.8760	.0327	.0029	32
29	.25010	.96822	.25831	.8713	.0328	3.9984	31
30	.25038	.96815	.25862	3.8667	1.0329	3.9939	30
31	.25066	.96807	.25893	.8621	.0330	.9894	29
32	.25094	.96800	.25924	.8574	.0330	.9850	28
33	.25122	.96793	.25955	.8528	.0331	.9805	27
34	.25151	.96785	.25986	.8482	.0332	.9760	26
35	.25179	.96778	.26017	3.8436	1.0333	3.9716	25
36	.25207	.96771	.26048	.8390	.0334	.9672	24
37	.25235	.96763	.26079	.8345	.0334	.9627	23
38	.25263	.96756	.26110	.8299	.0335	.9583	22
39	.25291	.96749	.26141	.8254	.0336	.9539	21
40	.25319	.96741	.26172	3.8208	1.0337	3.9495	20
41	.25348	.96734	.26203	.8163	.0338	.9451	19
42	.25376	.96727	.26234	.8118	.0338	.9408	18
43	.25404	.96719	.26266	.8073	.0339	.9364	17
44	.25432	.96712	.26297	.8027	.0340	.9320	16
45	.25460	.96704	.26328	3.7983	1.0341	3.9277	15
46	.25488	.96697	.26359	.7938	.0341	.9234	14
47	.25516	.96690	.26390	.7893	.0342	.9190	13
48	.25544	.96682	.26421	.7848	.0343	.9147	12
49	.25573	.96675	.26452	.7804	.0344	.9104	11
50	.25601	.96667	.26483	3.7759	1.0345	3.9061	10
51	.25629	.96660	.26514	.7715	.0345	.9018	9
52	.25657	.96652	.26546	.7671	.0346	.8976	8
53	.25685	.96645	.26577	.7627	.0347	.8933	7
54	.25713	.96638	.26608	.7583	.0348	.8890	6
55	.25741	.96630	.26639	3.7539	1.0349	3.8848	5
56	.25769	.96623	.26670	.7495	.0349	.8805	4
57	.25798	.96615	.26701	.7451	.0350	.8763	3
58	.25826	.96608	.26732	.7407	.0351	.8721	2
59	.25854	.96600	.26764	.7364	.0352	.8679	1
60	.25882	.96592	.26795	3.7320	1.0353	3.8637	0
M	Cosine	Sine	Cotan.	Tan.	Cosec.	Secant	M

M	Sine	Cosine	Tan.	Cotan.	Secant	Cosec.	M
0	.25882	.96592	.26795	3.7320	1.0353	3.8637	60
1	.25910	.96585	.26826	.7277	.0353	.8595	59
2	.25938	.96577	.26857	.7234	.0354	.8553	58
3	.25966	.96570	.26888	.7191	.0355	.8512	57
4	.25994	.96562	.26920	.7147	.0356	.8470	56
5	.26022	.96555	.26951	3.7104	1.0357	3.8428	55
6	.26050	.96547	.26982	.7062	.0358	.8387	54
7	.26078	.96540	.27013	.7019	.0358	.8346	53
8	.26107	.96532	.27044	.6976	.0359	.8304	52
9	.26135	.96524	.27076	.6933	.0360	.8263	51
10	.26163	.96517	.27107	3.6891	1.0361	3.8222	50
11	.26191	.96509	.27138	.6848	.0362	.8181	49
12	.26219	.96502	.27169	.6806	.0362	.8140	48
13	.26247	.96494	.27201	.6764	.0363	.8100	47
14	.26275	.96486	.27232	.6722	.0364	.8059	46
15	.26303	.96479	.27263	3.6679	1.0365	3.8018	45
16	.26331	.96471	.27294	.6637	.0366	.7978	44
17	.26359	.96463	.27326	.6596	.0367	.7937	43
18	.26387	.96456	.27357	.6554	.0367	.7897	42
19	.26415	.96448	.27388	.6512	.0368	.7857	41
20	.26443	.96440	.27419	3.6470	1.0369	3.7816	40
21	.26471	.96433	.27451	.6429	.0370	.7776	39
22	.26499	.96425	.27482	.6387	.0371	.7736	38
23	.26527	.96417	.27513	.6346	.0371	.7697	37
24	.26556	.96409	.27544	.6305	.0372	.7657	36
25	.26584	.96402	.27576	3.6263	1.0373	3.7617	35
26	.26612	.96394	.27607	.6222	.0374	.7577	34
27	.26640	.96386	.27638	.6181	.0375	.7538	33
28	.26668	.96378	.27670	.6140	.0376	.7498	32
29	.26696	.96371	.27701	.6100	.0376	.7459	31
30	.26724	.96363	.27732	3.6059	1.0377	3.7420	30
31	.26752	.96355	.27764	.6018	.0378	.7380	29
32	.26780	.96347	.27795	.5977	.0379	.7341	28
33	.26808	.96340	.27826	.5937	.0380	.7302	27
34	.26836	.96332	.27858	.5896	.0381	.7263	26
35	.26864	.96324	.27889	3.5856	1.0382	3.7224	25
36	.26892	.96316	.27920	.5816	.0382	.7186	24
37	.26920	.96308	.27952	.5776	.0383	.7147	23
38	.26948	.96301	.27983	.5736	.0384	.7108	22
39	.26976	.96293	.28014	.5696	.0385	.7070	21
40	.27004	.96285	.28046	3.5656	1.0386	3.7031	20
41	.27032	.96277	.28077	.5616	.0387	.6993	19
42	.27060	.96269	.28109	.5576	.0387	.6955	18
43	.27088	.96261	.28140	.5536	.0388	.6917	17
44	.27116	.96253	.28171	.5497	.0389	.6878	16
45	.27144	.96245	.28203	3.5457	1.0390	3.6840	15
46	.27172	.96238	.28234	.5418	.0391	.6802	14
47	.27200	.96230	.28266	.5378	.0392	.6765	13
48	.27228	.96222	.28297	.5339	.0393	.6727	12
49	.27256	.96214	.28328	.5300	.0393	.6689	11
50	.27284	.96206	.28360	3.5261	1.0394	3.6651	10
51	.27312	.96198	.28391	.5222	.0395	.6614	9
52	.27340	.96190	.28423	.5183	.0396	.6576	8
53	.27368	.96182	.28454	.5144	.0397	.6539	7
54	.27396	.96174	.28486	.5105	.0398	.6502	6
55	.27424	.96166	.28517	3.5066	1.0399	3.6464	5
56	.27452	.96158	.28549	.5028	.0399	.6427	4
57	.27480	.96150	.28580	.4989	.0400	.6390	3
58	.27508	.96142	.28611	.4951	.0401	.6353	2
59	.27536	.96134	.28643	.4912	.0402	.6316	1
60	.27564	.96126	.28674	3.4874	1.0403	3.6279	0
M	Cosine	Sine	Cotan.	Tan.	Cosec.	Secant	M

M	Sine	Cosine	Tan.	Cotan.	Secant	Cosec.	M
0	.27564	.96126	.28674	3.4874	1.0403	3.6279	60
1	.27592	.96118	.28706	.4836	.0404	.6243	59
2	.27620	.96110	.28737	.4798	.0405	.6206	58
3	.27648	.96102	.28769	.4760	.0406	.6169	57
4	.27675	.96094	.28800	.4722	.0406	.6133	56
5	.27703	.96086	.28832	3.4684	1.0407	3.6096	55
6	.27731	.96078	.28863	.4646	.0408	.6060	54
7	.27759	.96070	.28895	.4608	.0409	.6024	53
8	.27787	.96062	.28926	.4570	.0410	.5987	52
9	.27815	.96054	.28958	.4533	.0411	.5951	51
10	.27843	.96045	.28990	3.4495	1.0412	3.5915	50
11	.27871	.96037	.29021	.4458	.0413	.5879	49
12	.27899	.96029	.29053	.4420	.0413	.5843	48
13	.27927	.96021	.29084	.4383	.0414	.5807	47
14	.27955	.96013	.29116	.4346	.0415	.5772	46
15	.27983	.96005	.29147	3.4308	1.0416	3.5736	45
16	.28011	.95997	.29179	.4271	.0417	.5700	44
17	.28039	.95989	.29210	.4234	.0418	.5665	43
18	.28067	.95980	.29242	.4197	.0419	.5629	42
19	.28094	.95972	.29274	.4160	.0420	.5594	41
20	.28122	.95964	.29305	3.4124	1.0420	3.5559	40
21	.28150	.95956	.29337	.4087	.0421	.5523	39
22	.28178	.95948	.29368	.4050	.0422	.5488	38
23	.28206	.95940	.29400	.4014	.0423	.5453	37
24	.28234	.95931	.29432	.3977	.0424	.5418	36
25	.28262	.95923	.29463	3.3941	1.0425	3.5383	35
26	.28290	.95915	.29495	.3904	.0426	.5348	34
27	.28318	.95907	.29526	.3868	.0427	.5313	33
28	.28346	.95898	.29558	.3832	.0428	.5279	32
29	.28374	.95890	.29590	.3795	.0428	.5244	31
30	.28401	.95882	.29621	3.3759	1.0429	3.5209	30
31	.28429	.95874	.29653	.3723	.0430	.5175	29
32	.28457	.95865	.29685	.3687	.0431	.5140	28
33	.28485	.95857	.29716	.3651	.0432	.5106	27
34	.28513	.95849	.29748	.3616	.0433	.5072	26
35	.28541	.95840	.29780	3.3580	1.0434	3.5037	25
36	.28569	.95832	.29811	.3544	.0435	.5003	24
37	.28597	.95824	.29843	.3509	.0436	.4969	23
38	.28624	.95816	.29875	.3473	.0437	.4935	22
39	.28652	.95807	.29906	.3438	.0438	.4901	21
40	.28680	.95799	.29938	3.3402	1.0438	3.4867	20
41	.28708	.95791	.29970	.3367	.0439	.4833	19
42	.28736	.95782	.30001	.3332	.0440	.4799	18
43	.28764	.95774	.30033	.3296	.0441	.4766	17
44	.28792	.95765	.30065	.3261	.0442	.4732	16
45	.28820	.95757	.30096	3.3226	1.0443	3.4698	15
46	.28847	.95749	.30128	.3191	.0444	.4665	14
47	.28875	.95740	.30160	.3156	.0445	.4632	13
48	.28903	.95732	.30192	.3121	.0446	.4598	12
49	.28931	.95723	.30223	.3087	.0447	.4565	11
50	.28959	.95715	.30255	3.3052	1.0448	3.4532	10
51	.28987	.95707	.30287	.3017	.0448	.4498	9
52	.29014	.95698	.30319	3.2983	.0449	.4465	8
53	.29042	.95690	.30350	.2948	.0450	.4432	7
54	.29070	.95681	.30382	.2914	.0451	.4399	6
55	.29098	.95673	.30414	3.2879	1.0452	3.4366	5
56	.29126	.95664	.30446	.2845	.0453	.4334	4
57	.29154	.95656	.30478	.2811	.0454	.4301	3
58	.29181	.95647	.30509	.2777	.0455	.4268	2
59	.29209	.95639	.30541	.2742	.0456	.4236	1
60	.29237	.95630	.30573	3.2708	1.0457	3.4203	0

M	Cosine	Sine	Cotan.	Tan.	Cosec.	Secant	M

M	Sine	Cosine	Tan.	Cotan.	Secant	Cosec.	M
0	.29237	.95630	.30573	3.2708	1.0457	3.4203	60
1	.29265	.95622	.30605	.2674	.0458	.4170	59
2	.29293	.95613	.30637	.2640	.0459	.4138	58
3	.29321	.95605	.30668	.2607	.0460	.4106	57
4	.29348	.95596	.30700	.2573	.0461	.4073	56
5	.29376	.95588	.30732	3.2539	1.0461	3.4041	55
6	.29404	.95579	.30764	.2505	.0462	.4009	54
7	.29432	.95571	.30796	.2472	.0463	.3977	53
8	.29460	.95562	.30828	.2438	.0464	.3945	52
9	.29487	.95554	.30859	.2405	.0465	.3913	51
10	.29515	.95545	.30891	3.2371	1.0466	3.3881	50
11	.29543	.95536	.30923	.2338	.0467	.3849	49
12	.29571	.95528	.30955	.2305	.0468	.3817	48
13	.29598	.95519	.30987	.2271	.0469	.3785	47
14	.29626	.95511	.31019	.2238	.0470	.3754	46
15	.29654	.95502	.31051	3.2205	1.0471	3.3722	45
16	.29682	.95493	.31083	.2172	.0472	.3690	44
17	.29710	.95485	.31115	.2139	.0473	.3659	43
18	.29737	.95476	.31146	.2106	.0474	.3627	42
19	.29765	.95467	.31178	.2073	.0475	.3596	41
20	.29793	.95459	.31210	3.2041	1.0476	3.3565	40
21	.29821	.95450	.31242	.2008	.0477	.3534	39
22	.29848	.95441	.31274	.1975	.0478	.3502	38
23	.29876	.95433	.31306	.1942	.0478	.3471	37
24	.29904	.95424	.31338	.1910	.0479	.3440	36
25	.29932	.95415	.31370	3.1877	1.0480	3.3409	35
26	.29959	.95407	.31402	.1845	.0481	.3378	34
27	.29987	.95398	.31434	.1813	.0482	.3347	33
28	.30015	.95389	.31466	.1780	.0483	.3316	32
29	.30043	.95380	.31498	.1748	.0484	.3286	31
30	.30070	.95372	.31530	3.1716	1.0485	3.3255	30
31	.30098	.95363	.31562	.1684	.0486	.3224	29
32	.30126	.95354	.31594	.1652	.0487	.3194	28
33	.30154	.95345	.31626	.1620	.0488	.3163	27
34	.30181	.95337	.31658	.1588	.0489	.3133	26
35	.30209	.95328	.31690	3.1556	1.0490	3.3102	25
36	.30237	.95319	.31722	.1524	.0491	.3072	24
37	.30265	.95310	.31754	.1492	.0492	.3042	23
38	.30292	.95301	.31786	.1460	.0493	.3011	22
39	.30320	.95293	.31818	.1429	.0494	.2981	21
40	.30348	.95284	.31850	3.1397	1.0495	3.2951	20
41	.30375	.95275	.31882	.1366	.0496	.2921	19
42	.30403	.95266	.31914	1334	.0497	.2891	18
43	.30431	.95257	.31946	.1303	.0498	.2861	17
44	.30459	.95248	.31978	1271	.0499	.2831	16
45	.30486	.95239	.32010	3.1240	1.0500	3.2801	15
46	.30514	.95231	.32042	1209	.0501	.2772	14
47	.30542	.95222	.32074	.1177	.0502	.2742	13
48	.30569	.95213	.32106	.1146	.0503	.2712	12
49	.30597	.95204	.32138	.1115	.0504	.2683	11
50	.30625	.95195	.32171	3.1084	1.0505	3.2653	10
51	.30653	.95186	.32203	.1053	.0506	.2624	9
52	.30680	.95177	.32235	.1022	.0507	.2594	8
53	.30708	.95168	.32267	.0991	.0508	.2565	7
54	.30736	.95159	.32299	.0960	.0509	.2535	6
55	.30763	.95150	.32331	3.0930	1.0510	3.2506	5
56	.30791	.95141	.32363	.0899	.0511	.2477	4
57	.30819	.95132	.32395	.0868	.0512	.2448	3
58	.30846	.95124	.32428	.0838	.0513	.2419	2
59	.30874	.95115	.32460	.0807	.0514	.2390	1
60	.30902	.95106	.32492	3.0777	1.0515	3.2361	0

M	Cosine	Sine	Cotan.	Tan.	Cosec.	Secant	M

18°

M	Sine	Cosine	Tan.	Cotan.	Secant	Cosec.	M
0	.30902	.95106	.32492	3.0777	1.0515	3.2361	60
1	.30929	.95097	.32524	.0746	.0516	.2332	59
2	.30957	.95088	.32556	.0716	.0517	.2303	58
3	.30985	.95079	.32588	.0686	.0518	.2274	57
4	.31012	.95070	.32621	.0655	.0519	.2245	56
5	.31040	.95061	.32653	3.0625	1.0520	3.2216	55
6	.31068	.95051	.32685	.0595	.0521	.2188	54
7	.31095	.95042	.32717	.0565	.0522	.2159	53
8	.31123	.95033	.32749	.0535	.0523	.2131	52
9	.31150	.95024	.32782	.0505	.0524	.2102	51
10	.31178	.95015	.32814	3.0475	1.0525	3.2074	50
11	.31206	.95006	.32846	.0445	.0526	.2045	49
12	.31233	.94997	.32878	.0415	.0527	.2017	48
13	.31261	.94988	.32910	.0385	.0528	.1989	47
14	.31289	.94979	.32943	.0356	.0529	.1960	46
15	.31316	.94970	.32975	3.0326	1.0530	3.1932	45
16	.31344	.94961	.33007	.0296	.0531	.1904	44
17	.31372	.94952	.33039	.0267	.0532	.1876	43
18	.31399	.94942	.33072	.0237	.0533	.1848	42
19	.31427	.94933	.33104	.0208	.0534	.1820	41
20	.31454	.94924	.33136	3.0178	1.0535	3.1792	40
21	.31482	.94915	.33169	.0149	.0536	.1764	39
22	.31510	.94906	.33201	.0120	.0537	.1736	38
23	.31537	.94897	.33233	.0090	.0538	.1708	37
24	.31565	.94888	.33265	.0061	.0539	.1681	36
25	.31592	.94878	.33298	3.0032	1.0540	3.1653	35
26	.31620	.94869	.33330	.0003	.0541	.1625	34
27	.31648	.94860	.33362	2.9974	.0542	.1598	33
28	.31675	.94851	.33395	.9945	.0543	.1570	32
29	.31703	.94841	.33427	.9916	.0544	.1543	31
30	.31730	.94832	.33459	2.9887	1.0545	3.1515	30
31	.31758	.94823	.33492	.9858	.0546	.1488	29
32	.31786	.94814	.33524	.9829	.0547	.1461	28
33	.31813	.94805	.33557	.9800	.0548	.1433	27
34	.31841	.94795	.33589	.9772	.0549	.1406	26
35	.31868	.94786	.33621	2.9743	1.0550	3.1379	25
36	.31896	.94777	.33654	.9714	.0551	.1352	24
37	.31923	.94767	.33686	.9686	.0552	.1325	23
38	.31951	.94758	.33718	.9657	.0553	.1298	22
39	.31978	.94749	.33751	.9629	.0554	.1271	21
40	.32006	.94740	.33783	2.9600	1.0555	3.1244	20
41	.32034	.94730	.33816	.9572	.0556	.1217	19
42	.32061	.94721	.33848	.9544	.0557	.1190	18
43	.32089	.94712	.33880	.9515	.0558	.1163	17
44	.32116	.94702	.33913	.9487	.0559	.1137	16
45	.32144	.94693	.33945	2.9459	1.0560	3.1110	15
46	.32171	.94684	.33978	.9431	.0561	.1083	14
47	.32199	.94674	.34010	.9403	.0562	.1057	13
48	.32226	.94665	.34043	.9375	.0563	.1030	12
49	.32254	.94655	.34075	.9347	.0565	.1004	11
50	.32282	.94646	.34108	2.9319	1.0566	3.0977	10
51	.32309	.94637	.34140	.9291	.0567	.0951	9
52	.32337	.94627	.34173	.9263	.0568	.0925	8
53	.32364	.94618	.34205	.9235	.0569	.0898	7
54	.32392	.94608	.34238	.9208	.0570	.0872	6
55	.32419	.94599	.34270	2.9180	1.0571	3.0846	5
56	.32447	.94590	.34303	.9152	.0572	.0820	4
57	.32474	.94580	.34335	.9125	.0573	.0793	3
58	.32502	.94571	.34368	.9097	.0574	.0767	2
59	.32529	.94561	.34400	.9069	.0575	.0741	1
60	.32557	.94552	.34433	2.9042	1.0576	3.0715	0

M	Cosine	Sine	Cotan.	Tan.	Cosec.	Secant	M

71°

19°

M	Sine	Cosine	Tan.	Cotan.	Secant	Cosec.	M
0	.32557	.94552	.34433	2.9042	1.0576	3.0715	60
1	.32584	.94542	.34465	.9015	.0577	.0690	59
2	.32612	.94533	.34498	.8987	.0578	.0664	58
3	.32639	.94523	.34530	.8960	.0579	.0638	57
4	.32667	.94514	.34563	.8933	.0580	.0612	56
5	.32694	.94504	.34595	2.8905	1.0581	3.0586	55
6	.32722	.94495	.34628	.8878	.0582	.0561	54
7	.32749	.94485	.34661	.8851	.0584	.0535	53
8	.32777	.94476	.34693	.8824	.0585	.0509	52
9	.32804	.94466	.34726	.8797	.0586	.0484	51
10	.32832	.94457	.34758	2.8770	1.0587	3.0458	50
11	.32859	.94447	.34791	.8743	.0588	.0433	49
12	.32887	.94438	.34824	.8716	.0589	.0407	48
13	.32914	.94428	.34856	.8689	.0590	.0382	47
14	.32942	.94418	.34889	.8662	.0591	.0357	46
15	.32969	.94409	.34921	2.8636	1.0592	3.0331	45
16	.32996	.94399	.34954	.8609	.0593	.0306	44
17	.33024	.94390	.34987	.8582	.0594	.0281	43
18	.33051	.94380	.35019	.8555	.0595	.0256	42
19	.33079	.94370	.35052	.8529	.0596	.0231	41
20	.33106	.94361	.35085	2.8502	1.0598	3.0206	40
21	.33134	.94351	.35117	.8476	.0599	.0181	39
22	.33161	.94341	.35150	.8449	.0600	.0156	38
23	.33189	.94332	.35183	.8423	.0601	.0131	37
24	.33216	.94322	.35215	.8396	.0602	.0106	36
25	.33243	.94313	.35248	2.8370	1.0603	3.0081	35
26	.33271	.94303	.35281	.8344	.0604	.0056	34
27	.33298	.94293	.35314	.8318	.0605	.0031	33
28	.33326	.94283	.35346	.8291	.0606	.0007	32
29	.33353	.94274	.35379	.8265	.0607	2.9982	31
30	.33381	.94264	.35412	2.8239	1.0608	2.9957	30
31	.33408	.94254	.35445	.8213	.0609	.9933	29
32	.33435	.94245	.35477	.8187	.0611	.9908	28
33	.33463	.94235	.35510	.8161	.0612	.9884	27
34	.33490	.94225	.35543	.8135	.0613	.9859	26
35	.33518	.94215	.35576	2.8109	1.0614	2.9835	25
36	.33545	.94206	.35608	.8083	.0615	.9810	24
37	.33572	.94196	.35641	.8057	.0616	.9786	23
38	.33600	.94186	.35674	.8032	.0617	.9762	22
39	.33627	.94176	.35707	.8006	.0618	.9738	21
40	.33655	.94167	.35739	2.7980	1.0619	2.9713	20
41	.33682	.94157	.35772	.7954	.0620	.9689	19
42	.33709	.94147	.35805	.7929	.0622	.9665	18
43	.33737	.94137	.35838	.7903	.0623	.9641	17
44	.33764	.94127	.35871	.7878	.0624	.9617	16
45	.33792	.94118	.35904	2.7852	1.0625	2.9593	15
46	.33819	.94108	.35936	.7827	.0626	.9569	14
47	.33846	.94098	.35969	.7801	.0627	.9545	13
48	.33874	.94088	.36002	.7776	.0628	.9521	12
49	.33901	.94078	.36035	.7751	.0629	.9497	11
50	.33928	.94068	.36068	2.7725	1.0630	2.9474	10
51	.33956	.94058	.36101	.7700	.0632	.9450	9
52	.33983	.94049	.36134	.7675	.0633	.9426	8
53	.34011	.94039	.36167	.7650	.0634	.9402	7
54	.34038	.94029	.36199	.7625	.0635	.9379	6
55	.34065	.94019	.36232	2.7600	1.0636	2.9355	5
56	.34093	.94009	.36265	.7575	.0637	.9332	4
57	.34120	.93999	.36298	.7550	.0638	.9308	3
58	.34147	.93989	.36331	.7525	.0639	.9285	2
59	.34175	.93979	.36364	.7500	.0641	.9261	1
60	.34202	.93969	.36397	2.7475	1.0642	2.9238	0

M	Cosine	Sine	Cotan.	Tan.	Cosec.	Secant	M

70°

M	Sine	Cosine	Tan.	Cotan.	Secant	Cosec.	M	M	Sine	Cosine	Tan.	Cotan.	Secant	Cosec.	M
0	.34202	.93969	.36397	2.7475	1.0642	2.9238	60	0	.35837	.93358	.38386	2.6051	1.0711	2.7904	60
1	.34229	.93959	.36430	.7450	.0643	.9215	59	1	.35864	.93348	.38420	.6028	.0713	.7883	59
2	.34257	.93949	.36463	.7425	.0644	.9191	58	2	.35891	.93337	.38453	.6006	.0714	.7862	58
3	.34284	.93939	.36496	.7400	.0645	.9168	57	3	.35918	.93327	.38486	.5983	.0715	.7841	57
4	.34311	.93929	.36529	.7376	.0646	.9145	56	4	.35945	.93316	.38520	.5960	.0716	.7820	56
5	.34339	.93919	.36562	2.7351	1.0647	2.9122	55	5	.35972	.93306	.38553	2.5938	1.0717	2.7799	55
6	.34366	.93909	.36595	.7326	.0648	.9098	54	6	.36000	.93295	.38587	.5916	.0719	.7778	54
7	.34393	.93899	.36628	.7302	.0650	.9075	53	7	.36027	.93285	.38620	.5893	.0720	.7757	53
8	.34421	.93889	.36661	.7277	.0651	.9052	52	8	.36054	.93274	.38654	.5871	.0721	.7736	52
9	.34448	.93879	.36694	.7252	.0652	.9029	51	9	.36081	.93264	.38687	.5848	.0722	.7715	51
10	.34475	.93869	.36727	2.7228	1.0653	2.9006	50	10	.36108	.93253	.38720	2.5826	1.0723	2.7694	50
11	.34502	.93859	.36760	.7204	.0654	.8983	49	11	.36135	.93243	.38754	.5804	.0725	.7674	49
12	.34530	.93849	.36793	.7179	.0655	.8960	48	12	.36162	.93232	.38787	.5781	.0726	.7653	48
13	.34557	.93839	.36826	.7155	.0656	.8937	47	13	.36189	.93222	.38821	.5759	.0727	.7632	47
14	.34584	.93829	.36859	.7130	.0658	.8915	46	14	.36217	.93211	.38854	.5737	.0728	.7611	46
15	.34612	.93819	.36892	2.7106	1.0659	2.8892	45	15	.36244	.93201	.38888	2.5715	1.0729	2.7591	45
16	.34639	.93809	.36925	.7082	.0660	.8869	44	16	.36271	.93190	.38921	.5693	.0731	.7570	44
17	.34666	.93799	.36958	.7058	.0661	.8846	43	17	.36298	.93180	.38955	.5671	.0732	.7550	43
18	.34693	.93789	.36991	.7033	.0662	.8824	42	18	.36325	.93169	.38988	.5649	.0733	.7529	42
19	.34721	.93779	.37024	.7009	.0663	.8801	41	19	.36352	.93158	.39022	.5627	.0734	.7509	41
20	.34748	.93769	.37057	2.6985	1.0664	2.8778	40	20	.36379	.93148	.39055	2.5605	1.0736	2.7488	40
21	.34775	.93758	.37090	.6961	.0666	.8756	39	21	.36406	.93137	.39089	.5583	.0737	.7468	39
22	.34803	.93748	.37123	.6937	.0667	.8733	38	22	.36433	.93127	.39122	.5561	.0738	.7447	38
23	.34830	.93738	.37156	.6913	.0668	.8711	37	23	.36460	.93116	.39156	.5539	.0739	.7427	37
24	.34857	.93728	.37190	.6889	.0669	.8688	36	24	.36488	.93105	.39189	.5517	.0740	.7406	36
25	.34884	.93718	.37223	2.6865	1.0670	2.8666	35	25	.36515	.93095	.39223	2.5495	1.0742	2.7386	35
26	.34912	.93708	.37256	.6841	.0671·	.8644	34	26	.36542	.93084	.39257	.5473	.0743	.7366	34
27	.34939	.93698	.37289	.6817	.0673	.8621	33	27	.36569	.93074	.39290	.5451	.0744	.7346	33
28	.34966	.93687	.37322	.6794	.0674	.8599	32	28	.36596	.93063	.39324	.5430	.0745	.7325	32
29	.34993	.93677	.37355	.6770	.0675	.8577	31	29	.36623	.93052	.39357	.5408	.0747	.7305	31
30	.35021	.93667	.37388	2.6746	1.0676	2.8554	30	30	.36650	.93042	.39391	2.5386	1.0748	2.7285	30
31	.35048	.93657	.37422	.6722	.0677	.8532	29	31	.36677	.93031	.39425	.5365	.0749	.7265	29
32	.35075	.93647	.37455	.6699	.0678	.8510	28	32	.36704	.93020	.39458	.5343	.0750	.7245	28
33	.35102	.93637	.37488	.6675	.0679	.8488	27	33	.36731	.93010	.39492	.5322	.0751	.7225	27
34	.35130	.93626	.37521	.6652	.0681	.8466	26	34	.36758	.92999	.39525	.5300	.0753	.7205	26
35	.35157	.93616	.37554	2.6628	1.0682	2.8444	25	35	.36785	.92988	.39559	2.5278	1.0754	2.7185	25
36	.35184	.93606	.37587	.6604	.0683	.8422	24	36	.36812	.92978	.39593	.5257	.0755	.7165	24
37	.35211	.93596	.37621	.6581	.0684	.8400	23	37	.36839	.92967	.39626	.5236	.0756	.7145	23
38	.35239	.93585	.37654	.6558	.0685	.8378	22	38	.36866	.92956	.39660	.5214	.0758	.7125	22
39	.35266	.93575	.37687	.6534	.0686	.8356	21	39	.36893	.92945	.39694	.5193	.0759	.7105	21
40	.35293	.93565	.37720	2.6511	1.0688	2.8334	20	40	.36921	.92935	.39727	2.5171	1.0760	2.7085	20
41	.35320	.93555	.37754	.6487	.0689	.8312	19	41	.36948	.92924	.39761	.5150	.0761	.7065	19
42	.35347	.93544	.37787	.6464	.0690	.8290	18	42	.36975	.92913	.39795	.5129	.0763	.7045	18
43	.35375	.93534	.37820	.6441	.0691	.8269	17	43	.37002	.92902	.39828	.5108	.0764	.7026	17
44	.35402	.93524	.37853	.6418	.0692	.8247	16	44	.37029	.92892	.39862	.5086	.0765	.7006	16
45	.35429	.93513	.37887	2.6394	1.0694	2.8225	15	45	.37056	.92881	.39896	2.5065	1.0766	2.6986	15
46	.35456	.93503	.37920	.6371	.0695	.8204	14	46	.37083	.92870	.39930	.5044	.0768	.6967	14
47	.35483	.93493	.37953	.6348	.0696	.8182	13	47	.37110	.92859	.39963	.5023	.0769	.6947	13
48	.35511	.93482	.37986	.6325	.0697	.8160	12	48	.37137	.92848	.39997	.5002	.0770	.6927	12
49	.35538	.93472	.38020	.6302	.0698	.8139	11	49	.37164	.92838	.40031	.4981	.0771	.6908	11
50	.35565	.93462	.38053	2.6279	1.0699	2.8117	10	50	.37191	.92827	.40065	2.4960	1.0773	2.6888	10
51	.35592	.93451	.38086	.6256	.0701	.8096	9	51	.37218	.92816	.40098	.4939	.0774	.6869	9
52	.35619	.93441	.38120	.6233	.0702	.8074	8	52	.37245	.92805	.40132	.4918	.0775	.6849	8
53	.35647	.93431	.38153	.6210	.0703	.8053	7	53	.37272	.92794	.40166	.4897	.0776	.6830	7
54	.35674	.93420	.38186	.6187	.0704	.8032	6	54	.37299	.92784	.40200	.4876	.0778	.6810	6
55	.35701	.93410	.38220	2.6164	1.0705	2.8010	5	55	.37326	.92773	.40233	2.4855	1.0779	2.6791	5
56	.35728	.93400	.38253	.6142	.0707	.7989	4	56	.37353	.92762	.40267	.4834	.0780	.6772	4
57	.35755	.93389	.38286	.6119	.0708	.7968	3	57	.37380	.92751	.40301	.4813	.0781	.6752	3
58	.35782	.93379	.38320	.6096	.0709	.7947	2	58	.37407	.92740	.40335	.4792	.0783	.6733	2
59	.35810	.93368	.38353	.6073	.0710	.7925	1	59	.37434	.92729	.40369	.4772	.0784	.6714	1
60	.35837	.93358	.38386	2.6051	1.0711	2.7904	0	60	.37461	.92718	.40403	2.4751	1.0785	2.6695	0

M	Cosine	Sine	Cotan.	Tan.	Cosec.	Secant	M	M	Cosine	Sine	Cotan.	Tan.	Cosec.	Secant	M

22°

M	Sine	Cosine	Tan.	Cotan.	Secant	Cosec.	M
0	.37461	.92718	.40403	2.4751	1.0785	2.6695	60
1	.37488	.92707	.40436	.4730	.0787	.6675	59
2	.37514	.92696	.40470	.4709	.0788	.6656	58
3	.37541	.92686	.40504	.4689	.0789	.6637	57
4	.37568	.92675	.40538	.4668	.0790	.6618	56
5	.37595	.92664	.40572	2.4647	1.0792	2.6599	55
6	.37622	.92653	.40606	.4627	.0793	.6580	54
7	.37649	.92642	.40640	.4606	.0794	.6561	53
8	.37676	.92631	.40673	.4586	.0795	.6542	52
9	.37703	.92620	.40707	.4565	.0797	.6523	51
10	.37730	.92609	.40741	2.4545	1.0798	2.6504	50
11	.37757	.92598	.40775	.4525	.0799	.6485	49
12	.37784	.92587	.40809	.4504	.0801	.6466	48
13	.37811	.92576	.40843	.4484	.0802	.6447	47
14	.37838	.92565	.40877	.4463	.0803	.6428	46
15	.37865	.92554	.40911	2.4443	1.0804	2.6410	45
16	.37892	.92543	.40945	.4423	.0806	.6391	44
17	.37919	.92532	.40979	.4403	.0807	.6372	43
18	.37946	.92521	.41013	.4382	.0808	.6353	42
19	.37972	.92510	.41047	.4362	.0810	.6335	41
20	.37999	.92499	.41081	2.4342	1.0811	2.6316	40
21	.38026	.92488	.41115	.4322	.0812	.6297	39
22	.38053	.92477	.41149	.4302	.0813	.6279	38
23	.38080	.92466	.41183	.4282	.0815	.6260	37
24	.38107	.92455	.41217	.4262	.0816	.6242	36
25	.38134	.92443	.41251	2.4242	1.0817	2.6223	35
26	.38161	.92432	.41285	.4222	.0819	.6205	34
27	.38188	.92421	.41319	.4202	.0820	.6186	33
28	.38214	.92410	.41353	.4182	.0821	.6168	32
29	.38241	.92399	.41387	.4162	.0823	.6150	31
30	.38268	.92388	.41421	2.4142	1.0824	2.6131	30
31	.38295	.92377	.41455	.4122	.0825	.6113	29
32	.38322	.92366	.41489	.4102	.0826	.6095	28
33	.38349	.92354	.41524	.4083	.0828	.6076	27
34	.38376	.92343	.41558	.4063	.0829	.6058	26
35	.38403	.92332	.41592	2.4043	1.0830	2.6040	25
36	.38429	.92321	.41626	.4023	.0832	.6022	24
37	.38456	.92310	.41660	.4004	.0833	.6003	23
38	.38483	.92299	.41694	.3984	.0834	.5985	22
39	.38510	.92287	.41728	.3964	.0836	.5967	21
40	.38537	.92276	.41762	2.3945	1.0837	2.5949	20
41	.38564	.92265	.41797	.3925	.0838	.5931	19
42	.38591	.92254	.41831	.3906	.0840	.5913	18
43	.38617	.92242	.41865	.3886	.0841	.5895	17
44	.38644	.92231	.41899	.3867	.0842	.5877	16
45	.38671	.92220	.41933	2.3847	1.0844	2.5859	15
46	.38698	.92209	.41968	.3828	.0845	.5841	14
47	.38725	.92197	.42002	.3808	.0846	.5823	13
48	.38751	.92186	.42036	.3789	.0847	.5805	12
49	.38778	.92175	.42070	.3770	.0849	.5787	11
50	.38805	.92164	.42105	2.3750	1.0850	2.5770	10
51	.38832	.92152	.42139	.3731	.0851	.5752	9
52	.38859	.92141	.42173	.3712	.0853	.5734	8
53	.38886	.92130	.42207	.3692	.0854	.5716	7
54	.38912	.92118	.42242	.3673	.0855	.5699	6
55	.38939	.92107	.42276	2.3654	1.0857	2.5681	5
56	.38966	.92096	.42310	.3635	.0858	.5663	4
57	.38993	.92084	.42344	.3616	.0859	.5646	3
58	.39019	.92073	.42379	.3597	.0861	.5628	2
59	.39046	.92062	.42413	.3577	.0862	.5610	1
60	.39073	.92050	.42447	2.3558	1.0864	2.5593	0
M	Cosine	Sine	Cotan.	Tan.	Cosec.	Secant	M

67°

23°

M	Sine	Cosine	Tan.	Cotan.	Secant	Cosec.	M
0	.39073	.92050	.42447	2.3558	1.0864	2.5593	60
1	.39100	.92039	.42482	.3539	.0865	.5575	59
2	.39126	.92028	.42516	.3520	.0866	.5558	58
3	.39153	.92016	.42550	.3501	.0868	.5540	57
4	.39180	.92005	.42585	.3482	.0869	.5523	56
5	.39207	.91993	.42619	2.3463	1.0870	2.5506	55
6	.39234	.91982	.42654	.3445	.0872	.5488	54
7	.39260	.91971	.42688	.3426	.0873	.5471	53
8	.39287	.91959	.42722	.3407	.0874	.5453	52
9	.39314	.91948	.42757	.3388	.0876	.5436	51
10	.39341	.91936	.42791	2.3369	1.0877	2.5419	50
11	.39367	.91925	.42826	.3350	.0878	.5402	49
12	.39394	.91913	.42860	.3332	.0880	.5384	48
13	.39421	.91902	.42894	.3313	.0881	.5367	47
14	.39448	.91891	.42929	.3294	.0882	.5350	46
15	.39474	.91879	.42963	2.3276	1.0884	2.5333	45
16	.39501	.91868	.42998	.3257	.0885	.5316	44
17	.39528	.91856	.43032	.3238	.0886	.5299	43
18	.39554	.91845	.43067	.3220	.0888	.5281	42
19	.39581	.91833	.43101	.3201	.0889	.5264	41
20	.39608	.91822	.43136	2.3183	1.0891	2.5247	40
21	.39635	.91810	.43170	.3164	.0892	.5230	39
22	.39661	.91798	.43205	.3145	.0893	.5213	38
23	.39688	.91787	.43239	.3127	.0895	.5196	37
24	.39715	.91775	.43274	.3109	.0896	.5179	36
25	.39741	.91764	.43308	2.3090	1.0897	2.5163	35
26	.39768	.91752	.43343	.3072	.0899	.5146	34
27	.39795	.91741	.43378	.3053	.0900	.5129	33
28	.39821	.91729	.43412	.3035	.0902	.5112	32
29	.39848	.91718	.43447	.3017	.0903	.5095	31
30	.39875	.91706	.43481	2.2998	1.0904	2.5078	30
31	.39901	.91694	.43516	.2980	.0906	.5062	29
32	.39928	.91683	.43550	.2962	.0907	.5045	28
33	.39955	.91671	.43585	.2944	.0908	.5028	27
34	.39981	.91659	.43620	.2925	.0910	.5011	26
35	.40008	.91648	.43654	2.2907	1.0911	2.4995	25
36	.40035	.91636	.43689	.2889	.0913	.4978	24
37	.40061	.91625	.43723	.2871	.0914	.4961	23
38	.40088	.91613	.43758	.2853	.0915	.4945	22
39	.40115	.91601	.43793	.2835	.0917	.4928	21
40	.40141	.91590	.43827	2.2817	1.0918	2.4912	20
41	.40168	.91578	.43862	.2799	.0920	.4895	19
42	.40195	.91566	.43897	.2781	.0921	.4879	18
43	.40221	.91554	.43932	.2763	.0922	.4862	17
44	.40248	.91543	.43966	.2745	.0924	.4846	16
45	.40275	.91531	.44001	2.2727	1.0925	2.4829	15
46	.40301	.91519	.44036	.2709	.0927	.4813	14
47	.40328	.91508	.44070	.2691	.0928	.4797	13
48	.40354	.91496	.44105	.2673	.0929	.4780	12
49	.40381	.91484	.44140	.2655	.0931	.4764	11
50	.40408	.91472	.44175	2.2637	1.0932	2.4748	10
51	.40434	.91461	.44209	.2619	.0934	.4731	9
52	.40461	.91449	.44244	.2602	.0935	.4715	8
53	.40487	.91437	.44279	.2584	.0936	.4699	7
54	.40514	.91425	.44314	.2566	.0938	.4683	6
55	.40541	.91414	.44349	2.2548	1.0939	2.4666	5
56	.40567	.91402	.44383	.2531	.0941	.4650	4
57	.40594	.91390	.44418	.2513	.0942	.4634	3
58	.40620	.91378	.44453	.2495	.0943	.4618	2
59	.40647	.91366	.44488	.2478	.0945	.4602	1
60	.40674	.91354	.44523	2.2460	1.0946	2.4586	0
M	Cosine	Sine	Cotan.	Tan.	Cosec.	Secant	M

66°

M	Sine	Cosine	Tan.	Cotan.	Secant	Cosec.	M
0	.40674	.91354	.44523	2.2460	1.0946	2.4586	60
1	.40700	.91343	.44558	.2443	.0948	.4570	59
2	.40727	.91331	.44593	.2425	.0949	.4554	58
3	.40753	.91319	.44627	.2408	.0951	.4538	57
4	.40780	.91307	.44662	.2390	.0952	.4522	56
5	.40806	.91295	.44697	2.2373	1.0953	2.4506	55
6	.40833	.91283	.44732	.2355	.0955	.4490	54
7	.40860	.91271	.44767	.2338	.0956	.4474	53
8	.40886	.91260	.44802	.2320	.0958	.4458	52
9	.40913	.91248	.44837	.2303	.0959	.4442	51
10	.40939	.91236	.44872	2.2286	1.0961	2.4426	50
11	.40966	.91224	.44907	.2268	.0962	.4411	49
12	.40992	.91212	.44942	.2251	.0963	.4395	48
13	.41019	.91200	.44977	.2234	.0965	.4379	47
14	.41045	.91188	.45012	.2216	.0966	.4363	46
15	.41072	.91176	.45047	2.2199	1.0968	2.4347	45
16	.41098	.91164	.45082	.2182	.0969	.4332	44
17	.41125	.91152	.45117	.2165	.0971	.4316	43
18	.41151	.91140	.45152	.2147	.0972	.4300	42
19	.41178	.91128	.45187	.2130	.0973	.4285	41
20	.41204	.91116	.45222	2.2113	1.0975	2.4269	40
21	.41231	.91104	.45257	.2096	.0976	.4254	39
22	.41257	.91092	.45292	.2079	.0978	.4238	38
23	.41284	.91080	.45327	.2062	.0979	.4222	37
24	.41310	.91068	.45362	.2045	.0981	.4207	36
25	.41337	.91056	.45397	2.2028	1.0982	2.4191	35
26	.41363	.91044	.45432	.2011	.0984	.4176	34
27	.41390	.91032	.45467	.1994	.0985	.4160	33
28	.41416	.91020	.45502	.1977	.0986	.4145	32
29	.41443	.91008	.45537	.1960	.0988	.4130	31
30	.41469	.90996	.45573	2.1943	1.0989	2.4114	30
31	.41496	.90984	.45608	.1926	.0991	.4099	29
32	.41522	.90972	.45643	.1909	.0992	.4083	28
33	.41549	.90960	.45678	.1892	.0994	.4068	27
34	.41575	.90948	.45713	.1875	.0995	.4053	26
35	.41602	.90936	.45748	2.1859	1.0997	2.4037	25
36	.41628	.90924	.45783	.1842	.0998	.4022	24
37	.41654	.90911	.45819	.1825	.1000	.4007	23
38	.41681	.90899	.45854	.1808	.1001	.3992	22
39	.41707	.90887	.45889	.1792	.1003	.3976	21
40	.41734	.90875	.45924	2.1775	1.1004	2.3961	20
41	.41760	.90863	.45960	.1758	.1005	.3946	19
42	.41787	.90851	.45995	.1741	.1007	.3931	18
43	.41813	.90839	.46030	.1725	.1008	.3916	17
44	.41839	.90826	.46065	.1708	.1010	.3901	16
45	.41866	.90814	.46101	2.1692	1.1011	2.3886	15
46	.41892	.90802	.46136	.1675	.1013	.3871	14
47	.41919	.90790	.46171	.1658	.1014	.3856	13
48	.41945	.90778	.46206	.1642	.1016	.3841	12
49	.41972	.90765	.46242	.1625	.1017	.3826	11
50	.41998	.90753	.46277	2.1609	1.1019	2.3811	10
51	.42024	.90741	.46312	.1592	.1020	.3796	9
52	.42051	.90729	.46348	.1576	.1022	.3781	8
53	.42077	.90717	.46383	.1559	.1023	.3766	7
54	.42103	.90704	.46418	.1543	.1025	.3751	6
55	.42130	.90692	.46454	2.1527	1.1026	2.3736	5
56	.42156	.90680	.46489	.1510	.1028	.3721	4
57	.42183	.90668	.46524	.1494	.1029	.3706	3
58	.42209	.90655	.46560	.1478	.1031	.3691	2
59	.42235	.90643	.46595	.1461	.1032	.3677	1
60	.42262	.90631	.46631	2.1445	1.1034	2.3662	0
M	Cosine	Sine	Cotan.	Tan.	Cosec.	Secant	M

M	Sine	Cosine	Tan.	Cotan.	Secant	Cosec.	M
0	.42262	.90631	.46631	2.1445	1.1034	2.3662	60
1	.42288	.90618	.46666	.1429	.1035	.3647	59
2	.42314	.90606	.46702	.1412	.1037	.3632	58
3	.42341	.90594	.46737	.1396	.1038	.3618	57
4	.42367	.90581	.46772	.1380	.1040	.3603	56
5	.42394	.90569	.46808	2.1364	1.1041	2.3588	55
6	.42420	.90557	.46843	.1348	.1043	.3574	54
7	.42446	.90544	.46879	.1331	.1044	.3559	53
8	.42473	.90532	.46914	.1315	.1046	.3544	52
9	.42499	.90520	.46950	.1299	.1047	.3530	51
10	.42525	.90507	.46985	2.1283	1.1049	2.3515	50
11	.42552	.90495	.47021	.1267	.1050	.3501	49
12	.42578	.90483	.47056	.1251	.1052	.3486	48
13	.42604	.90470	.47092	.1235	.1053	.3472	47
14	.42630	.90458	.47127	.1219	.1055	.3457	46
15	.42657	.90445	.47163	2.1203	1.1056	2.3443	45
16	.42683	.90433	.47199	.1187	.1058	.3428	44
17	.42709	.90421	.47234	.1171	.1059	.3414	43
18	.42736	.90408	.47270	.1155	.1061	.3399	42
19	.42762	.90396	.47305	.1139	.1062	.3385	41
20	.42788	.90383	.47341	2.1123	1.1064	2.3371	40
21	.42815	.90371	.47376	.1107	.1065	.3356	39
22	.42841	.90358	.47412	.1092	.1067	.3342	38
23	.42867	.90346	.47448	.1076	.1068	.3328	37
24	.42893	.90333	.47483	.1060	.1070	.3313	36
25	.42920	.90321	.47519	2.1044	1.1072	2.3299	35
26	.42946	.90308	.47555	.1028	.1073	.3285	34
27	.42972	.90296	.47590	.1013	.1075	.3271	33
28	.42998	.90283	.47626	.0997	.1076	.3256	32
29	.43025	.90271	.47662	.0981	.1078	.3242	31
30	.43051	.90258	.47697	2.0965	1.1079	2.3228	30
31	.43077	.90246	.47733	.0950	.1081	.3214	29
32	.43104	.90233	.47769	.0934	.1082	.3200	28
33	.43130	.90221	.47805	.0918	.1084	.3186	27
34	.43156	.90208	.47840	.0903	.1085	.3172	26
35	.43182	.90196	.47876	2.0887	1.1087	2.3158	25
36	.43208	.90183	.47912	.0872	.1088	.3143	24
37	.43235	.90171	.47948	.0856	.1090	.3129	23
38	.43261	.90158	.47983	.0840	.1092	.3115	22
39	.43287	.90145	.48019	.0825	.1093	.3101	21
40	.43313	.90133	.48055	2.0809	1.1095	2.3087	20
41	.43340	.90120	.48091	.0794	.1096	.3073	19
42	.43366	.90108	.48127	.0778	.1098	.3059	18
43	.43392	.90095	.48162	.0763	.1099	.3046	17
44	.43418	.90082	.48198	.0747	.1101	.3032	16
45	.43444	.90070	.48234	2.0732	1.1102	2.3018	15
46	.43471	.90057	.48270	.0717	.1104	.3004	14
47	.43497	.90044	.48306	.0701	.1106	.2990	13
48	.43523	.90032	.48342	.0686	.1107	.2976	12
49	.43549	.90019	.48378	.0671	.1109	.2962	11
50	.43575	.90006	.48414	2.0655	1.1110	2.2949	10
51	.43602	.89994	.48449	.0640	.1112	.2935	9
52	.43628	.89981	.48485	.0625	.1113	.2921	8
53	.43654	.89968	.48521	.0609	.1115	.2907	7
54	.43680	.89956	.48557	.0594	.1116	.2894	6
55	.43706	.89943	.48593	2.0579	1.1118	2.2880	5
56	.43732	.89930	.48629	.0564	.1120	.2866	4
57	.43759	.89918	.48665	.0548	.1121	.2853	3
58	.43785	.89905	.48701	.0533	.1123	.2839	2
59	.43811	.89892	.48737	.0518	.1124	.2825	1
60	.43837	.89879	.48773	2.0503	1.1126	2.2812	0
M	Cosine	Sine	Cotan.	Tan.	Cosec.	Secant	M

M	Sine	Cosine	Tan.	Cotan.	Secant	Cosec.	M
0	.43837	.89879	.48773	2.0503	1.1126	2.2812	60
1	.43863	.89867	.48809	.0488	.1127	.2798	59
2	.43889	.89854	.48845	.0473	.1129	.2784	58
3	.43915	.89841	.48881	.0458	.1131	.2771	57
4	.43942	.89828	.48917	.0443	.1132	.2757	56
5	.43968	.89815	.48953	2.0427	1.1134	2.2744	55
6	.43994	.89803	.48989	.0412	.1135	.2730	54
7	.44020	.89790	.49025	.0397	.1137	.2717	53
8	.44046	.89777	.49062	2.0382	.1139	.2703	52
9	.44072	.89764	.49098	.0367	.1140	.2690	51
10	.44098	.89751	.49134	2.0352	1.1142	2.2676	50
11	.44124	.89739	.49170	.0338	.1143	.2663	49
12	.44150	.89726	.49206	.0323	.1145	.2650	48
13	.44177	.89713	.49242	.0308	.1147	.2636	47
14	.44203	.89700	.49278	.0293	.1148	.2623	46
15	.44229	.89687	.49314	2.0278	1.1150	2.2610	45
16	.44255	.89674	.49351	.0263	.1151	.2596	44
17	.44281	.89661	.49387	.0248	.1153	.2583	43
18	.44307	.89649	.49423	.0233	.1155	.2570	42
19	.44333	.89636	.49459	.0219	.1156	.2556	41
20	.44359	.89623	.49495	2.0204	1.1158	2.2543	40
21	.44385	.89610	.49532	.0189	.1159	.2530	39
22	.44411	.89597	.49568	.0174	.1161	.2517	38
23	.44437	.89584	.49604	.0159	.1163	.2503	37
24	.44463	.89571	.49640	.0145	.1164	.2490	36
25	.44489	.89558	.49677	2.0130	1.1166	2.2477	35
26	.44516	.89545	.49713	.0115	.1167	.2464	34
27	.44542	.89532	.49749	.0101	.1169	.2451	33
28	.44568	.89519	.49785	.0086	.1171	.2438	32
29	.44594	.89506	.49822	.0071	.1172	.2425	31
30	.44620	.89493	.49858	2.0057	1.1174	2.2411	30
31	.44646	.89480	.49894	.0042	.1176	.2398	29
32	.44672	.89467	.49931	.0028	.1177	.2385	28
33	.44698	.89454	.49967	.0013	.1179	.2372	27
34	.44724	.89441	.50003	1.9998	.1180	.2359	26
35	.44750	.89428	.50040	1.9984	1.1182	2.2348	25
36	.44776	.89415	.50076	.9969	.1184	.2333	24
37	.44802	.89402	.50113	.9955	.1185	.2320	23
38	.44828	.89389	.50149	.9940	.1187	.2307	22
39	.44854	.89376	.50185	.9926	.1189	.2294	21
40	.44880	.89363	.50222	1.9912	1.1190	2.2282	20
41	.44906	.89350	.50258	.9897	.1192	.2269	19
42	.44932	.89337	.50295	.9883	.1193	.2256	18
43	.44958	.89324	.50331	.9868	.1195	.2243	17
44	.44984	.89311	.50368	.9854	.1197	.2230	16
45	.45010	.89298	.50404	1.9840	1.1198	2.2217	15
46	.45036	.89285	.50441	.9825	.1200	.2204	14
47	.45062	.89272	.50477	.9811	.1202	.2192	13
48	.45088	.89258	.50514	.9797	.1203	.2179	12
49	.45114	.89245	.50550	.9782	.1205	.2166	11
50	.45140	.89232	.50587	1.9768	1.1207	2.2153	10
51	.45166	.89219	.50623	.9754	.1208	.2141	9
52	.45191	.89206	.50660	.9739	.1210	.2128	8
53	.45217	.89193	.50696	.9725	.1212	.2115	7
54	.45243	.89180	.50733	.9711	.1213	.2103	6
55	.45269	.89166	.50769	1.9697	1.1215	2.2090	5
56	.45295	.89153	.50806	.9683	.1217	.2077	4
57	.45321	.89140	.50843	.9668	.1218	.2065	3
58	.45347	.89127	.50879	.9654	.1220	.2052	2
59	.45373	.89114	.50916	.9640	.1222	.2039	1
60	.45399	.89101	.50952	1.9626	1.1223	2.2027	0
M	Cosine	Sine	Cotan.	Tan.	Cosec.	Secant	M

M	Sine	Cosine	Tan.	Cotan.	Secant	Cosec.	M
0	.45399	.89101	.50952	1.9626	1.1223	2.2027	60
1	.45425	.89087	.50989	.9612	.1225	.2014	59
2	.45451	.89074	.51026	.9598	.1226	.2002	58
3	.45477	.89061	.51062	.9584	.1228	.1989	57
4	.45503	.89048	.51099	.9570	.1230	.1977	56
5	.45528	.89034	.51136	1.9556	1.1231	2.1964	55
6	.45554	.89021	.51172	.9542	.1233	.1952	54
7	.45580	.89008	.51209	.9528	.1235	.1939	53
8	.45606	.88995	.51246	.9514	.1237	.1927	52
9	.45632	.88981	.51283	.9500	.1238	.1914	51
10	.45658	.88968	.51319	1.9486	1.1240	2.1902	50
11	.45684	.88955	.51356	.9472	.1242	.1889	49
12	.45710	.88942	.51393	.9458	.1243	.1877	48
13	.45736	.88928	.51430	.9444	.1245	.1865	47
14	.45761	.88915	.51466	.9430	.1247	.1852	46
15	.45787	.88902	.51503	1.9416	1.1248	2.1840	45
16	.45813	.88888	.51540	.9402	.1250	.1828	44
17	.45839	.88875	.51577	.9388	.1252	.1815	43
18	.45865	.88862	.51614	.9375	.1253	.1803	42
19	.45891	.88848	.51651	.9361	.1255	.1791	41
20	.45917	.88835	.51687	1.9347	1.1257	2.1778	40
21	.45942	.88822	.51724	.9333	.1258	.1766	39
22	.45968	.88808	.51761	.9319	.1260	.1754	38
23	.45994	.88795	.51798	.9306	.1262	.1742	37
24	.46020	.88781	.51835	.9292	.1264	.1730	36
25	.46046	.88768	.51872	1.9278	1.1265	2.1717	35
26	.46072	.88755	.51909	.9264	.1267	.1705	34
27	.46097	.88741	.51946	.9251	.1269	.1693	33
28	.46123	.88728	.51983	.9237	.1270	.1681	32
29	.46149	.88714	.52020	.9223	.1272	.1669	31
30	.46175	.88701	.52057	1.9210	1.1274	2.1657	30
31	.46201	.88688	.52094	.9196	.1275	.1645	29
32	.46226	.88674	.52131	.9182	.1277	.1633	28
33	.46252	.88661	.52168	.9169	.1279	.1620	27
34	.46278	.88647	.52205	.9155	.1281	.1608	26
35	.46304	.88634	.52242	1.9142	1.1282	2.1596	25
36	.46330	.88620	.52279	.9128	.1284	.1584	24
37	.46355	.88607	.52316	.9115	.1286	.1572	23
38	.46381	.88593	.52353	.9101	.1287	.1560	22
39	.46407	.88580	.52390	.9088	.1289	.1548	21
40	.46433	.88566	.52427	1.9074	1.1291	2.1536	20
41	.46458	.88553	.52464	.9061	.1293	.1525	19
42	.46484	.88539	.52501	.9047	.1294	.1513	18
43	.46510	.88526	.52538	.9034	.1296	.1501	17
44	.46536	.88512	.52575	.9020	.1298	.1489	16
45	.46561	.88499	.52612	1.9007	1.1299	2.1477	15
46	.46587	.88485	.52650	.8993	.1301	.1465	14
47	.46613	.88472	.52687	.8980	.1303	.1453	13
48	.46639	.88458	.52724	.8967	.1305	.1441	12
49	.46664	.88444	.52761	.8953	.1306	.1430	11
50	.46690	.88431	.52798	1.8940	1.1308	2.1418	10
51	.46716	.88417	.52836	.8927	.1310	.1406	9
52	.46741	.88404	.52873	.8913	.1312	.1394	8
53	.46767	.88390	.52910	.8900	.1313	.1382	7
54	.46793	.88376	.52947	.8887	.1315	.1371	6
55	.46819	.88363	.52984	1.8873	1.1317	2.1359	5
56	.46844	.88349	.53022	.8860	.1319	.1347	4
57	.46870	.88336	.53059	.8847	.1320	.1335	3
58	.46896	.88322	.53096	.8834	.1322	.1324	2
59	.46921	.88308	.53134	.8820	.1324	.1312	1
60	.46947	.88295	.53171	1.8807	1.1326	2.1300	0
M	Cosine	Sine	Cotan.	Tan.	Cosec.	Secant	M

M	Sine	Cosine	Tan.	Cotan.	Secant	Cosec.	M
0	.46947	.88295	.53171	1.8807	1.1326	2.1300	60
1	.46973	.88281	.53208	.8794	.1327	.1289	59
2	.46998	.88267	.53245	.8781	.1329	.1277	58
3	.47024	.88254	.53283	.8768	.1331	.1266	57
4	.47050	.88240	.53320	.8754	.1333	.1254	56
5	.47075	.88226	.53358	1.8741	1.1334	2.1242	55
6	.47101	.88213	.53395	.8728	.1336	.1231	54
7	.47127	.88199	.53432	.8715	.1338	.1219	53
8	.47152	.88185	.53470	.8702	.1340	.1208	52
9	.47178	.88171	.53507	.8689	.1341	.1196	51
10	.47204	.88158	.53545	1.8676	1.1343	2.1185	50
11	.47229	.88144	.53582	.8663	.1345	.1173	49
12	.47255	.88130	.53619	.8650	.1347	.1162	48
13	.47281	.88117	.53657	.8637	.1349	.1150	47
14	.47306	.88103	.53694	.8624	.1350	.1139	46
15	.47332	.88089	.53732	1.8611	1.1352	2.1127	45
16	.47357	.88075	.53769	.8598	.1354	.1116	44
17	.47383	.88061	.53807	.8585	.1356	.1104	43
18	.47409	.88048	.53844	.8572	.1357	.1093	42
19	.47434	.88034	.53882	.8559	.1359	.1082	41
20	.47460	.88020	.53919	1.8546	1.1361	2.1070	40
21	.47486	.88006	.53957	.8533	.1363	.1059	39
22	.47511	.87992	.53995	.8520	.1365	.1048	38
23	.47537	.87979	.54032	.8507	.1366	.1036	37
24	.47562	.87965	.54070	.8495	.1368	.1025	36
25	.47588	.87951	.54107	1.8482	1.1370	2.1014	35
26	.47613	.87937	.54145	.8469	.1372	.1002	34
27	.47639	.87923	.54183	.8456	.1373	.0991	33
28	.47665	.87909	.54220	.8443	.1375	.0980	32
29	.47690	.87895	.54258	.8430	.1377	.0969	31
30	.47716	.87882	.54295	1.8418	1.1379	2.0957	30
31	.47741	.87868	.54333	.8405	.1381	.0946	29
32	.47767	.87854	.54371	.8392	.1382	.0935	28
33	.47792	.87840	.54409	.8379	.1384	.0924	27
34	.47818	.87826	.54446	.8367	.1386	.0912	26
35	.47844	.87812	.54484	1.8354	1.1388	2.0901	25
36	.47869	.87798	.54522	.8341	.1390	.0890	24
37	.47895	.87784	.54559	.8329	.1391	.0879	23
38	.47920	.87770	.54597	.8316	.1393	.0868	22
39	.47946	.87756	.54635	.8303	.1395	.0857	21
40	.47971	.87742	.54673	1.8291	1.1397	2.0846	20
41	.47997	.87728	.54711	.8278	.1399	.0835	19
42	.48022	.87715	.54748	.8265	.1401	.0824	18
43	.48048	.87701	.54786	.8253	.1402	.0812	17
44	.48073	.87687	.54824	.8240	.1404	.0801	16
45	.48099	.87673	.54862	1.8227	1.1406	2.0790	15
46	.48124	.87659	.54900	.8215	.1408	.0779	14
47	.48150	.87645	.54937	.8202	.1410	.0768	13
48	.48175	.87631	.54975	.8190	.1411	.0757	12
49	.48201	.87617	.55013	.8177	.1413	.0746	11
50	.48226	.87603	.55051	1.8165	1.1415	2.0735	10
51	.48252	.87588	.55089	.8152	.1417	.0725	9
52	.48277	.87574	.55127	.8140	.1419	.0714	8
53	.48303	.87560	.55165	.8127	.1421	.0703	7
54	.48328	.87546	.55203	.8115	.1422	.0692	6
55	.48354	.87532	.55241	1.8102	1.1424	2.0681	5
56	.48379	.87518	.55279	.8090	.1426	.0670	4
57	.48405	.87504	.55317	.8078	.1428	.0659	3
58	.48430	.87490	.55355	.8065	.1430	.0648	2
59	.48455	.87476	.55393	.8053	.1432	.0637	1
60	.48481	.87462	.55431	1.8040	1.1433	2.0627	0

M	Cosine	Sine	Cotan.	Tan.	Cosec.	Secant	M

M	Sine	Cosine	Tan.	Cotan.	Secant	Cosec.	M
0	.48481	.87462	.55431	1.8040	1.1433	2.0627	60
1	.48506	.87448	.55469	.8028	.1435	.0616	59
2	.48532	.87434	.55507	.8016	.1437	.0605	58
3	.48557	.87420	.55545	.8003	.1439	.0594	57
4	.48583	.87405	.55583	.7991	.1441	.0583	56
5	.48608	.87391	.55621	1.7979	1.1443	2.0573	55
6	.48633	.87377	.55659	.7966	.1445	.0562	54
7	.48659	.87363	.55697	.7954	.1446	.0551	53
8	.48684	.87349	.55735	.7942	.1448	.0540	52
9	.48710	.87335	.55774	.7930	.1450	.0530	51
10	.48735	.87320	.55812	1.7917	1.1452	2.0519	50
11	.48760	.87306	.55850	.7905	.1454	.0508	49
12	.48786	.87292	.55888	.7893	.1456	.0498	48
13	.48811	.87278	.55926	.7881	.1458	.0487	47
14	.48837	.87264	.55964	.7868	.1459	.0476	46
15	.48862	.87250	.56003	.7856	.1461	2.0466	45
16	.48887	.87235	.56041	.7844	.1463	.0455	44
17	.48913	.87221	.56079	.7832	.1465	.0444	43
18	.48938	.87207	.56117	.7820	.1467	.0434	42
19	.48964	.87193	.56156	.7808	.1469	.0423	41
20	.48989	.87178	.56194	1.7795	1.1471	2.0413	40
21	.49014	.87164	.56232	.7783	.1473	.0402	39
22	.49040	.87150	.56270	.7771	.1474	.0392	38
23	.49065	.87136	.56309	.7759	.1476	.0381	37
24	.49090	.87121	.56347	.7747	.1478	.0370	36
25	.49116	.87107	.56385	1.7735	1.1480	2.0360	35
26	.49141	.87093	.56424	.7723	.1482	.0349	34
27	.49166	.87078	.56462	.7711	.1484	.0339	33
28	.49192	.87064	.56500	.7699	.1486	.0329	32
29	.49217	.87050	.56539	.7687	.1488	.0318	31
30	.49242	.87035	.56577	1.7675	1.1489	2.0308	30
31	.49268	.87021	.56616	.7663	.1491	.0297	29
32	.49293	.87007	.56654	.7651	.1493	.0287	28
33	.49318	.86992	.56692	.7639	.1495	.0276	27
34	.49343	.86978	.56731	.7627	.1497	.0266	26
35	.49369	.86964	.56769	1.7615	1.1499	2.0256	25
36	.49394	.86949	.56808	.7603	.1501	.0245	24
37	.49419	.86935	.56846	.7591	.1503	.0235	23
38	.49445	.86921	.56885	.7579	.1505	.0224	22
39	.49470	.86906	.56923	.7567	.1507	.0214	21
40	.49495	.86892	.56962	1.7555	1.1508	2.0204	20
41	.49521	.86877	.57000	.7544	.1510	.0194	19
42	.49546	.86863	.57039	.7532	.1512	.0183	18
43	.49571	.86849	.57077	.7520	.1514	.0173	17
44	.49596	.86834	.57116	.7508	.1516	.0163	16
45	.49622	.86820	.57155	1.7496	1.1518	2.0152	15
46	.49647	.86805	.57193	.7484	.1520	.0142	14
47	.49672	.86791	.57232	.7473	.1522	.0132	13
48	.49697	.86776	.57270	.7461	.1524	.0122	12
49	.49723	.86762	.57309	.7449	.1526	.0111	11
50	.49748	.86748	.57348	1.7437	1.1528	2.0101	10
51	.49773	.86733	.57386	.7426	.1530	.0091	9
52	.49798	.86719	.57425	.7414	.1531	.0081	8
53	.49823	.86704	.57464	.7402	.1533	.0071	7
54	.49849	.86690	.57502	.7390	.1535	.0061	6
55	.49874	.86675	.57541	1.7379	1.1537	2.0050	5
56	.49899	.86661	.57580	.7367	.1539	.0040	4
57	.49924	.86646	.57619	.7355	.1541	.0030	3
58	.49950	.86632	.57657	.7344	.1543	.0020	2
59	.49975	.86617	.57696	.7332	.1545	.0010	1
60	.50000	.86603	.57735	1.7320	1.1547	2.0000	0

M	Cosine	Sine	Cotan.	Tan.	Cosec.	Secant	M

M	Sine	Cosine	Tan.	Cotan.	Secant	Cosec.	M	M	Sine	Cosine	Tan.	Cotan.	Secant	Cosec.	M
0	.50000	.86603	.57735	1.7320	1.1547	2.0000	60	0	.51504	.85717	.60086	1.6643	1.1666	1.9416	60
1	.50025	.86588	.57774	.7309	.1549	1.9990	59	1	.51529	.85702	.60126	.6632	.1668	.9407	59
2	.50050	.86573	.57813	.7297	.1551	.9980	58	2	.51554	.85687	.60165	.6621	.1670	.9397	58
3	.50075	.86559	.57851	.7286	.1553	.9970	57	3	.51578	.85672	.60205	.6610	.1672	.9388	57
4	.50101	.86544	.57890	.7274	.1555	.9960	56	4	.51603	.85657	.60244	.6599	.1674	.9378	56
5	.50126	.86530	.57929	1.7262	1.1557	1.9950	55	5	.51628	.85642	.60284	1.6588	1.1676	1.9369	55
6	.50151	.86515	.57968	.7251	.1559	.9940	54	6	.51653	.85627	.60324	.6577	.1678	.9360	54
7	.50176	.86500	.58007	.7239	.1561	.9930	53	7	.51678	.85612	.60363	.6566	.1681	.9350	53
8	.50201	.86486	.58046	.7228	.1562	.9920	52	8	.51703	.85597	.60403	.6555	.1683	.9341	52
9	.50226	.86471	.58085	.7216	.1564	.9910	51	9	.51728	.85582	.60443	.6544	.1685	.9332	51
10	.50252	.86457	.58123	1.7205	1.1566	1.9900	50	10	.51753	.85566	.60483	1.6534	1.1687	1.9322	50
11	.50277	.86442	.58162	.7193	.1568	.9890	49	11	.51778	.85551	.60522	.6523	.1689	.9313	49
12	.50302	.86427	.58201	.7182	.1570	.9880	48	12	.51803	.85536	.60562	.6512	.1691	.9304	48
13	.50327	.86413	.58240	.7170	.1572	.9870	47	13	.51827	.85521	.60602	.6501	.1693	.9295	47
14	.50352	.86398	.58279	.7159	.1574	.9860	46	14	.51852	.85506	.60642	.6490	.1695	.9285	46
15	.50377	.86383	.58318	1.7147	1.1576	1.9850	45	15	.51877	.85491	.60681	1.6479	1.1697	1.9276	45
16	.50402	.86369	.58357	.7136	.1578	.9840	44	16	.51902	.85476	.60721	.6469	.1699	.9267	44
17	.50428	.86354	.58396	.7124	.1580	.9830	43	17	.51927	.85461	.60761	.6458	.1701	.9258	43
18	.50453	.86339	.58435	.7113	.1582	.9820	42	18	.51952	.85446	.60801	.6447	.1703	.9248	42
19	.50478	.86325	.58474	.7101	.1584	.9811	41	19	.51977	.85431	.60841	.6436	.1705	.9239	41
20	.50503	.86310	.58513	1.7090	1.1586	1.9801	40	20	.52002	.85416	.60881	1.6425	1.1707	1.9230	40
21	.50528	.86295	.58552	.7079	.1588	.9791	39	21	.52026	.85400	.60920	.6415	.1709	.9221	39
22	.50553	.86281	.58591	.7067	.1590	.9781	38	22	.52051	.85385	.60960	.6404	.1712	.9212	38
23	.50578	.86266	.58630	.7056	.1592	.9771	37	23	.52076	.85370	.61000	.6393	.1714	.9203	37
24	.50603	.86251	.58670	.7044	.1594	.9761	36	24	.52101	.85355	.61040	.6383	.1716	.9193	36
25	.50628	.86237	.58709	1.7033	1.1596	1.9752	35	25	.52126	.85340	.61080	1.6372	1.1718	1.9184	35
26	.50653	.86222	.58748	.7022	.1598	.9742	34	26	.52151	.85325	.61120	.6361	.1720	.9175	34
27	.50679	.86207	.58787	.7010	.1600	.9732	33	27	.52175	.85309	.61160	.6350	.1722	.9166	33
28	.50704	.86192	.58826	.6999	.1602	.9722	32	28	.52200	.85294	.61200	.6340	.1724	.9157	32
29	.50729	.86178	.58865	.6988	.1604	.9713	31	29	.52225	.85279	.61240	.6329	.1726	.9148	31
30	.50754	.86163	.58904	1.6977	1.1606	1.9703	30	30	.52250	.85264	.61280	1.6318	1.1728	1.9139	30
31	.50779	.86148	.58944	.6965	.1608	.9693	29	31	.52275	.85249	.61320	.6308	.1730	.9130	29
32	.50804	.86133	.58983	.6954	.1610	.9683	28	32	.52299	.85234	.61360	.6297	.1732	.9121	28
33	.50829	.86118	.59022	.6943	.1612	.9674	27	33	.52324	.85218	.61400	.6286	.1734	.9112	27
34	.50854	.86104	.59061	.6931	.1614	.9664	26	34	.52349	.85203	.61440	.6276	.1737	.9102	26
35	.50879	.86089	.59100	1.6920	1.1616	1.9654	25	35	.52374	.85188	.61480	1.6265	1.1739	1.9093	25
36	.50904	.86074	.59140	.6909	.1618	.9645	24	36	.52398	.85173	.61520	.6255	.1741	.9084	24
37	.50929	.86059	.59179	.6898	.1620	.9635	23	37	.52423	.85157	.61560	.6244	.1743	.9075	23
38	.50954	.86044	.59218	.6887	.1622	.9625	22	38	.52448	.85142	.61601	.6233	.1745	.9066	22
39	.50979	.86030	.59258	.6875	.1624	.9616	21	39	.52473	.85127	.61641	.6223	.1747	.9057	21
40	.51004	.86015	.59297	1.6864	1.1626	1.9606	20	40	.52498	.85112	.61681	1.6212	1.1749	1.9048	20
41	.51029	.86000	.59336	.6853	.1628	.9596	19	41	.52522	.85096	.61721	.6202	.1751	.9039	19
42	.51054	.85985	.59376	.6842	.1630	.9587	18	42	.52547	.85081	.61761	.6191	.1753	.9030	18
43	.51079	.85970	.59415	.6831	.1632	.9577	17	43	.52572	.85066	.61801	.6181	.1756	.9021	17
44	.51104	.85955	.59454	.6820	.1634	.9568	16	44	.52597	.85050	.61842	.6170	.1758	.9013	16
45	.51129	.85941	.59494	1.6808	1.1636	1.9558	15	45	.52621	.85035	.61882	1.6160	1.1760	1.9004	15
46	.51154	.85926	.59533	.6797	.1638	.9549	14	46	.52646	.85020	.61922	.6149	.1762	.8995	14
47	.51179	.85911	.59572	.6786	.1640	.9539	13	47	.52671	.85004	.61962	.6139	.1764	.8986	13
48	.51204	.85896	.59612	.6775	.1642	.9530	12	48	.52695	.84989	.62003	.6128	.1766	.8977	12
49	.51229	.85881	.59651	.6764	.1644	.9520	11	49	.52720	.84974	.62043	.6118	.1768	.8968	11
50	.51254	.85866	.59691	1.6753	1.1646	1.9510	10	50	.52745	.84959	.62083	1.6107	1.1770	1.8959	10
51	.51279	.85851	.59730	.6742	.1648	.9501	9	51	.52770	.84943	.62123	.6097	.1772	.8950	9
52	.51304	.85836	.59770	.6731	.1650	.9491	8	52	.52794	.84928	.62164	.6086	.1775	.8941	8
53	.51329	.85821	.59809	.6720	.1652	.9482	7	53	.52819	.84912	.62204	.6076	.1777	.8932	7
54	.51354	.85806	.59849	.6709	.1654	.9473	6	54	.52844	.84897	.62244	.6066	.1779	.8924	6
55	.51379	.85791	.59888	1.6698	1.1656	1.9463	5	55	.52868	.84882	.62285	1.6055	1.1781	1.8915	5
56	.51404	.85777	.59928	.6687	.1658	.9454	4	56	.52893	.84866	.62325	.6045	.1783	.8906	4
57	.51429	.85762	.59967	.6676	.1660	.9444	3	57	.52918	.84851	.62366	.6034	.1785	.8897	3
58	.51454	.85747	.60007	.6665	.1662	.9435	2	58	.52942	.84836	.62406	.6024	.1787	.8888	2
59	.51479	.85732	.60046	.6654	.1664	.9425	1	59	.52967	.84820	.62446	.6014	.1790	.8879	1
60	.51504	.85717	.60086	1.6643	1.1666	1.9416	0	60	.52992	.84805	.62487	1.6003	1.1792	1.8871	0
M	Cosine	Sine	Cotan.	Tan.	Cosec.	Secant	M	M	Cosine	Sine	Cotan.	Tan.	Cosec.	Secant	M

32°

M	Sine	Cosine	Tan.	Cotan.	Secant	Cosec.	M
0	.52992	.84805	.62487	1.6003	1.1792	1.8871	60
1	.53016	.84789	.62527	.5993	.1794	.8862	59
2	.53041	.84774	.62568	.5983	.1796	.8853	58
3	.53066	.84758	.62608	.5972	.1798	.8844	57
4	.53090	.84743	.62649	.5962	.1800	.8836	56
5	.53115	.84728	.62689	1.5952	1.1802	1.8827	55
6	.53140	.84712	.62730	.5941	.1805	.8818	54
7	.53164	.84697	.62770	.5931	.1807	.8809	53
8	.53189	.84681	.62811	.5921	.1809	.8801	52
9	.53214	.84666	.62851	.5910	.1811	.8792	51
10	.53238	.84650	.62892	1.5900	1.1813	1.8783	50
11	.53263	.84635	.62933	.5890	.1815	.8775	49
12	.53288	.84619	.62973	.5880	.1818	.8766	48
13	.53312	.84604	.63014	.5869	.1820	.8757	47
14	.53337	.84588	.63055	.5859	.1822	.8749	46
15	.53361	.84573	.63095	1.5849	1.1824	1.8740	45
16	.53386	.84557	.63136	.5839	.1826	.8731	44
17	.53411	.84542	.63177	.5829	.1828	.8723	43
18	.53435	.84526	.63217	.5818	.1831	.8714	42
19	.53460	.84511	.63258	.5808	.1833	.8706	41
20	.53484	.84495	.63299	1.5798	1.1835	1.8697	40
21	.53509	.84479	.63339	.5788	.1837	.8688	39
22	.53533	.84464	.63380	.5778	.1839	.8680	38
23	.53558	.84448	.63421	.5768	.1841	.8671	37
24	.53583	.84433	.63462	.5757	.1844	.8663	36
25	.53607	.84417	.63503	1.5747	1.1846	1.8654	35
26	.53632	.84402	.63543	.5737	.1848	.8646	34
27	.53656	.84386	.63584	.5727	.1850	.8637	33
28	.53681	.84370	.63625	.5717	.1852	.8629	32
29	.53705	.84355	.63666	.5707	.1855	.8620	31
30	.53730	.84339	.63707	1.5697	1.1857	1.8611	30
31	.53754	.84323	.63748	.5687	.1859	.8603	29
32	.53779	.84308	.63789	.5677	.1861	.8595	28
33	.53803	.84292	.63830	.5667	.1863	.8586	27
34	.53828	.84276	.63871	.5657	.1866	.8578	26
35	.53852	.84261	.63912	1.5646	1.1868	1.8569	25
36	.53877	.84245	.63953	.5636	.1870	.8561	24
37	.53901	.84229	.63994	.5626	.1872	.8552	23
38	.53926	.84214	.64035	.5616	.1874	.8544	22
39	.53950	.84198	.64076	.5606	.1877	.8535	21
40	.53975	.84182	.64117	1.5596	1.1879	1.8527	20
41	.53999	.84167	.64158	.5586	.1881	.8519	19
42	.54024	.84151	.64199	.5577	.1883	.8510	18
43	.54048	.84135	.64240	.5567	.1886	.8502	17
44	.54073	.84120	.64281	.5557	.1888	.8493	16
45	.54097	.84104	.64322	1.5547	1.1890	1.8485	15
46	.54122	.84088	.64363	.5537	.1892	.8477	14
47	.54146	.84072	.64404	.5527	.1894	.8468	13
48	.54171	.84057	.64446	.5517	.1897	.8460	12
49	.54195	.84041	.64487	.5507	.1899	.8452	11
50	.54220	.84025	.64528	1.5497	1.1901	1.8443	10
51	.54244	.84009	.64569	.5487	.1903	.8435	9
52	.54268	.83993	.64610	.5477	.1906	.8427	8
53	.54293	.83978	.64652	.5467	.1908	.8418	7
54	.54317	.83962	.64693	.5458	.1910	.8410	6
55	.54342	.83946	.64734	1.5448	1.1912	1.8402	5
56	.54366	.83930	.64775	.5438	.1915	.8394	4
57	.54391	.83914	.64817	.5428	.1917	.8385	3
58	.54415	.83899	.64858	.5418	.1919	.8377	2
59	.54439	.83883	.64899	.5408	.1921	.8369	1
60	.54464	.83867	.64941	1.5399	1.1924	1.8361	0

M	Cosine	Sine	Cotan.	Tan.	Cosec.	Secant	M

57°

33°

M	Sine	Cosine	Tan.	Cotan.	Secant	Cosec.	M
0	.54464	.83867	.64941	1.5399	1.1924	1.8361	60
1	.54488	.83851	.64982	.5389	.1926	.8352	59
2	.54513	.83835	.65023	.5379	.1928	.8344	58
3	.54537	.83819	.65065	.5369	.1930	.8336	57
4	.54561	.83804	.65106	.5359	.1933	.8328	56
5	.54586	.83788	.65148	1.5350	1.1935	1.8320	55
6	.54610	.83772	.65189	.5340	.1937	.8311	54
7	.54634	.83756	.65231	.5330	.1939	.8303	53
8	.54659	.83740	.65272	.5320	.1942	.8295	52
9	.54683	.83724	.65314	.5311	.1944	.8287	51
10	.54708	.83708	.65355	1.5301	1.1946	1.8279	50
11	.54732	.83692	.65397	.5291	.1948	.8271	49
12	.54756	.83676	.65438	.5282	.1951	.8263	48
13	.54781	.83660	.65480	.5272	.1953	.8255	47
14	.54805	.83644	.65521	.5262	.1955	.8246	46
15	.54829	.83629	.65563	1.5252	1.1958	1.8238	45
16	.54854	.83613	.65604	.5243	.1960	.8230	44
17	.54878	.83597	.65646	.5233	.1962	.8222	43
18	.54902	.83581	.65688	.5223	.1964	.8214	42
19	.54926	.83565	.65729	.5214	.1967	.8206	41
20	.54951	.83549	.65771	1.5204	1.1969	1.8198	40
21	.54975	.83533	.65813	.5195	.1971	.8190	39
22	.54999	.83517	.65854	.5185	.1974	.8182	38
23	.55024	.83501	.65896	.5175	.1976	.8174	37
24	.55048	.83485	.65938	.5166	.1978	.8166	36
25	.55072	.83469	.65980	1.5156	1.1980	1.8158	35
26	.55097	.83453	.66021	.5147	.1983	.8150	34
27	.55121	.83437	.66063	.5137	.1985	.8142	33
28	.55145	.83421	.66105	.5127	.1987	.8134	32
29	.55169	.83405	.66147	.5118	.1990	.8126	31
30	.55194	.83388	.66188	1.5108	1.1992	1.8118	30
31	.55218	.83372	.66230	.5099	.1994	.8110	29
32	.55242	.83356	.66272	.5089	.1997	.8102	28
33	.55266	.83340	.66314	.5080	.1999	.8094	27
34	.55291	.83324	.66356	.5070	.2001	.8086	26
35	.55315	.83308	.66398	1.5061	1.2004	1.8078	25
36	.55339	.83292	.66440	.5051	.2006	.8070	24
37	.55363	.83276	.66482	.5042	.2008	.8062	23
38	.55388	.83260	.66524	.5032	.2010	.8054	22
39	.55412	.83244	.66566	.5023	.2013	.8047	21
40	.55436	.83228	.66608	1.5013	1.2015	1.8039	20
41	.55460	.83211	.66650	.5004	.2017	.8031	19
42	.55484	.83195	.66692	.4994	.2020	.8023	18
43	.55509	.83179	.66734	.4985	.2022	.8015	17
44	.55533	.83163	.66776	.4975	.2024	.8007	16
45	.55557	.83147	.66818	1.4966	1.2027	1.7999	15
46	.55581	.83131	.66860	.4957	.2029	.7992	14
47	.55605	.83115	.66902	.4947	.2031	.7984	13
48	.55629	.83098	.66944	.4938	.2034	.7976	12
49	.55654	.83082	.66986	.4928	.2036	.7968	11
50	.55678	.83066	.67028	1.4919	1.2039	1.7960	10
51	.55702	.83050	.67071	.4910	.2041	.7953	9
52	.55726	.83034	.67113	.4900	.2043	.7945	8
53	.55750	.83017	.67155	.4891	.2046	.7937	7
54	.55774	.83001	.67197	.4881	.2048	.7929	6
55	.55799	.82985	.67239	1.4872	1.2050	1.7921	5
56	.55823	.82969	.67282	.4863	.2053	.7914	4
57	.55847	.82952	.67324	.4853	.2055	.7906	3
58	.55871	.82936	.67366	.4844	.2057	.7898	2
59	.55895	.82920	.67408	.4835	.2060	.7891	1
60	.55919	.82904	.67451	1.4826	1.2062	1.7883	0

M	Cosine	Sine	Cotan.	Tan.	Cosec.	Secant	M

56°

34°

M	Sine	Cosine	Tan.	Cotan.	Secant	Cosec.	M
0	.55919	.82904	.67451	1.4826	1.2062	1.7883	60
1	.55943	.82887	.67493	.4816	.2064	.7875	59
2	.55967	.82871	.67535	.4807	.2067	.7867	58
3	.55992	.82855	.67578	.4798	.2069	.7860	57
4	.56016	.82839	.67620	.4788	.2072	.7852	56
5	.56040	.82822	.67663	1.4779	1.2074	1.7844	55
6	.56064	.82806	.67705	.4770	.2076	.7837	54
7	.56088	.82790	.67747	.4761	.2079	.7829	53
8	.56112	.82773	.67790	.4751	.2081	.7821	52
9	.56136	.82757	.67832	.4742	.2083	.7814	51
10	.56160	.82741	.67875	1.4733	1.2086	1.7806	50
11	.56184	.82724	.67917	.4724	.2088	.7798	49
12	.56208	.82708	**.67960**	.4714	.2091	.7791	48
13	.56232	.82692	.68002	.4705	.2093	.7783	47
14	.56256	.82675	.68045	.4696	.2095	.7776	46
15	.56280	.82659	.68087	1.4687	1.2098	1.7768	45
16	.56304	.82643	.68130	.4678	.2100	.7760	44
17	.56328	.82626	.68173	.4669	.2103	.7753	43
18	.56353	.82610	.68215	.4659	.2105	.7745	42
19	.56377	.82593	.68258	.4650	.2107	.7738	41
20	.56401	.82577	.68301	1.4641	1.2110	1.7730	40
21	.56425	.82561	.68343	.4632	.2112	.7723	39
22	.56449	.82544	.68386	.4623	.2115	.7715	38
23	.56473	.82528	.68429	.4614	.2117	.7708	37
24	.56497	.82511	.68471	.4605	.2119	.7700	36
25	.56521	.82495	.68514	1.4595	1.2122	1.7693	35
26	.56545	.82478	.68557	.4586	.2124	.7685	34
27	.56569	.82462	.68600	.4577	.2127	.7678	33
28	.56593	.82445	.68642	.4568	.2129	.7670	32
29	.56617	.82429	.68685	.4559	.2132	.7663	31
30	.56641	.82413	.68728	1.4550	1.2134	1.7655	30
31	.56664	.82396	.68771	.4541	.2136	.7648	29
32	.56688	.82380	.68814	.4532	.2139	.7640	28
33	.56712	.82363	.68857	.4523	.2141	.7633	27
34	.56736	.82347	.68899	.4514	.2144	.7625	26
35	.56760	.82330	.68942	1.4505	1.2146	1.7618	25
36	.56784	.82314	.68985	.4496	.2149	.7610	24
37	.56808	.82297	.69028	.4487	.2151	.7603	23
38	.56832	.82280	.69071	.4478	.2153	.7596	22
39	.56856	.82264	.69114	.4469	.2156	.7588	21
40	.56880	.82247	.69157	1.4460	1.2158	1.7581	20
41	.56904	.82231	.69200	.4451	.2161	.7573	19
42	.56928	.82214	.69243	.4442	.2163	.7566	18
43	.56952	.82197	.69286	.4433	.2166	.7559	17
44	.56976	.82181	.69329	.4424	.2168	.7551	16
45	.57000	.82165	.69372	1.4415	1.2171	1.7544	15
46	.57023	.82148	.69415	.4406	.2173	.7537	14
47	.57047	.82131	.69459	.4397	.2175	.7529	13
48	.57071	.82115	.69502	.4388	.2178	.7522	12
49	.57095	.82098	.69545	.4379	.2180	.7514	11
50	.57119	.82082	.69588	1.4370	1.2183	1.7507	10
51	.57143	.82065	.69631	.4361	.2185	.7500	9
52	.57167	.82048	.69674	.4352	.2188	.7493	8
53	.57191	.82032	.69718	.4343	.2190	.7485	7
54	.57214	.82015	.69761	.4335	.2193	.7478	6
55	.57238	.81998	.69804	1.4326	1.2195	1.7471	5
56	.57262	.81982	.69847	.4317	.2198	.7463	4
57	.57286	.81965	.69891	.4308	.2200	.7456	3
58	.57310	.81948	.69934	.4299	.2203	.7449	2
59	.57334	.81932	.69977	.4290	.2205	.7442	1
60	.57358	.81915	.70021	1.4281	1.2208	1.7434	0
M	Cosine	Sine	Cotan.	Tan.	Cosec.	Secant	M

55°

35°

M	Sine	Cosine	Tan.	Cotan.	Secant	Cosec.	M
0	.57358	.81915	.70021	1.4281	1.2208	1.7434	60
1	.57381	.81898	.70064	.4273	.2210	.7427	59
2	.57405	.81882	.70107	.4264	.2213	.7420	58
3	.57429	.81865	.70151	.4255	.2215	.7413	57
4	.57453	.81848	.70194	.4246	.2218	.7405	56
5	.57477	.81832	.70238	1.4237	1.2220	1.7398	55
6	.57500	.81815	.70281	.4228	.2223	.7391	54
7	.57524	.81798	.70325	4220	.2225	.7384	53
8	.57548	.81781	.70368	.4211	.2228	.7377	52
9	.57572	.81765	.70412	.4202	.2230	.7369	51
10	.57596	.81748	.70455	1.4193	1.2233	1.7362	50
11	.57619	.81731	.70499	.4185	.2235	.7355	49
12	.57643	.81714	.70542	.4176	.2238	.7348	48
13	.57667	.81698	.70586	.4167	.2240	.7341	47
14	.57691	.81681	.70629	.4158	.2243	.7334	46
15	.57714	.81664	.70673	1.4150	1.2245	1.7327	45
16	.57738	.81647	.70717	.4141	.2248	.7319	44
17	.57762	.81630	.70760	.4132	.2250	.7312	43
18	.57786	.81614	.70804	.4123	.2253	.7305	42
19	.57809	.81597	.70848	.4115	.2255	.7298	41
20	.57833	.81580	.70891	1.4106	1.2258	1.7291	40
21	.57857	.81563	.70935	.4097	.2260	.7284	39
22	.57881	.81546	.70979	.4089	.2263	.7277	38
23	.57904	.81530	.71022	.4080	.2265	.7270	37
24	.57928	.81513	.71066	.4071	.2268	.7263	36
25	.57952	.81496	.71110	1.4063	1.2270	1.7256	35
26	.57975	.81479	.71154	.4054	.2273	.7249	34
27	.57999	.81462	.71198	.4045	.2276	.7242	33
28	.58023	.81445	.71241	1.4037	.2278	.7234	32
29	.58047	.81428	.71285	.4028	.2281	.7227	31
30	.58070	.81411	.71329	1.4019	1.2283	1.7220	30
31	.58094	.81395	.71373	.4011	.2286	.7213	29
32	.58118	.81378	.71417	.4002	.2288	.7206	28
33	.58141	.81361	.71461	.3994	.2291	.7199	27
34	.58165	.81344	.71505	.3985	.2293	.7192	26
35	.58189	.81327	.71549	1.3976	1.2296	1.7185	25
36	.58212	.81310	.71593	.3968	.2298	.7178	24
37	.58236	.81293	.71637	.3959	.2301	.7171	23
38	.58259	.81276	.71681	.3951	.2304	.7164	22
39	.58283	.81259	.71725	.3942	.2306	.7157	21
40	.58307	.81242	.71769	1.3933	1.2309	1.7151	20
41	.58330	.81225	.71813	.3925	.2311	.7144	19
42	.58354	.81208	.71857	.3916	.2314	.7137	18
43	.58378	.81191	.71901	.3908	.2316	.7130	17
44	.58401	.81174	.71945	.3899	.2319	.7123	16
45	.58425	.81157	.71990	1.3891	1.2322	1.7116	15
46	.58448	.81140	.72034	.3882	.2324	.7109	14
47	.58472	.81123	.72078	.3874	.2327	.7102	13
48	.58496	.81106	.72122	.3865	.2329	.7095	12
49	.58519	.81089	.72166	.3857	.2332	.7088	11
50	.58543	.81072	.72211	1.3848	1.2335	1.7081	10
51	.58566	.81055	.72255	.3840	.2337	.7075	9
52	.58590	.81038	.72299	.3831	.2340	.7068	8
53	.58614	.81021	.72344	.3823	.2342	.7061	7
54	.58637	.81004	.72388	.3814	.2345	.7054	6
55	.58661	.80987	.72432	1.3806	1.2348	1.7047	5
56	.58684	.80970	.72477	.3797	.2350	.7040	4
57	.58708	.80953	.72521	.3789	.2353	.7033	3
58	.58731	.80936	.72565	.3781	.2355	.7027	2
59	.58755	.80919	.72610	.3772	.2358	.7020	1
60	.58778	.80902	.72654	1.3764	1.2361	1.7013	0
M	Cosine	Sine	Cotan.	Tan.	Cosec.	Secant	M

54°

36°

M	Sine	Cosine	Tan.	Cotan.	Secant	Cosec.	M
0	.58778	.80902	.72654	1.3764	1.2361	1.7013	60
1	.58802	.80885	.72699	.3755	.2363	.7006	59
2	.58825	.80867	.72743	.3747	.2366	.6999	58
3	.58849	.80850	.72788	.3738	.2368	.6993	57
4	.58873	.80833	.72832	1.3730	.2371	.6986	56
5	.58896	.80816	.72877	1.3722	1.2374	1.6979	55
6	.58920	.80799	.72921	.3713	.2376	.6972	54
7	.58943	.80782	.72966	.3705	.2379	.6965	53
8	.58967	.80765	.73010	.3697	.2382	.6959	52
9	.58990	.80747	.73055	.3688	.2384	.6952	51
10	.59014	.80730	.73100	1.3680	1.2387	1.6945	50
11	.59037	.80713	.73144	.3672	.2389	.6938	49
12	.59060	.80696	.73189	.3663	.2392	.6932	48
13	.59084	.80679	.73234	.3655	.2395	.6925	47
14	.59107	.80662	.73278	.3647	.2397	.6918	46
15	.59131	.80644	.73323	1.3638	1.2400	1.6912	45
16	.59154	.80627	.73368	.3630	.2403	.6905	44
17	.59178	.80610	.73412	.3622	.2405	.6898	43
18	.59201	.80593	.73457	.3613	.2408	.6891	42
19	.59225	.80576	.73502	.3605	.2411	.6885	41
20	.59248	.80558	.73547	1.3597	1.2413	1.6878	40
21	.59272	.80541	.73592	.3588	.2416	.6871	39
22	.59295	.80524	.73681	.3580	.2419	.6865	38
23	.59318	.80507	.73681	.3572	.2421	.6858	37
24	.59342	.80489	.73726	.3564	.2424	.6851	36
25	.59365	.80472	.73771	1.3555	1.2427	1.6845	35
26	.59389	.80455	.73816	.3547	.2429	1.6838	34
27	.59412	.80437	.73861	.3539	.2432	.6831	33
28	.59435	.80420	.73906	.3531	.2435	.6825	32
29	.59459	.80403	.73951	.3522	.2437	.6818	31
30	.59482	.80386	.73996	1.3514	1.2440	1.6812	30
31	.59506	.80368	.74041	.3506	.2443	.6805	29
32	.59529	.80351	.74086	.3498	.2445	.6798	28
33	.59552	.80334	.74131	.3489	.2448	.6792	27
34	.59576	.80316	.74176	.3481	.2451	.6785	26
35	.59599	.80299	.74221	1.3473	1.2453	1.6779	25
36	.59622	.80282	.74266	.3465	.2456	.6772	24
37	.59646	.80264	.74312	.3457	.2459	.6766	23
38	.59669	.80247	.74357	.3449	.2461	.6759	22
39	.59692	.80230	.74402	.3440	.2464	.6752	21
40	.59716	.80212	.74447	1.3432	1.2467	1.6746	20
41	.59739	.80195	.74492	.3424	.2470	.6739	19
42	.59762	.80177	.74538	.3416	.2472	.6733	18
43	.59786	.80160	.74583	.3408	.2475	.6726	17
44	.59809	.80143	.74628	.3400	.2478	.6720	16
45	.59832	.80125	.74673	1.3392	1.2480	1.6713	15
46	.59856	.80108	.74719	1.3383	.2483	.6707	14
47	.59879	.80090	.74764	.3375	.2486	.6700	13
48	.59902	.80073	.74809	.3367	.2488	.6694	12
49	.59926	.80056	.74855	.3359	.2491	.6687	11
50	.59949	.80038	.74900	1.3351	1.2494	1.6681	10
51	.59972	.80021	.74946	.3343	.2497	.6674	9
52	.59995	.80003	.74991	.3335	.2499	.6668	8
53	.60019	.79986	.75037	.3327	.2502	.6661	7
54	.60042	.79968	.75082	.3319	.2505	.6655	6
55	.60065	.79951	.75128	1.3311	1.2508	1.6648	5
56	.60088	.79933	.75173	.3303	.2510	.6642	4
57	.60112	.79916	.75219	.3294	.2513	.6636	3
58	.60135	.79898	.75264	.3286	.2516	.6629	2
59	.60158	.79881	.75310	.3278	.2519	.6623	1
60	.60181	.79863	.75355	1.3270	1.2521	1.6616	0

M	Cosine	Sine	Cotan.	Tan.	Cosec.	Secant	M

53°

37°

M	Sine	Cosine	Tan.	Cotan.	Secant	Cosec.	M
0	.60181	.79863	.75355	1.3270	1.2521	1.6616	60
1	.60205	.79846	.75401	.3262	.2524	.6610	59
2	.60228	.79828	.75447	.3254	.2527	.6603	58
3	.60251	.79811	.75492	.3246	.2530	.6597	57
4	.60274	.79793	.75538	.3238	.2532	.6591	56
5	.60298	.79776	.75584	1.3230	1.2535	1.6584	55
6	.60320	.79758	.75629	.3222	.2538	.6578	54
7	.60344	.79741	.75675	.3214	.2541	.6572	53
8	.60367	.79723	.75721 ·	.3206	.2543	.6565	52
9	.60390	.79706	.75767	.3198	.2546	.6559	51
10	.60413	.79688	.75812	1.3190	1.2549	1.6552	50
11	.60437	.79670	.75858	.3182	.2552	.6546	49
12	.60460	.79653	.75904	.3174	.2554	.6540	48
13	.60483	.79635	.75950	.3166	.2557	.6533	47
14	.60506	.79618	.75996	.3159	.2560	.6527	46
15	.60529	.79600	.76042	1.3151	1.2563	1.6521	45
16	.60552	.79582	.76088	.3143	.2565	.6514	44
17	.60576	.79565	.76134	.3135	.2568	.6508	43
18	.60599	.79547	.76179	.3127	.2571	.6502	42
19	.60622	.79530	.76225	.3119	.2574	.6496	41
20	.60645	.79512	.76271	1.3111	1.2577	1.6489	40
21	.60668	.79494	.76317	.3103	.2579	.6483	39
22	.60691	.79477	.76364	.3095	.2582	.6477	38
23	.60714	.79459	.76410	.3087	.2585	.6470	37
24	.60737	.79441	.76456	.3079	.2588	.6464	36
25	.60761	.79424	.76502	1.3071	1.2591	1.6458	35
26	.60784	.79406	.76548	.3064	.2593	.6452	34
27	.60807	.79388	.76594	.3056	.2596	.6445	33
28	.60830	.79371	.76640	.3048	.2599	.6439	32
29	.60853	.79353	.76686	.3040	.2602	.6433	31
30	.60876	.79335	.76733	1.3032	1.2605	1.6427	30
31	.60899	.79318	.76779	.3024	.2607	.6420	29
32	.60922	.79300	.76825	.3016	.2610	.6414	28
33	.60945	.79282	.76871	.3009	.2613	.6408	27
34	.60968	.79264	.76918	.3001	.2616	.6402	26
35	.60991	.79247	.76964	1.2993	1.2619	Ⅰ.6396	25
36	.61014	.79229	.77010	.2985	.2622	.6389	24
37	.61037	.79211	.77057	.2977	.2624	1.6383	23
38	.61061	.79193	.77103	.2970	.2627	.6377	22
39	.61084	.79176	.77149	.2962	.2630	.6371	21
40	.61107	.79158	.77196	1.2954	1.2633	1.6365	20
41	.61130	.79140	.77242	.2946	.2636	.6359	19
42	.61153	.79122	.77289	.2938	.2639	.6352	18
43	.61176	.79104	.77335	.2931	.2641	.6346	17
44	.61199	.79087	.77382	.2923	.2644	.6340	16
45	.61222	.79069	.77428	1.2915	1.2647	1.6334	15
46	.61245	.79051	.77475	.2907	.2650	.6328	14
47	.61268	.79033	.77521	.2900	.2653	.6322	13
48	.61290	.79015	.77568	.2892	.2656	.6316	12
49	.61314	.78998	.77614	.2884	.2659	.6309	11
50	.61337	.78980	.77661	1.2876	1.2661	1.6303	10
51	.61360	.78962	.77708	.2869	.2664	.6297	9
52	.61383	.78944	.77754	.2861	.2667	.6291	8
53	.61405	.78926	.77801	.2853	.2670	.6285	7
54	.61428	.78908	.77848	.2845	.2673	.6279	6
55	.61451	.78890	.77895	1.2838	1.2676	1.6273	5
56	.61474	.78873	.77941	.2830	.2679	.6267	4
57	.61497	.78855	.77988	.2822	.2681	.6261	3
58	.61520	.78837	.78035	.2815	.2684	.6255	2
59	.61543	.78819	.78082	.2807	.2687	.6249	1
60	.61566	.78801	.78128	1.2799	1.2690	1.6243	0

M	Cosine	Sine	Cotan.	Tan.	Cosec.	Secant	M

52°

38°

M	Sine	Cosine	Tan.	Cotan.	Secant	Cosec.	M
0	.61566	.78801	.78128	1.2799	1.2690	1.6243	60
1	.61589	.78783	.78175	.2792	.2693	.6237	59
2	.61612	.78765	.78222	.2784	.2696	.6231	58
3	.61635	.78747	.78269	.2776	.2699	.6224	57
4	.61658	.78729	.78316	.2769	.2702	.6218	56
5	.61681	.78711	.78363	1.2761	1.2705	1.6212	55
6	.61703	.78693	.78410	.2753	.2707	.6206	54
7	.61726	.78675	.78457	.2746	.2710	.6200	53
8	.61749	.78657	.78504	.2738	.2713	.6194	52
9	.61772	.78640	.78551	.2730	.2716	.6188	51
10	.61795	.78622	.78598	1.2723	1.2719	1.6182	50
11	.61818	.78604	.78645	.2715	.2722	.6176	49
12	.61841	.78586	.78692	.2708	.2725	.6170	48
13	.61864	.78568	.78739	.2700	.2728	.6164	47
14	.61886	.78550	.78786	.2692	.2731	.6159	46
15	.61909	.78532	.78834	1.2685	1.2734	1.6153	45
16	.61932	.78514	.78881	.2677	.2737	.6147	44
17	.61955	.78496	.78928	.2670	.2739	.6141	43
18	.61978	.78478	.78975	.2662	.2742	.6135	42
19	.62001	.78460	.79022	.2655	.2745	.6129	41
20	.62023	.78441	.79070	1.2647	1.2748	1.6123	40
21	.62046	.78423	.79117	.2639	.2751	.6117	39
22	.62069	.78405	.79164	.2632	.2754	.6111	38
23	.62092	.78387	.79212	.2624	.2757	.6105	37
24	.62115	.78369	.79259	.2617	.2760	.6099	36
25	.62137	.78351	.79306	1.2609	1.2763	1.6093	35
26	.62160	.78333	.79354	.2602	.2766	.6087	34
27	.62183	.78315	.79401	.2594	.2769	.6081	33
28	.62206	.78297	.79449	.2587	.2772	.6077	32
29	.62229	.78279	.79496	.2579	.2775	.6070	31
30	.62251	.78261	.79543	1.2572	1.2778	1.6064	30
31	.62274	.78243	.79591	.2564	.2781	.6058	29
32	.62297	.78224	.79639	.2557	.2784	.6052	28
33	.62320	.78206	.79686	.2549	.2787	.6046	27
34	.62342	.78188	.79734	.2542	.2790	.6040	26
35	.62365	.78170	.79781	1.2534	1.2793	1.6034	25
36	.62388	.78152	.79829	.2527	.2795	.6029	24
37	.62411	.78134	.79876	.2519	.2798	.6023	23
38	.62433	.78116	.79924	.2512	.2801	.6017	22
39	.62456	.78097	.79972	.2504	.2804	.6011	21
40	.62479	.78079	.80020	1.2497	1.2807	1.6005	20
41	.62501	.78061	.80067	.2489	.2810	.6000	19
42	.62524	.78043	.80115	.2482	.2813	.5994	18
43	.62547	.78025	.80163	.2475	.2816	.5988	17
44	.62570	.78007	.80211	.2467	.2819	.5982	16
45	.62592	.77988	.80258	1.2460	1.2822	1.5976	15
46	.62615	.77970	.80306	.2452	.2825	.5971	14
47	.62638	.77952	.80354	.2445	.2828	.5965	13
48	.62660	.77934	.80402	.2437	.2831	.5959	12
49	.62683	.77915	.80450	.2430	.2834	.5953	11
50	.62706	.77897	.80498	1.2423	1.2837	1.5947	10
51	.62728	.77879	.80546	.2415	.2840	.5942	9
52	.62751	.77861	.80594	.2408	.2843	.5936	8
53	.62774	.77842	.80642	.2400	.2846	.5930	7
54	.62796	.77824	.80690	.2393	.2849	.5924	6
55	.62819	.77806	.80738	1.2386	1.2852	1.5919	5
56	.62841	.77788	.80786	.2378	.2855	.5913	4
57	.62864	.77769	.80834	.2371	.2858	.5907	3
58	.62887	.77751	.80882	.2364	.2861	.5901	2
59	.62909	.77733	.80930	.2356	.2864	.5896	1
60	.62932	.77715	.80978	1.2349	1.2867	1.5890	0

M	Cosine	Sine	Cotan.	Tan.	Cosec.	Secant	M

51°

39°

M	Sine	Cosine	Tan.	Cotan.	Secant	Cosec.	M
0	.62932	.77715	.80978	1.2349	1.2867	1.5890	60
1	.62955	.77696	.81026	.2342	.2871	.5884	59
2	.62977	.77678	.81075	.2334	.2874	.5879	58
3	.63000	.77660	.81123	.2327	.2877	.5873	57
4	.63022	.77641	.81171	.2320	.2880	.5867	56
5	.63045	.77623	.81219	1.2312	1.2883	1.5862	55
6	.63067	.77605	.81268	.2305	.2886	.5856	54
7	.63090	.77586	.81316	.2297	.2889	.5850	53
8	.63113	.77568	.81364	.2290	.2892	.5845	52
9	.63135	.77549	.81413	.2283	.2895	.5839	51
10	.63158	.77531	.81461	1.2276	1.2898	1.5833	50
11	.63180	.77513	.81509	.2268	.2901	.5828	49
12	.63203	.77494	.81558	.2261	.2904	.5822	48
13	.63225	.77476	.81606	.2254	.2907	.5816	47
14	.63248	.77458	.81655	.2247	.2910	.5811	46
15	.63270	.77439	.81703	1.2239	1.2913	1.5805	45
16	.63293	.77421	.81752	.2232	.2916	.5799	44
17	.63315	.77402	.81800	.2225	.2919	.5794	43
18	.63338	.77384	.81849	.2218	.2922	.5788	42
19	.63360	.77365	.81898	.2210	.2926	.5783	41
20	.63383	.77347	.81946	1.2203	1.2929	1.5777	40
21	.63405	.77329	.81995	.2196	.2932	.5771	39
22	.63428	.77310	.82043	.2189	.2935	.5766	38
23	.63450	.77292	.82092	.2181	.2938	.5760	37
24	.63473	.77273	.82141	.2174	.2941	.5755	36
25	.63495	.77255	.82190	1.2167	1.2944	1.5749	35
26	.63518	.77236	.82238	.2160	.2947	.5743	34
27	.63540	.77218	.82287	.2152	.2950	.5738	33
28	.63563	.77199	.82336	.2145	.2953	.5732	32
29	.63585	.77181	.82385	.2138	.2956	.5727	31
30	.63608	.77162	.82434	1.2131	1.2960	1.5721	30
31	.63630	.77144	.82482	.2124	.2963	.5716	29
32	.63653	.77125	.82531	.2117	.2966	.5710	28
33	.63675	.77107	.82580	.2109	.2969	.5705	27
34	.63697	.77088	.82629	.2102	.2972	.5699	26
35	.63720	.77070	.82678	1.2095	1.2975	1.5694	25
36	.63742	.77051	.82727	.2088	.2978	.5688	24
37	.63765	.77033	.82776	.2081	.2981	.5683	23
38	.63787	.77014	.82825	.2074	.2985	.5677	22
39	.63810	.76996	.82874	.2066	.2988	.5672	21
40	.63832	.76977	.82923	1.2059	1.2991	1.5666	20
41	.63854	.76958	.82972	.2052	.2994	.5661	19
42	.63877	.76940	.83022	.2045	.2997	.5655	18
43	.63899	.76921	.83071	.2038	.3000	.5650	17
44	.63921	.76903	.83120	.2031	.3003	.5644	16
45	.63944	.76884	.83169	1.2024	1.3006	1.5639	15
46	.63966	.76865	.83218	.2016	.3010	.5633	14
47	.63989	.76847	.83267	.2009	.3013	.5628	13
48	.64011	.76828	.83317	.2002	.3016	.5622	12
49	.64033	.76810	.83366	.1995	.3019	.5617	11
50	.64056	.76791	.83415	1.1988	1.3022	1.5611	10
51	.64078	.76772	.83465	.1981	.3025	.5606	9
52	.64100	.76754	.83514	.1974	.3029	.5600	8
53	.64123	.76735	.83563	.1967	.3032	.5595	7
54	.64145	.76716	.83613	.1960	.3035	.5590	6
55	.64167	.76698	.83662	1.1953	1.3038	1.5584	5
56	.64189	.76679	.83712	.1946	.3041	.5579	4
57	.64212	.76660	.83761	.1939	.3044	.5573	3
58	.64234	.76642	.83811	.1932	.3048	.5568	2
59	.64256	.76623	.83860	.1924	.3051	.5563	1
60	.64279	.76604	.83910	1.1917	1.3054	1.5557	0

M	Cosine	Sine	Cotan.	Tan.	Cosec.	Secant	M

50°

40°

M	Sine	Cosine	Tan.	Cotan.	Secant	Cosec.	M
0	.64279	.76604	.83910	1.1917	1.3054	1.5557	60
1	.64301	.76586	.83959	.1910	.3057	.5552	59
2	.64323	.76567	.84009	.1903	.3060	.5546	58
3	.64345	.76548	.84059	.1896	.3064	.5541	57
4	.64368	.76530	.84108	.1889	.3067	.5536	56
5	.64390	.76511	.84158	.1882	1.3070	1.5530	55
6	.64412	.76492	.84208	.1875	.3073	.5525	54
7	.64435	.76473	.84257	.1868	.3076	.5520	53
8	.64457	.76455	.84307	.1861	.3080	.5514	52
9	.64479	.76436	.84357	.1854	.3083	.5509	51
10	.64501	.76417	.84407	1.1847	1.3086	1.5503	50
11	.64523	.76398	.84457	.1840	.3089	.5498	49
12	.64546	.76380	.84506	.1833	.3092	.5493	48
13	.64568	.76361	.84556	.1826	.3096	.5487	47
14	.64590	.76342	.84606	.1819	.3099	.5482	46
15	.64612	.76323	.84656	.1812	1.3102	1.5477	45
16	.64635	.76304	.84706	.1805	.3105	.5471	44
17	.64657	.76286	.84756	.1798	.3109	.5466	43
18	.64679	.76267	.84806	.1791	.3112	.5461	42
19	.64701	.76248	.84856	.1785	.3115	.5456	41
20	.64723	.76229	.84906	1.1778	1.3118	1.5450	40
21	.64745	.76210	.84956	.1771	.3121	.5445	39
22	.64768	.76191	.85006	.1764	.3125	.5440	38
23	.64790	.76173	.85056	.1757	.3128	.5434	37
24	.64812	.76154	.85107	.1750	.3131	.5429	36
25	.64834	.76135	.85157	1.1743	1.3134	1.5424	35
26	.64856	.76116	.85207	.1736	.3138	.5419	34
27	.64878	.76097	.85257	.1729	.3141	.5413	33
28	.64900	.76078	.85307	.1722	.3144	.5408	32
29	.64923	.76059	.85358	.1715	.3148	.5403	31
30	.64945	.76041	.85408	1.1708	1.3151	1.5398	30
31	.64967	.76022	.85458	.1702	.3154	.5392	29
32	.64989	.76003	.85509	.1695	.3157	.5387	28
33	.65011	.75984	.85559	.1688	.3161	.5382	27
34	.65033	.75965	.85609	.1681	.3164	.5377	26
35	.65055	.75946	.85660	1.1674	1.3167	1.5371	25
36	.65077	.75927	.85710	.1667	.3170	.5366	24
37	.65100	.75908	.85761	.1660	.3174	.5361	23
38	.65121	.75889	.85811	.1653	.3177	.5356	22
39	.65144	.75870	.85862	.1647	.3180	.5351	21
40	.65166	.75851	.85912	1.1640	1.3184	1.5345	20
41	.65188	.75832	.85963	.1633	.3187	.5340	19
42	.65210	.75813	.86013	.1626	.3190	.5335	18
43	.65232	.75794	.86064	.1619	.3193	.5330	17
44	.65254	.75775	.86115	.1612	.3197	.5325	16
45	.65276	.75756	.86165	1.1605	1.3200	1.5319	15
46	.65298	.75737	.86216	.1599	.3203	.5314	14
47	.65320	.75718	.86267	.1592	.3207	.5309	13
48	.65342	.75700	.86318	.1585	.3210	.5304	12
49	.65364	.75680	.86368	.1578	.3213	.5290	11
50	.65386	.75661	.86419	1.1571	1.3217	1.5294	10
51	.65408	.75642	.86470	.1565	.3220	.5289	9
52	.65430	.75623	.86521	.1558	.3223	.5283	8
53	.65452	.75604	.86572	.1551	.3227	.5278	7
54	.65474	.75585	.86623	.1544	.3230	.5273	6
55	.65496	.75566	.86674	.1537	1.3233	1.5268	5
56	.65518	.75547	.86725	.1531	.3237	.5263	4
57	.65540	.75528	.86775	.1524	.3240	.5258	3
58	.65562	.75509	.86826	.1517	.3243	.5253	2
59	.65584	.75490	.86878	.1510	.3247	.5248	1
60	.65606	.75471	.86929	1.1504	1.3250	1.5242	0

| M | Cosine | Sine | Cotan. | Tan. | Cosec. | Secant | M |

49°

41°

M	Sine	Cosine	Tan.	Cotan.	Secant	Cosec.	M
0	.65606	.75471	.86929	1.1504	1.3250	1.5242	60
1	.65628	.75452	.86980	.1497	.3253	.5237	59
2	.65650	.75433	.87031	.1490	.3257	.5232	58
3	.65672	.75414	.87082	.1483	.3260	.5227	57
4	.65694	.75394	.87133	.1477	.3263	.5222	56
5	.65716	.75375	.87184	.1470	1.3267	1.5217	55
6	.65737	.75356	.87235	.1463	.3270	.5212	54
7	.65759	.75337	.87287	.1456	.3274	.5207	53
8	.65781	.75318	.87338	.1450	.3277	.5202	52
9	.65803	.75299	.87389	.1443	.3280	.5197	51
10	.65825	.75280	.87441	1.1436	1.3284	1.5192	50
11	.65847	.75261	.87492	.1430	.3287	.5187	49
12	.65869	.75241	.87543	.1423	.3290	.5182	48
13	.65891	.75222	.87595	.1416	.3294	.5177	47
14	.65913	.75203	.87646	.1409	.3297	.5171	46
15	.65934	.75184	.87698	.1403	1.3301	1.5166	45
16	.65956	.75165	.87749	.1396	.3304	.5161	44
17	.65978	.75146	.87801	.1389	.3307	.5156	43
18	.66000	.75126	.87852	.1383	.3311	.5151	42
19	.66022	.75107	.87904	.1376	.3314	.5146	41
20	.66044	.75088	.87955	1.1369	1.3318	1.5141	40
21	.66066	.75069	.88007	.1363	.3321	.5136	39
22	.66087	.75049	.88058	.1356	.3324	.5131	38
23	.66109	.75030	.88110	.1349	.3328	.5126	37
24	.66131	.75011	.88162	.1343	.3331	.5121	36
25	.66153	.74992	.88213	1.1336	1.3335	1.5116	35
26	.66175	.74973	.88265	.1329	.3338	.5111	34
27	.66197	.74953	.88317	.1323	.3342	.5106	33
28	.66218	.74934	.88369	.1316	.3345	.5101	32
29	.66240	.74915	.88421	.1309	.3348	.5096	31
30	.66262	.74895	.88472	.1303	1.3352	1.5092	30
31	.66284	.74876	.88524	.1296	.3355	.5087	29
32	.66305	.74857	.88576	.1290	.3359	.5082	28
33	.66327	.74838	.88628	.1283	.3362	.5077	27
34	.66349	.74818	.88680	.1276	.3366	.5072	26
35	.66371	.74799	.88732	1.1270	1.3369	1.5067	25
36	.66393	.74780	.88784	.1263	.3372	.5062	24
37	.66414	.74760	.88836	.1257	.3376	.5057	23
38	.66436	.74741	.88888	.1250	.3379	.5052	22
39	.66458	.74722	.88940	.1243	.3383	.5047	21
40	.66479	.74702	.88992	1.1237	1.3386	1.5042	20
41	.66501	.74683	.89044	.1230	.3390	.5037	19
42	.66523	.74664	.89097	.1224	.3393	.5032	18
43	.66545	.74644	.89149	.1217	.3397	.5027	17
44	.66566	.74625	.89201	.1211	.3400	.5022	16
45	.66588	.74606	.89253	1.1204	1.3404	1.5018	15
46	.66610	.74586	.89306	.1197	.3407	.5013	14
47	.66631	.74567	.89358	.1191	.3411	.5008	13
48	.66653	.74548	.89410	.1184	.3414	.5003	12
49	.66675	.74528	.89463	.1178	.3418	.4998	11
50	.66697	.74509	.89515	1.1171	1.3421	1.4993	10
51	.66718	.74489	.89567	.1165	.3425	.4988	9
52	.66740	.74470	.89620	.1158	.3428	.4983	8
53	.66762	.74450	.89672	.1152	.3432	.4979	7
54	.66783	.74431	.89725	.1145	.3435	.4974	6
55	.66805	.74412	.89777	.1139	1.3439	1.4969	5
56	.66826	.74392	.89830	.1132	.3442	.4964	4
57	.66848	.74373	.89882	.1126	.3446	.4959	3
58	.66870	.74353	.89935	.1119	.3449	.4954	2
59	.66891	.74334	.89988	.1113	.3453	.4949	1
60	.66913	.74314	.90040	1.1106	1.3456	1.4945	0

| M | Cosine | Sine | Cotan. | Tan. | Cosec. | Secant | M |

48°

M	Sine	Cosine	Tan.	Cotan.	Secant	Cosec.	M
0	.66913	.74314	.90040	1.1106	1.3456	1.4945	60
1	.66935	.74295	.90093	.1100	.3460	.4940	59
2	.66956	.74275	.90146	.1093	.3463	.4935	58
3	.66978	.74256	.90198	.1086	.3467	.4930	57
4	.66999	.74236	.90251	.1080	.3470	.4925	56
5	.67021	.74217	.90304	1.1074	1.3474	1.4921	55
6	.67043	.74197	.90357	.1067	.3477	.4916	54
7	.67064	.74178	.90410	.1061	.3481	.4911	53
8	.67086	.74158	.90463	.1054	.3485	.4906	52
9	.67107	.74139	.90515	.1048	.3488	.4901	51
10	.67129	.74119	.90568	1.1041	1.3492	1.4897	50
11	.67150	.74100	.90621	.1035	.3495	.4892	49
12	.67172	.74080	.90674	.1028	.3499	.4887	48
13	.67194	.74061	.90727	.1022	.3502	.4882	47
14	.67215	.74041	.90780	.1015	.3506	.4877	46
15	.67237	.74022	.90834	1.1009	1.3509	1.4873	45
16	.67258	.74002	.90887	.1003	.3513	.4868	44
17	.67280	.73983	.90940	.0996	.3517	.4863	43
18	.67301	.73963	.90993	.0990	.3520	.4858	42
19	.67323	.73943	.91046	.0983	.3524	.4854	41
20	.67344	.73924	.91099	1.0977	1.3527	1.4849	40
21	.67366	.73904	.91153	.0971	.3531	.4844	39
22	.67387	.73885	.91206	.0964	.3534	.4839	38
23	.67409	.73865	.91259	.0958	.3538	.4835	37
24	.67430	.73845	.91312	.0951	.3542	.4830	36
25	.67452	.73826	.91366	1.0945	1.3545	1.4825	35
26	.67473	.73806	.91419	.0939	.3549	.4821	34
27	.67495	.73787	.91473	.0932	.3552	.4816	33
28	.67516	.73767	.91526	.0926	.3556	.4811	32
29	.67537	.73747	.91580	.0919	.3560	.4806	31
30	.67559	.73728	.91633	1.0913	1.3563	1.4802	30
31	.67580	.73708	.91687	.0907	.3567	.4797	29
32	.67602	.73688	.91740	.0900	.3571	.4792	28
33	.67623	.73669	.91794	.0894	.3574	.4788	27
34	.67645	.73649	.91847	.0888	.3578	.4783	26
35	.67666	.73629	.91901	1.0881	1.3581	1.4778	25
36	.67688	.73610	.91955	.0875	.3585	.4774	24
37	.67709	.73590	.92008	.0868	.3589	.4769	23
38	.67730	.73570	.92062	.0862	.3592	.4764	22
39	.67752	.73551	.92116	.0856	.3596	.4760	21
40	.67773	.73531	.92170	1.0849	1.3600	1.4755	20
41	.67794	.73511	.92223	.0843	.3603	.4750	19
42	.67816	.73491	.92277	.0837	.3607	.4746	18
43	.67837	.73472	.92331	.0830	.3611	.4741	17
44	.67859	.73452	.92385	.0824	.3614	.4736	16
45	.67880	.73432	.92439	1.0818	1.3618	1.4732	15
46	.67901	.73412	.92493	.0812	.3622	.4727	14
47	.67923	.73393	.92547	.0805	.3625	.4723	13
48	.67944	.73373	.92601	.0799	.3629	.4718	12
49	.67965	.73353	.92655	.0793	.3633	.4713	11
50	.67987	.73333	.92709	1.0786	1.3636	1.4709	10
51	.68008	.73314	.92763	.0780	.3640	.4704	9
52	.68029	.73294	.92817	.0774	.3644	.4699	8
53	.68051	.73274	.92871	.0767	.3647	.4695	7
54	.68072	.73254	.92926	.0761	.3651	.4690	6
55	.68093	.73234	.92980	1.0755	1.3655	1.4686	5
56	.68115	.73215	.93034	.0749	.3658	.4681	4
57	.68136	.73195	.93088	.0742	.3662	.4676	3
58	.68157	.73175	.93143	.0736	.3666	.4672	2
59	.68178	.73155	.93197	.0730	.3669	.4667	1
60	.68200	.73135	.93251	1.0724	1.3673	1.4663	0

M	Cosine	Sine	Cotan.	Tan.	Cosec.	Secant	M

M	Sine	Cosine	Tan.	Cotan.	Secant	Cosec.	M
0	.68200	.73135	.93251	1.0724	1.3673	1.4663	60
1	.68221	.73115	.93306	.0717	.3677	.4658	59
2	.68242	.73096	.93360	.0711	.3681	.4654	58
3	.68264	.73076	.93415	.0705	.3684	.4649	57
4	.68285	.73056	.93469	.0699	.3688	.4644	56
5	.68306	.73036	.93524	1.0692	1.3692	1.4640	55
6	.68327	.73016	.93578	.0686	.3695	.4635	54
7	.68349	.72996	.93633	.0680	.3699	.4631	53
8	.68370	.72976	.93687	.0674	.3703	.4626	52
9	.68391	.72956	.93742	.0667	.3707	.4622	51
10	.68412	.72937	.93797	1.0661	1.3710	1.4617	50
11	.68433	.72917	.93851	.0655	.3714	.4613	49
12	.68455	.72897	.93906	.0649	.3718	.4608	48
13	.68476	.72877	.93961	.0643	.3722	.4604	47
14	.68497	.72857	.94016	.0636	.3725	.4599	46
15	.68518	.72837	.94071	1.0630	1.3729	1.4595	45
16	68539	.72817	.94125	.0624	.3733	.4590	44
17	.68561	.72797	.94180	.0618	.3737	.4586	43
18	.68582	.72777	.94235	.0612	.3740	.4581	42
19	.68603	.72757	.94290	.0605	.3744	.4577	41
20	.68624	.72737	.94345	1.0599	1.3748	1.4572	40
21	.68645	.72717	.94400	.0593	.3752	.4568	39
22	.68666	.72697	.94455	.0587	.3756	.4563	38
23	.68688	.72677	.94510	.0581	.3759	.4559	37
24	.68709	.72657	.94565	.0575	.3763	.4554	36
25	.68730	.72637	.94620	1.0568	1.3767	1.4550	35
26	.68751	.72617	.94675	.0562	.3771	.4545	34
27	.68772	.72597	.94731	.0556	.3774	.4541	33
28	.68793	.72577	.94786	.0550	.3778	.4536	32
29	.68814	.72557	.94841	.0544	.3782	.4532	31
30	.68835	.72537	.94896	1.0538	1.3786	1.4527	30
31	.68856	.72517	.94952	.0532	.3790	.4523	29
32	.68878	.72497	.95007	.0525	.3794	.4518	28
33	.68899	.72477	.95062	.0519	.3797	.4514	27
34	.68920	.72457	.95118	.0513	.3801	.4510	26
35	.68941	.72437	.95173	1.0507	1.3805	1.4505	25
36	.68962	.72417	.95229	.0501	.3809	.4501	24
37	.68983	.72397	.95284	.0495	.3813	.4496	23
38	.69004	.72377	.95340	.0489	.3816	.4492	22
39	.69025	.72357	.95395	.0483	.3820	.4487	21
40	.69046	.72337	.95451	1.0476	1.3824	1.4483	20
41	.69067	.72317	.95506	.0470	.3828	.4479	19
42	.69088	.72297	.95562	.0464	.3832	.4474	18
43	.69109	.72277	.95618	.0458	.3836	.4470	17
44	.69130	.72256	.95673	.0452	.3839	.4465	16
45	.69151	.72236	.95729	1.0446	1.3843	1.4461	15
46	.69172	.72216	.95785	.0440	.3847	.4457	14
47	.69193	.72196	.95841	.0434	.3851	.4452	13
48	.69214	.72176	.95896	.0428	.3855	.4448	12
49	.69235	.72156	.95952	.0422	.3859	.4443	11
50	.69256	.72136	.96008	1.0416	1.3863	1.4439	10
51	.69277	.72115	.96064	.0410	.3867	.4435	9
52	.69298	.72095	.96120	.0404	.3870	.4430	8
53	.69319	.72075	.96176	.0397	.3874	.4426	7
54	.69340	.72055	.96232	.0391	.3878	.4422	6
55	.69361	.72035	.96288	1.0385	1.3882	1.4417	5
56	.69382	.72015	.96344	.0379	.3886	.4413	4
57	.69403	.71994	.96400	.0373	.3890	.4408	3
58	.69424	.71974	.96456	.0367	.3894	.4404	2
59	.69445	.71954	.96513	.0361	.3898	.4400	1
60	.69466	.71934	.96569	1.0355	1.3902	1.4395	0

M	Cosine	Sine	Cotan.	Tan.	Cosec.	Secant	M

M	Sine	Cosine	Tan.	Cotan.	Secant	Cosec.	M
0	.69466	.71934	.96569	1.0355	1.3902	1.4395	60
1	.69487	.71914	.96625	.0349	.3905	.4391	59
2	.69508	.71893	.96681	.0343	.3909	.4387	58
3	.69528	.71873	.96738	.0337	.3913	.4382	57
4	.69549	.71853	96794	.0331	.3917	.4378	56
5	.69570	.71833	.96850	1.0325	1.3921	1.4374	55
6	.69591	.71813	.96907	.0319	.3925	.4370	54
7	.69612	.71792	.96963	.0313	.3929	.4365	53
8	.69633	.71772	.97020	.0307	.3933	.4361	52
9	.69654	.71752	.97076	.0301	.3937	.4357	51
10	.69675	.71732	.97133	1.0295	1.3941	1.4352	50
11	.69696	.71711	.97189	.0289	.3945	.4348	49
12	.69716	.71691	.97246	.0283	.3949	.4344	48
13	.69737	.71671	97302	.0277	.3953	.4339	47
14	.69758	71650	.97359	.0271	.3957	.4335	46
15	.69779	.71630	.97416	1.0265	1.3960	1.4331	45
16	.69800	.71610	.97472	.0259	.3964	.4327	44
17	.69821	.71589	.97529	.0253	.3968	.4322	43
18	.69841	.71569	.97586	.0247	.3972	.4318	42
19	.69862	.71549	.97643	.0241	.3976	.4314	41
20	.69883	.71529	.97700	1.0235	1.3980	1.4310	40
21	.69904	.71508	.97756	.0229	.3984	.4305	39
22	.69925	.71488	.97813	.0223	.3988	.4301	38
23	.69945	.71468	.97870	.0218	.3992	.4297	37
24	.69966	.71447	.97927	.0212	.3996	.4292	36
25	.69987	.71427	.97984	1.0206	1.4000	1.4288	35
26	.70008	.71406	.98041	.0200	.4004	.4284	34
27	.70029	.71386	.98098	.0194	.4008	.4280	33
28	.70049	.71366	.98155	.0188	.4012	.4276	32
29	.70070	.71345	.98212	.0182	.4016	.4271	31
30	.70091	.71325	.98270	1.0176	1.4020	1.4267	30
31	.70112	.71305	.98327	.0170	.4024	.4263	29
32	.70132	.71284	.98384	.0164	.4028	.4259	28
33	.70153	.71264	.98441	.0158	.4032	.4254	27
34	.70174	.71243	.98499	.0152	.4036	.4250	26
35	.70194	.71223	.98556	1.0146	1.4040	1.4246	25
36	.70215	.71203	.98613	.0141	.4044	.4242	24
37	.70236	.71182	.98671	.0135	.4048	.4238	23
38	.70257	.71162	.98728	.0129	.4052	.4233	22
39	.70277	.71141	.98786	.0123	.4056	.4229	21
40	.70298	.71121	.98843	1.0117	1.4060	1.4225	20
41	.70319	.71100	.98901	.0111	.4065	.4221	19
42	.70339	.71080	.98958	.0105	.4069	.4217	18
43	.70360	.71059	.99016	.0099	.4073	.4212	17
44	.70381	.71039	.99073	.0093	.4077	.4208	16
45	.70401	.71018	.99131	1.0088	1.4081	1.4204	15
46	.70422	.70998	.99189	.0082	.4085	.4200	14
47	.70443	.70977	.99246	.0076	.4089	.4196	13
48	.70463	.70957	.99304	.0070	.4093	.4192	12
49	.70484	.70936	.99362	.0064	.4097	.4188	11
50	.70505	.70916	.99420	1.0058	1.4101	1.4183	10
51	.70525	.70895	.99478	.0052	.4105	.4179	9
52	.70546	.70875	.99536	.0047	.4109	.4175	8
53	.70566	.70854	.99593	.0041	.4113	.4171	7
54	.70587	.70834	.99651	.0035	.4117	.4167	6
55	.70608	.70813	.99709	1.0029	1.4122	1.4163	5
56	.70628	.70793	.99767	.0023	.4126	.4159	4
57	.70649	.70772	.99826	.0017	.4130	.4154	3
58	.70669	.70752	.99884	.0012	.4134	.4150	2
59	.70690	.70731	.99942	.0006	.4138	.4146	1
60	.70711	.70711	1.0000	1.0000	1.4142	1.4142	0

M	Cosine	Sine	Cotan.	Tan.	Cosec.	Secant	M

Index

Index

Edited by Suzanne L. Cheatle

Other Bestsellers From TAB

☐ **WORKING WITH FIBERGLASS: Techniques and Projects—Wiley**

With the expert instruction provided by this guide, you can use fiberglass to make model boats, flower pots, even garden furniture and hot tubs at a fraction of the commercially-made price! These complete step-by-step instructions on laminating and molding make it simple to construct a wide variety of projects—including projects not available in manufactured versions. 224 pp., 252 illus. 7″ × 10″.

Paper $11.95   **Hard $19.95**
Book No. 2739

☐ **THE COMPLETE BOOK OF HOME WELDING**

Highlights new arc welding equipment and singlephase wire feeders that greatly simplify the welding process and make it feasible for even novice do-it-yourselfers. The author provides actual step-by-step welding projects complete with detailed illustrations that makes even complicated welding projects amazingly easy to perform. Just a few of the things you'll be able to construct and repair include garden carts, car racks, trailers, spiral staircases, wood-burning stoves, piping systems, auto engines, and others. You'll find endless applications for your new skill! 496 pp., 464 illus.

Paper $19.95   **Hard $29.95**
Book No. 2717

☐ **THE ELECTROPLATER'S HANDBOOK**

If you want to plate any kind of object for any purpose, this is the guide to have! It's an invaluable guide whether you're a model railroad builder, auto or antique restorer, amateur jeweler, coin collector, science buff, radio and electronics builder, silversmith, metal caster, artist, sculptor, potter, small manufacturer, stained glass worker, inventor, or even a parent who wants to bronze baby shoes! 224 pp., 136 illus.

Paper $12.95   **Hard $18.95**
Book No. 2610

☐ **MAKING KNIVES AND TOOLS—2nd Edition—Blandford**

Here is the completely revised and expanded new second edition of a guidebook that has become the "Bible" in its field. Written by a highly respected metalworking/woodworking craftsman, it shows you how you can make almost any type of edged tool or knife, at amazingly affordable cost! You'll learn how to make pro-quality knives and tools from plain kitchen knives to shaping tools. 256 pp., 187 illus.

Paper $12.95   **Hard $18.95**
Book No. 1944

☐ **CANVAS AND UPHOLSTERY PROJECTS FOR BOATS AND RVs—Wiley**

This easy-to-follow guide to modern canvas and upholstery techniques for boats and RVs thoroughly covers everything you need to know to do a professional job . . . from the tools needed to the basic hand *sewing* stitches such as herringbone, roundstitch, and slip stitch . . . from the materials you'll need and where to get them, to operating, choosing, and repairing a heavy-duty upholstery machine. 320 pp., 327 illus.

Paper $15.95   **Hard $22.95**
Book No. 2719

☐ **BEGINNING BLACKSMITHING, WITH PROJECTS—Converse**

This illustration-packed handbook includes everything from a history of blacksmithing to traditional blacksmithing techniques. Jim Converse explains types of welds, where to buy a forge and anvil, and how to set up and maintain a small shop. The projects included will teach you, hands-on, all the fundamentals of the blacksmithing. 288 pp., 260 illus. 7″ × 10″.

Paper $12.95   **Hard $18.95**
Book No. 2651

HOW TO CAST SMALL METAL AND RUBBER PARTS—2nd Edition—Cannon

Using this excellent sourcebook, you can easily make defect-free castings and at an amazingly low cost . . . obsolete or vintage car parts, hood ornaments, garden tools, kitchen utensils, automotive parts, replacing antique parts, reproducing sculpture, and other art! Includes all-new information on casting polyurethane rubber parts. There's even a listing of sources for supplies and equipment. 176 pp., 143 illus.

Paper $9.95   **Hard $15.95**
Book No. 2614

☐ **CASTING ALUMINUM—Ammen**

Cast your own automotive or other replacement parts . . . reproduce antique objects . . . cast all kinds of decorative and useful objects in aluminum for your own use, or to sell! It's far easier than you'd imagine! C.W. Ammen leads you step-by-step through every detail in the aluminum-casting process from assembling (and even making) needed equipment to producing your own perfect cast aluminum pieces for hobby or small business purposes! 252 pp., 200 illus.

Paper $11.95   **Hard $18.95**
Book No. 1910

Other Bestsellers From TAB